BLACK LIVES,
WHITE LIVES

BLACK LIVES, WHITE LIVES

THREE DECADES OF
RACE RELATIONS IN AMERICA

with two new essays:
The Author's Story
Where Are the People Now?

BOB BLAUNER

University of California Press / Berkeley / Los Angeles / London

University of California Press
Berkeley and Los Angeles, California
University of California Press, Ltd.
London, England

© 1989 by
The Regents of the University of California

Printed in the United States of America
2 3 4 5 6 7 8 9

First Paperback Printing 1990

Added to the Second Printing: *The Author's Story*
and *Where Are the People Now?*

Library of Congress Cataloging-in-Publication Data

Blauner, Bob.
  Black lives, white lives.

  Bibliography: p.
  1. United States—Race relations.   2. Racism—United
States—History—20th century.   3. Afro-Americans—
Civil rights.   I. Title.
E185.615.B556   1989   305.8'00973   88-27769
ISBN 0-520-06261-2 (alk. paper)
ISBN 0-520-06950-1 (pbk: alk. paper)

To the memory of my mother, Esther Blauner (1899–1986),
and to the future of my children, Marya and Jonathan:
may they live in a peaceful world.

Contents

PART TWO   1978–1987
GROWING OLDER IN THE SEVENTIES AND EIGHTIES

Acknowledgments

For a project as long as mine, the list of people who made a real difference to its completion is staggering, and I apologize in advance to those whom I may have left out.

First I want to thank the research staff from the late 1960s, in particular David Wellman, who directed the interviewers: Hardy Frye, Alex Papillon, Lincoln Bergman, Sheila Gibson Stevens, H. Edward Price, and Maurice Haltom. Imaginative and committed, they each had the technical and personal skills that made it possible for people to share with them their lives and deep beliefs. I am also indebted to them for helping me locate people for the followup interviews in the late 1970s. And at numerous stages of the project Wellman and Frye have also taken time from their very busy schedules to comment on my work in progress.

I have benefited greatly from the suggestions of an ongoing discussion group that has included Troy Duster, Lillian Rubin, David Matza, Elliot Currie, Norma Wikler, and David Minkus, in addition to David Wellman. Robert Alford read the manuscript at a time when I specially needed his wise advice. Todd Gitlin gave me useful criticism and support for the project. Helena Hershel's enthusiasm for my approach to this book has been important to me. Lois Benjamin's suggestions were extremely valuable; I have learned much from our exchange of ideas. Tomás Almaguer, Barbara Christian, and Earl Lewis directed me to some of the more recent literature in the field. Others who have read all or parts of the work include Michael Hout, June Murray-Gill, Steve Millner, Linda Collins, Ron Takaki, Michael Messner, Beth Roy, Angie Fa, and Eloise Dunlap. Peter Carroll made a number of important contributions, including the idea of a third round of interviews and useful suggestions for cutting an excessively long manuscript. Margie Gilford checked census data and Joselyn Stuart helped with footnotes.

Throughout ten years of writing, I have been sustained emotionally and in countless other ways by my comrades in what must be the longest ongoing men's support group. Lloyd Churgin, Russell Ellis, Ron Elson, Bill Lawler, and David Deitch also read all or parts of the book. The friendship and critical suggestions of Bob Ehrlich, David Matza, Carole Julian, and Madeline Marcus have also been important to me.

Margaret Henderson typed most of the second-round interviews, with uncanny accuracy. Marcy McGaugh transcribed all of the third-round inter-views and typed innumerable versions of the manuscript in its later stages. She did first-rate work, and I have also valued her deep understanding of the book's content. Of the many typists who worked on earlier stages of the project, I give special thanks to Julie Lamont, Lois Macmillan, Susan Chu, Lynn Turner, and Olivia Inaba.

Virtually all the typing was paid for by the Committee on Research at the University of California; the committee's long and patient support has been indispensable. The first phase of the research was financed by a grant from the National Institute of Mental Health. Support from the Ford Foundation in 1978 was important in making possible the second round of interviews. And a Rockefeller Foundation fellowship in 1980–81 helped supplement two quar-ters of sabbatical leave from my teaching duties at the University of Califor-nia, Berkeley. I want to thank also the staff members of the Department of Sociology at the university for their work and personal kindnesses.

I feel honored to have worked closely with James H. Clark, the director of the University of California Press. His continuing belief that a book would someday emerge—through all the diverse outlines, drafts, and passing years—was indispensable to my own ability to concentrate on the task at hand, that of turning the massive primary materials and sometimes inchoate idea of their organization into a workable result. I also enjoyed working with Laird Easton and Mary Renaud at the Press and want to thank my sister Sonia Saxon for help with the last-minute preparations. In the final stages the manuscript was immeasurably improved by Amy Einsohn's outstanding copyediting.

I especially thank Marya and Jonathan for their patience and understand-ing of a father who always had a book to write.

My biggest debt is to the people whose life stories make up the book. They were willing to be interviewed not only once, but three times over the course of what must have seemed like a never-ending study. I want to thank them for their candor and their cooperation, and to single out, by pseudonym, three Sacramentoans who provided useful advice and help in introducing me to some of the people in the book: Millie Harding, Harold Sampson, and espe-cially the late Florence Grier.

Introduction

This book is about the racial experience and consciousness of black and white Americans. What is unique about it is the attempt to explore race and racism within the context of people's lives over the course of almost twenty years, a period spanning three decades each of which has had its own distinctive political and cultural climate. The subjects in this book were interviewed in 1968, again in 1978–79, and for a third time in 1986. The sixteen blacks and twelve whites speak in their own words about how their lives unfolded, how their political beliefs and racial attitudes changed or remained the same, and how they assess the social transformations they have witnessed. The long span of the study permits us to hold in view both historical shifts in the zeitgeist, or spirit of the time, and the processes of personal aging, as the individuals grow older, influenced by—and in turn contributing to—larger social changes.

On the day Martin Luther King, Jr., was assassinated, April 4, 1968, we had already interviewed almost half of the blacks in the study and had just begun to interview the whites. The timing of our work intersected with the national tragedy to create a natural experiment, an unintended research design that enabled us to compare the reactions of blacks and whites to King's death and also to observe the effect of his assassination on people's opinions of his political philosophy and historical role.

There was a striking difference in the ways blacks and whites reacted. Most blacks we talked to mourned not only the civil rights leader himself but also the ray of hope that he promised, his dream that a just and integrated society might still be realized. How profoundly the assassination affected black people is suggested by the bursts of eloquence that the topic evoked. Even a year later, almost every black person could tell us exactly what they were doing at the moment they heard the news. A forty-year-old state office worker in Sacramento remembered that she was standing on a chair in her kitchen, reaching up to get something out of a cupboard, when the radio made an announcement. An eighteen-year-old in the Watts section of Los Angeles heard the news from a gym coach, who interrupted a schoolyard basketball game: "Everyone just froze for about fifteen seconds, everyone just stood there . . . and we just stopped playing completely. Everyone sat down and wondered what's going to happen in Watts. . . . It's just going to boil like a volcano and blow up."

1

Virtually all the blacks we talked to felt an immediate and deep sense of loss, very much like a death in the family. Even people who did not entirely support his policies strongly identified with Dr. King and his bereaved wife. Before the assassination many people had disparaged King's leadership, arguing that his moderate style and nonviolent philosophy had outlived their usefulness. Other criticisms concerned King's opposition to the Vietnam war, his support of the striking sanitation workers in Memphis, and his plans for a Poor People's March on Washington.[1]

After April 4, these criticisms were muted by grief and by identification: "They kill part of me when they kill [John] Kennedy; they kill the other part of me when they kill Martin Luther King," said a hospital worker in her fifties. Sorrow was infused by anger, even in some middle-aged black men who had been brought up in the South and been taught to suppress the very awareness of that potentially dangerous emotion. Many redoubled their determination to continue the struggle for racial justice. One unusually eloquent speaker proudly noted that King's work had finally buried the myth that southern blacks were docile and would not fight back.

We heard surprisingly little generalized hatred of whites, but many blacks were repelled by what they saw as white people's pretense of sorrow and concern. Yet many whites we interviewed didn't even try to pretend sorrow or regret. A firefighter told us that his co-workers cheered when they heard that King had died. And when I reinterviewed people in 1979, in the second stage of this study, a suburban Sacramento housewife said that when she told her husband the news back in 1968, he said, "They ought to shoot more of them." But such outright hostility was not typical. Overall, King's death was just not that important to most white people. Almost no one introduced his or her reaction by fixing the moment in time when they first heard the news, and their thoughts and feelings were more abstract, less personal.

Although quite a few whites appreciated King's historical role, for some it was a grudging appreciation. "I thought he was a good man, but I think he did a helluva lot more harm than good," said a white resident of a predominantly black housing project. And a printer in his late sixties granted that King was a "very great man," but immediately qualified his praise by saying that "he was not the pacifist that he claimed to be," but instead was "one of the most inflammatory speakers" he had ever heard. Still other whites saw the martyred leader as a sinister force, a firebrand, and they held him personally responsible for the country's racial troubles, including the violence following the assassination. Many whites felt resentful, even jealous, of the time television devoted in the wake of the assassination to documentaries about King and the civil rights movement.

It is also true that television educated some people. And there were other whites, particularly some of the San Francisco hippies we interviewed, who were deeply moved by the death of King. One young woman said: "Most men until then had either gone to one side or the other. And he was still there keeping the two middle-class masses [black and white] talking to each other. And keeping them with hope. And then he was gone. A great big silence, a big emptiness. I remember the day; it seemed very quiet. [I felt] sort of abandoned."

As these responses to the assassination suggest, blacks and whites were sharply divided in 1968. A month before the assassination, the Kerner Commission had warned the country: "Our nation is moving toward two societies, one black, one white—separate and unequal."* During interviews conducted with the same respondents in 1978 and 1979, in the second phase of this study, great differences in outlook still remained, with many whites believing that King's dream of a racially just society had already come to pass, while blacks were adamant that relatively little progress had been made. But in their feelings about King himself, the two groups had come somewhat closer together. Whites sounded less extreme in their racial attitudes, perhaps in part because they were no longer confronted by a strong and aggressive black movement and because the public clamor and pressure for racial equality had abated. By 1979 the suburban husband who had wanted "more of them" killed had, his wife now said, "mellowed to the blacks." Her neighbors, she added, "look back and respect Martin Luther King's work" even though "they felt very strongly against him during the time he was on his sit-down strikes." Among blacks who had derided King in 1968 as irrelevant or overly conciliatory, opinions had also changed. A longshoreman who came close to calling King an "Uncle Tom" before the assassination—"turning one cheek, then the other, you'll never get nothing over, brother"—now likened him to Marcus Garvey in historical importance (though not, of course, in political strategy) and added that blacks would have been in a much better situation had King lived.

By the summer of 1986, when I interviewed people for the third time, King's birthday had become a national holiday, and the passage of time had softened some of the opposition to the man and his beliefs. The holiday itself is an extremely significant achievement—even if not recognized by all states. But as King has been turned into an official hero, his political agenda has been reduced to the advocacy of nonviolence. The national celebration, ironically, makes it easier to avoid facing squarely the evils of racism, economic injustice, and war that he struggled against. Furthermore, the canonization of Dr. King distorts the historical memory. The strong tendency to portray King as virtually synonymous with civil rights leads people to overlook the move-

*The National Advisory Commission on Civil Disorders was appointed by President Lyndon Johnson to examine the causes of the riots in the urban ghettos during the mid-sixties. The commission was chaired by Otto Kerner, Jr., then the governor of Illinois.

ment's other brave and effective leaders and foot soldiers. Ronald Reagan, in particular, has used the holiday to suggest a national consensus about racial justice. But in truth no such consensus existed in the sixties, and none exists today.

Through the oral histories in this book I have tried to evoke the late sixties as those years were experienced then, as a period rife with conflict when America seemed to be dividing into two camps: those who were for "the system" and those who were against it. The first set of interviews took place from late 1967 through early 1969, at a time when relations between blacks and whites were becoming so polarized that many people contemplated the prospect of a race war and speculated about what they would do when it broke out. Racial conflict had intensified during the sixties, and by 1968 people's nerves were on edge, their sensibilities razor-sharp, their convictions passionate. As the conventions that customarily inhibited frank discussion of sensitive issues relaxed in the "anything goes" mood of the sixties, people were eager to talk about race—but, in such a highly charged climate, only with someone from their own racial group. With few exceptions, we therefore used white interviewers to talk to our white respondents and blacks to interview blacks.

Our interest was racial consciousness, not only in its unusually pointed manifestations that year, but also as it developed in the course of people's lives. We chose the method of a racial life history to explore the ways in which various beliefs and assumptions, implicit as well as explicit, became a part of the way people viewed themselves, their society, and other groups. We looked at the role of race and racism in the everyday lives of blacks and whites—in school experiences, at work, with the law, and in other institutional areas. We were interested in the personal as well as the political, but especially the connection between the two, concurring with C. Wright Mills that investigating the relation between public issues and private troubles is sociology's special mandate.

So in addition to the life story, we focused equally on the racial politics of the day and asked people what they thought about civil rights leaders, integration, black power, nationalism, nonviolence, and other issues then under debate. We asked blacks about racism: how they coped with it day-to-day, how it affected their manhood and womanhood and the relations between the sexes. They talked about black culture, about the ways they were different from or the same as whites, and which aspects of the black experience were ethnic strengths to be preserved, which were group weaknesses. Whites were asked how they explained the inequality between the races, whether they believed racism existed or not, how they saw their own involvement in it, how important "whiteness" was as a part of their personal identity, and how they made sense of and reacted to the growing assertiveness and militancy of black people. We had a special interest in probing the tacit theories people had about the disadvantaged status of racial minorities. Did they blame the system for failing to provide equal opportunity, or did they fault the minority group's culture and characteristics? *

Collectively, these interviews provide a picture of a decade of intensified consciousness and rapid social change in which the impact of the historical moment on individual lives was unusually transparent. They also show people "going through changes," as the phrase went, changes in their political viewpoints, self-awareness, and personal commitments. But what happened to these new values and opinions as the political climate shifted in the 1970s? Curious about this, I began reinterviewing some of the same people in 1978.

By that time I sensed that the climate had changed enough so that I might be able to interview blacks as well as whites. It's also true that I didn't have much choice; in the prosperous sixties a grant from the National Institute of Mental Health had financed the interviewing staff. Even more important, I wanted the chance to talk to the people whose life stories I had been working on and was learning so much from. I was apprehensive at first, particularly about interviewing the more nationalistic and angry blacks, the more conservative or racist whites. But I didn't have to be. Most people were pleased, almost flattered, to be remembered by a research project after so many years. No one refused to be interviewed and I sensed that only two—one white, one black—were holding back their real opinions. (They do not appear in the book.)

One goal of the followup interview was to bring the life history up to date, to catch up on changes as well as continuities in work, economic welfare, family situation, and life-style. I also asked people about personal issues— how they had grown or changed in their sense of self, how satisfied they were with their lives, how they were dealing with growing older.

Second, I was interested in consciousness. We were in a more conservative time, a more private era, and a period of *relative* racial peace and harmony. Racial issues were no longer on the front page, and public events in general did not capture people's imaginations or intrude into their personal lives as they had in the sixties. Now the most pressing issues seemed to be economic: inflation and the soaring price of gasoline. So I was interested in finding out what had happened to black anger, militancy, and nationalist leanings. And what had whites learned about minority groups in the intervening years? Had people's views changed with the new times, or were the perspectives of the sixties still a part of them?

---

*This question underlies one of the leading theoretical debates among sociologists of race and ethnic relations over the past thirty years. "System-blaming" explanations are called *structural*: they tend to attribute racial stratification to imperatives of social and economic structures, including racial discrimination. *Cultural* explanations emphasize internal characteristics of the ethnic group, such as family patterns, values, and other traditions.

Finally, I wanted to find out how people looked back on the 1960s from the vantage point of a very different era. How did they assess the decade's impact on American society, on racial equality, and on their own lives? I was searching for the legacy of the sixties and its special racial consciousness: was its explosive impact as ephemeral as it appeared toward the end of the seventies, or had it left significant traces on the lives and worldviews of the people who had lived through its unique intensity?

During the 1980s the policies and philosophy of the Reagan presidency both reflected and set the national tone on racial matters. The administration cut programs for the poor, relaxed enforcement of various civil rights laws and executive orders, and tried—with some success—to roll back much of the momentum minority groups had gained during the 1960s and 1970s. The problem of "reverse racism" against white males was given a higher priority than affirmative action, the mandates of the Civil Rights Commission and the Equal Employment Opportunity Commission were revised, many conservatives were appointed to the nation's courts, and race-related issues such as crime, drugs, and welfare gained center stage. Throughout the 1980s we have seen both a resurgence of bigotry and racist acts and a noticeable increase in racial awareness and protest. Among the signs have been the anti-apartheid movement, the rise in incidents of racial violence and harassment (including the case of Bernhard Goetz), the unprecedented outbreaks of racism on college campuses, and events in Howard Beach, New York, and Forsyth County, Georgia.

I had originally intended my final contact in 1986 to be only a brief telephone update. But seven years had passed and we were in a new decade, possibly even in a new period of race relations. I therefore decided to do a third round of substantial face-to-face interviews, although only a small portion of that material appears in this book.

Black Lives, White Lives is not a definitive study of the course of our nation's racial consciousness since the 1960s. The 28 people who appear in this book were chosen from an initial group of more than 350 persons, but almost all were residents of the San Francisco Bay Area or Sacramento, California. Northern California, of course, has the same kinds of racial problems as the rest of America, but for reasons of history and geography, they do not always express themselves as starkly.* In California, as in the entire western region, the employment and educational levels of blacks are above the national average. Furthermore, since the 1970s the most severe problems of race and class have involved children, teenagers, and young adults living in the inner cities. Because of my longitudinal research design, I did not interview this new gen-

---

*Until forty years ago blacks were a numerically small group in California, and historically they have not been the state's most oppressed minority; that burden has variously fallen on the native Indians, the Mexicans, and the Chinese.

eration in the second and third phases of this study. Many of the older people talk about these youth, but the age group most locked out of the American Dream does not have its own voice in this book.

Nonetheless, the experiences recounted here exemplify many of the central themes of racial and social change in American society since the 1960s. They give us a window to view the shifting racial landscape of the past three decades.

The people in this book speak in their own words. Originally I had intended a more conventional sociological analysis written in the third person, but as Julie Lamont, one of our typists, commented on the transcript of Florence Grier's 1968 interview: "The woman, and therefore the interview, is magnificent; no words but her own could do her justice." I had to agree, not only for the very articulate Mrs. Grier but for the others as well.

My role has been to organize and edit the transcripts in order to present as faithfully as possible each person's life story and consciousness, while highlighting those sociological themes I deem most significant and retaining some sense of the interview itself as an interpersonal encounter. Although I have had to abridge extremely long transcripts, I've tried to keep enough detail so that readers can make their own analyses of the material, and I've tried to keep enough of the flavor of the original to suggest the spontaneous, meandering, and even sometimes inconsistent way people think and talk. To protect people's privacy, I have changed their names (with the exception of Elena Albert) and in a few cases have also changed place names and occupations.

I have placed my own summaries and interpretations in the introductions to each part and in brief commentary within the interview chapters, as well as in a concluding essay where I draw some lessons from this twenty-year project.

PART ONE

1968

SURVIVING
THE SIXTIES

Integration or Black Power?
The Great Debate

From the Montgomery bus boycott of 1956 through the early 1960s, the civil rights movement achieved considerable success in combating legal segregation in public facilities in the South. But by 1963, when the movement began concentrating on voter registration and other issues of political equality, progress became more difficult. Further, the tactics that had successfully challenged southern segregation—boycotts, sit-ins, marches, and freedom rides—had little relevance to the de facto segregation, economic inequality, and social problems of the northern ghettos. Where integration did proceed, the pace of change was unbearably slow. Those blacks who gained entry into previously segregated occupations, neighborhoods, or schools were often frustrated and disillusioned by the hostility or indifference of whites, and the white backlash could only be expected to intensify as integration spread.

In response the movement became more and more militant. An impatient, vigorous drive to integrate gave way to an increasingly angry black nationalism. The Student Nonviolent Coordinating Committee (SNCC), formed in the wake of the 1960 sit-ins, was at first a militant interracial organization devoted to integration. But between 1963 and 1965 SNCC's separatist faction gained the upper hand, and whites were excluded from the group.

This change of course from integration to separatism was heralded by the emergence of Black Power in 1966. As articulated by SNCC leader Stokely Carmichael and other young militants, Black Power stressed self-determination, the right of ethnic minorities to define their group identity and to make the decisions that affected their lives. Since the rules of the "system" were biased, the advocates of Black Power would invent their own rules, use "any means necessary," in the words of Malcolm X, the militants' theoretician and martyred hero.

In the black community this new mood provoked an intense debate about

priorities and strategies for change. Should Afro-Americans continue to demand their right to participate fully in every aspect of American life, in essence following the white middle-class model for mobility and success? Or,
since they would never be accepted as equal citizens in a racist society, would
always be a group apart, should they instead turn inward and develop the
strengths and potential of the black community as an economic, political, and
cultural force that could stand on its own? "A decade of racial dialectics—of
the cut and thrust of white racism and Black Power," as Thomas Blair explains, had touched the emotional roots of an ethnic ambivalence.[1] As the
promise of America seemed to wither in violent conflicts—a divisive war, disruptions on college campuses, and political assassinations—blacks pondered
James Baldwin's rhetorical question: "Would you want to integrate into a
burning house?"

Integration versus separatism (or black nationalism)—a "choice" that
proved to be oversimplified when posed as mutually exclusive alternatives—
emerged as the central issue in the black politics of the late 1960s. This controversy had, of course, dominated black political thought for more than a century, but, except for the Garvey movement in the 1920s, the integrationist-
separatist debate had been confined to a small circle of intellectuals.* In the
sixties the discussion moved out onto the streets—and onto television, which
played a critical role in defining and publicizing what had been a private
in-group debate. Television focused on the most extreme positions, playing
up, even exaggerating, the differences between them.[2] The media coverage
emphasized personalities and turned leaders into symbols: Martin Luther
King versus Malcolm X and the Black Muslims; later, King versus Stokely
Carmichael.

Though some of the people we interviewed stressed the complementarity
of the moderate and the militant strategies, the pendulum was clearly swinging to the younger generation of nationalists, especially in the North and
West. Pro-integration leaders like Whitney Young of the Urban League and
Roy Wilkins of the NAACP seemed outmoded compared to Carmichael or
the Black Panthers. And even Martin Luther King was called a "has-been."

Black Power, Violence, and the Police

In 1968 almost all the blacks we interviewed, including the moderates, favored some form of Black Power.† The slogan had stimulated wide interest,

---

*The dispute was an underlying theme in the leadership struggle between Booker T. Washington
and W. E. B. Du Bois early in the century. Later Marcus Garvey, Elijah Muhammad, and
Malcolm X represented the separatist impulse, whereas the NAACP and the modern civil rights
movement worked for integration into the mainstream.
†Ten years later, however, several people complained of the intense pressure they had felt during
the late sixties to support militant positions.

but it was too ambiguous a term to be a focal point for developing a unified political strategy. To moderate blacks, Black Power meant building up black business; to liberals, it denoted greater electoral participation and more educational and employment opportunities. To cultural nationalists and many intellectuals, Black Power signified the right of black people to define their own group realities, choose their priorities, write their history, create a culture. Political nationalists stressed the importance of building autonomous all-black institutions—schools, businesses, police—in their communities. Militants of various tendencies equated Black Power with fighting back against racist provocations. In the vehemence of militant rhetoric, many whites—and not a few blacks—sensed undertones of violence.

The shift from integration to Black Power confused whites. They wondered what blacks really wanted, what they would do next. Schooled by traditions of racist thought to view blacks categorically, whites expected them to speak with one voice and had difficulty appreciating their personal, philosophical, and political diversity. If blacks wanted to build their own separate communities, whites asked, why are they still demanding special treatment in the system—at work or at school?

In the separatist rhetoric of the Black Power advocates, whites also saw a rejection of consensual values, particularly the national myth of the melting pot. And by tirelessly pointing the finger at America's racist structure, black militants challenged the commonly held idea that a minority group could find equality and justice through the normal workings of the American way. Further, the militants were no longer willing to wait for the fate of their people to slowly improve as the result of aggregate personal efforts and sacrifices made by specific individuals; they wanted immediate equality for all blacks.

In challenging basic American values and myths, Black Power advocates antagonized virtually every strand of white opinion. The greatest opposition came from liberals, whose integrationist credo was offended by Black Power's separatist emphasis. "Color-blind" liberals especially objected to the idea that power blocs should be based on race. Conservatives tended to be more comfortable than liberals with frank talk about power, but few welcomed its association with people of color. More explicit racists insisted that power should remain with whites. Even most white radicals, otherwise sympathetic to black militancy, expressed skepticism, seeing Black Power as a threat to the fragile bonds among the sixties' anti-establishment movements or as an obstacle to the Marxist dream of working-class unity or the counterculture's vision of universal love.

The idea of Black Power also tapped into deep-seated fears and anxieties, highly emotional associations between race and violence. Whites had difficulty accepting that Black Power was what blacks said it was: community control, economic autonomy, and political self-determination. Though some learned to appreciate these meanings, most suspected that Black Power was a disguised call to use violence to achieve black domination. Black rioting in the cities, the appearance of nationalist groups "taking up the gun," and the pervasive talk—as well as the reality—of political and personal violence gave shape to racist fears. In such a highly charged atmosphere, most whites did not make a sharp distinction between a principled adherence to nonviolence and a more open-ended political strategy. They saw instead the aggressive potential in any militant action, sensed the threat of violence even in nonviolent civil disobedience.

At the same time many blacks were hard pressed to maintain their own commitment to nonviolence. The strategy of "turning the other cheek" appealed to religious ideals and to an Afro-American redemptive humanism that had been a strikingly successful tactic in the early stages of the civil rights movement. But temperateness was increasingly seen as ineffective, cowardly, even as unmanly. Nonviolence had not prevented civil rights workers in the South from being beaten and killed; in the North nonviolence had little to offer the younger generation of low-income blacks, particularly the street youth who saw in groups like the Black Panthers a more appropriate vehicle for their rebellious mentality.

When "riots"—more often termed "rebellions" or "revolts" by politically conscious militants—first erupted in 1964 and 1965, even moderate blacks were sympathetic, understanding the depth of the anger that lay behind the outbursts. Many of these blacks were hopeful that such extreme measures would spur fundamental reforms. By the time we began our interviews, however, people were very critical of the violence. Their objections were not based on a moral condemnation so much as a cost-benefit analysis: what was the political payoff of rioting, when only their own communities were being destroyed, their own people dominating the list of dead and wounded?

This may explain why the summer of 1967 was the last of the "long hot summers." Although some of the decade's heaviest rioting followed the assassination of Dr. King in April 1968, there were no major ghetto revolts during the summers of 1968 or 1969, years when racial tension was otherwise at its peak. Rather, riotlike actions in the late sixties moved away from the "Watts model" toward more focused settings: high schools, colleges, and especially prisons. There were also organized actions by black nationalist groups against the police in a number of cities. Many blacks to whom we talked in 1968 were moving toward an acceptance of this kind of controlled, focused violence. Not without conflict, however. They searched their souls to find ways to reconcile their ethical values with the growing feeling that desperate measures were necessary, especially to deal with the police.

The police were major actors in the racial drama. Because they were on the front lines, trying to contain riots, seeing that civil rights and other demonstrations operated within the law, and making arrests in racially sensitive situations, their role was often controversial. Blacks and whites viewed them quite differently. Most blacks saw law enforcement as the country's most racist institution. Though they appreciated the need for public safety and deterring criminals, they resented being harassed by white cops and were disturbed by widespread allegations of brutality. As law enforcement became more politicized, targeting militant organizations such as the Black Panthers, many blacks began to view white police forces as colonial armies of occupation.

For many whites, in contrast, the police were the "thin blue line" protecting them from anarchy, revolution, and black violence. Often with friends or relatives on the local force, whites tended to identify with police officers, seeing them as workers with a job to do, decent men besieged by belligerent blacks, overzealous antiwar activists, and rebellious college students. A solid majority of whites approved the actions of the Chicago police in suppressing radical antiwar demonstrators at the Democratic Convention in 1968; blacks overwhelmingly disapproved.[3] A year earlier, after the decade's worst riots in Detroit and Newark, a Harris poll showed that whites had supported, by a ratio of 2.5 to 1, the police's shooting of looters; blacks had disapproved by the same ratio.[4] And unlike black people, most whites did not agree with the Kerner Commission's premise that urban riots were spontaneous manifestations of discontent arising from discrimination and prejudice. Instead, whites suspected that the violence was the result of agitation by communists or by leaders such as King and Carmichael—to many whites the political differences between moderate and militant black leadership seemed unimportant.

Black Identity and White Consciousness

Throughout the 1960s blacks were becoming more aware of their systematic oppression, of the institutional character of the racism that marked the parameters of their existence—their present lives as well as past histories. It was common then to say that no black person had to learn this, for each had lived it directly, his or her consciousness of oppression forged in the pain of survival. The interviews we conducted suggest that this was more true for the older southern-reared generation, which had experienced the clearcut lines of traditional segregation. But there were quite a few others, mostly northern-raised youth or Californians, who told us that they had never been discriminated against, never really knew what "all the fuss was about" until the movements and the mood of the sixties began their education in race relations, giving them for the first time a sense of racial grievance.

Along with an intensifying awareness of racism came a new attitude toward black ethnic identity. Many of our interviews capture the still-fresh excitement of this discovery, as positive feelings like pride and identification replace negative ones like self-doubt and alienation. Pride in blackness and the new identification with "black culture" also suggested a solution to the dilemma of integration. On the one hand, to get one's fair share of society's benefits, it was necessary to participate, at least to a certain extent, in the mainstream, which was, after all, "the only game in town." On the other hand, if integration meant "becoming white," compromising one's ethnicity and deepest self, it seemed less and less worth the price. During the late sixties, black pride, black culture, and Black Power promised to give Afro-Americans a way to negotiate this dilemma, to feel that they were setting some of the terms of the assimilation bargain.

Many blacks we talked to remained skeptical about the existence of a black culture—until the 1960s the standard view had been that slavery and assimilation had eliminated most vestiges of distinctive ethnicity—but others celebrated its growing recognition. They searched for their culture's themes and essential features and inventoried its strengths and weaknesses. Black Power with its separatist overtones was appealing because it promised to nourish and preserve the uniqueness of the black experience. This fear that the communal solidarity of black life would be lost in the American melting pot also contributed to the widespread ambivalence toward integration in the late 1960s.

The word *black* itself symbolized this new outlook, and its rapid acceptance showed the power of this "cultural revolution." In our earliest interviews, everyone—black and white alike—referred to people of Afro-American descent primarily as *Negroes*. By late 1968 (for blacks) and by the summer of 1969 (for whites) the dominant, almost exclusive, usage was *black* people.

In emphasizing race and racism so markedly, in flaunting their blackness so aggressively, the black militants forced many whites to confront the fatefulness of skin color and its social implications. Living in a multiracial society with democratic ideals and a color-blind ideology, whites as the dominant group had not experienced race and racism as pressing realities in their everyday lives. Especially since de facto segregation limited regular contacts with racial minorities, American whites had been able to confine their "whiteness" to remote corners of their consciousness, identifying themselves primarily as Americans, or as Irish or Italians, Catholics or Baptists. Outside the South (and the minds of transplanted southerners), whiteness per se was rarely a significant component of personal identity. (The very phrase "white identity" seems strange and jarring.) In the 1960s, however, blacks made it harder for whites to keep their racial identities so conveniently compartmentalized. Black actions impinged on white lives directly: at work, in the community, above all in politics and public life. The black demand that Euro-Americans own up to their whiteness met resistance. People who saw themselves as fair-minded and committed to equality and individual responsibility did not want

to face the possibility that their social position, even in p⸺
product of racial privilege.

This issue of who was responsible for racial inequality w⸺
one, because it was tied to the practical matter of who would pay ⸺
social change. In broad terms, whites addressed the question in one o⸺
ways.[5] First, they could accept personal responsibility for racism, viewing
themselves and their families, friends, and fellow workers as personally impli-
cated in the problems of black Americans. Having acknowledged their own
racist bias, they could decide how best to act on this new self-understanding.
And a few whites did wrestle with these agonies, sometimes in affecting ways,
like the hippies we talked to who considered themselves racists just because
they *noticed* differences of color.

But other whites didn't feel like racists. They thought of themselves as decent human beings, as people deserving what little they had achieved in their
lives, not as oppressors or exploiters. Some adopted a sociological explanation
of racism, condemning the society itself as a racially oppressive one. Among
the people we interviewed, the liberals and the radicals in particular took this
position and supported, if only ambivalently, fundamental social change to
create racial justice.

Fundamental social change, however, threatened whites' own interests,
and most whites found the analysis of racism as an impersonal force, an attribute of a system rather than of individuals, too abstract, too removed from
their personal experience, or just plain wrong. So the majority took a third
view. They neutralized the reality of racism by minimizing their own color
privileges and denying their personal prejudices. Rather than indicting themselves or the social system, they "blamed the victim," locating the barriers to
racial equality in the characteristics of the minority group.[6] With traditional
racism discredited as an ideology, few people now blamed the "deficits" of
blacks on biology or genetics. More fashionable was some version of "cultural
deprivation." Blacks were not able to advance like other groups because they
lacked the critical attributes necessary for success: education, motivation,
good work habits, discipline, and family cohesiveness.[7]

Why There Was No Race War

Underlying and facilitating racial and social ferment in the 1960s was an unprecedented economic boom. Employers' needs for more workers dovetailed
with civil rights pressures to bring down discriminatory barriers, and blacks
entered new industries and occupations. Paradoxically, these changes were
too slow for the excluded minorities, whose expectations had been raised
throughout the decade, and at the same time too fast for the white majority,
whose interests seemed threatened by the prospect of racial change. As the

nation moved slowly toward greater equality, conflict increased rather than lessened.

Conflict particularly intensified in day-to-day personal encounters. In every sphere of life, blacks challenged the spoken and unspoken assumptions that had governed race relations for generations. No longer were they accepting an inferior position, especially in the racial struggle itself. Those sympathetic whites who had once played important, even leading, roles in racial politics found themselves unwelcome in civil rights organizations.

For centuries blacks had lived in fear of whites. Now whites were afraid of blacks, their political militancy, their new aggressiveness, their potential violence. Whereas whites, as the "superior race," had long rejected blacks, now black people—especially the separatists—were rejecting whites, as political allies, as carriers of values, as models to be emulated.* Instead of taking racial insults, blacks were calling the names—"whitey," "honky," "racist"—and whites were learning how it felt to be the object of racial hatred, to be viewed categorically rather than as individuals. To many, it seemed as if the customary relationship between the races was being turned on its head.

Still, communication between blacks and whites was not closed. In the workplace, whites were hearing from black co-workers viewpoints on Black Power and other issues that countered the more alarming ideas they picked up from television and other whites. But whites sensed a change in black attitudes and demeanor, an anger and a withdrawal that were hard to deal with. Their most common complaint was that blacks were becoming too "touchy."

In other places where the races met—in high schools and the streets of mixed neighborhoods—racial tension was even more pronounced. In San Francisco's Haight-Ashbury white hippies complained of the frequent street hassles provoked by blacks. As one very pro-black hippy put it, poignantly but without a trace of irony: "It's so hard to be white these days." For their part, blacks, even moderates still committed to racial harmony, integration, and nonviolence, took some measure of delight in these reversals.

The great fear of whites was that blacks would go all the way and turn the tables. They thought blacks wanted to dominate them, just as they had been dominated. On both sides fear and paranoia were rife. Many blacks talked of genocidal plots, of concentration camps being readied. Whites thought that black militants were organizing armed insurrection, that their goal was to seize power through violent revolution. Especially after the assassination of Martin Luther King, people of both races worried that a civil war between whites and blacks might break out.[8] One white man we talked to regretted the prospect of having to shoot some of his Negro friends; other whites contem-

---

*Prodded by cultural nationalists who exploited the long-suppressed hunger for ethnic self-respect, the positive affirmation of black identity at times crossed the line separating pride from chauvinistic claims of black superiority.

plated going over to the black side; interracial couples agonized over their special predicament. At bottom, most people really didn't think it would come to a civil war, but the specter of racial holocaust aggravated the despair and pessimism of many blacks and intensified the fear of many whites.

Despite the widening color gap, racial division was never total, even during the polarized year of 1968. Though the polls found blacks consistently more opposed than whites to the war in Vietnam, some black conservatives sounded very much like white backlashers, supporting both the war and the actions of the Chicago police. And some whites were highly critical of the police and supportive of black militancy. Thus the forces that seemed to be dividing the society into two camps—either for or against "the system"—were not simply racial. The division was based rather on a collision between differing political priorities and philosophical assumptions about American society and social change.

On one side were those whose sense of urgency about racial problems transcended other concerns and values. Viewing racism and racial inequality as American democracy's most vital unfinished business, this group wanted to take advantage of the unique opportunity for a fundamental breakthrough that had been opened by the civil rights movement and, later, by the black militants. For those who held this position, the goal of incorporating blacks in the system was so paramount that it justified drastic changes in institutions and values to accommodate the special needs and interests of the previously excluded minorities. If such changes threatened an already fragile social order, the risk was worth taking, since it was these very institutions and values—whatever their democratic presumptions or "positive functioning"— that maintained a racially stratified society. Not surprisingly, this position was held by many (though not necessarily most) blacks, along with a small (though not necessarily insignificant) segment of the white population.

The "other side" had different priorities. Whether or not they supported the goal of racial equality, their major concern was the defense of a society whose integrity and stability seemed threatened by the divisiveness, the widespread violence, and the near anarchy of the time. For this group what was at stake was the democratic process itself. And because black militants insisted on setting their own rules and procedures and refused to accept conventional understandings of how to effect change, they were perceived as a threat to basic precepts of America's political culture. If black demands had merit, they must be accommodated to the consensual values of the society; racial minorities could not expect privileges unavailable to other groups. Most whites probably agreed with this point of view, and so did more than a few blacks and other minorities. Of course, there were people of both races who would not have subscribed to either position. They were somewhere in the middle, politically apathetic or uninterested in racial issues.

The events of the late 1960s challenged many people's unexamined assumptions and made them think about America and its social problems, especially race, on a deeper level. In the pages that follow we hear ordinary people, not just intellectuals, struggling to make sense of the racial crisis, advancing theories to explain racial inequality, the urban riots, the differences between minority groups. We hear people thinking with critical perspectives about social issues, learning from the conflicts and the public discourse of the 1960s, and experiencing for the first time the excitement of participating in historically significant events and contributing to social change. It is my hope that these oral histories preserve some of this excitement and heightened consciousness, and especially the urgency with which issues of race and racism were being debated by blacks and whites alike.

CHAPTER 1

The Politics of Manhood and the Southern Black Experience

Black militants projected an image of aggressive masculinity: to be a man was to confront and resist white people in a direct and forceful manner. After Watts and other riots, young black men often said that fighting back against the police was the first time in their lives they felt like men. Organizations such as the Black Panthers played upon this manhood theme in their strident rhetoric, their uniforms and weaponry, and of course in their almost exclusively male leadership.

Southern whites had long demanded docility of black men: the etiquette of hat in hand, the downward look, the nervous shuffle. Black women, though equally oppressed and exploited, were not as threatening to white men and white power and were permitted more latitude in expression and movement within the interstices of a racist system. Florence Grier's story, which opens this chapter, documents this double standard; she also describes how racism and discrimination made it almost impossible for black men to carry out the roles expected of males in a patriarchal society, that of providing for and protecting their wives and children. This may explain why manhood was a political and personal issue for Afro-Americans long before the sixties and well before the women's movement brought to the surface a "masculinity crisis" for white middle-class men.

But manhood was *not* a burning issue for the whites we talked to. Whereas blacks brought up the topic spontaneously and discussed it with intensity and passion, whites mentioned manhood only when asked directly. And among whites, conventional definitions of manhood, emphasizing the "good provider," prevailed, while blacks described a real man as someone who speaks up for what is right and is willing to fight for his principles. The mainstream ideas of men's economic responsibility and personal power were not irrelevant to blacks, but their idea of manhood had a deeper, more politicized, even philosophical, resonance: in addition to resisting racial injustice, a man had the fundamental right to claim a sense of personal dignity in his dealings with the world, to be viewed as a human being of intrinsic worth, whatever his color.[1]

The accounts of southern black life in this chapter are as much social histories of race relations as life histories of persons. Indeed, one lesson of the politics of the late sixties was that the personal and the political cannot be separated. Current events lent a special urgency to individual biographies, with people recalling the most minute details of a story of racial injustice or resistance that had taken place thirty, forty, even fifty years ago with the immediacy of an incident that had occurred last week. Florence Grier, living in Sacramento, California, and seeing television reports of blacks in Watts attacking bus drivers, remembers how southern drivers wielded total and arbitrary authority—one left her stranded during a ten-minute restroom stop— and figures that some of the black rioters must be recalling similar treatment in the South. For Mrs. Grier, like many other southern-born blacks who had left home decades earlier, her childhood shaped her assessment of the North and framed her attitudes toward the events of the sixties.

Hardy Frye, who conducted all the interviews in this chapter, is also of southern origin. Born in Alabama, Frye had worked with King's nonviolent movement as a young man and later became an organizer for SNCC. He moved to Los Angeles in the early sixties and was on the streets during the 1965 Watts riots. In March 1968, at the time of these interviews, Frye was attending college in Sacramento and working in the same community group as Florence Grier.

Florence Grier

"My father was from Alabama"

Florence Grier was in her early twenties when she left Oklahoma for California in 1942. Now, at age forty-five and the mother of five children, she is unemployed and on welfare. Like so many other black women of her generation, Grier has worked as a domestic most of her life. But she doesn't want to clean, wash, and cook for white people any longer. She began "day work" at the age of eleven, shortly after her mother died.

It didn't take me very long to learn that there was *nobody* . . . better than Negroes. As a girl, I'd walk into [white people's] homes, and they didn't know how to cook, they didn't know how to talk, they were more stupid than I. And it just didn't take me very long to find out that the only difference in this particular woman and myself was that she was white—and that she had the opportunity to live on the other side of town—and she could have access to better jobs. And I knew this when I was a girl! So I *never* grew up with this inferiority complex, this feeling that they were better.

I learned so many things about white women over the years. I learned to separate the poor white trash from the middle class from the upper crust—I call the upper crust "Mrs. Roosevelt." And I got to the place where I could walk into a woman's house, and I could tell by her clothes, the way that they were in the closets, the kind of things that she wore . . . the particular characteristics of the person.

The woman who is "Mrs. Roosevelt," she doesn't bother to tell you how to dust her furniture! If you don't know how to do it, she doesn't want to be bothered with you in the first place. She asks your qualifications, and you'll say that you're capable, then she shows you where the stuff is, shows you the instructions, and she leaves you there with it.

Then you've got the middle-class woman who had just worked and got her wealth or whatever she has. She stands and watches every move you make with a rag to make sure you don't scratch this, because she paid dearly for it. You see. She has this need for an inflated ego, so she wants the windows and everything shined like brass. She wants everything just up to par—because *her whole life* is bound up in this need to show off to the neighbors. This is the middle-class woman!

I've worked for these women who are middle class. You work all day long. Then she goes to the store and gets three grapefruit . . . one for daddy, and one for Lucy, and one for [her]self, and none for you. You're just . . . you're just a cleaning woman! You're not even worth fooling with! And of course, I sort of had a little ugly quirk. Whenever I worked in some of these homes I'd make sure that I ate up two portions of somebody's food. If there was just three grapefruit there, I'd make sure to eat one whole grapefruit myself.

The *poor* white . . . you're coming in the back door! (*Laughs bitterly.*) And the poor white is the one who keep his foot on your head all the time! He needs to be better than you. If you accidentally happen to call one of 'em, say, Sarah, she will remind you that she is Mrs. Jones. There's just no end to the stupid things that they can't do. They always need to look at the clock when you come in the door. "You're three minutes late! You're four minutes late!" And this woman can figure out seven minutes . . . to the three dollars and two cents that she owes you! This is how you can classify poor white trash from the middle class from the person who has. Because she can't afford to hire you! This is the kind that might not feed your brother! She can have him out there in the yard, and she will just ignore him as though he's a dog.

California is flooded with poor whites from the South. I've worked for them. If you go into some of these cannery stores, they'll bump into you trying to get to the counter! They eat everything the Negroes eat: pigs' feet, ears, and everything the same. My culture stems from [their] culture. Period! And the only culture that I really know when I hear this subculture business . . . the way that we have to live . . . is this inhuman condition that they have forced on us. The colored man and the white man—put him down there together in the gutters of Mississippi—that "culture" is the same.

When she was fourteen Florence had a run-in with a poor white woman who wanted her to work late Thursday afternoon, the customary half-day off for domestics.

When I said, "I'm not getting a half a day, and this is what you promised me when I took this job," she said, "Well, you're just a little bit too smart! For your smartness . . . you're just gonna get a dollar, ninety-five cents!" And I said, "If that nickel will do any good, you keep it! But I'm gonna be sure to tell every other Negro maid in town the kind of person you are." I have to admit to you I was afraid! Because to hit back or do too much talking you could get murdered. You just don't look a white woman in the face and tell her that she was doing you wrong!

We didn't have any 1954 desegregation idea—to help you with any idea of rising up. We hadn't any law to go to! Who could you run to and say help me? You lived for the day that you could just make enough money to get outta town, to get away from that. And you know, it's kinda funny when I hear sometimes on the news, on the talk shows, and it seems that Rap Brown and Stokely Carmichael and a few other of the militants are awakening the Negroes up to things that they hadn't known. You've *always* known this. You've never needed anybody to tell you that you weren't happy!

Oklahoma is not exactly in the Deep South. But Oklahoma is segregated, and you have the same experience in Oklahoma as you have in Arkansas, Tennessee, Texas, or anyplace else. I don't know what they do now, but at that time, you went in the back door. The people in Oklahoma, most of 'em in the area that I lived, were a poor type people. You worked, and if you had a brother or anybody, he would clean the yard and you would have to give him his lunch in the backyard. This was one of the things that I resented so much in Oklahoma! He could do yard work, but he could never get any further than the back porch! I don't care if it was December, snow on the ground, or anything, he sat out on the steps, and eat his lunch.

And I have seen this: A young Negro male, sixteen, seventeen, eighteen years old, is working in the garden. And the white woman squat down in the yard in front of this boy, just an open advance to him. I'm looking right between her legs, and the boy's looking between her legs! And all I have to do is just look up at him and see him sweating! I'm sure that there are hundreds and hundreds of other Negro women have had this experience. And she go up in her house and take her clothes off. And I remember saying to this particular boy, "Now you gonna get an invitation to go upstairs . . . but you better keep your butt away from up there! Because if this man happens to drive up in the driveway and catch you upstairs, you're gonna get lynched. So you just sweat it out, buddy!" These are just some of the little experiences that the Negro male has had.

I didn't like the attitude that I was a nobody. When I think of some of the things that we did—if the Negro really wanted to have killed the white man! I've had an aunt who was so mad because she wanted to go home . . . at the right time . . . she just turned right around and *spit* over in the cake! She said, "This is for you!" Right in the cake! "You don't like me and you think that you're better? You're gonna eat all the spit that I can get in this cake!" This is something inside that you want to do that. You can't do anything else because you don't want to die! You see? And they come out to the kitchen [and] say to her, "Oooohhh, well, this was a wonderful cake!" I've even seen this happen, Hardy! If you think that the Negro's been baffled all these years, *he just couldn't do anything else!*

I've seen youngsters that I've taken care of until they got three or four years old, I've seen the youngster gradually withdraw. After I've taken care of the baby until he's big enough to say "Florence," and he's big enough to notice me when he gets out in public . . . and he'd meet me up in Kress, and he'd say, "Momma! There's Florence!" And then she'd say, "Shhhh! Shut up! You're not supposed to be with her up here!" And . . . gradually . . . he would get to the place where he wouldn't, he wouldn't speak to me so much— in public. He would be just as sweet as he wanted to be when I came in the back door, but then when I went to town that would be a different little boy! Now this little boy had been sitting in my lap, this little boy had been sleeping in my bed—I'd been taking him out to my servant quarters—but when he would get to town he would have to change his whole attitude. And this is the way that they teach these youngsters prejudice and selfishness. He learns by the time he's five years old that "Florence is a nigger."

When school was out I would hire myself out as a maid to people going off on vacations, from Oklahoma to Wyoming to Kansas to Texas. And the white woman always will leave you there in the house with this—with the white male. If I had the time to sit down and tell you the stories of the white men that have walked around in the house with me! An eleven-year-old girl. It's nothing for them to walk around in their shorts and talk to me as though they were my brother or something like that! Because I held my integrity, it wasn't because her husband was so good! It was because of my integrity, not the husband's! I could go into any part of the house, sit down and talk and hold discussions with the white male. But the Negro male could never come farther than the back porch!

There are some bigots I've worked for. If he's a good bigot, then he's not touchable. He'll get up in the morning and have his shirt and tie on just the way he's supposed to have 'em on. He'll get up and close the door. You know how you would do if there's somebody that you don't want to be bothered with, 'cause you're so high that you can't be reached. But when he comes down, all the way downstairs and grunts and goes backward and forward through the living room . . . all outta his territory, into the part that you're into. . . . You just don't go parading around with a strange maid this way. He's not my brother. It's not something that you can really put your hands on. But I know that there're a lot of women would recognize this.

I'm working in this house. And maybe the whites, the two of 'em had planned to give me a box of chocolates over Christmas. But I want a bicycle for my little boy. And I go into the dining room or wherever he is sitting, and I said that I had planned on getting a bicycle for my little boy. When I can go and say that I'd like to have a certain thing done . . . and . . . just leave it in the air! And I can get it. To tell you the truth, Hardy, it's kind of a pleasure. You know. He can be tricked. It's the coyness of a woman. It has given me a sense of satisfaction over the years that he can be bought. You have to be a white man to understand what I'm saying!

Hardy, a man is a man. And I (*wry laugh*) really haven't found any difference in 'em. Only that the white man will want an undercover situation. It's not to be talked about or anything. And this is not poor white men—this is white men *period*. "Have you ever had experience with a white man?" This is one of the approaches that they would ask you. "What do you think about white men?" Coming down through the kitchen 'n' you're cooking dinner or something like that. And "Have you ever had . . . sexual relations with a white man?" Or "If you're nice to me"—you're getting, say you're getting a dollar an hour—"Wouldn't you like to make your check a little bit bigger?"

■ *They'll make these statements?*

Yeah! Of course a colored man would do the same things. I honestly don't see any difference other than the color of the man's skin. My experience has been, the most beautiful men in the world, the most tender and loving men in the world, the kindest men in the world—I have found to be white. The most kindest men in the world, some of the most beautiful men in the world—I've found to be colored. If the man is educated, if he has the right background—a sense of what I call a gentleness and kindness. Moral principles and that sort of thing. It has nothing to do with color at all!

My father was from Alabama. And even now he is so thoroughly oriented to using a front that a white person, twenty-five years old, could walk up to him and he would say, "Yes sir, how do you do?" He could be the milkman or anybody.

This is what happens to the little Negro boy in the South. His first experience with whites is when he goes to town to buy something with his parents. And then he learns—by his mother constantly telling him to keep his hands off—not to make too much noise, "because you're gonna get thrown out of here!" The tension that the mother has . . . she keeps a steady hand on him—*all the time.* If he gets too far out and makes too much noise, he just might get the worst spanking!

I didn't always realize what was happening and why our youngsters are not this Stokely kind—this aggressive look-you-between-the-eyes, this Muhammad Ali sort of Negro. Your kind! That will look this man in the face. This is the new Negro! The Negro is not used to *this* Negro! I mean my father's type, and I would be willing to say some of my age are not used to seeing this kind of Negro. Look this white man in the face and tell him he's a dirty rat! (*Heavy dialect and mimicking great fear:*) "Man! What is this cat trying to do? He's going get us all *killed!*"

You take myself, for instance, having this complete way of thinking from the South. You can't get all this out of a person at one time! After you've spent, say, twenty or twenty-five years in this segregated attitude. There's a feeling of withdrawal. And I sense that in Dr. King. When Dr. King talks he weighs all of his words very heavily. Dr. King is conditioned to think two or three times before he makes a statement. Because you're used to making it sound palatable to the white man. Even *I* do it! You start to thinking, "Now why did I say it this way?!" You know. And then you see the young Negro, and baby! (*Laughs.*) This is a new Negro!

He won't think two or three times! He hasn't had to go in that white man's kitchen . . . he hasn't had to go bow for him, he hasn't had to wash windows 'n' dig in his yard or anything like this. He hasn't had this complete conditioning that is passed on by your parents! "Now you weigh it really heavy, because you gotta decide whether you gonna get your head [or] . . . your teeth knocked in!" Oh, how many times have I heard my grandmother say, I've heard old colored women say, when they were whipping kids with a stick: "Now I'm gonna beat the hell out of you to keep that white man from killing you! I'm gonna bend you now!"

And there are men . . . when the insurance agent comes in . . . rather than look that man in the face and tell him that "I can't afford that insurance and I don't want any of it now" . . . he would have me to go to the door—

■ *Your father did it?*

My father! My father, my brother . . . my brother wouldn't do it now, but there are men who are my age—or less, and you've got some in the South now—that rather than look this white man in the face and show him . . . You can't hide the hate . . . and resentment that you feel all the time! The nigger with the big white eyes. It'd be kind of hard for you. . . . When you don't like a thing I can tell it right away!

- *Me, you mean?*

Yeah, Because you get a slit in your eyes, you know. And when you're happy, your eyes are just nice and round. I can register it right away! And rather than look this white man in the face and let him see how he feels, he'll hold his head down. He's not holding his head down all the time because he's afraid. He don't want to register what he feels. Because he might be kicked in the teeth.

What we call a man is somebody who makes a living the way we think he's supposed to make a living—keeps up with the rat race. But that's not my idea of a man. My idea is a man who's free to express and bring out his real understanding of what life is.

The standard of the white man has said, "The man is the head of his family." But this Negro male image . . . is squashed. He's lost his manhood, that part that's supposed to be aggressive according to our society! We've already beat that out of him, because you don't want the white man to beat him. Then when he goes to work, he's gotta practically bow down. He's called a *boy* and all the other things.

A lot of Negro men didn't have any jobs, and the job that you had was the only thing that kept the family together! The only thing that the husband was for was to produce kids! And to comfort you. You see? And it does something to you when you find out that you're the boss of everything. You see the man bending to do whatever you say do. Because the money is in your hand. Whether it's two dollars a week or whether it's one dollar a week—you got the money and he's got none! You buy the groceries, you even buy his cigarettes because he's got no money! And of course, a lot of times this makes the man mad. You're just mad because nothing is going right for you. My own husband . . . would just get up and walk out! You're taking all of his authority away from him, you see? Well, there's nothing for him to do but bash out a window or get up and walk off and just get mad or stay out for three or four weeks. And then he can't explain all the time. I've seen my own daddy before we came out here—on the Fourth of July, when I think about it now—he couldn't bring us some firecrackers. And rather than come home and face it and say, "I haven't got any firecrackers," he just stayed gone three or four days.

There is this need, deep need, that the Negro has had for years and years and years. I go to school and every five minutes, if you bring up a conversation, you hear a Rap Brown and a Stokely Carmichael. And you get a real thrill when a Stokely gets up and tells [Lyndon] Johnson that he's a buffoon. He stands up and looks this man right between the eyes and he says, "I am the excellency of God's dignity. I am just as much a man as any other man." This man is the man that we've been waiting for. *All* Negro girls, they're looking for this kind of man. I hate this man when I see this man in the white man. I see this kind of man in Robert Kennedy! I see these guys in George Wallace. I see this kind of a guy in Ronald Reagan! You know? But this guy, who stands up, a Stokely Carmichael, who defies the whole nation . . . and you watch this man . . . *petrify* . . . *magnetize* . . . *all* the *Congress*. And when Stokely breaks wind—if they could see the wind (*laughing*), they'd shoot it, man!

This is the kind of man that you've always had, but you've just crushed this stuff and it's just coming out now. This is the kind of man that will *never* be crushed! This is the kind of man that you need in every state! Just one Stokely Carmichael and one Rap Brown, one Hardy Frye. And Stokely hasn't shot a single gun, has he? All he do is work on this Man's conscience.

> Mrs. Grier's 1968 interview continues in chapter 3,
> where she talks about organizing against police
> racism in Sacramento. For her ideas ten years
> later, see chapter 8.

LIVING IN a racist society presents people with a constant dilemma of whether to submit to a particular injustice out of expediency or habit, or whether to rebel against it. The political history of blacks in America can be analyzed in terms of this dialectical tension between accommodation and protest. Certain historical periods, like the 1960s, encouraged resistance, but more typically acts of resistance and rebellion had to be covert, lest they invite more repression. And since white southerners had a stake in portraying the Negro people as contented with their lot, even the memories of acts of resistance were often suppressed.

A subterranean tradition of rebellion nevertheless persisted, and in the 1960s black people actively reclaimed their past. We heard an unexpected number of "fighting back" stories, particularly when older southern-born blacks talked about their childhoods. It seemed as if there was an unsung Nat Turner in everyone's lineage: a father, grandfather, brother, or uncle who had defended his family with a gun, protested Jim Crow laws, fought off white policemen, or talked back to the boss.

But even though many southern blacks did resist, most had little choice but to live with the situation, placing their hopes on their children, and in the process "catching hell"—like the parents of Len Davis, whose story follows. Others, like Davis himself, a thirty-year-old postal worker originally from Florida, chose the alternative of going North. He tells of the high hopes of young blacks who left the South, only to discover a different brand of racism in the North. This theme of disillusionment with the hypocritical North, and an almost nostalgic preference for the straightforward racism of the South, was alluded to by virtually all the southern-born blacks we talked to.

Len Davis

"Promised Land is just like the old plantation"

Why do Negroes leave the South? It's just like getting out of slavery. When you get to the Promised Land, you free, man. You can do what you want to and go where you want to, say what you want to. And you don't have to worry about somebody throwing a bomb in your house because you stand up for your rights.

And it's really a letdown when you get there, man. Promised Land is just like the old plantation, really. You still haven't got any more rights. They're all a bunch of phony rights. They're a little bit better, but it's not like what you've been thinking. And that's what makes you mad.

I lived on the East Coast, New York, the northern cities, about five years. And I've been out here [Sacramento] five years. And it isn't different. You've still got that old niggertown. And look at Harlem. The biggest niggertown in the world. And Fillmore district in San Francisco. Oak Park in Sacramento. And the white man, he'll still come out there with his pistol on his side. And walk around like he owned the whole world. And anything that you got down there, you've got it here. It's not as open, you know. There's a lot of under-cover. Underhand business and sneaky business. Really, I got a lot of respect for Governor George Wallace. 'Cause he just says, "I hate niggers," you know.

I'm really glad I was raised in the South. I'm a step ahead of all this north-ern shit, this California shit. I knew all these race problems when we were just youngsters, wherein they don't know anything. [They] think, "I'm sure glad I'm not down there because they don't lynch here. I'm in the Promised Land. I can do this and I can do that, and there won't be any problem." Then all of a sudden—snap—it comes to them, that they aren't in no better shape than that guy that's being lynched down in the South. As a matter of fact I think that has something to do with the riots now. It's not going on in the South. It's the kids in the North, they get to thinking, shit, I'm in worse shape than they are.

We were a little more together down South. You had to be. All the Negroes were in one community. Everything they did, they did it together. You went to the same schools. You couldn't go and eat dinner downtown at a white res-taurant. It was you on one side of town and whites on the other side.

In every town down South there's a section called the quarter. And you go down there, and nine times out of ten there's one street that stands out in that community. And we had one called Maple Street. And man, those cops would come down there on Saturday night. Wow, they'd just whip heads if they felt like it. I've seen guys half drunk that would straighten up when they seen these cops walking down the street. Two of them would walk down a community of nothing but Negroes, you know. A hundred Negroes. And Negroes, they're supposed to be—oh, they cut you and shoot you and all that stuff. But there was no fear in these cops. That's what I could never understand.

What they did and said was gospel. They were cops, and they had so much respect, man, I think that the thought that they were mistreating you was wiped out of your mind. In most of the adults. Now the youngsters my age, I think we started the change. I think we started the people to thinking, you know. Right there in the early fifties. But man, anybody that was twenty years old or more, in the early fifties—they were terrible. They had been brainwashed that this white man was really a protector. They *had* to think that way in order to make it. I'm no psychiatrist or anything, but I think that you can just block something out of your mind, you know. And start looking at the good side of it. In other words, I'm not being suppressed, I'm not being discriminated against, I'm just being protected. And I think that's the only way that the Negro could have made it back in those days. He couldn't go to bed thinking in the night that, man, this man is treating me like a dog.

I saw a couple of cases where they took four boys to court—they were caught with a white woman. They didn't rape her, but they were seen with her. So they said all four raped her. They got life sentences. Sheriff Simmons killed a couple of them on the way to prison. I guess I was about fourteen. It was a big thing in my hometown. Everybody was afraid to go out, you know. You just stayed on your side of town.

I knew a lot of guys that had these type of jobs that you could get then—working in a drugstore or as a delivery boy—where you come into contact with whites. And these guys walked a chalk line. "I better not say anything about this raping or anything." Whereas today, even in Florida, and especially in California, they talk about it on their job. Just like talking about who won the baseball game.

And what I got out of it, being a kid, was that those guys got out of their place. Even our parents participated in making us think that those boys were wrong for even being in the *presence* of this white woman. Whether they raped her or not. We were brainwashed, in other words.

In high school everything is happy-go-lucky. You play. You want to know why you can't go where you can, show the whites that you are just as good as they are. Athletically, scholastically, either way, you know. But once you get out of high school, you want that same job that the white boy can get without taking a test. And just a better economic standard, that's all. You're belittled because of your race. And you're more aware of it now, once you're out of high school. That happy-go-lucky feeling—that everything is lovely—and it *was* lovely, but you didn't know all the things your parents had to go through even to keep you in school back in those days. And then once you become an adult you find out. All that hell that they caught trying to keep you in school. And man, you *really* hate.

The thing that kept me going was that I'm going to get away from here one day. If I'd known then what I know now I'd have stayed there and fought them. When I left it was in my mind that there was no hope. That you can't fight these people. They've got the stronghold, let them have it.

> Len Davis's 1968 narrative continues in chapter 7,
> and his 1981 and 1987 followup interviews are in
> chapter 13.

"YOU SHOW a little grit and you lands in jail," Paul Robeson sang in "Old Man River." The southern prison farms were crowded with "uppity" black men who had refused to conform to the traditional role, who had "gotten out of their place." Howard Spence, whose story closes this chapter, was an NAACP field representative who investigated dozens of the kinds of lynchings that had terrorized Len Davis as a boy: "Some of them are so rash I don't want to talk about them," Spence told interviewer Hardy Frye.

Howard Spence

"I wouldn't want to treat anybody like I've been treated in Mississippi"

Howard Spence was sixty-five years old in 1968. He was born in Mississippi; one grandfather was a slave, the other the slave owner, "a white man named Spence." He grew up on a plantation, the eldest son of nine children. Poverty and his parents' separation forced him to quit school in the sixth grade. To support the family, he picked cotton and cut ties for the Illinois Central. The railroad's construction had been supervised by his white grandfather, using the labor of his former slaves.

At seventeen, shortly after World War I, he was one of many blacks of his generation who left the South in search of greater opportunity. He moved to Chicago, where he shined shoes, worked in factories, operated the candy concession for the elevated railway, and chauffeured for rich Jewish families on the

*North Shore. He learned to read and write and became a sleeping-car porter.
After World War II Spence returned to Mississippi, opened a service station,
and served as an NAACP field secretary, investigating lynchings and pioneer-
ing the registration of black voters. He played a pivotal role in bringing the
Emmett Till murder to national attention. Such activities placed him on the
Klan's death list, so in the mid-1950s he left Mississippi for a second time to
settle in Sacramento, California, where he became a respected figure among
that city's black activists.*

*When he talked to interviewer Hardy Frye, "Mr. Spence"—as he was
called, in keeping with the traditional black southern respect for age—was feeling deeply sad and dejected. The race war that seemed imminent during the
spring of 1968 threatened to destroy the meaning of his life, a life that had been
devoted to constructive racial progress.*

*Growing up in Mississippi, he "always had to remember that the white was
the boss. Was superior."*

Today when I hear so much about school busing and the teachers and what
they're learning, I can always remember how the whites would pass us as we
were going to school. We had to honor those people—that they were something special, that we were different, that we were tainted. All of this had a
psychological effect on keeping us in a *cramped* condition. I don't know that it
was an *inferior* condition; it was a cramped condition to live in. Back in the
days when I began to grow up and would go to town, I had to step off the
street, step in the mud, to let white people pass by. These are things that had a
terrible bearing on me.

I had a cousin that came back from World War I with wrapped leggings on.
And I saw white people telling this man to stay off the streets with the uniform
on. In my little town. And these things had a bearing on me that made me
wonder just *where* do I fit into this American society.

There was nothing to give us the motivation and the drive that we should
have had. You mustn't be an incentive farmer, you must look to others. Teach
us that we were never able to take care of ourselves without the aid of the
commissary or the store. This is known to the older Negroes, not to the young
people. They don't know anything about what has happened in Mississippi.

*Working as a sleeping-car porter opened up new vistas and experiences that set
him off from others of his generation, both from his Mississippi cousin who
"never changed" and from northern black workers who drank up their paychecks
most Saturday nights. "I loved the trains. The railroad was my salvation."*

*On the tops of passenger cars and in the hobo camps, he met lawyers, engi-
neers, and doctors who had lost everything during the Great Depression. He
learned how temporary and temporal are wealth and status, and he resolved to*

*do something more meaningful with his life, to plan for the long range and stop
living day by day.*

*When he moved back to Mississippi, only 40 of the 10,000 Negroes in the
half-black town were registered to vote and none actually voted. He became
active in the Mississippi Registered Voters League. In one year alone they registered 490 new voters, despite the white registrars' asking blacks such questions
as how many seeds in a watermelon, how high is up, and how many bubbles in
a bar of soap.*

*As an NAACP field representative Spence also investigated lynchings. At
first he wouldn't even discuss them. But then he starts talking about Emmett
Till, a fourteen-year-old black boy from Chicago who was visiting relatives in
Mississippi.*

I happened to be deeply involved in the Emmett Till case. The lad that
was taken out of Lennox, Mississippi, and murdered. By these whites. Had
it not been for Medgar Evers, who was NAACP secretary at the time, asking
me to go investigate, it would have just been another "case" that's been forgot. I sometimes think that the Emmett Till case was the beginning of the
Montgomery bus boycott. It was the beginning of a lot of incidents in the
South that began to make the Negro aware of the fact that he would *have* to
get out and expose himself to these racists—to these people that were gonna
kill him.

I had my old 1940 raggedy Chevrolet coupe. And I drove over to the farm
where these people were. Now in order to be disguised, to keep from being
killed, I had put on some overalls, put in some cotton padding, and I began to
talk about picking cotton until I got a chance to ask them about Emmett Till.
They began to whisper the facts. "Oh, he's in the river. But that'll be all there
is to it."

Now when I went back to Greenwood, my telephone was already tapped.
That Saturday night there was about an eight-foot cross burned right in front
of my place. On my lawn. It tied in with Gus Coate—no, the Reverend
George Lee murder.

Now after I had made this trip I rushed to Jackson. And there was a Detroit
newspaper—I don't know which one—reporter in Medgar Evers's office. And
this man made one remark that will forever be with me. He said never before
has a case of this kind been able to escape the borders of Mississippi. "*Now*
we're gonna see that this one gets out: because the report that you have given
us will be in the Detroit press tomorrow." And from there on the Emmett Till
case began to take just a flurry of action.

They began to search the river; they began to search from place to place;
they got everybody together. And as a result he was found in the Tallahatchie
River. When they brought him to Greenwood, what we had formerly thought
was a bullet hole—it was explained to us that it was a bit that had been drilled

through the child's head. This is a fact—I'm only talking about facts. These men [two white men confessed to the crime in *Look* magazine after a jury acquitted them] admitted that never was there a time that this boy stopped pressing this. Even to his last breath, he was still resisting. And this was something exciting to them—this is why they went to the river. There was an old gin, fan wheel, there—this is what they had for him. I'm just wondering now how many shackles will we find in the Tallahatchie River.

I want to tell you the truth. I felt my life wasn't worth a penny with a hole in it. I looked at any minute to be shot down in the night. Now there was twelve men on the list to be killed. I happened to be one. Dr. Howard, Reverend George Lee, and on down the line. Now they killed about six of these men. I probably would have been there to be killed, but due to my wife's health—what had actually happened to her *because* of these conditions—I left.

Now these are some of the things that make me know that racism can be frightening. And when I try to work with young people in California and Sacramento and we try to formulate plans to help the poor and we show this complacent feeling—this lack of being serious about what we're doing . . . I just think back at these people that have made more progress than we have under such *terrible* conditions. Now one more incident to show what racism is—this will not take long.

It was these two white cousins out of Parchman. They broke out of jail and off the [penal] farm. They went to McAdams, Mississippi, and they killed this whole family. We don't know why they picked this family. There was a wife, a husband, and there were two children that was killed, and a girl fourteen years old was shot through the right breast. The father was shot in the stomach with a forty-five. The mother held the child that was shot—the fourteen-year-old girl. The strange thing was that at no time was any effort made to apprehend these people that committed this act. After the press got ahold of it and began to get it out, *then* they caught them. They were only returned to jail. That was all that happened to the white men that committed this crime. These are just incidents of racism that I have given to you. I could name one after the other all day long.

This is how you crush a man till he accepts the fact that he feels inferior to you. I think the older people, they'll never grow out of this thing. They're still suffering under this same feeling. In the South especially. Now a lot of them come here because they expect the handout, they expect little things. They don't believe in creating. Like I'm talking about the work part of it. This farm life—there's nothing wrong with the farm life if we could have expanded it. We learned to do a lot of things, we learned to make our way. We learned to create things. Any person who can do something with their hands . . . don't have to be the timid one.

I've always advocated work, menial work. Labor. It can be dignified and become a factor in our gaining recognition and position, to become a part of this rich society. I'm trying to say this: we've *always* had to do work, and we've had to work for little—very little—I can remember when I worked for fifteen cents a day. I can remember splitting rails for twenty-five cents a ton. This was a terrible hard, manual, muscle work.

The young Negro is not particularly interested in me telling him all of these things. He wants to know, Why did we take it? "Why were you so long waking up? Why should I have to know about all of this when I'm *supposed* to be getting these things? These laws are for people, these laws are for *us.*" So we older people are really indicted by the youth. And I think rightly so; I feel kind of guilty.

- *Why do you feel guilty?*

I believe there could have been more done for our young people. When we were talking about raising money for some foreign mission in Africa, we didn't have an accredited college in Mississippi. Why, if that's the only education you've got, you know you won't fit into the society. Tougaloo, Jackson State—these places we've founded since then. And the part that frightens me now is that these young people—I don't think it's because they have a better idea. They have an idea that none of the whole thing needs to exist. Just wipe it off. And get a clean slate. Even in our neighborhood work here, we're empty for ideas as to what to do about the problem. Now when I read and when I listen to the radio, as I have today, about all the preparations being made to put down the riots, to murder and slaughter in the streets, I am absolutely frightened. I think the people that are advocating it haven't given a thought to what's going to happen when the blood starts.

I'd rather starve than have a race war. We don't understand what this thing would actually mean. To the mass of people. The disruption, the despair, and the effect that's gonna have on the Negro that don't feel like he's involved. He's gonna be *affected* by this thing; he's gonna have to take a stand, one way or the other. What are they gonna do? Once they start killing Negroes? Stop? The Negroes might escalate the whole thing, they might surprise them, like they are in Vietnam. Gee whiz, I thought the war was over in Vietnam. And these little people that have nothing but a hand grenade or a popgun or firecrackers, they come up and changed the scene for the whole business.

I find the leading magazines every week, I'm faced with these stories, wondering why it is that they're just now coming out with the truth. It's been a fact for years. And it's having a damaging effect on our society. And I don't think any of it is hardly worth saving. Now I'm almost ready to give up. Because I have worked hard, I've tried to do something to help clear up the situation. And I don't see any way. (*His voice is very soft and sad.*)

I was listening carefully this morning when they were accusing Stokely Carmichael of teaching the black people to hate white people. And I wonder what is so frightening about this. When all of these years *they* have been taught to hate black people. My God, the boys that I grew up with—white boys that we used to go swimming with in the mudhole and run the snakes and turtles out, swam together—when he was twelve years old, I'm wondering why I missed him for a couple of weeks. And when he come back he was ready for me to start calling him Mister. *Who* had been talking to him? How come? What made him feel now that he's twelve years old and I'm twelve years old and I got to say Mister? To him. Now you see, somebody's teaching somebody something else. So we used to walk downtown together and get an ice cream cone together, eat together, play together.

If racism went in reverse, I'd rather be the slave myself. I'd rather see a war that would destroy everything than to see us have to practice racism. There's no sense in it. I wouldn't want to treat anybody like I've been treated in Mississippi. I wouldn't get much credit no doubt, from the young people, for saying this.

I think Black Power is absolutely what we've got to have. And you can call it cynical, but you have to have a base that we can operate with. Power is about the only thing that gets respect. Now whether it had to be *Black* Power—I think political power is what it really means. And I've always advocated this. How are you gonna talk to this establishment from a base of weakness? Nobody listens to a weak person in the first place.

- *What about Stokely?*

Well, I like the boy. When a man try to be peaceful, try to be accepted on his merits—he has an education—I would like to know why people are so frightened because he changed. I'd change too. I remember when the man was beat up and put into jail. They say get an education, clean up, straighten up. We done all of these things. And *still* we're not accepted. So what is left for the boy to do? I think before they talk about Stokely Carmichael they should talk about the Ku Klux Klan.

I'm really afraid. I don't see nothing but violence because this is what they want. They're preparing for it. I had a man approach me the other night. Said, "Well, they're getting ready to mow the Negroes down in the streets." Okay. Has he ever thought that maybe they're playing into the Negroes' hands? Maybe a man can get in a condition where he feels that death is more acceptable than the conditions that he's living in. Are they going to do him a favor? By shooting him down in the streets? If they get out there and blast them down with machine guns, it'll be the shot that is heard around the world. What consequences it'll have I don't know. I'm not a scholar of that type.

But he is a community activist, concerned with and involved in virtually every problem faced by Sacramento blacks. He has campaigned for children's playgrounds, against police brutality, and especially for jobs.

All Stokely Carmichael is telling you, the way I understand it, is that if we will be set aside in the ghetto, let's make something out of that ghetto. This is what we're talking about here in Oak Park right now. We know that there's enough repair jobs—if it wasn't for the restrictions of the City Planning Commission and the establishment—we could give out jobs to young people and train them how to work. So what happens? The unions won't hire us. The city planners keep restrictions over us. And here is a kind of waste of what could be talent, what would be something to help cut out some of our unemployment.

You know what makes me sick is these things they change. Now you know this word *ghetto*. This belonged to the Jewish people, according to the things that I have read about it. Now they've attached it to the Negro. Now, we always had *quarters*. The quarters used to be this little row of houses after houses on the plantation. This was during slave times, where all the Negroes were kept, where they could go there, and one word would go right down the line. There were no white skins there at all. So I sometimes become amazed at the names that they give. Seems like it's just to confuse us. I don't let people confuse me with a Jewish ghetto. Because what makes ours different is that we are black and very distinguished from other people. It's so easy to put all of us together. But if a Jew learns how to speak English and gets some money, that's it. He's lost in this whole situation. They can't pick him out. It doesn't make any difference *what* we do. I don't care how much money we get.

As long as this whole thing—color—is taught, it has priority over everything else. Any case that comes up, even *we* have accepted that, we want to know, Is it colored or white? White and black thing is something that we are not going to get rid of in these times. Because nobody is going to accept the fact that they have to accept a black person on his own merits. It's not gonna happen here; I said it before the Supreme Court decision, I say it now, if they want to place me on the record with Stokely Carmichael I'll *still* say it. You'll not be accepted in this society with black skin.

He works as a janitor at a local college.

One of the security men said to me, "Spence, why is it that the Negro lived in Africa all these years, he never thought of making a wheel or anything?" And really, I got upset. And he saw that. Now, just last week the same man came into the boiler plant and we sat down for a conversation and coffee. He said, "Did you see in the paper today where this doctor that transplanted this heart—he got some of his ideas from the two Negro janitors that worked in the building?" I said, "You look to me like you're backing up on your own thoughts." Now, I have been able to read stories of the great historians about Timbuktu, the cultures they had. I have shared my home with African boys, and talked about the different cultures. I can't accept the fact that we haven't had any culture. I will accept the fact that the first thing that they did when they brought us to this country was to destroy what little thought we had of it.

Imitating the white man—or trying to imitate him—this has been one of the best gimmicks that he ever put up. Trying to get us to wear our hair like his, make us dress up every Sunday, give us all these expensive ideas and keep the money from us. I'm beginning to think that maybe we *might* revive or reconstruct something that you could call our culture. But otherwise I wouldn't want to commit myself to trying to talk about it because it's brand new to me. It's *all* up in confusion. I do like some of the things that we have changed. Because I don't see how in the world you can use powder on a black person to make him look like a white person. And if we're gonna search for anything I think we ought to be ourselves.

- *What is ourselves?*

Be a black man. My concept of this is be yourself. Since we are black, I don't kill any time with being black. I don't waste any time thinking or worrying about being black. What I'm trying to do is to express myself—express this inner urge that I have. The urgency of being an individual.

And you couldn't hardly be an individual without accepting the fact that you are part of a group. Right now we are beginning to find ourselves being congealed or brought together. When somebody like Stokely Carmichael—he wouldn't have to say, "Hate white people." All he's got to do is tell us to start loving one another. And this is frightening, especially to white people.

And I want to tell you something, Hardy. If I didn't believe that we had the greatest capacity—I mean black people—for changes, for forgiving, for love . . . We have the capacity to desire to live after all of these crushing defeats that we have went through. Not many people do. Not many people will accept life . . . the American people themselves only accept it on a certain basis. If they can't be boss, if they can't run the show, just tear it up.

In my younger days, when you went to church you heard soul music. You heard music that was born out of respect—born out of people that was trying to express themselves in a song, what they could not express in action. So they sung, "Oh Lord, won't you help me?" They sung "I'll Overcome" and all these things. We sung it in the cotton factories and in the fields where people wasn't allowed to express themselves. But when I was in Birmingham last year and I saw this church that had been blasted that killed these children, it made me begin to hate the thought of religion. Because I think it's been used as a gimmick. As serious as we have been about our religion, as much as our people, the soul people, want to think that this has been a help to them, and I want to respect them for having something to hold on to, I think it was a gimmick. The whole religious system—even the whites'. A lot of baloney as far as I'm concerned. To do unto others as you'd have others do unto you was here long before this Man ever thought about it. And he got us all tangled up in this mess.

Let me ask you this question: if a people were too dumb to have a ballot after the Civil War, if we were too ignorant to vote, what made anyone think that we were smart enough to read the Bible? My goodness, it's much more complicated to read and understand the Bible than it is to go up there and cast a ballot for somebody you want. But they freely gave it to us—because, I think, and I'm suspicious now, that they knew that all we could do was get tangled up in it. And as a result everywhere you go you find this Negro bogged down in churches and the biggest money that he spends is for building churches. Yet in that same community you find vice, crime, you find heresy, you find torn families. The things that a religion should congeal and bring together.

I feel like being a man is a great thing. When I was a boy I always felt if I could grow up to be a man: I felt *man* meant independence. It meant that you were grown. And to be a man you should accept certain responsibilities. Now I accept the responsibility of raising my family, tutoring my children, being able to own land or own a business, work and develop this business like *I* would like to see it. I've had several and I have run head-on into a lot of obstacles. Because of the double standard. Whereas I couldn't get certain concessions or certain relaxed restrictions as some other poor man with a skin color different from mine.

Now when these things are not denied you, you've got no excuse. Even though we've been slaves, all of this thing we've had, after you're grown up into a world where you can read, you can write, you can study, you can think—you've got no business asking anybody to pity you. I don't want any special favors because I'm black. I want a favor because I'm *entitled* to this favor as a man. Or as a citizen. Or as a product that's going to support this structure that we're talking about. I want to contribute something to that by being a man that can take a man's place in my home. I want to be a *man* that my son can admire.

I can only see myself as the breadwinner. I am the decision maker. I am the trunk. I am the man that has the say. Now it isn't that I don't consider my family and my wife. Yes, we counsel together. I'm criticized sometimes. But the decisions come from me. I wish there were more black men that could stand up and say, look, I'm gonna make the living. I'm gonna work. I'm gonna bring in the bread. My position and my experience gives me this authority. And when we relax this authority we lose, because the woman becomes the spokesman. I have some boys I'm working with. And do you want to know something? The problem in that home is that the mother has a louder voice, more of a say, than the father. I think this is one of the quickest ways to destroy people, when you can get a man to relinquish his position as a responsible leader of his home.

■ *Daniel Moynihan says the black community is a matriarchal society.*[2]

It's an invention of the white man. He done it when she was working in his kitchen, when he *allowed* her to take a plate to the man. She would cook for him, [he'd] give her nothing, so he didn't mind her taking enough out of his kitchen to feed the other part of the family, the man included. The man couldn't get a job. This is the way of castrating—bring this man down to a level where he just can't feel that he's a grown man. He'll act it out. I don't act it out. I don't grin with anybody. I don't care whether he's white or black. Even though I was brought up in the black, I didn't do it there, because I didn't get tickled. I was always fearful. As long as I don't say anything, you can't indict me. So I would just take it and walk off. But he couldn't make me believe that I wasn't a better man than him. Because I was able to take his abuse and take the things that he would do to me. That was inhuman. Dehumanizing. These things were used to keep us from being men. Listen, it took a lot to do this. You got to give these people a lot of credit.

I can remember when the white man would allow Negroes to see him shooting craps or playing mumblety-peg with his pocketknife. But when he got ready to talk business you had to get out. He didn't allow you to hear him when he talked about the people, what they're gonna do about ruling. He taught us to copy his vices, but kept you from his virtues. And the average Negro man at that time figured it was something if he could act drunk like a white man. If he could do some of the sins of the white man. He didn't talk about college and development and such as this before the Negro. But he was always talking about something that would be degrading. I know, because I've been around it.

> For followup interviews with Howard Spence in 1979 and 1986, see chapter 8.

CHAPTER 2

Whites on the Front Lines
of Racial Conflict

T he racial views of whites in the late sixties lacked the sociological scope of black consciousness; except among radicals of the left or right, attitudes toward race were not integrated into a comprehensive worldview or connected to a social critique of American society. Whites tended to explain the racial crisis in personal terms, emphasizing the motivations of individuals, rather than looking at social forces and group relations. And while the 1960s had revitalized the ideological traditions of black political thought, the two frameworks that had organized white thinking on racial questions were virtually in disarray.

The legitimacy of *conservative racism*, the doctrine that unabashedly proclaims the inferiority of the darker races, had been steadily eroding as a result of New Deal liberalism, the war against Nazism and fascism, the anticolonial movements of the postwar period, and the progress of racial minorities in the United States. But *liberal equalitarianism*, the "color-blind" philosophy that race and color are irrelevant personal characteristics, was also in crisis. The liberal outlook was sorely tested in the racially conscious sixties, as the black movement became more militant and nationalistic, and white supporters of civil rights felt the threat of racial violence.*

In the absence of a comprehensive ideology, most whites improvised their racial viewpoints in response to the demands blacks made, the actions they staged, the shifts in their outlook. Whites reacted rather than acted, and they often reacted defensively and personally. Many were angry at the black militants for disrupting their lives, for overturning what they thought had been harmonious and peaceful race relations, and for forcing them to address difficult issues of fairness and equality.

*As a politics of moderation, liberalism was hard pressed also by the overall polarization of the sixties, particularly by the failure of its leading figures to oppose the unpopular war in Vietnam.

In northern California, it was particularly the Black Panther Party, founded by Huey Newton and Bobby Seale in Oakland in 1966, that aroused the ire of many white people. The Panthers put forward a comprehensive economic and social program for black autonomy. But it was advocating that Afro-Americans carry arms to defend themselves against police racism that won them public attention. To dramatize the issue of police brutality, they donned black leather jackets and berets, brandished shotguns and revolvers, and "invaded" the California State Assembly during a debate on the right of private citizens to bear arms. The Panthers also patrolled the police: when Panthers saw or heard about an officer stopping a black citizen for questioning, they would come armed with weapons and law books to observe the proceedings.

The Panthers' activities touched on the lives of the whites who speak in this chapter. Joe Rypins, an avid hunter and collector of sporting guns, blames their militancy for the new restrictions on the carrying of guns. Gladys Hunt explains that the trial of Huey Newton for the murder of an Oakland police officer has so polarized race relations that she fears her black neighbors will riot when the expected conviction is handed down; Hunt is also enraged at what she sees as Newton's unfair demands for lenient treatment. For Joan Keres, in contrast, Newton is the hero who "started the Revolution." Provoked by the rhetoric of Black Power, fearful of burning cities and the specter of racial warfare, the whites in this chapter, liberal as well as conservative, were also wrestling with their own violent impulses.

Each of the four people in this chapter was involved in close relations with black people, at work or off the job. The majority of Joe Rypins's fellow longshoremen were black; Gladys Hunt worked for an antipoverty program in the predominantly black housing project where she also lived; Joan Keres was living in an integrated neighborhood and her first boyfriend was black; and Virginia Lawrence, a teacher in an inner-city school, pursued an integrated social life. Although such interracial contact made these four atypical, their position on the "front lines" of racial conflict imparts a special acuity and intensity to their observations.

Joe Rypins

"Stokely Carmichael ain't no better than me"

Interviewer Alex Papillon had an exceptional ability to confront white people about their racial attitudes as well as a relentless curiosity about their lives, despite the fact that he was an outspoken black nationalist, a member of the original Black Panther circle. I met him in one of my classes after he transferred to the University of California, and I asked him to join our project. Papillon was also working as a longshoreman on San Francisco's waterfront. There he met Joe Rypins, a young man of the same age (twenty-nine) but with a very different background. While Papillon's father was a sandblaster, the senior Rypins was an executive with a large corporation; in his son's words, he was "filthy rich," "real powerful around town," on the school board, the Chamber of Commerce, "and all that bullshit."

Alex and Joe, both exceptionally large men, also have strong egos. They think of themselves as tough, ready to fight if crossed. Working together in the hold, they were able to talk about racial politics. This interview takes place in Joe Rypins's home.

I

I totally disagree with the Panthers and Stokely Carmichael: he ain't no more man or no better than me in no way, shape, or form. And he wants to be. The way I understand Stokely Carmichael, he wants to be the all-powerful race messiah of the black people. And he got his hammer in his hand and if he falls, then that guy's head comes off. And I just don't go for that, man. Nobody needs to have that kind of power.

I'd shoot that mo— son of a gun, if I had half a chance. I'd shoot him dead in the head. 'Cause the cat's nothing but a troublemaker, see? You can't name one single thing that Stokely Carmichael does—that *I* know about—that's constructive. He don't do nothing but get that shit stick and stir the pot. Everything he does is to tear something down. Now I ain't saying what he's tearing down is right, but he ain't building nothing. There's a couple of Stokely Carmichaels over at [the union hiring hall], but I don't pay no attention. Mostly 'cause you can't fight in the hall. (*Laughs.*)

■ *What about the Black Panthers' idea of arming the black community?*

I kind of go along with that. As long as it would be used in the way it was originally intended. Arm black people to protect themselves. Give a guy a twelve-gauge shotgun and teach him how to use it. See? If some son of a bitch come in his front door, he knows just what to do. Take care of business. But you don't need to go around stirring up shit with it, see? Like them dudes that went up there to the legislature in Sacramento. I think that was a big mistake.

It was a mistake, Joe says, because "they're messing it up for me." In his bedroom are more than forty sports rifles, pistols, and shotguns; he even makes his own hunting guns. But after the Panthers marched into the state legislature with their shotguns, the authorities began strictly enforcing weapons regula-

tions. When Joe goes hunting, he now has to make sure his gun is unloaded, in its holster, on the seat next to him, in plain view. He used to be able to stop for coffee and doughnuts wearing his gun, but now he has to remove and unload it. "All that bullshit, just because of them dudes that went up there making like gangbusters."

The original idea I had on Black Power was this guy that got himself knocked off—what was his name? Malcolm X. I think he advocated a totally separate black community, all powerful. Within themselves. And I thought that was wrong. It can't never create nothing but a problem, people fighting. And you can't have two wholly separate communities and both communities have all the best advantages. There aren't that many best advantages available.

The way I see Black Power is simply black people bringing themselves to a position where if the restaurant owner says in Alabama, "I won't serve colored people," that colored man is going to say, "You serve me, mister." And ain't nothing that guy can do about it—he got to serve him. And Black Power says that all opportunities in this world will be even. And Black Power is the means of achieving this evenness—equality. The black man is registering his independence, his indignation with his treatment. Black Power is the banding together of that group.

The riots? I don't know whether stealing, break the window out of a store, whether all that's necessary or not. Maybe there's no other way people are getting that stuff. I never been to Watts, I never been to Chicago, I ain't been no place. It ain't right to steal. But maybe this guy that owns that store has been giving them a screwing, really putting it on people. He's supposed to get robbed. But I don't go for this throwing rocks at the firemen. That cat's in there risking his ass to put out your fire, and somebody hit him over the head with a rock. That's wrong as two left feet. And lighting fires is wrong. And hiding up in a building and shooting at everybody, that's wrong.

■ *But you would shoot Stokely?*

In a minute.

■ *But these dudes shooting the cops wouldn't be the same?*

Well, uh. (*Long pause.*) I don't know what's taking place. Maybe the cops got a couple colored guys up against the wall hitting them in the head with a stick, and his partner will shoot the cop. Well, I say that cop's *supposed* to be shot.

As for police brutality, first thing I better say is my brother's a cop. But there's got to be some truth to it. There can't be all that much smoke without some kind of fire. And I know that a lot of times cops are put on so much by what they see that it makes them brutal. Makes them hard. Guys tells them,

"I've got a right" and "I've got all this and you can't do that." And rather than put up with a bunch of bullshit from somebody—teeny boppers at the draft thing*—hit him in the mouth, shut him up, throw him in there, you know. 'Cause I think an honest cop's job is just like riding down a sewer in a glass-bottom boat. You see all the worst.

Joe doesn't have much respect for Martin Luther King, Jr., and his nonviolent philosophy. He calls King a "do-nothing" and says that all the March on Washington did was wear out a lot of shoes. Still, he likes King as a person a lot better than Stokely Carmichael. He can't abide the way Carmichael puts himself above everybody, including him, while "Martin Luther King is not trying to be better than me."

- *Why is how they relate to you more important than what they're doing for black people?*

What Martin Luther King is doing cannot possibly ever come back on me. Because he's not doing nothing. He's leading a march down the street. Well, walk down the street. I don't give a fat rat's ass. But what Stokely Carmichael is doing is better for the black people because he's stirring them up. He gives them energy and ambition to do something. You see? And if I was a black man, I would have to relate to Stokely Carmichael, because he's getting me going, see? And he's getting all the brothers going. He's making things roll. But as he relates to me, and I am white, what Stokely Carmichael does is stir up a lot of shit that might break out into something that might *involve* me.

- *Involve you how?*

A riot. I'm driving down the streets in Oakland and somebody throws a rock through my window. Oh, I'd be mad. Ohhh, I'd be mad. See? I get pretty hot. I don't mess with nobody else, I don't expect them to mess with me. What Stokely Carmichael does is likely to involve me in something I dislike. As opposed to what Martin Luther King does. He's not going to involve me in a riot, a fight, burn my house down, something like that.

II

Direct action has always been Joe Rypins's personal style. When he was eleven, some nineteen-year-old boys threw a cherry bomb into his parents' yard on the Fourth of July. Joe went out and hit the boys with a board, while his father chose the telephone as his weapon—he called the police. Three days before high school graduation Joe was expelled for decking his history teacher in the class-

*At a mass demonstration against the Vietnam war at the Oakland Induction Center in 1967, the police used considerable force to "control" the youthful, predominantly white demonstrators.

room. *Though he got As and Bs on exams, he'd end up with Ds and Fs because he wouldn't do the homework, the "meticulous writing and all that bullshit. If somebody tells you something and you have that knowledge, ain't no reason you should have to turn around and write a fifty-page letter about the son of a bitch." During those school years he had no real experience with "races or prejudices or anything of this."*

The Germans and the Jews were not one and the same, I knew this. And colored people and white people, they were not one and the same. I knew this. But I had no contact, San Vicente was all white—was then, anyway.

■ *If you had no contact, how did you know the difference?*

I don't know. I knew there was colored people and white people, that's all I knew. And white people didn't like colored people. I knew that.

■ *How did you know that?*

(*Somewhat defensively, but without hesitation.*) I really don't know specifically. You know, it's just there. It wasn't in the family. I guess you just hear people talking, that's all. We used to play football with Richmond High. We had some night games and everybody used to say, "Be sure to get out of Richmond after the game right away when it's dark, 'cause the niggers will get you." I don't know what they're talking about, except I don't want no ass-kicking, so I'd get out of town.

We didn't have any colored people here in San Vicente. And none in school. We had some Puerto Rican people. And a lot of Spanish people. A few Chinese and Oriental people. Jewish people. We had all kinds of people, except we didn't have colored people. It was no thing, you know.

And then when they *were* around or when I was around Negroes, like at the football games with Castlemont, then everybody was scared of them, so I guess I was.

■ *Why were they scared, do you know?*

(*Voice rising an octave.*) I don't know. I really don't know. It's funny now. (*Laughs nervously.*) It was different. There were no people like that around here. There were none of your people here in town. And all my life I never knew any of your people. And when you go to a football game there's hundreds of them, see? I don't know what it was. (*Mimics black speech.*) "I'm going to kick your ass."

■ *You said that they were different.*

I never met a single colored person in conversation until I went in the service. Does that help straighten it out, what I'm trying to tell you?

I was eighteen years old. And I don't know from nothing about nothing. I'm still on the bottle. I never had a piece of ass in my life. That first night in boot camp, it was miserable. I didn't want to be there. It's cold. Gave you one blanket. No mattress cover. I was ready to die. This corporal—I panicked every time he comes around. And the guy comes in: "Turn the lights off and get to sleep." And I was almost asleep and these three colored guys from Los Angeles turn the lights on and they're playing cards. I said, "Hey man, shut that light off. Before that guy comes back here and kills us all." And that colored guy comes down off that bed and walked over to me. He hit me right in the mouth so hard I didn't know what was happening. And right then and there I became prejudiced, man. I said them colored things, they're no good at all. I hate them people. (*Both laugh.*)

It was a very strong reaffirmation. Of what I had always heard and what I always knew, when I was going to school in San Vicente: "Watch out for the niggers. They get you."

Although some Asians and Mexicans now live in San Vicente, there are still virtually no blacks. Yet less than a mile away, across the creek that forms a natural border between Joe's suburb and the adjacent city, is a large and growing black community. At first Joe insisted that the creek itself had obstructed integration, but then he admitted that a real estate clique ("on the elite side of town") kept blacks out. He strongly disapproves of the practice: "If a man can afford to live where I live, I don't give a shit if he's green with purple spots. As long as he doesn't throw his garbage over my fence."

Joe lives just a few blocks from his parents. His father isn't prejudiced, he says, but his mother might be a bit; he recalls some remarks she made while he was growing up. They never had any Negro people over to the house, though the "other races" came in, and his father did have some Negro friends at work. They pause so Joe can say good-night to his two young children.

If my daughter was old enough to get married right now, I wouldn't like it to be a black man for one reason, and that would be the children. Because white people will put them children down. White kids. Kids are the hardest people in the world on other kids, mentally. If you get three or four young kids against another kid, that kid's got it bad. You know, he can suffer greatly. And now if my daughter has a colored husband and they have children—I'm not familiar with birth processes, but do kids come out light-colored or what? I didn't ever pay any attention. (*Nervous laugh.*) But it couldn't possibly be anything but disaster to the children.

- *What if the kids were raised in the black community?*

I don't know. I don't know that much about the black community.

- *What if they weren't ostracized, if they found a place in the black community?*

Great. If they have a place there. You see? Kids got to have everything, 'cause kids are all we got, see? There ain't nothing else. Once you're gone, man, that's all you have left. So you got to do for them. I mean if you got to beat them, you got to beat them—but for *their* good. Whatever's best for kids, that's what I'm for.

I just don't think it would work anywhere in this day and age, really. Because what are you going to do? Go down in—where is the black community? West Oakland. What are you gonna do, spend a whole life there? You can't have that.

Let's say one of them will come out colored and the other come out white. Now the kid has friends come in. "This is my brother." What's going on here? Now he's going to talk about them two kids, see? So where are they gonna go where this won't take place?

- *What if* both *of them came out dark complected?*

Then those two kids got a place, see? Then they have a community of their own. I just don't know the full story. I don't know the Negro people—how they feel. All I know is how white people feel. It would be disastrous.

I don't think you're ever going to get over this . . . interracial thing. As long as this earth rolls around, there's going to be a majority of white people against intermixing of the races. But as with regard to everyday life, if colored people are *ever* going to have the opportunities that everybody has—you know, if my opportunities are your opportunities, if my son's opportunities are your son's opportunities—if we're ever to have that situation, wholly and totally, which is I think what everybody's after, then it's got to be in the schools. Intermarriages are really quite a rare thing. And nothing that small could ever be as important as something as big as integration in the schools. Integration—you go to school where the closest one is. My kid go to school down on the corner, 'cause that's the closest one around. If he had to go across town, I'd be a mad son of a bitch. Someone would pay for it.

The majority of the people in the world are white; they're all down on the colored people. Or most of them. They say, well, I'm going to stick up for this guy, but don't let him marry my sister. I'm not saying they're hypocrites. They want to do right. But inwardly they have this prejudice. They just keep it in. That's most white people. Them that let it out are sons of bitches, I guess. If I met them I just go away from them 'cause I don't like people that are that radical.

III

After his discharge from the Marines, Joe went to work packing auto parts. Whenever he saw a chance for more money, he changed jobs. A year ago, at a truck plant, he got in a fight and was fired. Now he's found his ideal job: the union controls all work assignments, and the men have almost complete freedom to set their hours, choose their work crews, and refuse a job they don't like. So if Joe feels like it, he can stay home, sleep in, and if he wants to take off and go hunting, nobody's going to complain. Only working in the woods in British Columbia would be more appealing; his ideal life-style would be to survive totally on his own—without grocery stores, law enforcement, or other social institutions.

On the waterfront, man, you're free. With your ideas. You're a free thing. You move around. Up and down the ladder, in and out of the hatch. Nobody messes with you down there, as a general rule. You're down there with four other guys and you guys are responsible for the way you put that stuff in there. Or the way you take it out. You want to dig down, dig down.

People say, "Hey, that cat's pretty smart for the way he done that." In their heads they think, "Yeah, that guy's right." And a man likes to be right. A man hates to be wrong. Some men if they're wrong they get embarrassed. If they're wrong they get mad. They got to have some reaction to being wrong. And all men like to have other men say, "That guy's right. He did the right thing." All men like to be praised. Everybody's vain. To a degree. Me, you, everybody.

Followup interviews with Joe Rypins in 1979 and 1987 appear in chapter 11.

Gladys Hunt

"You break your neck to do something, and they give you a hard time"

Lincoln Bergman conducted this interview and the one following. A white leftist from a radical background, Bergman had been close to black people while growing up in San Francisco. In 1968 he was on the staff of The Movement, *a magazine sponsored by Students for a Democratic Society, which was trying to mobilize white support for the Black Panther Party.*

Bergman had intended to interview Gladys Hunt and her husband at the same time. But Lewis Hunt is glued to the television, watching the preliminaries leading up to the nomination of Hubert Humphrey at the Democratic Convention. Gladys also keeps her eye on the TV, but the event that most concerns her is the summer-long trial of Black Panther leader Huey Newton. She is particularly offended by Newton's supporters demanding that all charges against him be dropped before the trial. Gladys predicts that blacks will riot in her Oakland housing project when the expected guilty verdict is returned. It is a time of unusual tension, even for the summer of 1968.

I don't know what it is anymore, but I find myself being less and less tolerant. And I think it's happening to a lot of white people. Before, we could go along with it, and we could even try to halfway understand what they must've been going through. Because *nobody*, nobody, can put themselves in the place of a black man and say, "Yeah, I know how you feel." Because you're not black, you *don't* know how they feel. But we can try to understand; we can try to help. And then when we get pushed back when we try to help, this is what I resent.

It just seems that they want to take over completely! I think there's a lot of fine black people; now don't get me wrong! There are! And there's some very well educated—these are the kinds of people that should be leading the black people. Not a bunch of rabble-rousers like the Black Panthers . . . patrol the streets with guns . . . and running on the Peace and Freedom.* To me this is not freedom; this is insanity. I can stand to listen to their ideas. But Christ Almighty, who in the hell hasn't been persecuted since the world began? The Jews were persecuted, the Irish people. We [she is English] were thrown out of Ireland. And the Indians . . . who in the hell hasn't been persecuted? We all have! Thousands of years back!

Every race has its dignity; every race has its culture. We all have our music, we all have our customs. The Irish people have theirs, the Jewish people have theirs, their culture, their customs. They have their music, their books. They have their scientists. Every race. And so does the Negro race. We *all* have a culture. And we're all here struggling. And God knows we all might just as well join hands and fight the battle together.

This Black Panther bit . . . to really police their neighborhoods, I could see it. But when they try to take over the state legislature and try to take over the Oakland Police Department, this is a form of terrorism. At Huey Newton's trial . . . them goddamned Black Panthers are out there going through their military maneuvers trying to coerce. To me this is not *justice*. And if he killed a guy, if he really did kill that guy . . . Huey Newton ain't a goddamned bit better than I am! I'd have to stand trial for shooting a cop! So what makes *him* better? Because he's black?

Cops? I think they're okay. I really do! And I think they take a helluva beating from a lot of people and I don't think they deserve it.

LEWIS: But in Chicago? It was on television today . . . a riot, a demon-

---

*In 1968 the Panthers entered into an electoral coalition with the predominantly white, California-based Peace and Freedom Party. The Panthers provided a number of candidates for national office on the Peace and Freedom ticket, including Eldridge Cleaver for president and Huey Newton ("running" from inside Oakland's county jail) for Congress.

stration in Lincoln Park where the police got real violent . . . with newsmen and photographers as well as demonstrators—

GLADYS: I don't see it that way, Lewis. I think the cops get paid to do a job. He don't wanta go out there and be afraid he's gonna have his goddamned skull broken, or somebody shoot 'im or something. They just *look* at a kid and right away they're screaming police brutality. Sure, there's some cases where some cops get overanxious and they kinda rough the kids up. But this is not all the time! This is just a remote incident. And I believe the cops deserve a lot more credit than they're getting.

Right down here a year ago, I saw a colored kid advance on a cop with a drawn weapon and walk right up taunting him and teasing him. That cop stood there. And if he shot, God knows he'd a probably missed the kid that was doing the tormenting and hurt an innocent bystander—that park was loaded with kids. And this is no kid! This kid was in his twenties!

Growing up in an all-Irish Boston neighborhood, Gladys faced prejudice herself. In those days, she recalls, black people stayed in the South End, but with open housing today they move everywhere. The housing project where she lives was once 80 percent white; now fewer than ten white families remain. All her kids' friends have moved, and if she and Lewis go out at night they never know how many windows will have been knocked out when they return. And it doesn't help to leave the dog outside; the kids just throw rocks at him.

We've had it as rough as they had. For six and a half years we lived on a goddamned pension, before I went to work. We don't have a car. The cars driving through this project belong to colored people. They don't belong to white people. Like some joker that's got six or seven kids, he can sit around and collect welfare and drive a big Cadillac. But it's not strictly a black problem, 'cause there's some Caucasian stinkers and there's some Mexican-Americans that have a whole bunch of kids and sit around and drive big Lincolns.

Four years ago she volunteered to work in the poverty program. She was hired as a paid office worker a year ago. It's helped her financially, but otherwise has been disillusioning.

Four years ago I thought, Jesus, here's my chance to really do something! Maybe I can help a little bit, get a kid a job or something like that. But it's not working out that way. I've stayed 'til four in the morning. I haven't had a lunch hour for three weeks. I haven't had one day off since May. Those guys come in, take time off, take sick-leave days off; they get their full checks; nobody says a word. I take an hour off of work—"What the hell you doing taking an hour?" Goddamnit, if they want me to start screaming about inequities, this kid can scream about inequities too.

Last summer they had forty jobs, that's all they had. They had kids by the hundreds come in there, and do you think they'd be honest enough to tell them, "Well, we've got the forty and that's it"? They kept those poor kids coming. They talk about the white people being deceptive. Now what do you call that? It's *them* . . . that's deceiving their own people. The white people are doing more for the black man today than their own kind!

I'm the only Caucasian there. And there's some of those gals that're real good friends of mine. We get along well and they understand me and I understand them. And if I got something to say I'm gonna say it to 'em. But I *am not* one of them. And some of my best friends aren't Negroes. (*Laughs.*)

And me, protesting that I'm not a racist, and maybe that's what I'm sounding like. You know, I've taken so much now. And I mean I used to sympathize; I really did! I really felt sorry for 'em; I thought, you know, this is not fair! To see 'em like this. . . . Don't got any jobs, and my God! The kids can't seem to get anywhere in school; the teachers are giving 'em a hard time! And Christ, you break your neck to do something and then they—they give you a hard time!

I think we're gonna have another Civil War on our hands. Because these people today are doing things and getting away with 'em. I don't think they should have a law for the black people, a law for the Mexican-Americans, a law for the Irish people, a law for the Jewish people; I think if we've got one law it should be for *everybody!* What's right and just for me . . . is right and just for anybody else. I ask no more, I expect no more. (*Pounds table.*) I believe they should have anything that's gonna make 'em happy. . . . But let 'em go about it the right way, and don't start shoving other people around just to get what they want. Hell, they was shoved around a hundred years ago! That's not my problem! My folks were shoved around; I was shoved around when I was a kid.

They cannot get their way overnight. Because the white people have had enough of it. I know I'm coming to the end of my rope with it. I find myself fighting back. *By God,* I'm gonna give 'em every bit as good as they give me.

All this crap every four years. (*Turning to the television.*) People could care less. This is a goddamned circus! I like George Wallace because he's got guts. He keeps saying he's not a racist. . . . Well, maybe he is.

She might not even vote this year. All the big politicians are millionaires: Governor Reagan—who's been cutting welfare funds—the Kennedys, Rockefeller, Harriman, Harry Truman, Lyndon Johnson. "Politics is really dirty," she has concluded, and the convention has been rigged for Humphrey.

Did you hear Inouye speak? "Look," he says, "my folks were interned in California during World War II." This guy lost an arm . . . during the Japanese war, World War II. But he said, "I didn't burn my American citizenship." He said, "I didn't burn my draft card." He said, "I didn't tear up my birth certificate." He told 'em, "This is *no* way to get things done!" (*Pounds table again.*) And then he really slapped the hell outta those militants last night! He said, "You've *got to obey the law!*" He says you can't have revolt in your streets; he says you can't have murder in your streets. He says you can't be afraid to *walk the streets anymore!*

When I moved here twelve years ago, Lincoln, I would never think anything of coming up the avenue at twelve-thirty, one o'clock at night by myself. And now I wouldn't even walk down to the corner after nine o'clock, I'm so afraid. The young punks . . . they've just scared the *hell* out of me! And I never used to be afraid like that. I'd go over to Bennie's to have a drink—right over here at the corner bar. And Lewis'd be home and *here* I'd be waltzing in . . . by myself . . . twelve-thirty or one. . . . Just walking up the avenue, crossing open fields . . . just swinging my purse and just minding my own business and walk right up here!

■ *No more, huh?*

No more! You damn well right no more! No more! Not when they run right up on your goddamned porch at six o'clock in the evening and grab ya. And I'm really afraid for Dorothy [her daughter]; that's why I want to move. I really am. And that's an *awful* thing to say.

> The Hunts moved East shortly after this interview. I was unable to find them ten years later.

Joan Keres

"Sometimes you wish you were black"

Though more of a political radical than a cultural radical, interviewer Lincoln Bergman had access to the counterculture through a sister and brother who had become hippies. Their utopia was a color-blind society based on love and peace, but the hippies we talked to were fascinated by racial differences. Perhaps because they thought of themselves as pro-minority, they seemed even quicker than other whites to generalize about the characteristics of blacks, whom they viewed as unspoiled primitives. In essence, the hippies repeated conventional stereotypes of blacks ("natural rhythm" and super-sexuality) but evaluated them as positive rather than negative traits.

Sometimes you wish you were black, don't you? Once in a while, a little bit? You know, I like the black way a lot. Like that Mothers of Invention song,

"I'm Not White." There's a whole lot of times I wish I could say I'm not white. When that Spanish man was yelling, "You whites are all no good," I couldn't say, "Right."

Like a surprising number of the young hippy women Bergman interviewed, Joan said her first boyfriend had been black—a "hippy type" she met in high school. Fellow students accepted them, but she never introduced him to her parents. Because she couldn't be herself around them, couldn't smoke dope or "do a lot of things," she began running away from home when she was sixteen. A year later she dropped out of school, fed up with the regimentation, the back-wardness, the lack of creativity.

Joan found a new life in San Francisco's Haight-Ashbury. People she met gave her things and there were free meals; she panhandled, sold papers, and modeled for extra money. Picked up as a runaway, she was roughed up by the police, sent to juvenile hall for two weeks, and then returned to her parents. For a while she worked as a typist and a filing clerk, but office jobs bored her. She ran away again. "I had to live my life 'cause it was mine and I had to do it the way I wanted to do it." She's now eighteen and out of her parents' control. Bergman asks her if she finally feels free.

I'm not really clear what that means anymore. Like I can do whatever I want to, I guess, 'cause I'm white. But I just know I'm not real free, like Bob Dylan's song, "The Birds Not Free from the Chains of the Sky." If you keep yourself open and you're nice to people, people stomp on you. It's a real terrible thing. That you just can't trust everybody. I've been lied to and tricked and hurt.

Haight Street is ugly. Not very many beautiful people. Weird people, and they're not doing anything, empty-headed, and it's not a very happy place and not very safe. There's guns around. Sometimes the police come down, four cops on one side of the street, four cops on the other, and a paddy wagon in the middle, and they just stop everybody.

So she's moved to the Mission District, with her white boyfriend, Jeff. They've sold marijuana a few times, to middle-class white kids, when they needed money. Once a black man pulled a knife on her and stole their dope, "'cause they don't have any money."

A lot of hippies are prejudiced. A whole lot. A big hippy, he was saying some shit about Negro people breaking windows on Haight Street. I got up-tight at them. And like a friend of Tim and Nancy, she talks real negatively about black people, too.

■ *How do you feel about the riots?*

That's not the right way to do it anymore, you know. They're just destroying too much of their own. They've grown weaker, and a big riot, that just gives the police more opportunity to kill more black people.

- *And the right way to do it?*

The way the Black Panthers say. Work in small groups. Just kill a few cops secretly.

- *Is that okay?*

No, it's not okay. It's fucked-up, of course. But you can't stop them unless you kill them.

The Black Panthers, I think they're the best thing going. Huey P. Newton, he started it all. Started the Black Panthers. And started like the Revolution. He just stood up and he wasn't afraid.

- *If a race war broke out in this country, what would you do?*

If all black and white people were fighting it out? Maybe I'd be behind the scene, on the black side. If I had to do the paperwork and I wouldn't have to be out there fighting. Or I'd just split, far into the country. I mean, what can I do? I'd be killed if I was out on the street, and I couldn't shoot the black people. What would you do, Linc?

- *I don't know. You have to see how the things developed and what political forces were at work and where you could fit in best. You would help in a hospital or that kind of thing?*

Yeah, that's what I would do. Help in a hospital. So I wasn't out on the street being killed. Unless they had uniforms and then if I could fight, I'd fight.

- *If you had the power to change things?*

Maybe I'd send all the white people back to Europe after they gave in. I'd give all the black people what they wanted. Well, you just can't force southerners to like black people or else go to jail and everything. I mean, they can't help it. It's deep-rooted hate they have. So I would have to try and rehabilitate them some way. Jeff always thinks of like putting a cop in the closet and making him take acid and blasting out music real loud.

Acid opens up all your senses, and you're just turned on to everything that's around you. It's changed my life. When I was taking a lot of acid I was just real super-positive. And tried to really like everybody, you know. But then you realize you just can't change people. It doesn't matter how much you love 'em, it's just not enough.

I'm happy being white. I'm not very super ego-proud, but I mean I like it okay. I think I'm fine. A lot of beautiful white people, just like the black people and Chinese people. White people have soul too. Chinese people have soul.

- *Are Negroes different from white people?*

They look different, act different, talk different. They came from a different part of the world, they had a whole different heredity. They're more relaxed, they just move more easier or freer or something. They don't walk
standing up so straight. But it depends on the Negro, because middle-class
Negroes are a lot different than poor. Now Jeff doesn't like this when I say it,
but like Africa, it's real much music and stuff, and that's a big part of black
people's heritage. Don't you think, Lincoln, that they could possibly have
natural rhythm?

People just don't have natural feelings about their bodies. They think it's
dirty. They have to cover it up. And [men and women], they just don't get
along too well. Their faces aren't very happy with one another, and they're
mad for so long. And I know through books and stuff that most of the women
are frigid, and they're just not open to each other. White women are sort of
marshmallow or plastic.

I'd like to be an out-of-sight woman and maybe live in the country, have
happy children, you know, bring them up out-of-sight. Love 'em and pay attention to them and be their friend and try and understand. And not possess
them. They call it protection, but it's really possession. Try and keep them
open to new things. Keep their curiosity going. That's what children have and
then something happens to it.

> For followup interviews with Joan Keres in 1978
> and 1986, see chapter 13.

Virginia Lawrence

"I was the wrong color in my black man's eyes"

*A teacher in her mid-forties, Virginia Lawrence begins her life history with a
story, told in almost biblical language.*

My mother, albeit she was born in a generation where it was very hard to
carry out her feelings, had some very fundamentally egalitarian feelings. And
she communicated them to me. And one thing I can remember her telling
me, when I was quite young, was that her great-grandmother, my great-great-
grandmother, had been the wife of a very wealthy plantation owner in the
South. And she had borne seventeen children, which was all she was supposed to do. The children were raised by Negro women, of course. And at
some point in the lives of these seventeen children, she gathered them all
around her and said to them, "Something is very wrong. Something is very
wrong that black people should be treated differently from white people. And

you, my children, you may get by. But sometime there will be a high price to pay for this. And you must do something about it." And my mother's grandmother was one of these seventeen children, and heard that said. And it skipped a generation, because my mother's father was a very, very prejudiced man. And my mother's mother died when she was six months old, so she was raised by her grandmother. And she conveyed this all to my mother, and somehow or other, outside of a framework of any kind of real equal social contact—my parents never entertained any Negroes in their home—she conveyed it to me.

Except for the Negro domestic who always ate with them at the table and was "honored as a person," her family lived an all-white existence. Not until attending an integrated high school in Oakland did she make her first Negro friend. Virginia was responsible for an important school program and it "meant an enormous amount" to be able to give a prominent place to "a very fine Negro singer." Outbreaks of racial conflict at school pained and confused her, and she discussed them with her mother.

In college she became active in liberal organizations, dated a Negro boy, and had very close Japanese friends. The injustice of the internment of Japanese-Americans during World War II "just hurt me in all the places where I'm tender and sensitive." Her sorority sisters considered her bizarre. After a Jewish pledge she sponsored was voted down, Virginia quit the sorority.

She married while still in college. Virginia remembers the excitement of those early days when she and her husband had Negro friends over and talked about race into the early hours of the morning. But beneath the facade of their perfect middle-class marriage, she and her husband were not close: "I didn't even know what his dreams were or his concept of the world." "One day, when I was about thirty-three, I remember opening the door of my house and looking out into the garden, and saying to myself, 'I am not really who I am. And the only gift I can really give my children is who I am. And I got to do some things about my life so that this gift can be given.'"

She divorced, moved into an integrated neighborhood, and began to carry out her part in the family story. She has a circle of intimate friends, centered in her church, with whom she feels free to "express any idea on earth with regard to race or anything else." The church is integrated; her best friend is black.

Ten years ago she began a new career teaching junior high school. Her students, by choice, are ninth graders with learning problems. She teaches 125 students on a one-to-one basis, in part through the programmed text she's developed, in part by being concerned with each student: "If I feel a rub and a grind and an agony, it's because we can spend the money that we spend on the machinery of war, and have the pupil-teacher ratio as lousy as it is."

The men in her life are primarily, though not exclusively, black. Indeed, the interviewer, Alex Papillon, is precisely the kind of forceful, aggressive black man to whom Virginia is attracted.

A Negro man joined our faculty just a year ago. He was located down the hall from me. And there was a party, advertised among the entire faculty, at a place out behind the hills, where it's really white. And finally he decided that he'd go, and I finally decided I'd go, and so we rode together.

And I can remember the experience of walking in that place . . . for which I was not fully prepared. Because I had assumed that this faculty had finally accepted the fact that we would be integrated—at least for faculty social events. And as John and I walked in together . . . the people were sitting at cocktail tables . . . it was . . . exactly like walking into a stone wall . . . which would *not* open up. And I thought I was out of my mind. I thought I was imagining it all. And then a friend said, "Oh, Virginia, it was just awful. I could *feel* it." And finally some benevolent soul gave us a place to sit down. But I can remember our walking in and all these faces just looked at us absolutely blankly as though we didn't even exist. Now, I wasn't born yesterday, and I've belonged to an interracial church for years, and I've gone to all kinds of interracial gatherings, and I've experienced the Negro cold front look at me—as I have been one of the very few white people. So it's not that I'm naive. But I will never forget the chill of that experience . . . in a place where we were officially welcome.

We sat at the end of a table . . . across from each other. John refused to dance with me, which made me furious. 'Cause I thought if we were gonna make a scene, we might as well make a good one. Our Negro vice-principal did not come, because he had finally decided he couldn't stand it. So John was it, and I was with him, and pretty soon we got up and went into Berkeley and had three drinks! (*Laughs.*)

I went with a Negro man for six years. And there's a kind of look in people's eyes sometimes, as you walk down the street or you sit in a restaurant, which is unmistakable. I can remember sitting in a restaurant once and the look of just utter disgust on the face of a white woman in an adjoining booth. I was really startled by how uncivilized it was. Now—in Berkeley, if you want to be noticed, it's a little disappointing to discover that nobody stares at you anymore. (*Laughs.*)

With a lot of kids I just don't experience very much hostility. When they come into my classroom they know that I'm known to be trustworthy. And one thing I have to let them know is that I'm not always trustworthy in some absolute sense. I go to quite a little trouble to help them realize that I will make mistakes and it's part of their responsibility to help contain some of my errors.

■ *Have you noticed problems that relate to one racial or economic group?*

Kids with problems have problems. Kids who have had to move from school to school, a lot of problems. We're not in a very poor district, [but] the poor kids, black or white, have a rougher time. If they're on welfare, they have a harder time learning. And where there's a real chaotic family situation, it shows up at school. And this is true irrespective of color.

■ *Many teachers say black kids are not interested in the curriculum.*

All my kids lack interest because they've got some other problems that are much more primary than color. Now I'm not ignoring the fact, Alex, that color can be a problem! Like a lot of our Negro kids have a helluva time making it in the school because teachers do some very terrible things to them sometimes! Or the kids have had enough negative experience that they *imagine* things. I've spent a lot of time trying to help the Negro kids learn how to handle themselves so that they don't invite too much disaster. But I spent a lot of time with white kids doing this also. I have four classes filled with discipline problems—and they come in all colors, sizes, shapes, and heritages! And you asked me about educational interest—this is determined by *many* other things. Besides race. Some of my Negro kids come from families where their parents are so obsessed with education that they're on the big rebellious kick not to get educated at any cost! And some of the Negro kids come from very, very stable homes where there's plenty of money, and they're going along having a fine time. Others of them are rebelling just as middle-class white kids rebel against *their* middle-class family.

When Virginia says that she couldn't possibly tell him how many blacks are in her classes without counting them tomorrow, Alex becomes impatient with her tendency to downplay race. But for Virginia Lawrence the significant divisions among people are those of values, and they are based usually on social class, not on race. She mentions a Negro friend in her church who's "hung up on the distribution of color in the choir. She counts [people] and says, 'Did you notice today?' 'Did I notice what today?' I couldn't care less as long as the people can sing, you know."

I sit in the teachers' lunchroom occasionally, which I can only stand on a fairly infrequent basis, and I hear some of the deprecatory things teachers say, and I marvel that they can stand themselves. There's an art teacher that really honestly thinks the line should be drawn down the middle of Oakland and they should have theirs—as good a school, of course, but they should have theirs and we should have ours. And almost any of the deprecating names that anybody has ever heard applied to Negroes, I have heard used by some of these faculty members. Almost any negative stereotype that you can think of in terms of the capacity to learn or the kinds of homes they must've come from. So that a teacher goes into shock when he discovers that a kid comes from an intellectual Negro home. And then there's the comment, "Well, he's a Negro kid, but he's *nice!* Really, he's the *nicest* kid."

But she finds some rays of hope: the guidance counselors aren't so bad anymore, and the physical education teachers work well with all the pupils, Negro and white. On the faculty, there are a number of "Rocks of Gibraltar with sound feelings about their fellow human beings," and the new principal told her, "We're in the twentieth century and if some people just can't stand it, they go." She also praises the members of the faculty human relations committee that she organized and a small dedicated group that plans the student dances.

The whole dance situation has very profound racial overtones because five years ago the kids who were interested in dancing were the Negro kids. And the women's P.E. department just shut a dance off in the middle for the most incredible thing! Now, I think *this* was racial. Gradually, gradually, we've gotten some very well integrated dances and our kids have hassled the whole music situation—between surfer and soul music and all this bit—in a very open way over a five-year period. And they've really done a marvelous job!

I think some of the teachers who talk about "the disgusting dances" . . . I have a feeling if these were all white kids dancing exactly the same way, we wouldn't get quite the same comments . . . about quote-unquote "their way of dancing." I wish I could remember some direct things that were said, but unfortunately, it's just never all that direct. Part of it *is* atmosphere. *You (referring to Alex's blackness)* know that. Part of it you can't grab your hand on; part of it's the sentence that isn't said; part of it's just the feeling; part of it's the gesture!

I can remember a group of teachers standing in the hall, and a Negro girl went down the hall in an incredibly short skirt. And there were a number of derogatory comments made. And then a little white girl who was in the accelerated program—a gifted program or some damn thing—came down the hall in an even shorter skirt. And one of the men teachers said, "Aw, she's a little doll."

I think there is something about sexuality here. Put clothes on those natives!

■ *This business of sexuality, is it something you feel the whites are injecting into the situation, or is this sexuality in the situation?*

I think it's mostly projection. The Negro kids have got this thing about dancing, which they spend gew-gobs of time doing. And there's all kind of explanations of why some Negro kids dance well. But there're other Negroes who can't dance worth a damn and who suffer over it. And I watch some of the able white kids who're well coordinated and got a lot of rhythm, and I watch them dance and they're just as sexy, if that's what you want to see in 'em. All young things have a certain fresh, raw sexuality that is really quite a delight!

There's something very psychological about the American white's use of the American Negro. As though all the side of one's self conceived of as darker—the shadow self, in Jungian terms—has been loaded onto an available race—which by a fortuitous chance is darker. And anything which in this Puritan structure, the white felt like he couldn't touch or look at or feel or really accept in himself, got loaded onto the race which he was using or misusing. The real issue is the condition of each of us—we are not really in touch with our own thing. If we were in touch with our own thing, *who the hell* would have time to bother with race?

The way my life is lived, I run into more Negro men who appeal to me than whites. The school system attracts relatively passive white men, but it is a place for the able Negro man right now. And some of the Negro men I meet in the school system are really very aggressive, powerful men. 'Cause this is one place that'll take 'em.

I have my job, ninety percent because of my contacts with the Negro world. The guy sitting in that personnel office began to ask me about myself, who I knew that taught in Oakland, and I just happened to think of Negroes. To my amazement he picked up the phone and made arrangements for me to be in the internship program at Cal. See, anybody who doesn't know that there's a Negro power structure doesn't know what today's world consists of.

One of the myths that got shattered is that if you're involved with Negroes, you're sunk economically. [People had told her] "You can't possibly get a job, you'll never keep a job." "How could you do this to your children? Your children will be discriminated against." "After all, if you marry a Negro he won't even be their real father." All kinds of junk, like "this person is lower than you."

Although she did have to change her son's school because of the negative comments about her black lover, Harold, her son grew to make "excellent use" of Harold, and in time her four children have all become open, autonomous, thriving individuals. At times she felt the pain wasn't worth it, but today it's all "just a delight"; the vision she saw looking out into her garden years ago has come to pass.

After seven years she and Harold separated. She blames value conflicts, based on economic origins. Harold had risen from abject poverty in the South, from the bottom of the Negro class system, and he saw immediate gratification as more important than long-range planning. For Virginia, this produced "a kind of instability very characteristic of Negro families." But Harold said their problem was that she was white.

The man who told me this (*pounds the table*) and I had spent *years* in social experience together. We didn't run into any profound problems at all as a result of race. Don't tell me I'm the wrong color. Not when we've shared all the things we have to share. Not when we managed to go through the mechanics of life without a ripple in terms of any serious kind of color experience. Say to me, "Look, I really can't cope with the situation." I'll love you for that, I'll respect that. This takes courage to say. But for God's sake, don't tell me I'm the wrong color.

After the separation, she had a peculiar experience. She felt she had been thrown back in time, into several centuries of racial anguish in America and was experiencing everything as a Negro woman might have.

I felt as I felt they must have felt . . . that in some very important, significant, gut-level way, race or color was really not the issue, and it was being used. And this ties in with my feeling of the irrelevance of race. Because who I care about relates to my vision; it just doesn't matter about what they look like or a whole lot of other things. And it's as though these women were realizing that the men who told them this did not have a vision! And they used race as an excuse!

For a week and then every Saturday I did nothing but write and that relieved me somewhat of my pain. And then another thing happened which was very unexpected. I realized I was so angry I could kill. And I remember searching the street for Negroes to kill. I didn't care what Negro. Any Negro would do. I was *sooooo* angry. And so wounded. And it was all so irrational.

Now, I didn't kill. And perhaps it's just the fact that I admitted I wanted to kill, that saved me from doing any violence to anyone. And gradually the feeling receded and I focused on the one person. I would not have been so surprised if immediately I wanted to kill him. What shocked me, what horrified me, is that anybody who was black would do. Anybody. I remember phoning Spencer, with whom I have this soul feeling. I said, "You know, look, I'm really in trouble. If you were here, I might want to kill you. You know, you'd go with the rest." And then I understood, you know, how this thing spreads out, and how the innocent become involved. And I guess that's one thing that just gave me an enormous insight into the anger that is exposed in riots—and wanton killings, what we think are wanton. I know what their roots are now. Nobody has to explain it to me. I was the wrong color in my black man's eyes.

Virginia Lawrence's story continues in chapter 9.

CHAPTER 3

Four Black Women and the
Consciousness of the Sixties

For black Americans, the consciousness of the sixties was predominantly a racial consciousness. Below the surface, however, were important issues of class and gender. The four women in this chapter are strong, resourceful, articulate, and highly engaged in public life, and although they do not speak in the language of the feminist movement, they share an outlook with some implicitly feminist characteristics. Even more striking is the class consciousness implicit in these accounts, and indeed in the words of many, if not most, blacks in this book. Although race consciousness and class consciousness are usually viewed as antithetical, American blacks in the late 1960s were voicing a social critique that bore some marked affinities to the classical proletarian outlook of the Marxist tradition, including a skeptical and critical attitude toward authority in general and toward hierarchical relations of class and power. Many looked beyond color to question all the institutions and practices of American society, seeking to explain events in terms of group forces, rather than individual motivations, and searching for collective strategies for fundamental change in the social order. From their experience with racism, Afro-Americans have developed an antipathy toward other forms of exploitation and oppression and an ability to identify with a wide range of disadvantaged people.

Florence Grier, whose story continues in this chapter, became aware of the significance of social class—as well as race and gender—while still a young girl, but she did not become politically active until 1967, when she saw the Sacramento police use excess force to quell social protest. Her first political act was an attempt to protect black youths from police entanglement by urging their mothers to keep them off the street. Until then she had been something of a racial moderate, but in a period of only months she became more and more militant, embracing much of the radical mood of late-sixties black nationalism. Millie Harding, whose story follows Grier's, had become politically involved as a teenager in the 1950s—perhaps that is one reason she maintained some distance and skepticism regarding the black militants, neither awed by their rhetoric nor swayed by the fads and fashions in black politics and culture.

Although we found generalized anti-white attitudes among many people, particularly the youth (see chapter 5), the women in this chapter do not totally condemn or reject white people as a group. Angry and increasingly distrustful, they resent discrimination and insensitivity, express strong racial pride and ethnic identification, but remain integrationists also. Their racial awareness and political consciousness thus do not follow the simplistic contours of polarized integrationist and nationalist perspectives emphasized by the mass media and by social analysts at the time.

Florence Grier

"I'm tired of being scared"

Almost every night, Florence Grier has been on the streets, trying to keep things calm, or in the car patrol monitoring the actions of the police. Her community group has taken a leaf from the Panthers' book. Once last summer she saw police arrest six young men for breaking windows at a place where they couldn't possibly have been. She reported this, yet the authorities wouldn't listen. She spent five weeks at the trial and testified, but the men were found guilty.

The interview begins on one of the car patrols. Hardy Frye has his tape recorder on as they drive around Oak Park, on an early spring evening in 1968.

I

I saw the Sacramento police lie through their teeth last summer. And even Officer Travis, the colored policeman, had to lie through his teeth, sitting right on that stand. Honestly, Hardy, I feel the way Mr. Muhammad feels, that they oughta turn every single black man loose. For the simple reason that he has not been treated equally! When you say to me that a colored man's got a record, it just doesn't mean anything to me. He's got a record because he's black.

We've got a little thing going over here at Sacramento High now because of the inability of the principal and the teachers to understand that you have double standards for Negro youngsters. About twenty youngsters got into a fracas about three weeks ago. The principal calls the police force. Takes down these thirteen to fourteen of your little boys to the police station. Immediately you get our boys' names on the record as juvenile delinquents and it's never taken off. Whenever they want to find out anything on 'em, you dig his high school record up. This is what he faces when he goes to get a job at the post office, this is what he faces when he goes to get a job on the garbage, this is what he faces all over. And I honestly feel this deep in my heart, the Negro male has got a long way to go to get justice from the white man.

Circling McClatchy Park, she catches sight of a familiar police car.

If they don't get rid of Lieutenant Rivers, we gonna have some hell in Oak Park. 'Cause he's a racist, Hardy. He's a racist, you hear? One of the little boys last summer called him a dirty name and made a break across the park there to the recreation center. And Lieutenant Rivers ran out because he couldn't stand to have this little fourteen-year-old boy call him a dirty name. And they took him over and pistol-whipped him.

■ *What do you think it's gonna take to change 'em?*

Want me to tell you the absolute truth about it? I'm the mother of five kids, but I think that the Negro at this particular time will have to take the Black Panther route. And that's killing, isn't it? Hardy, I'm gonna be frank with you, because I'm frustrated now! But if we can't get this white man to think no other way—and I'm a mother—if we can't get him to see any other way—kill some policemen, the way that they're killing us.

I really am feeling this from my heart—let some of them die. They kill and they are exonerated. Nothing is done about it. They shoot 'em in the back, they take 'em and put 'em in jail, and they take 'em outta jail. They do all kinds of things to 'em and nobody does anything about it! The way I feel is this: it's bad to say it, and I hope that I can change it, but until some of . . . you, you get enough of them killed—. . . I believe in love! I'm a Christian! But at this particular time, I'm frustrated! You kill some of them. Now if that's Black Pantherism, that's the way I feel about it. And I'm scared, Hardy! I'm scared, but I'm tired of being scared now!

If I said what I wanted to say, and I didn't have my kids to think about, I'd get me a sign and I'd go up in front of the City Council there. As far as I'm concerned I don't think any Negroes have got any business in Vietnam. Period. You're not fighting for anything in Vietnam. You don't have equal rights. You go over to Vietnam and kill those people over there and come back here . . . if you get in a certain section of Sacramento with a white woman, one of those racist policemen just might blow your brains out!

There have been so many things left out of the books about the Negro, and you have got *so many* stupid white people. I heard one woman come on the radio the other day. She says (*high, mincing tone*), "Would you tell me where there's a Negro that won't bite?" They haven't been taught this: that Negroes are human, with all the hopes and aspirations, the gentleness and love and tenderness and need that they have.

And another thing that I'm disgusted about. My little Will is thirteen, and when he goes to school, he likes to play basketball. And if dark catches Will outside, I have to do a lot of praying. I resent that the police sit around California Junior High and Sacramento High and these different schools where they've got our kids integrated, and Will can come along as innocent as he is and don't even know whether, as black as he is, he don't even know whether he's black right now! Because I haven't—I'm, I'm reluctant to have him dig into Negro history! He's free as a breeze now, and he's getting along good in school. . . . And I hate to tell him that he's black, and I don't want him to dig too far into Negro history to see just exactly who he is because I'm afraid that with his capacity for thinking, if he ever digs into the political books the way you guys are doing, he'll be a Stokely and a Rap Brown as sure as he's what he is! I never say, "You read this, Will!" I can let [my daughter] read it because she's gonna be somebody's wife! (*Hard laugh.*)

And I resent the fact that if Will goes to school right now, between here and California Junior High, some stupid idiot like Lieutenant Rivers could pick him up—because five or six of 'em come down the street, and he's got a natural hairdo, and decide that they want to stop 'em! Some of these stupid white women along the way decide that there're too many of those Negroes making all that noise coming along from school—the school that they have transferred our kids across town to! And Will at thirteen, he's tall, my son's never encountered the police under any circumstances. . . . Some of these idiots might pick him up, and if he protests, throw him against the wall, and put him in jail, and have his life ruined and have him hate everybody.

II

They've stopped on Stockton Boulevard at a Japanese-owned drive-in to get some coffee.

I didn't make any mistakes about Black Power when I first heard the word. To me it didn't mean anything about getting you some guns and going out and raising hell. My understanding of Black Power was "work together." I see Black Power as a cry for the Negro to use whatever means he can economically. Let me give you an example.

We women that are on welfare, if each one of these five hundred women in Sacramento, black women, would just donate a dollar apiece on the first of the month—it's just a package of cigarettes. You put that down on that old piece of house the real estate agents have bought from these poor white people that are scared of the Negroes coming, and make yourself a nursery. Put your women in there if they get some work and need somebody to take care of the baby. And buy another house and buy another house until you own that entire block. Now that's my idea of Black Power!

If you're working in these employment agencies, when those little black boys come through there, see to it you get him a job. If he can't pass that test, do it the way the Japanese and the Chinese do! Tell him how to pass the white man's test! Take these kids in and drill 'em on the arithmetic. This is what I call Black Power! Okay, put your money together and put up a carpenter's school and put out some carpenters. This is what I call Black Power.

And buy this stuff, the way I see the Japanese doing here on Tenth Avenue. They're not doing a lot of talking down on Tenth Street, just keeping their mouths shut. And when you look up, Japanese own this, Japanese own that, Japanese own this! Move over here in the Negro section of town, put up a store and sell chitlins and neckbones and everything to you. And then move over to his section of town the way they're doing. Trade with black people. This is what Black Power means!

Put a man like Attorney Cox in the City Council! Negroes in Del Paso Heights, Negroes out here in Oak Park, Negroes all around! You get together and put your vote and then tell Cox what you intend for him to do. But make sure he talks the way Adam Clayton Powell talks.

Political and economic power. And accidentally shoot a few police. You understand what I'm saying? Let a few of 'em come up dead. And don't nobody talk. That's what I call Black Power!

■ *People are saying that Black Power means reverse racism.*

Is this reverse racism if you buy it, you rent it, you get it whatever way you can—so you own it? I don't believe in racism. But there comes a time when you got to get your foot off my neck. I don't see that it's reverse racism. It's survival.

I want to live! I want to see blacks live! I want to see blacks rise up! I've thought about the concentration camps. (*Sighs.*) In my heart, I'm getting to the place where I don't care. Make this white man own up to that he's a racist. And let all the world see he's a racist and putting us in some concentration camps.

(*Shouting very emotionally.*) This may not be the right way to feel, but that's the way I feel!

■ *I'm just asking you!* (Shouting.) *I just want your honest opinion.*

I'm just telling you! Concentration camps don't scare me anymore. Maybe we'll get in the concentration camps, and some of those Negroes will get together and get some confidence. The Japanese came outta there with some confidence and they came out with some shoemakers, and they came out with some television repairmen, washing repairmen, and things like that.

III

At Florence's house. The streets are quiet now.

I don't hate . . . the white man. Something inside of me understands that he was taught that. And I have a real deep smirk of, some sense of satisfaction—it might be self-righteousness—but I have a real good feeling that I love him and—and I feel bigger than he is. You can't make me hate *every* white man! Even though I'd kill a policeman! The way that they just keep killing. But I can't hate everybody I see. I can't just throw all white people in a package and say that none of 'em are any good. Way down inside, I love—I love people. All kinds of people. And I feel that by them beating us and doing all the ugly things that they did to us, we've had an experience of learning what it really feels to have empathy with people. This is where this *deep* ability to bring out the interpretation of a song [comes from]!

There is a difference in the rhythm of the Negro and the white. There's a difference in the way that they sing. But I also know that if you listen to a real good hillbilly song, they have that same feeling that the Negro has. It's a deep sensitive feeling. And we don't have any more soul than anybody else. But I know what they call soul . . . something about a feeling of kindness and love and understanding of suffering. Everybody's got that, Hardy. There's a couple of women here in Sacramento, they're white, they've got soul. This is just depth of feeling, sensitivity. The way that I feel toward all babies. You can't give me a baby—whether the baby is white—I've nursed all kinds of babies, and I feel the same for all.

- *How did you sustain yourself in a system like this?*

I think it is a miracle how millions and millions of Negroes survived . . . all the suffering and frustration. I believe I made it by [my] deep sense of religion . . . that says man has a Creator that gives him the strength to move on. I've seen my sisters drop on the floor from nothing to eat. You eat wild greens and you eat in these second-hand stores. You make ends meet with what you have. I think that the Negro, if he really sits down and thinks of how he had to make it, he would know that he's not an inferior race! To go through the things that we've gone through is to be whipped.

When I think of nine children and *nobody* been to jail. And my father went to fourth grade and most of us finished high school. Why, I finished high school! I had to borrow the dress that I wore! I had to borrow shoes that I wore! Somebody had to give me the two dollars to get the cap and gown.

The house that I lived in, I've laid in the house and looked out in the air and watched the snow fall. I laid in the springs and just piled the rags and things all on top of the springs. We slept four and five in a bed. We didn't have the incest and the rape and all these stupid things that you hear people talking about . . . that Negroes are animals and all that. We had a lot of love! We had a lot of sharing! We had to eat a lot of sweet potatoes (*laughs*) and neckbones and pig's feet and—lots of second-hand clothes, and work in people's kitchens. See, I'm forty-five, and I've worked all my life in kitchens, hotels, laundries, served dinners, done janitor's work. And the experiences I've had . . .

And seeing, just really seeing that they're none of 'em . . . I haven't met a single white man better than you! I haven't met a single white woman who was better than I was! None! The only thing that she had that I didn't have was schooling. The only thing that she had that I didn't have was an opportunity to open a store, or open a little place over in the Negro area. This is the only thing that they had!

> See chapter 8 for Mrs. Grier's interviews in 1979 and 1981.

Millie Harding

"This is no dream world, baby"

Florence Grier's friend and fellow community activist, Millie Harding was born and raised in Alabama, where she learned at an early age to protect herself from white men.

For all the years that I can remember, one thing we have never been able to take away—or castrate a Negro man of—has been his courage and his guts. Now, they can call him a pimp or anything else they want, but he know he can hold his own out there on the street, or in the service, or anyplace else. He's never been called a coward. But I watch the kids now, even on the junior high school level, and any time five or six guys band together and because someone disagrees with their trend of thought, just jump on him and beat him to a pulp . . . this is cowardice.

It's April 1968, only a week after the assassination. Martin Luther King was her ideal of a real man, she tells interviewer Frye. "The man had a way about him no other men have. He not only reached us, he reached them." The day after Dr. King was shot, the militants called a strike at her daughter's school.

They got the two or three hundred kids that were interested, and they told the other kids, "If you don't walk, man, we're going to take care of you." Well, this is saying to me I don't have the right to think. You do my thinking for me, and you tell me what to do. I told my child, "I'm not going to tell you to walk and I'm not going to tell you to sit. Whatever your judgment is, I stand by you on it." She said, "I don't think we should walk out until we hear what the administration has to say first."

I told George the other day, "Baby, you talk about white power got his foot on my neck, then you're gonna get Black Power and you gonna have *your* foot on my neck!" Hell, I might as well stay with white power, at least he's got what I need.

The African-Americans, the Muslims, are sitting here hollering, "Give us five states. Give us a black country." I don't want any part of it. They want absolute control of those people in those five states, Hardy. They're not going to tolerate any dissension from me or you. They ain't going to tolerate as much as we feeding the white man. If you don't go along, they going to wipe you out. Now, the Man out there, he may not agree with you, and in some parts of the country he try to wipe you out too, but we do have freedom to say, "Well, man, I don't like the way you're running things." If he thought all the Negroes would go, he'd give you five states before you could bat your eye. Because he'd prefer to have you in one spot where he can keep his eye on you. But if we'd go and settle for something like this, what have all the generations of the past four hundred years died for? If my husband went to war and my relatives in the South died so I could have my being the way I see fit, and then I'm going to get into a country like the Indians on the reservation? No, thank you. I want to have the same privileges and the same freedoms that he had. This is what we've been fighting for all these years, to be able to live right in the middle of that Man, right next door up there with [Governor] Ronald Reagan or President Johnson and still snap my fingers and eat my cornbread and collard greens with my fingers if I feel like it.

Like Florence Grier, Millie Harding is very involved in monitoring the police.

I've seen young policemen who have been on the force two or three weeks, just plain old scared. . . . If you know you've got a cat that's got prejudices against black people, then you do not put him in Oak Park. You send him out to Town and Country, by Reagan and them. But I think the policemen are like anybody else. I think they're human. I've seen the bad side of the policemen and I've seen the good side.

The night my sister got married, my son and four or five of the little friends he runs around buddy-buddy with was out on the corner. Now that day there had been several break-ins so they were patrolling the area pretty hard. Now these little guys—we stood right out here across by that wire fence and watched 'em—they were running upside the [police] cars, kicking at 'em, and saying, "Hey, whitey, what you doing over here, get your so-and-sos out of here before we blow one of these cars up." They'd walk out in front of the car and just stand there. So I told [my husband], "Now, if the officers went to pick one up, he'd have trouble. All five would rally to that one, and he'd have to end up hitting somebody across the head."

■ *You think the policeman would've had a right to hit him?*

This was the only way he could take him in. I'll put myself in the officer's place and what he gets paid a month, and now if *I* walked up on that kid, I'd know he was bluffing, but the cop don't know this. 'Cause he don't live here with him every day. The kids don't realize, when they playing these little games out there, that these people are trained to kill. And our kids have not been taught. . . . One thing about the people in the South is they were taught back there, you respect an officer, as long as he respects you.

I don't think the people [there] had the fear of the police that the people here have. I remember we were coming from church one night and a group of white boys shot my mother in the hip. The police came to take a report and they propped on the front porch, just kind of shooting the breeze. And my stepdaddy came in, he couldn't stand those people, so he told them, "Man, you get your feet off my bannister, you didn't come here to socialize."

The officer asked my mother, "Are you sure it was a group of kids that shot you? Or was it some of the paddies that you work for that you had an affair with?" And my stepdad was standing there, and he hit the officer in the mouth. They didn't bother him that night. They knew that the community was heated up. [Later] they put him in jail.

■ *But that Sacramento officer, you can't say that he respects you any more than the police in Alabama did.*

But you can't expect an officer's gonna respect you when he say to you, "Now you have no business taking that man's stuff out of his store, you put it back." And [you answer]: "You m-f, who are you to tell me what to do?" Now what is he supposed to do? These people are paid to keep the peace. And if he don't keep the peace, we get mad, and if he keep the peace, we get mad. You either have to say that the man is going to come here and keep peace or tell the man, "I don't want no cops in here and you all get out on the street and keep the peace." But if you too scared to talk to a few kids at Soul City, I know you don't want to keep the peace.

"Soul City" is a street corner where a group of young men had been hassling women who were passing by. Mrs. Harding's community group decided to talk

directly to the troublemakers rather than calling the police. But none of the
men in her organization would volunteer. They were afraid of retaliation. So
she took the job.

I said to them, "The library is here, and my child likes to go up there.
Now, it seems ridiculous she got to fight her way through because she does not
care to have you guys manhandle her. If you're standing all across the sidewalk the way you guys do, and someone asks you to move—you got to get
cussed out—this is ridiculous. Now, I am a woman. I oughta have the right to
choose who I want to put his hands all over me. Just because I don't want you
to paw me, I don't think you should tear [me] to pieces, verbally or physically."

"The girls over in the Recreation are white, but they still girls in our community, and let's show that man that you can also give his woman respect,
even though he don't give yours none. That man respects his woman, he
makes you respect her. Yet you will not give us the same respect. Maybe we
don't act as feminine as the Caucasian woman, but then the Caucasian
woman have a lot more reason to act feminine. Because we're out here in
some woman's kitchen or on one of those steady jobs working just like you to
make ends meet. So I don't have time to do my nails twice a week and roll my
hair and look pretty all the time. This is no dream world, baby. And yet because I go so far out for you as my man, I expect you, when I walk on the
street, to give me that kind of respect. I am your woman and you are something special to me." And they cut it out, pronto.

There isn't one of my guys out here that I can say, "Well, you just no good.
You just lazy, you ain't working because you just don't want to." Because I
don't evaluate my guys this way.

She is thirty-three, the mother of ten children. A woman's life, she says, is "a
vicious circle . . . you never really own yourself anymore. You got part of you
split over here to be part of the children. Each child is an individual and needs
different types of treatment. You've got a husband and you've got to groove
with his moods because he also has a rough time out there making a living.
[But] Negro women are a lot more sensitive toward our men than they are to-
ward us."

■ *How about the riots?*

I don't believe in a riot if it's going to end up like in Watts. A bunch of kids
jump up and say, "Man, let's go out there and throw a few rocks or a few
molotovs." All my kids are shot down and laying in the streets and their blood
running in the dust, and them people walks off loose and fancy free. If that's
the kind of riot you talking about, I don't want any part of it. Oh, it makes

them notice you're there, but it doesn't accomplish anything. Because he's only proven one more time that he can control you.

But a riot is fine if you've got good planning. If you're talking in terms of a community uniting, hit 'em from every area at the same time . . . I feel this is going to be necessary. As long as we sit and talk, I don't think they're ever going to do anything. This country has only understood violence. He can sit there and promise you from now till Jesus comes. And never produce anything, 'cause he's going to tell you, "Well, it takes time." What kind of time? We ain't got that kind of time.

> For followup interviews with Millie Harding in
> 1979 and 1986, see chapter 8.

BOTH VERA Brooke and Elena Albert, whose stories follow, talked about the experience of being called "nigger" as a young schoolchild. For many blacks, such an incident may be their first inkling that their color will affect their fate in a significant way. Later, more dramatic examples of discrimination may occur, events that mark major turning points in the development of their attitude toward the world, as when Malcolm X's white eighth-grade teacher advised him to give up the idea of becoming a lawyer in favor of a more "realistic goal for a nigger," like becoming a carpenter.[1] After that, he says, "I drew away from white people."

"Something happened in my childhood I've never forgotten" is how Elena Albert prefaces her story of winning a race and being given a prize far inferior to those the white kids received. Such incidents of differential treatment evoke deep feelings of disappointment, even disillusionment, and a sense of grievance at the unfairness of double standards. Young people want to believe that life is fair and that society lives up to its ideals. Prejudice and discrimination dramatize the fact that things aren't what they seem, that there is an enormous gap between society's pretensions and the way things really are. The discovery of the prevalence of hypocrisy in social and political life prompts a reevaluation of all that has preceded: isolated incidents now seem part of a definable pattern. "Everything began to make sense," Vera Brooke says, when an overt act of discrimination spurred her to realize that it was not her father who was creating problems, but the white system.

Growing up in the era of civil rights and black power, Vera Brooke first resisted the spirit of 1960s activism, then fully embraced it. Almost forty years older than Ms. Brooke, Elena Albert became politically and racially conscious in much less favorable circumstances, in the western mountain states early in the century. For Mrs. Albert, the consciousness of the sixties was the culmination of her life-long quest for a black identity.

Vera Brooke

"Those that came from a different social experience I feared"

Vera Brooke was an upper-division student at the University of California in April 1968. Like many other privileged blacks at that time, she felt caught between her middle-class status and her belief in racial solidarity; at the time of this interview she was learning to overcome her fear of lower-class blacks. Such class divisions were a major obstacle to black unity, with the movement speaking more to the needs and possibilities of middle-class blacks than to the situation of the poor.

The interviewer was Sheila Gibson, a graduate student in sociology, one of the first black women doctoral students in the department's history. Gibson was born in Berkeley and her family had deep roots in the Bay Area's middle-class black community. She had known Vera since childhood, and their families had been friends.

Vera's parents were college graduates who had been involved in civil rights activities as far back as the 1940s and whose families had lived in California for several generations. As a child, Vera felt apart from her peers.

When girls were wearing tighter and shorter skirts and wearing their hair down, I was still in braids. And still wearing oxfords and white socks to junior high school. I was relatively good in sports and I loved to skate. But I didn't have boyfriends, and they sort of took me as "one of the fellows." When class pictures were taken nobody except my girlfriends wanted [my] picture. The sort of indirect and awkward comments that boys will make to girls at this age were never directed to me.

Twice I gave a party at home and the black students who came out of curiosity—"What kind of party would this chick give?"—would always be very upset that my parents were around. My parties were always very boring because my parents would set up sandwich spreads and soft drinks. I was always fat and I had a real hangup behind being physically acceptable. But I really liked to dance.

It was the only area of expression that I felt uninhibited. And I could shake my behind and twist around any way I felt like because I was dancing. And I wouldn't walk the street that way, and I would never be flippant or insinuating in speech. But, man, when I got ready to dance, that was my thing! And Daddy would not have it. And I had a mean cha-cha going with my sister, and Daddy came in the room and I froze. He looked at me and didn't say anything. I was practicing up because I had been invited to go to this party by this guy, and this was my sophomore year, *like wow!* And of course Daddy was going to drive and pick me up at nine-thirty or something ungodly, but I was still going to go. And I had such a good time and a lot of people that had kind of cut me out of their social group were very surprised that I could dance so well. Despite the fact that I got good grades, spoke proper English, and didn't dress extreme.

A week later somebody was giving a party and Daddy said, "The fraternity is giving a program on job opportunities for black college students and I think you ought to hear it. As long as you are a minor, you may not like what I tell you to do, but you just have to do it. I don't want my daughter becoming a party girl." I was mad! I sat through that thing refusing to listen. And Daddy tried to draw me into a conversation about it afterwards, and I wasn't going to talk to him.

This began the pattern. I ceased talking to my father past necessary communication—you know, "Hello," "Goodbye," "Can I have my allowance?" I would never volunteer information about what I was doing, what I was reading, what I thought about things. Because every time I did he kept destroying things I had believed in.

I would sit and watch programs like the Dick Clark show and just swoon over people like Frankie Avalon. And he would say, "They're trying to sound like black singers." And I got interested in folksinging, and there was a big hefty white chick that used to sing out of Berkeley, her name was Barbara Dane. And Barbara sang blues, you know, and Daddy says, "Another one of those white chicks thinking she's some big black mamma." And [he] didn't like Dinah Shore, didn't like Peggy Lee, just everything I thought was so groovy was always somehow a little bit wrong. So I refused to talk about things that I'd done, because he'd say, "Aw, some black man already did that." But at the same time I was really inculcating what he was teaching. And using it sort of selfishly to gain acceptance from other young people. They would say something like, "Have you ever noticed how a lot of white kids try to sound like black singers?" and I'd say, "Oh, yes, Dinah Shore imitates Ella Fitzgerald, and Barbara Dane thinks she's Odetta." And people think that you're a very hip black chick—and I think subsconciously it began to, you know, form in my mind that the cat's right. He's not a super-sensitive black man, he's not super-puritanical.

I was raised primarily in an integrated middle-class situation. And I remember being told to talk a certain way, always pronounce words properly, don't talk like this, don't be loud, get your studies down, be home at a certain time. "I'd rather you didn't play with those children. I know they're nice children but their mothers aren't concerned with whether they swear or if they're properly dressed." I didn't see anything wrong with these kids. And I thought, Mom and Dad are sure hard to live with.

When we moved into North Oakland, I was put into classes that were quote-unquote upper-level, [where] there never were very many black classmates. Most of my friends were white or Japanese. I was always reading ahead of the class, and I got to be a librarian monitor.

I was invited to tell a story to the Board of Education, and now I look back on it, it was almost a model-Negro type thing. One of our prime black students, you know, from Jefferson Elementary School, a predominantly Negro neighborhood, who has surmounted the barriers of her social existence. I had a new dress and I told them a story, and they clapped.

Those that came from a different social experience I feared, mostly because they were just a rougher, tougher bunch. I remember laughing when they made funny comments in class, and later in the sixth grade I remember feeling—when they fumbled in answering and were very quickly cut off—"Why don't you let them finish? Maybe he knows the answer." And about sixth grade I began to feel the weight of "You think you're better than we are, don't you?" kind of a thing.

I wanted to be like them, but I didn't want to be like them. I wanted to be accepted, but I didn't want to have to go through this little in-group initiation process of being able to steal candy from the store, or sassing the bus driver, or losing a library book and not telling them. My parents were very happy about, like the way school was progressing, and I never got into fights. But my friends were beginning to make comments that being white, or being good, wasn't so good. And I was always caught in between.

When I got to high school, I became extremely nervous around the—shall we say—the less refined element, and I even remember developing a fear of walking down the hall when there were a lot of black students, guys and girls, just standing along the lockers and talking and being very, very aware that I didn't know these people, they weren't in any of my classes, they were very, very different from me, they thought I was very different. Conversations changed when I came into proximity. They looked at me funny when I walked down the hall with white friends. And I was torn between apologizing or explaining. "Look, you know, these are my friends—but it isn't because I want to be white. This chick is in my French class and we're talking about the assignments." Then I also became defensive, saying [to myself], "Why can't I have white friends? Who are you to decide who my friends are? You can't make me feel bad." And yet I did feel bad.

About this time a lot of black students complained that there wasn't a club in the high school for them. They didn't want to belong to a photo club, they didn't want to belong to a folk dance club because that was foul. They wanted to sit around and talk about what black people should talk about. Nobody would volunteer to organize it. So I did. And it was very awkward because most of the students who made up the Interracial Understanding Club were the very group of black students who did not consider me part of them. Yet I had to get up in front of them and moderate discussions, plan programs, really be in a position of being the Negro leader picked by the establishment, quote-unquote, to relate to the other blacks. And this became extremely difficult. And literally what the group became was a safety-in-numbers mechanism for blacks to sit around and talk about white students and feel safe because it was a sociological thing, it wasn't a personal thing.

There could be no clubs that were only for black students at this time. And the whites in the group would say things like, "How come Negro students don't want to learn? Why don't they join in the student government?" And black students would say things like, "Doesn't make any difference if I do or not, because you don't like me, and don't try to be my friend because I don't want to be your friend," and you know, "All you whites are all alike," or even extreme things that I found myself wincing at, like, "I don't like paddies, man." And I would think, you mustn't use that word, can't you express your-self in a more delicate manner? Please don't embarrass me by addressing my friends in this way because they will think that I think this way too, *and I do not think this way.* When in fact I really did, but I would never tell some chick I had been studying with for six months, "I don't dig paddies," you know, because Mama said you're not supposed to use the word.

Shopping with my parents, I would see some white girl that I knew and I'd say to Daddy, "Hey, there's Sally in my French class. She and I are really good friends." I'd say, "Hi Sally," and the hello was so different than in class. I'd say, "She's probably just in a hurry or shy because her parents are present." But Daddy was always pointing out: "She didn't invite you shopping. Ob-viously you're good in French and her grades are going up because she's study-ing with you."

I thought he was terribly sensitive. And unnecessarily hard on white people. And that's when I began to fight against the activities we were participating in concerning civil rights. I hated going to NAACP meetings. I didn't want to read *Ebony* magazine except for the fashion articles. I didn't want to listen to Martin Luther King's speeches.

I began to hate to go to restaurants because Daddy always made the waitress angry. And I began to recognize expressions on his face that something was going to happen to spoil Sunday dinner again. And I'd really get angry. Now I can see how it pained him, because I didn't understand what he was trying to show me and I was taking out on him what was really not him at all. I really made it hard on him. I would say things like, "You're too sensitive" or "Oh, Daddy, don't do that." We'd go somewhere and the waitress would bang the water glasses down, and Daddy would look at her and say something like, "It sure is a nice day, isn't it?" through clenched teeth, and I'd just want to hide.

The first time it really hit me that Daddy was not creating a problem was when we went with my grandparents to a resort place in the valley. She and grandpa had lived in this community for twenty years, and for the most part people accept them like another rural couple. And grandma's rock club had gone to this resort place for a picnic [before. But when we arrived,] the man said, "We're closed today," and cars were driving past and going inside. And Daddy got out of the car and got that same expression, and I thought, now we're going to have some stuff and spoil another weekend. And the man said to my grandmother, "How are you, hope everything's fine, I'm sorry we're only taking groups that made reservations today." Well, he kept making excuses until finally he got very angry and said, "We don't serve Negro people." Grandmother was the only Negro woman in this club, so of course they let the club in before. But an entire family of black people, they weren't going to let us in.

And it just hit me, it was *the* turning point when I realized that Daddy wasn't creating the problems, that they really existed. And because of the way I had been raised, the classes I had been in, and the friends I had had, I had been blinded, really, from seeing it. And now, you know, everything began to make sense. I could understand marches, speeches, complaints, committees, everything. And in the space of about a month I became extremely cynical. And I became much more tolerant of the less refined, less sophisticated reactions of these other black students.

She "integrated" a small white college, where only six of the sixty-five girls questioned by the dean were willing to room with her. Vera "couldn't stand" her first roommate who was always asking, "How do your people feel about this?"

So I got another and she was very angry with me. She was going to play Great White Mother, and I wasn't functioning. I was not culturally deprived and therefore I didn't suit her needs at all. My parents were college students, I could speak two foreign languages, I liked to read, I played the guitar. And I knew other people in town and the library better than she did.

Vera wouldn't laugh at the racist jokes students felt free to tell in her presence because she was "their favorite Negro and so relaxed." After one incident the dean's wife had her over for tea to explain that some students weren't used to being around Negroes. School officials were afraid she would write the NAACP.

I became very lonely for black people. The first day that woman walked in, and she introduced herself—her name was Bessie Simmons—I really liked her. She said, "Well, things might be changing, got some blackness in here." I

watched her a few minutes sweeping the floor and finally I said, "Mrs. Simmons, just a minute. I'd appreciate it very much if you wouldn't clean my
room." She said, "Oh, girl, I'm sweeping all these rooms, yours doesn't make
no difference." I said, "I've been brought up to clean my own room and
people don't wait on me. And if you want to come in here and take your coffee
break or have a cigarette, fine." And Bessie would be sitting in there talking,
and the supervisor would come down the hall. So we'd turn back to our
books, and there's Bessie pushing the mop. And soon as she'd go by, we'd start
talking.

My parents loved me and everything. But there was a certain cultural thing
about black people which I just didn't know about. And I saw Bessie's house
and it was very small, linoleum was cracking, the floor was very cold. She had
three children, her oldest daughter was pregnant out of wedlock, the two little
boys were just as cute as could be. Her husband drank on occasion but he
wasn't loud, you know, he wasn't negligent. He was a member of one of the
small churches there, and cornbread every night, grits and porkchops for
breakfast. That sort of thing. And I just dug it because, without really being
able to analyze it, here was a basic honestness in existence that I wasn't getting
on campus. And it was easier to get than at home. At home there were certain rituals you had to perform, and then you were acceptable. And there was
just sort of an earthiness here that I really latched on to. Because I was stuck
on this campus and I ran into so much gas during the day, and on weekends
it was so great to go to Bessie's. Get up and read funny papers to the kids. And
go to church with them and hear Bessie sing. Lord have mercy, could
Bessie sing!

I learned a lot of things at college I would not have learned at home. I
learned how to have confidence in my own selection of people, and even if
the cat looked rough and had a conk I could talk to him and we could go to
parties together, and I wasn't going to get raped. But for me the racial thing
was what was really very important. I learned in a very sophisticated manner
to maintain a general distrust of white people.

I could really see the kinds of assumptions they had about me. They assumed that I assumed that they were very desirable people to know. They were
doing me a favor by inviting me to go horseback riding. And I felt almost
superior, in a way, because I knew that the parties that I went to with black
students were much more fun, I knew that Bessie and her husband James
were much nicer than their parents. When their parents came up, they hardly
talked to me, got very busy, and I began to see what was coming down. I was a
little bit bitter at first. And I began to see it as a sort of necessary condition that
a lot of black people lived in all the time. No big thing, no unique experience.
And I began to understand why my father got tense when he went into restaurants, or became super-sensitive to nuances, why he would get mad when

people looked at him, why he was extremely curt with people who would come to service appliances at the house. Unfortunately, I got so involved in my living experience that I flunked all my final exams.

At the local community college the next year, students she had known in high school would say, "Oh, Vera went away to college and couldn't make it. Now she's back with us." Going to class was like walking the gauntlet.

"Man, you see that chick in the white dress?" "Uh huh, sure been looking a long time." "Too bad all you can do is look!" If some cat reached out and patted me on the ass, I'd probably faint . . . or jump straight up and scream.

Black consciousness was coming in, and I found myself feeling very silly for having all these hangups about talking to the cats at school. So the very next morning I was walking down the hall and some cat says, "Say, Mama, you sure are fine." And I said, "Oh, yeah?" and kept walking. And the cat did a double take, because he'd been saying it every morning for two semesters, you know. And then I made a point of walking over to the black table and sat down with my coffee. I didn't open a book, I didn't immediately get buried in a magazine. I just sat there. And people made friendly overtures, and after that I sat at the black table all the time. And I would smile and say hello to white students who walked by, but I forced myself to be with the black community. Even though it was imperfect in many ways, it was not as destructive as what I had experienced my freshman year.

And there was also a certain ease and comfort behind the very direct and graphic banter of black people. If you stay within your middle-class bag, it's very crude and very offensive. But like when you've been around it for a while, it's a very easy kind of thing. And nobody's talking about raping you, man, and obviously there's a situation of display and recognition. The group of brothers watch the cat's technique. All the little leers and sly smiles when they light your cigarettes, or somebody'd say, "Hey, give me the sugar, no, give me some sugar," and you'd reach over the sugar bowl and he'd say, "That's not what I meant." If I'm a black woman, [and] there's a black man around, he's going to relate to me in that way, that's his way, and it's got nothing to do with if I'm being provocative or not. And I began to enjoy it, you know, "Jesus, it's about time."

Vera Brooke's life history continues in chapter 13.

Elena Albert

"Something happened in my childhood
I've never forgotten"

Elena Albert is an amateur historian, active in a San Francisco organization devoted to Afro-American history, and it is with a historian's eye that she describes to interviewer Hardy Frye what it was like to grow up in Montana and Washington early in the twentieth century. There were so few black people that many—including members of her own family—had little choice but to intermarry.

When I was a little girl in Montana, it was the same as it had been in pioneer days. Negroes could homestead. My mother, my aunt, my grandmother, and my grandfather, each filed on a hundred sixty acres of land. And we had milk cows. My little cousin and I delivered milk in pails to people who lived on the other side of the railroad track. In those days there was no question about the milk being in sanitary containers or homogenized or anything. As soon as the milking was over at night, we delivered it to our customers. Now my grandmother was a little unusual for her day: she divorced my grandfather. She ran a boardinghouse near the railroad tracks—twenty-two rooms— it seems to have been customary out in the West that Negro women would go into having a boardinghouse or a restaurant. And my grandmother had roomers and boarders—white men who worked for the railroad. And there we lived together in the same house, eating our meals at the same time at the table. But Montana was a very, very ugly racist place.

My mother, the second time, married a German. My aunt for her second husband married a Norwegian. Of course, you know there were very, very few black people in Montana. So there was quite a lot of intermarriage in the family. But they were not able to get licenses in the state. They went to the eastern part of Washington. There an interracial couple could get a marriage license.

My mother taught me to read at home. I remember once she was showing me countries on the map. She showed me Norway, where our neighbor, Moe, had been born, and she showed us the country Sweden, and she said certain neighbors were from Sweden; and we had Irish neighbors, and she showed me Ireland. And I asked her, "Mother, which one is *our* country?" And in 1915, my mother said to me, "We don't have a country."

I couldn't understand that all my neighbors had a country. So many of them were immigrants, you see, so they talked about the country where they were born.

As a child, I realized that there *was* a difference between me and the other children at school. I was called "nigger" and "darky." And when I was small, I used to fight my schoolmates. Teachers never were sympathetic about it. Some of my contemporaries tell me that they were not ever aware of a difference when they were children. On the whole, having so many white relatives, I felt comfortable with white people, but I was always aware that I was treated differently. But generally speaking our neighbors were friendly, and it was not unpleasant . . . living out in the country, or in the small town, as far as our relationships with white people were concerned.

Of course, there were unspoken customs. We knew that we were not likely to get certain jobs. All my memories of Negro men working are shoeshiners, porters, janitors. The only man I know who had a job that was unusual and required a great deal of skill was a man whose name I don't even remember anymore. He was in charge of the transformer there, and he worked for the company that supplied electricity. It sticks in my mind because of his unusual job—he must've had some special training.

My uncle is only ten years older than I. So when he was in high school, he was determined that he would study bookkeeping, shorthand, typing. No one in the school approved of his taking those subjects. The head of the department told him, "You'll never get a job doing this." But he was determined, and he [did] take these subjects. And during World War I, when there was a drain of manpower, he did get the opportunity for which he had trained himself. He became secretary to the sheriff. And this seemed to us a very wonderful job. (*Highly amused.*)

When my uncle was still in high school, he went to work for Western Union delivering telegrams. And one of the operators, when they weren't busy, started to teach him the Morse code. But when the manager found out, he said that he was not to teach him. And there were certain places which by kind of an unspoken agreement we never entered at all! Certain restaurants where we didn't ever go in to get a meal. We just *knew* that we were not welcome there; we didn't make an issue of it.

In Montana there were so few of us that we really couldn't support a minister, but we did have a branch of the African Methodist church. Sometimes we didn't have a pastor, so my aunts would persuade us to go to the Presbyterian church. And something happened in my childhood I've never forgotten: there was a church picnic with contests where children would win the prizes. And I always ran so fast that I won the race. I remember no one gave me a prize. Finally the pastor felt he should do something. So he came over and he squatted down and he handed me a box of crackerjacks that had been *opened*. And I—I, I was, when I was a child, I was a . . . well, . . . spoiled, and, and quick-tempered. And I would not accept the box because it had been opened. I realized that this wasn't the prize that other winners got, you know.

I think it was *very* unpleasant to be a black child in the schools. I was always dropping out, and always being disciplined by my mother and the teachers. Because I just . . . rebelled. Once when I stopped going to sixth grade the teacher asked me why. And I said, "Oh, I can't get arithmetic." But finally I told her, "Well, the other kids don't want to hold my hand when we do these square dances." So she said to me, "Did you ever hear of a Negro general who was greater than George Washington?" I hadn't and she told me about the revolt in Haiti and about Christophe and Toussaint L'Ouverture. About that time I came across books where I could find something about my people other than what I was being taught in school. So I sort of started to hunt. Most of my friends didn't buy books except Paul Dunbar's collection of poetry. And many of the conclusions told me by white teachers I accepted without question. I was told that the Negro never did anything to win his freedom. So I didn't know until I was thirty about the Negro volunteers who fought in the Civil War. Or the black men who fought to win their freedom on both sides in the Revolutionary War.

In school where pupils touched hands or body contact, I realized the white children didn't want me to be in the game. So I learned a long time ago to give teacher an out, and I would say I didn't want to play games. As a result, I know nothing about any kind of athletics! (*Laughs.*) I turned to books, so that I learned to read well when I was small, and I formed the habit of finding companionship in books. I still do. And I don't really and truly enjoy working with other people. I like to do things alone. Because I had to when I was a child.

I have warm friendships with white people. I am deeply indebted to certain white individuals for the opportunity to have studied music, to have heard music, to have learned about books, to have studied books. I think maybe three or four white teachers have understood how lonely it was for me and really wanted to do something about it. But most of them didn't know what to do, so it didn't help. Once a teacher asked me to stay after school. And he was so embarrassed—he said, "Now we're studying about slavery, and I hope you won't feel hurt when the kids will talk about 'niggers.'" And I was so proud I didn't want him to know that I was hurt, so I said, "Oh, no. I don't mind at all!" But the only time that *my* people were mentioned in school were as . . . slaves. And the people who cultivated cotton. . . . Even then I knew that we were not all unskilled. For instance, my father was a blacksmith. And I knew even when I was a very young child about the beautiful ironwork in New Orleans.

This was extremely painful to me. This made me withdraw into myself. I—I, I would feel angry and thwarted. I was known to have a very bad temper. I was one of those kids in school who was a problem as far as discipline was concerned. Maybe it forced me to achieve a little more because my Negro relatives and friends would give me the impression that I represented the race.

And this I think is unfair. But this is the way my generation felt. So many never had the opportunity to learn to read, so all of my generation had the unspoken commitment to learn as much as we could in the white school—swallowing back.

■ *What's "swallowing back"?*

Not voicing resentment or anger. Not complaining at what we knew were obvious biases, because we felt we must share this with others of our race. And in those days, we felt that the key to our progress was education.

They moved westward again. In Spokane, Washington, her grandmother bought a house. When times got hard, she wanted to sell, but no one would buy a house from blacks. So the grandmother, who had been born a slave and fathered by a white master, passed for white to sell the house. Elena recalls going from room to room taking down the pictures of her darker relatives. Very dark herself, she had to stay away while the house was being sold. Struck by the enormity of racism, she joined the NAACP soon after—at age fourteen.

It wasn't until I dropped out of high school because I was so very unhappy, that I began to read books by Dr. Du Bois. I think it was just an accident, but in Everett, Washington, where we were living at that time, I found *The Souls of Black Folk* and *The Quest of the Silver Fleece*. And finally then, I began to realize . . . that I was a descendant of Africans. Then I lived for two or three years with a Baptist minister who had been born in slavery. He told me about life in Virginia, and he told me about people he had known who remembered Africa. So this was the first inkling I had of identity.

Then Marcus Garvey's movement caught on in the Far West. In Tacoma we had a chapter of the Universal Negro Improvement Association. An African came to tell us about our brothers in Africa. I remember he wore conventional street clothes, but he wasn't ordinary in any other way. His English was excellent. The impression after forty-some years that I have is of this man walking back and forth as he talked passionately of the enslavement of our brothers in Africa. And I began to feel that I had brothers and sisters in other parts of the world. The chapter of course went down after Garvey was imprisoned.* But one of the results was three Negro businesses: one, a little grocery store; another, as I remember, was a dry-cleaning plant. They endured for many, many years. Incidentally, *now* the young people are discovering Marcus Garvey. And evidently they find that he expressed much of what they are fighting for.

Because we lived where there were so few other colored families, there's

*In 1923 Garvey was convicted of mail fraud for having misused business funds. President Coolidge pardoned him in 1927 but had him deported to Jamaica, Garvey's native country.

been so many interracial marriages in my family. And I guess by and large
they worked out all right. But my mother, after having a German husband
and seeing her sisters married to white men—and one of her brothers to a
white woman—felt that I should have the opportunity to live where there
were more of our people, and she said to me, "I think there's been enough
intermarriage in our family. Now I want you to marry a Negro." So that was
one of the reasons we moved to the state of Washington—so that I'd have a
chance to know more about our own people. And I did marry a black man.
Now I think individuals should be allowed to make their own choice.

*Before she was married, she worked as a maid and a janitor as "most black
women did in the twenties." But her mother recognized Elena's talent and enrolled her at a Boston music school. The school wouldn't allow her to live in the
dormitory with the white girls; she was placed instead in a Negro home. "The
Boston I had read so much about . . . wasn't so liberal as I had thought. And I
thought of Paul Revere."*

*Having read also of William Monroe Trotter, Boston's militant black leader
and editor, she had expected to find Boston's Negroes "extremely progressive."
But it was the West Indians who had established businesses and were the successful entrepreneurs. She also met "real Bostonians," blacks whose families
had lived in the city for three generations. Although she shared their admiration for learning, even then, at age eighteen, she was critical of the way they
"tried to imitate middle-class white people . . . in their speech, in their homes,
in all their standards."*

My generation had the feeling that if by our speech, by our appearances,
by our . . . pretense of accepting the standards of middle-class white America,
then we might grow to be Americans. But *now* at *sixty*, I realize that there's no
reason I should try to be an imitation middle-class white woman. I am not.
When I studied music I very carefully erased from my singing (*very amused*)
the characteristics that were Negro . . . or black . . . or African in order to
sing operatic arias. Now I think that was a great mistake. I no longer see why I
should try to erase from my voice what is unique and what is different. If I had
to do it over again I would sing like Mahalia Jackson rather than Camilla
Williams, the operatic star.

Years ago when I did recitals, I sang folk music, the spirituals, and the work
songs, and I also sang the art music of Negro composers. In those days we
referred to ourselves as "Negro," some organizations like the church were "African," some were "colored," like the NAACP. In those days I would talk
about the origin of our music. And when I was talking in a poetic vein, I
referred to us as *black* people. And this gave me a great deal of pleasure. But
when I was very matter-of-fact I usually said "Negro." I don't really feel that to

use the word *Negro* identifies me only as a slave. When I stand before children now, what I wish to impart to the individual is an inner awareness of himself as the descendant of a people who have endured and who have a proud history. The independent individual is not deterred by a label. If you want to insist on always saying *black,* it seems a little bit artificial to me. (*Laughs.*)

In the United States where we have not had the opportunity as other people who came here to preserve a language from Africa, a religion from Africa, there still persists certain things that are in us. I think our instinct for life is more nearly right than the Puritan standard in this country. That work in itself is so admired—we haven't gone along with that. I believe our understanding of what is human and what is right and what is beautiful—the inner thing—is going to shape our society. I don't think that in America there is a definite *black* culture. I think there is the story of black people in America, but it's a part of the history of the United States.

She moved to San Francisco in 1959 and fell in love with the city. Now she lives in the Hunters Point section, a low-income, heavily black area near the bay. She wouldn't want to live in a white neighborhood, because it would be too reserved and impersonal: you couldn't walk up to someone and say, "Good morning, honey." As for the black movement, she supports Black Power and integration, admires both Stokely Carmichael and Martin Luther King. Sadly, King's assassination has made her realize that people do not "attain rights without actual physical violence." As for Black Power: "I don't think that the ability to shape our own destiny, to have a part in determining whether we are to have full citizenship rights is something that is revolutionary or extraordinary." And seeing Stokely Carmichael at Hunters Point belied his image in the white media. She was impressed with his "beautiful and loving spirit," the patience with which he explained to his young audience that black brothers who were policemen or who processed their hair were not necessarily enemies.

The Black Panthers? Now I don't suppose that a woman of my generation can *entirely* understand young men under thirty, but I'm going to say . . . I . . . admire their ideals, it gives me an entirely different concept of Negro manhood—that they say, "We will defend ourselves." I admire the Panthers; I feel that as a woman of sixty I ought to, that I have a great stake in the Huey Newton trial. I feel that I must support them; I feel that a part of me is there.

Although she's found in San Francisco some of the "same old western racial biases . . . police brutality, for instance," the contrast with Seattle astonished her: exciting black journalists, so many unusual magazines and newspapers like the Sun Reporter *and* The Movement, *blacks driving Yellow Cabs, a gen-*

eral feeling "that anything can happen." She's picketed banks, hotels, "Auto Row." * San Francisco has been an ideal place "to have lived through this exciting period, the first time in my life I've ever felt really a part of something where with my body I could protest and think maybe there might be a change."*

See chapter 13 for the followup interview with Elena Albert in 1978.

---

*From November 1963 to April 1964, CORE chapters from the city of Berkeley and the University of California campus, along with the Ad Hoc Committee to End Discrimination, organized mass picketing, sit-ins, and "shop-ins" in an attempt to force local businesses to hire black people. More than a thousand demonstrators were arrested in what was at that time the largest civil rights action outside the South; in March and April 1964 there were more than three hundred arrests on "Auto Row," the several blocks of San Francisco's Van Ness Avenue lined with new car dealerships.

CHAPTER 4

White Backlash: The Fear of
a Black Majority and
Other Nightmares

By the time we began interviewing in 1967, public opinion polls were recording a precipitous drop in white support for the black movement.[1] Congress, having passed pathbreaking civil rights legislation in 1964 and 1965, responded to the new mood by rejecting Lyndon Johnson's third package of civil rights bills. By 1968, three-fourths of white Americans agreed that "the Negro was being brought forward too fast."[2]

Racial change had to be gradual, many whites insisted, because blacks weren't ready for full equality and couldn't yet handle their freedom. Gladys Hunt, whose views in chapter 2 are a pungent expression of the backlash mentality, put it succinctly: "After a hundred years, all of a sudden you turn these people loose." To Hunt and many others, blacks were like children: the more you gave them, the more they wanted. It was essential, these whites felt, that the white majority—not the black minority—decide what changes were necessary and how fast to implement them.

The underlying anxiety was a fantasy of black domination, that blacks would become the numerical majority in certain cities or regions, reverse the tables, and exact revenge on white people. Racial integration could proceed as long as the numbers involved were small, but Gladys Hunt's predicament— feeling totally surrounded at home and at work—was unacceptable. In this chapter Maude Wiley expresses this fear of black domination in an unusually explicit manner.

Maude Wiley

"They're afraid the colored people are gonna move in and take over"

A housewife in her fifties, Maude Wiley first met blacks in sizable numbers during World War II when she worked in a Navy personnel office.

A good many had been brought up from the South. And this was a new experience for them; they were transported to a place where they felt they had some rights, there was no segregation there. And of course working for the Navy, they were supposed to be kept on an equal basis with the white people. Well, I think this went to their head. They became very overbearing. Because suddenly they had their freedom that they hadn't had in the South. And you'd start to board the bus, and they'd push you out of the way! I mean they lacked some of the social graces that the white people—I guess it would go back to their culture—that the white people had had the advantage of having. I felt like I could understand why they were acting this way. But there were certainly lots of people who it made just furious. They felt, well, these colored people were just pushing 'em away and trying to take *over*, you know, and be better than they were!

Today she works with black families as a volunteer in a Headstart program.

I think the colored people are really suspicious, even of the white people who are trying to work with them. They're wondering about their motives. There is so much *anger* in the Negro people toward the white people. Our whole country, we're walking on a powder keg right now.

I think the colored people are hurting themselves by these riots. Because finally we *are* beginning to work toward a lessening of racial discrimination; we *are* working to give the colored people in the South the vote. And to try to give them more advantages, and an equal education. I can understand why we are having riots. And I'm afraid that it's gonna continue on, because all this hate, and it's been bottled up for so long, and now that they are beginning to get a few advantages—and a little road upward—they're impatient to have more.

I hope you'll excuse me in using this analogy, but you take a dog . . .

She hesitates, a little embarrassed; the interviewer is black. But Hardy Frye encourages her to continue.

I'm—I'm sorry to use this, but this is just . . .

■ *Go ahead! I can take it.*

It's sort of an example. You take a dog that has been penned up, tied, chained . . . all his life! And then you turn him loose! Well, that dog . . . he has had no training; you can't take him in the house and expect him to behave like a dog that has been housebroken! Or perhaps he'll run loose, he'll have his *freedom* for the first time! He'll wanta run! He'll wanta . . . explore so much! It's the same thing with, with the . . . colored . . . with the Negro. In the last ten, fifteen years, he's beginning to really get his freedom.

I firmly believe that they should have all the advantages that we've had. But this is not done overnight. It's a long, slow process that has to start with education. The colored man has to be educated up to the same, or given the same advantages . . . as the white people have had—in education, in culture, and everything! But, you see, education takes a generation, doesn't it? I mean, it starts with the baby. The ones who are rioting and causing all the trouble, they really haven't had the background, the education.

I've had a very average education, you know. Yet I find it far more interesting to be with a person who can talk intelligently about various things. The white people who haven't had enough education, they're not as tolerant of the Negro. Don't you find this so? I mean, you mix with *both* types. Don't you find that the intellectuals are far more tolerant than the man on the street?

We should have open housing, if we're going to make any strides upward. But an awful lot of people are fearful that if one Negro family moves into a neighborhood, this brings others, and then their value as a property starts dropping. Because this *is* what has happened in many other communities such as Los Angeles. In the Figueroa, that used to be all strictly the white families. And then from Watts, where the colored people were living, they gradually started moving a little closer to that area, until now, I guess, that whole area is all colored, isn't it?

■ *Why did they try to sell? Why didn't they just stay?*

They're afraid the colored people are gonna get the upper hand; they're gonna move in and *take over.* So many of them will come that there'll be a majority of colored people instead of a majority of the whites.

■ *And there should always be a majority of the whites?*

Yes. Because they *are* white. A majority rules, you know. (*Laughs.*) I mean if you have a predominantly Negro society, then they're gonna make the rules and say what can be done, and . . . I think perhaps they're afraid that the Negro will want to get *even* with . . . what has happened to them in the past. I think even now, where you have a large grouping, and there are a few white people . . .

■ *What happens?*

Well, my daughter's boyfriend just came back from Vietnam. He says it's the Negro who discriminates against the white fellows over there. They will have *nothing* to do with the white fellows. And if there is ever any trouble between a white and a black over there, the Negroes will all band together to protect their interests, but he says we don't always have this with the white fellows.

There've been cases where they've . . . beaten up the white people. I think that's where your fear is. And for the working class, well, afraid that work is gonna be given to the colored man instead of the white man, and he'll be discriminated against. You know! I mean, just reversing the table! (*Laughs.*) The working class, they feel somehow or other, that they're better than the colored fellow and they should have the choice of everything. Don't ask me why.

■ *Let's talk about how* you *feel. Do you feel that's true?*

No. Not—not if, if . . . I feel if a colored person has had an equal education as I and lives in the same manner as I—why should there be any difference?

■ *I'm working on a Ph.D. Would I be accepted in your neighborhood?*

You'd be accepted by me. Now I don't know if you'd be accepted by all of them.

■ *Why not? I'm educated.*

This is what I can't understand! And I get awfully mad about it. With my husband. 'Cause I feel that a person should be judged by his education and what he is himself. Not his color. But not all white people agree with that. They judge them by the color of the skin. Which is wrong and is an attitude that has to be changed in the white people the same as the colored people.

I'm not sure if I would join a group that was predominantly Negro. Because then I would be (*laughs*), I would be a minority! (*Laughs.*) I might feel a little fear . . . that they don't trust us . . . that they wouldn't trust *me.* If I was sure and positive that I would be accepted, then I would feel free doing it. The trouble is that there is the suspicion between us. There is the suspicion that the colored people have to the white and the whites have to the colored.

Mrs. Wiley first became aware of prejudice as a little girl during World War I, when her German-born mother had to give up her language and her foreign ways because "the hatred was so strong." They lived in the suburbs of Los Angeles. White people there didn't associate with blacks or Japanese people. "I'm sure my mother never said, 'Don't mix with these.'" It just seemed the thing to do. Maude was always "friendly" to the few Negroes in her high school.

But I didn't mix with them socially. Because I had my white friends. Come to think of it, one of my good friends started going with a boy that appeared to be a colored boy. We couldn't understand *why* she was going with this boy. He insisted he wasn't, and their family even had blood tests to see if there was a Negro strain. They were French . . . far back. After they were married, I visited them.

When we started to build a house in Torrance, we had a draftsman and he was a colored fellow. I know there are lots of white people who wouldn't ask a colored person to be in the house. But I felt, well, if he could do the work there's no reason why I shouldn't.

My husband's attitude is very narrow. And he and I get into arguments about it. He feels that the colored people are being given too much leeway now. And that we're, the white people, are gonna have to step aside for the colored if it keeps on like this.

■ *Why does he feel that way?*

It's because of these inborn *prejudices.* Why do *most* people feel this way? It's just . . . there!

■ Inborn *prejudice?*

Well, not inborn. No, that's wrong. (*Laughs.*) I mean these prejudices that have started from the time you can first remember. The old idea that the whites are the superior race! I suppose every white person feels this way. It was the accepted thing . . . until you get older and you start questioning if this is right or not. I guess as I got older I became aware that there'd been a grave injustice done to them through the years. And since then, I've, well, I've tried . . . never to let any prejudice enter my mind.

For Mrs. Wiley's views in 1979 and 1986, see chapter 9.

AN UNDERLYING assumption about the white backlash—that many whites had abandoned the ideals of civil rights because of the urban riots and Black Power militancy—disquieted many Afro-Americans. Was the backlash really the new phenomenon that the media pundits had just discovered? Or was it simply a more respectable cover for an old-fashioned racism with a dangerous new twist, one that shifted responsibility for the racial crisis from the prejudices of the majority to the behavior of the minority? The case of George Hendrickson, whose story follows, would seem to favor the latter interpretation. Hendrickson's conservative racial views are rooted in a tradition of racial domination that has shaped the consciousness of Western thought, that of classical colonialism.

Hendrickson spoke to us in 1969. At the time black students at the University of California at Berkeley were striking to demand a Black Studies curriculum. Interviewer Ed Price was then a graduate student doing research on the radical right. More conservative politically than the rest of our staff, and with a clean-cut appearance, Ed was able to gain rapport with "establishment" groups such as civic leaders and owners of small businesses.

George Hendrickson

"The Congo nigger"

A printer in his late sixties, George Hendrickson spent his early childhood in India and other outposts of the British Empire. His father had been an English officer in the Boer War and then served as a colonial functionary. Young George learned Hindi from his private nurse—one of the "bunches of servants" in the household—long before he could speak English. He still recalls the "unbearable" Indian weather. When the family moved to the primitive backcountry of Canada, it was a complete turnaround: log cabins, no shoes, and knowing what it was "to have mush for breakfast, mush for lunch, and fried mush for supper." Discipline was severe in the one-room schools he attended, but he feels he received a better education than today's youngsters are getting. And he had enormous freedom "to camp, to fish, to swim, to go here, to go there, a better young boyhood than the kids are having today."

After serving in World War I, he mined coal and worked in lumber camps, sawmills, and paper mills. He learned printing so fast that he became a journeyman assistant in one year instead of four, and soon after a master pressman. He still finds his work quite challenging: "Every job is an experience in itself, so you're constantly thinking and figuring."

We've got several colored in our union. As long as they can pass the test, as long as they can handle work, it's okay. But they sent down thirty colored people to take the examination and not one of them passed. So they sent down thirty more, and one of those passed, and he wouldn't take the job, 'cause he's an educated man.

I do not look down upon the colored man. I look at him as a man. But when he crosses the line . . . not only do I look down on him, but I am very well aware that his own people look down upon him. A mixed marriage is not a healthy marriage. I have had a colored man come to my house. But if he was married to a white woman . . .

Now I'll bring out a point that escapes many, many people. When a colored man or woman marries a white, the children are not white, they are colored. I have a friend who I admire greatly. And he is as fair as I am. I worked with him for two or three weeks before I knew he was colored. Do you know that he always refers to himself as a colored man and a Negro? And this is the problem that these people are creating. They just don't realize it—that the offspring never become white. And as time goes by, they lose many friends, they lack the opportunity to make new friends because of this crossover. And their problems are very apt, as the years go by, to become unbearable.

■ *Have you ever had a colored person as a friend?*

No, never what you call this kind of socially close friendship. But I've been to dinner, I've sat with colored people right next to me, socially. I don't have any prejudice. But I do think that a race mistake is made when the line is crossed.

I was in a colored neighborhood three or four times this past week, getting ready for the garden show. [The] type of homes, the way they live, the general unruliness of the youngsters, the way they let the places run down—frequently, although not all of them by any means. I just wouldn't care to go and live there. But in a neighborhood like this we don't get those. So if a man comes in here, a colored man, and can pay forty thousand dollars for the home next door, I'm quite sure he's probably an educated man; he may be a doctor or a lawyer or an engineer. He's probably a very nice person. I don't think I would object.

My taxes, in just a small home, have tripled. In ten years. On this block, any one of these people'll tell you the same story. If it triples again, I'll be long gone. I can't even afford to retire on my social security and my not-too-bad little pension. And I'm getting more and more and more resentful of having to pay for broken windows and smashed typewriters and dirt and filth in buildings that have been taken over and burnt. Now these rats and these demonstration types, these militants are not going to get anywhere because they're in the minority and their tactics are wrong. In the long run you're going to find that these riots, these sit-ins, are going to fade and die.

For the right way to bring about change, he cites his participation on a commission concerned with water pollution in the early 1950s. "We didn't go and pound our fists on anybody's desk and say that there is water pollution and we want it stopped." Instead they asked key officials to establish a committee to research the problem. And because the committee members were powerful, knowledgeable people, state legislators listened and were willing to visit polluted beaches, lakes, and rivers. Tough state regulations were enacted as a result. This was one of the most meaningful experiences in George Hendrick-

son's life, and he uses it as a benchmark in discussing student protests and demonstrations.

As a chancellor sitting in the University of California, if anybody came in to me and pounded their fists on the desk and said, "We demand—" I'd grab the phone and call the police [and] the National Guard so fast it would make their heads swim. When a group takes over a building, [I'd] lock the doors, turn off the gas and lights. And when they're ready to come out, they have to register to show who they are and then the building should be examined and each individual should be sued for the entire amount of damage. But they won't do that, no. They stand out there and talk and talk and talk.

And I think also that the students that are doing this, certain types of students, are not educatable.

■ *What do you mean?*

Well, the university has been asked to permit a certain number of people to come in without the proper credits.* If these people haven't got the IQ necessary to pass the examination, then this is going to turn out inferior doctors, inferior engineers, inferior attorneys, inferior people in many types of employment as these men start practicing.

I don't think that every person has the mental ability to assimilate [knowledge]. I know my son can pick up a highly technical book and can sit there and read it for an hour or two. And if I pick up the same book, after the second page I'm in a fog. Perhaps a fellow with your education can sit down and read halfway through.

■ *Are these inborn characteristics?*

I think to some extent they are. In animals, you breed a horse for racing, you breed a dray horse for pulling a heavy wagon. But you can't get a racehorse out of one and a truck horse out of the other. So let's say that the truck horse is a working man and the racehorse is the professional.

■ *But is there a difference between the races?*

I think to some extent. My son always told me that the Chinese and the Japanese are the ones that are giving you the real competition when he was going to school. And you'll find that the *top* colored graduates will be about the middle of the class. And the further down you get, the more colored you have.

■ *But do blacks have the same opportunities?*

I don't know. On fairness, I don't. I think this is a matter of breeding *and*

---

*In order to recruit more minority students, the University of California had instituted a special program whereby 2 percent of the entering students would be selected on the basis of motivation, life experience, and creative potential, instead of grades and test scores.

training. Say a professor and a wife who is equally a college professor should produce a child who is more intellectually inclined and perhaps more intelligent, with higher IQs—of course this is not always the case . . . but on the average—than the son or daughter of a laborer or waitress, neither of them got through more than fifth or sixth grade. You don't start out with somebody that can't read and write and their son or daughter becomes a doctor or lawyer or something like that. There are exceptions, but the rule is they have to come up a step at a time. Finally, generation after generation, they'll get there.

    Now this may be environmental. I don't know. I think the colored has been held down tremendously. There was a time when the white men who taught the colored men how to read and write was subject to be put in jail. It wasn't right to bring the people over here in the first place. And of course you have another problem, too, one I think you haven't realized. The type of Negroes that was brought over here, in many of the Asian countries they refer to them as the lowest types. He was the Congo nigger.

■ *"Congo nigger"?*

He was easy to get. He wasn't warlike. He lacked the ability to organize himself in his community for his own defense. He was simply a river dweller who lived in the easiest possible way. Now look at the history of the Zulus. You don't find a Zulu here because they were a great people. They were organized, they had a government. It was a harsh government, a cruel government. They numbered probably three, four, five millions. They were a fighting people. They were also agricultural people. And they had armies that were quite substantial.

    And the Arab who came down into the Negro area didn't try to take a village of the Zulus and bring them over here. No, he took the easy ones. So what did we get over here? We've got the lowest, poorest type. And they made slaves of them. But you couldn't make a slave out of a Zulu. He'd stick your eye and cut his own throat. (*Laughs.*)

    I think Martin Luther King was a very great man, and a brilliant speaker. He was not the pacifist that he claimed to be. In fact, he was one of the most inflammatory speakers that I ever heard in my life. And all the time that he was preaching peace and preaching nonviolence, he was stirring the people to violent acts.

    I couldn't say whether he was doing it deliberately or not. He was dealing with an unfortunate group of people, let's face it, a group of illiterates. To hold their interest they had to have flag waving, they had to have the chanting, they had to have the parade, or they would simply disintegrate [as a] group. If he dealt with more definite terms, I don't think they would have the ability to see what he was trying to do.

    It's very similar to some of the colored churches. They chant and they sing. The first thing you know they are pounding their feet and clapping hands, and after a little while, rolling on the floor. You know this is emotional, this is what appeals to them because up to the present time they haven't developed the ability to follow a problem through to its conclusion.

- *What does it mean to you to be a white man?*

I've never thought of that. I don't think that it's either done me any good or any harm. Anything I have, I've got for myself. What little it is, not too much.

- *Do you think you'd have a harder time if you were colored?*

No. Like I said to you, they're in our union.

> Followup interviews with George Hendrickson in
> 1979 and 1986 are in chapter 9.

THROUGH THE early 1940s relatively few Afro-Americans lived in California. The most systematic racism was directed at the large Mexican population native to the state, and also at the enclaves of Chinese and Japanese, whose presence evoked "yellow peril" nightmares of Asia and its "boundless masses." Blacks also faced prejudice and discrimination, but were too few to be considered a serious threat. Demographics, a strong state economy, and favorable living conditions spared California from the kind of crowded black ghettos that in eastern cities intensified social problems and intergroup hostilities.

In the conflict-ridden late sixties, many white Californians regretted the passing of what they viewed as a golden age of racial harmony. Surprised by racial violence, these "native Californians" had not fully accepted the demographic changes that had occurred during and after World War II, when the shipyards and other wartime industries attracted large numbers of southern blacks to the state. The new migrants became the "critical mass" of the black population. To whites like William Singer, these relatively uneducated and lower-class southerners were perfect fodder for political agitation. By encouraging their discontent, the militants of the civil rights movement had subverted the racial harmony of the past.

William Singer

"We didn't have a great sense of racial awareness"

Ed Price and Will Singer talk in Singer's office during the spring of 1969.

I'm a third-generation native Californian. Which means I've been here a little while. The original Singer came from Saxony in 1846. He went on to the foothills, bought some acreage from John Frémont. He was a teamster and ran a livery business. And my grandfather operated the business [until] the automobile came along. And he rented automobiles as well as horse-drawn rigs and had a stage business carrying passengers to Yosemite Valley and he also hauled freight.

We really didn't have a great sense of racial awareness. There were blacks. They were just scattered. There was Duff and there was Old Mose and there were a lot of others; they came following 1849. Hell, Jim Beckworth, the great frontier scout, was a black man. How many people know that? And he accompanied Kit Carson, Frémont, and a whole lot of others. He got a pass named for him in Northern California. He got a town named for him.

In the lumber camps, in the mine communities, they worked together regardless of color. They depended on each other for proper performance. People in a small town, they look at themselves as a community. They are neighbors. All right, he may be dark, in complexion, a Negro, or he has an accent, which might be a Pole. I think these are all ways of describing and identifying people—you don't just point to him if he isn't there. I don't think that they do it to segregate people. Myself, and I think this is true for many people, never really became aware of the big division between black and white until we started this sort of agitation process, of singling people out and drawing lines between them. When you talk about racial segregation, I guess it was the Chinese. They spoke a different language to start with and they had a tendency to gather in their own little clusters. The Alien Exclusion Act was directed at the Chinese.

Even though his family had inherited wealth, his parents stressed the importance of work. As a youngster he handled three newspaper delivery routes at a time, picked up trash, and hoed weeds. After studying engineering, he became a business consultant and advised the big corporations entering the lumber industry which small mills to buy up and where to locate new ones. In his mid-forties and financially independent after selling the business, he's now the financial director for a county agency.

■ *Do you find that blacks tend to be more distrustful of government than whites?*

Not really. We've had some this way. But by and large we've gotten along very well with them. Other than the fact that their skin is black, I can't see that they're any different than anyone else. And we try to give them logical answers that they can understand, and they do. And many of these people are quite intelligent, and they haven't had the opportunity to do better. Someone may have been holding them back or they have been just too timid to take the chance. We really don't have an opportunity to discriminate against people. Because of the regulations and [our] purpose.

The Negro women and men that I've had in here, we've gotten along very well. In fact one of them, he was wasting his time here, he really had talent. And I think that I was instrumental in getting him employed by one of our major banks, the first appraiser that they ever hired. Believe me, it was difficult. These are hard-core institutions. "Is he really that good? You know it's going to be hard for people to accept." And I would say, "Jim, that's a pile of hogwash. The man is capable, he's adaptable, he will do a fine job for you, and this is the thing that is going to impress your clients. You're part of the conservative institution and you're not willing to accept change." To my knowledge, they've been satisfied with him.

We have a lot of whites that seem to think that we ought to cut off our hands because our ancestors years ago had a slave. And the activist group, they're going to remind these people that they're black, every day that they're alive. And I think that what they're doing is divisive. You keep pointing at these people. You're second-class, you're black, you belong over there, you're not a part of our society. These are the black militants, and I guess it's like selling soap. What is it we're buying this year? Fab? The one that's hawked the most is the first thing that comes to your mind. After a while you believe this is the only kind there is.

[The word *ghetto*] always used to apply to the Jewish quarter; it was in Warsaw. Now any place they have old houses, it's a ghetto. By the definition today. And I don't think you can call [Berkeley] a slum, not when you've seen New York, and some parts of Chicago, and certainly if you've been down in the South. [In Berkeley] we're closer and we have a better feeling for what is going on. There have been some cities that have not been able to deal with riots and burnings and lootings. They fail to recognize that you have to maintain a line of communication and be somewhat responsive to the needs of these people. Granted, you can't give them the whole damn city. But you can at least be responsive to them. At least give them the idea that they're getting a part of it.

Whatever is stimulating this revolt, it almost seems that they want to collar the institutions, destroy the progress that we've made. I think the Black Student Union [at the University of California] is really against the institution. And I don't really understand why any of these so-called soul, if you want to call them that, soul teachings or black history . . . I really don't know what it does for these people unless it promotes understanding. So fine, I have three units in black studies; I have maybe twelve or fifteen units in, say, Watusi, or whatever language it is, and all my meals have been cooked by an expert, a person that's hired to develop soul foods. With this sort of background, what are my alternatives later on? I don't know math, I don't know much about anything else. If you progress in your life, you have to be adaptable to change. So you have to have a broader scope. I think they're hurting themselves. Really the only purpose in raising these demands is it gives them a banner.

*Singer doesn't feel that the university discriminates against blacks. He notes
that blacks are being admitted who have not met all the entrance requirements,
and he wonders if Black English or the "broken speech" that he attributes to
their southern background prevents them from doing better in school.*

Those that came out of the South had a feeling of inferiority. This large
group of relatively unskilled people, they brought their awareness of segregation from the South. That really caused the problems. And brought the
awareness of racial differences with them. And it became part of our life here.
Those that were here before didn't have this [feeling of inferiority]. A good
friend of mine, a [black] real estate dealer, a third-generation Californian, he
always referred to 'em as "Kaiser blacks" [after one of the big World War II
shipyards]. That's trash. Even among their own, they had a distinction.

Even in the nineteen thirties, we've always had a substantial black community, somewhere around twenty-five to thirty percent. [Berkeley] was the
home base for the Pullman porters, the dining-car attendants. Berkeley was
the end of the line; they just dropped off the car. This was the last station for
Santa Fe—the Southern Pacific had one more station at Fortieth and San
Pablo [in Oakland]. And they were people of substantial means. When they
came off a run they always had money. Because of the tip situation. Presley
Winfield, the Pullman porter, he took his tips and put 'em into real estate and
when he died, Christ, I think there was over five hundred houses he owned in
Berkeley.

Thirty years ago, guys I went to school with, there was no great problem. It
was a mixture on the school grounds, athletics afterwards—you didn't recognize race as a factor. Blacks were heavily in athletics even then, but they were
also heavy scholastically. These fellows you associated with out of respect
more than anything else. You can legislate association, but you can't legislate
respect. When Leon Marsh got out of school, he went to work for the Berkeley Fire Department. He didn't have any problem. Now we have racial problems in the fire department.

For the 1978 followup interview with William
Singer, see chapter 9.

BECAUSE THE black movement in its militant late-sixties' phase challenged
the privileged status of whites in American society, it brought to the surface
deep-seated racial prejudices that in ordinary times were not expressed as
openly. But it would be a mistake to simply reduce the backlash to white racism. In their "nonnegotiable" demands, the militants were threatening fundamental premises of the political process, and in their broadside attacks on
white society they seemed to be trashing core values of American culture:

work, patriotism, even fair play. Will Singer's commitment to the color-blind ideal was a sincere one, and "law and order" was not to him simply a code word for racism.

By the late sixties, the backlash was beginning to take its toll even on radical supporters of the black movement like Bill and Diane Harcliff.

Bill Harcliff and Diane Harcliff

BILL: "It's just a strong apartheid on the street"

DIANE: "The whole racial thing makes me burst with sadness"

In the late 1960s racial tensions increased between white hippies and blacks in integrated neighborhoods like San Francisco's Haight-Ashbury. Young whites, who felt as powerless and outside the system as blacks, had earlier responded with enthusiasm to the civil rights struggle. Experiencing their parents' middle-class life-styles and values as empty, they found meaning in the energy and vitality of black culture and politics. But while the counterculture was celebrating peace and love, blacks were aggressively seeking power, which hippies equated with domination. Black Power was also a rejection of white support in the struggle to change society: black separatism excluded whites from a shared community, and black violence targeted them along with their "racist" parents as equally deserving victims.

Bill Harcliff is nineteen years old and Diane is eighteen. Involved in civil rights, Bill manages a branch store of an independent black business in the Haight-Ashbury neighborhood. Relations with blacks in Freedom Now (an offshoot of SNCC) were "mostly pretty good" because "they're all lefties and they're all against the war and all smoke pot." When blacks complained that there were too many hippy posters and psychedelic colors in the stores—"the whole thing should be for blacks"—the business decided that whites would work in white communities and blacks in theirs.

BILL: We began talking a lot of political theories and eventually we had to face the fact that one of the real issues was whether we personally want to work [with black people]. And I have to admit to you a, you know, a kind of essentially racist attitude—that I felt very paranoid about working with a black person in the store. Sitting at a desk with him and working out whether he can help pay the bills and what to do with the money.

I guess I'm in a very typical kind of like liberal hypocritical position, you know. 'Cause up until recently I, like many of us, felt definitely on the side of the Negroes. And just never thought too much about their not liking me. And recently it's been very fashionable for black people to hate white people. That's a shocker for a lot of people, you know.

Bill comes from an Eastern academic family, "sort of Quaker-pacifist-intellectual-radical." His older brother burned his draft card and was jailed for antiwar activities. During high school Bill adopted a bohemian life-style. He enjoyed being around black people and used to visit the ghetto often, imagining that he "was getting along well with these people." But when he was seventeen, he was arrested in Ohio for "looking funny." The white inmates warned him to stay away from the blacks. But the whites seemed like hicks, "kinda dull," and the blacks seemed hip, people with whom one could talk about marijuana and music. "I was very naive so I didn't know what was happening. And I got jumped by five queers and that really was a shocker. 'Cause it was very clearly a racial thing as well as a sexual thing."

That experience has been very much with me ever since. By and large if I encounter a black person somewhere—I guess I'll use the word "black person," I mean more the urban ghetto black person as, say, opposed to like an Uncle Tom sort of educated black person—my first reaction is to start looking for ways to stay out of their way. Rather than like a few years ago, I would've walked right up to them and shake hands and say, "Well, how're you? You know, we sure like you guys." (*Laughs.*) It's kind of a mixture of, if I stay out of his way everything'll be okay, plus a, you know, alienated kind of desire to get back together thing. So that if I'm walking down the street and encounter a black person and if they say "hi" or if they smile, like I react, I *over*-react, like I have again that white liberal strong feeling to be friends. Well (*turning to Diane*), want to talk for awhile?

DIANE: Well, I was born and raised in Salt Lake City, and if I were black I wouldn't live there. There aren't very many black people there. Because of the Mormon church. So actually, living in Haight-Ashbury is the most experience I've had.

I feel very tense kind of, and a lot of it is because I'm a girl, you know. If I walk around in this area, just everybody, you know, wants to fuck me, and it's very, very hard. But with black people it's even harder because there's just something very militant about the way they come on. White people are more polite about it, and it's familiar. I just don't know how to react to, to, "Hey, you, come over here, I wanna fuck you."

BILL: Just an hour before this, Diane was over in Golden Gate Park and five real young spade kids came over, like seven years old, and were coming on with a real strong sexual thing.

I want to get away from the racial hassle here. There's a lot of hassles living in Haight-Ashbury; one of them is the speed-freak hassle and the other is the straight people against hippies hassle. But I think the main one is Haight-Ashbury is basically a ghetto, really. Kind of a fringe ghetto, you know.

There's no future for white people here, that's all! And there may be more hostility here than other places. 'Cause hippies are coming on poor and diverting all the sympathy that rightfully ought to go to spades. You know, the hippies are dropping in at the Free Clinic and the free clothes thing and welfare. And I guess if I were a spade I'd be pretty pissed off. There's kind of a strong undercurrent of tension. I just sort of feel that at any time we could get bumped off. So I'm very interested in moving to Berkeley.

When I see a black person being friendly to a hippy, it kind of automatically brands him as a Tom in my mind. (*Laughs.*) Somewhat apart from the ghetto scene. You know, he must have middle-class parents or he must be a college cat, or something. The mainstream black person doesn't like the hippies. There's a lot of burning that goes on in the street, and if anyone's stupid enough to give 'em ten dollars, they say, "Thank you, brother," and walk away. (*Laughs.*)

It's funny because the hippy scene grew very directly out of Negro forms. You know, from jazz to hipsters to hippies. The whole terminology and the style and everything, very directly out of jazz music. And twenty or thirty years after, hippies have no awareness what their tradition is. I guess hippies and the blacks both have no awareness that there is a link between 'em. It's very funny. I can't think of a hip word that isn't a jazz word originally, you know. It's just a strong apartheid on the street.

DIANE: I was just gonna say the black people who hang around Haight Street aren't very hip people at all. Like they wear flashy colors and . . . it's very clothes-conscious and material-conscious and ride around in big fancy cars . . .

Even the black movement seems headed toward such "suburban" goals, she feels. The hip scene equally discourages her; much of it is ugly, stupid, even degenerate: for example, people taking acid just to get stoned.

BILL: The word that keeps coming to my mind is *dimwitted*. Bunch of stupid shits in Haight-Ashbury. When I first got involved, it was about '64, the people were usually former intellectuals or former radicals or former college people. They were all rebelling against this kind of thing, but they still knew some big words and they were smart and they had their eyes open and they could tell a certain degree of bullshit from reality. And it seems a lot of 'em are kinda almost hicks today. The average person on Haight Street is usually pretty dumb and kind of idle in a bad sort of way, rather than in the classical bohemian kind of way.

■ *What do you think of the Black Panthers?*

DIANE: Politically they're a good thing, but I don't think politics is a very good thing. I don't think that's the right way to work at it. The Black Panthers are very apartheid and very militant. And it sort of has to be that way, you know, at this point in history. There's no other way that a hundred years of putting people down can be wiped out. But I think personal changes would really do more good.

BILL: Well, my background is radical, so my first reaction is to defend these things. There is this kind of ridiculous national dialogue on Black Power, you know, and everybody's talking up the word. Nobody's talking about freedom! A big part of Black Power is self-respect: our own culture is beautiful. We don't need any white shit. I can see that Black Power's necessary, but I'm against power.

We're both kind of mystically oriented, you know. That means we see good and evil in very long-range terms, and not so much in immediate political, tangible terms. If someone tries to help himself by getting power, then he's barking up the wrong tree. He can only help himself by finding out where he's at, and some kind of internal changes, to which power is largely irrelevant. Power's really just a means at best for fooling yourself about being in this world, and at worst is a means for exploiting other people. And yet I think hunger and suffering are real too. And the white majority has gotta be shaken loose of whatever the black people need—like money or status or whatever. I've grown up as a pacifist, and even so I can't argue too much with the notion of black people getting themselves guns. There's gonna be a worse and worse kind of polarization.

■ *Like a race war possibly?*

In a sense there's a race war going on right now. I remember once we were standing around barefoot—most people on Haight Street are barefoot—and some little black kids came along, finding all the bottles they could and smashing 'em on the sidewalk and throwing emotional shit at us. They probably attach great political significance to that—that they're like guerrilla soldiers in the black-white war, you know, they're doing their little bit of sabotage. And that is probably true too.

Young black kids in this neighborhood seem to have a very strongly developed class consciousness on race. They're very aware that whites are their enemy. A lot of my friends have been jumped by gangs of seven-year-old black kids, and called honky and white-ass and . . . like a kid'll come up to me with a cap pistol, "You know, if this were a real gun I'd shoot your ass off, whitey."

I have to say I definitely am racist. And, you know, in spite of my liberal Quaker and all-men-are-equal-under-God kind of upbringing, the other day I caught myself doing something funny. This is in the park, in Golden Gate, it was kind of an encounter ground, not only between blacks and whites, but like between me and winos, speed freaks, and police, straight people. So a large part of my consciousness when I'm there is devoted to cubbyholing people: to tell whether I'm safe or not (*laughs*) or how I should come on. And I was looking at the ground and I saw someone, like peripheral vision, and I relaxed—somehow I had classified myself as safe. And I looked up and noticed that they had blond hair. And all the other things about them weren't safe: they were big and strong, they had a wine bottle, they had boots on. And so I noticed that I not only have a predilection toward whiteness, but toward blond hair too. (*All laugh.*) Yeah, I think I've got a lot of very deeply rooted racism in me. And that kind of leads me toward pessimism, you know. Racism goes very, very deep and it'll take a lot more than civil rights bills to do something about this country.

- *What about you? Do you feel you're a racist?*

DIANE: I don't *feel* I am, but I guess I really am. Because I can't see all people as being the same. It wouldn't be honest if I were to tell you that I did, because there is a cultural difference. There's a difference between people raised in the suburbs and people raised in the ghetto. And that difference makes me a racist.

It seems like it's a racist time. That's a hard thing for me to say—but it seems more important to me . . . to save my own soul than to save all and to erase the ghetto. I think that's how I really feel. And it's more important for everybody to save their own soul; I can see that human misery doesn't just come from material surroundings, you know.

The whole racial thing makes me just burst with sadness because there's nothing I can do about it that I can see. Except . . . wait. When Martin Luther King was killed I felt very *sad*. I also felt frightened for the nation. Because somehow I thought that would be the blow that would tear it apart. Which it has. There've been a bunch of riots that we haven't heard about. Because some were recorded, some were just kind of not.

> Bill Harcliff was interviewed again in 1981 and
> 1986; see chapter 9.

CHAPTER 5

Black Youth and the
Ghetto Streets

uring the 1960s an ideological battle was being waged for the minds of
the new black generation. With their political commitments not yet
formed, young people could not rely on long-held positions or on life experience to guide their way. They had to choose not only between ideologies, but
between different ways of living their lives. During the racially conscious late
sixties, this included the question of whether to associate only with fellow
blacks or with whites also, and whether to pursue the goals of American society as they entered adulthood or to reject these "white" values on racial
grounds. In this chapter Larry Dillard talks about why he has taken the separatist path, Sarah Williams why she chooses to be part of the system.

Youth is also the critical period in determining a person's life-long economic and social fortunes. After high school graduation most middle-class
youths go on to college, and most working-class youths immediately take a job
or join the military. But a significant proportion, if not the majority, of low-
income minority youths drop out before graduation and, unable to find a job,
many make a life for themselves on the streets.

A leading theme in the three male interviews in this chapter is the important role that the police play in the lives of black street youth. Larry Dillard
describes how street youths are under constant police surveillance. Some
schools even invite the police into classrooms to take away troublemakers,
thereby escalating disruptive behavior into a criminal matter. And Richard
Simmons talks about serving twenty days in jail for having questioned two
black officers about an arrest they were making. As Florence Grier emphasized in chapter 3, an arrest record reduces a youth's already remote chances
of finding a decent job. Like the failure to complete high school, an arrest
record—even with no convictions—can have lifelong economic and social
repercussions. Such considerations prompt Harold Sampson to assert that the

role of the police is "to maintain you in your place, to dehumanize you in every sense of the word."

For Sampson, an older observer of the youth scene, the issue of manhood is at the heart of the war between black youth and white cops, with the young men "equating defiance of authority with a show of masculinity." Similarly, what Richard Simmons respects most about his father is that he stands up to the police and argues with them if he's being treated unfairly. On the streets, a large part of the appeal of the Black Panthers was their fearless denunciation of, and their militant confrontations with, the police. Yet many street youths were also quite critical of the Panthers, as we see from Simmons's interview.

Richard Simmons

"White boys, they're always innocent"

Richard Simmons is eighteen and lives in Oak Park, "where the black brothers live." When he was six, his parents separated. Richard's mother, a deeply religious person, one of "the saved," stayed in the South; his father brought the family to California.

My father, he's not like some people's parents, too old. We sit and kid around and talk about the Man. He agrees with me about that. He don't let the police treat him like I've seen some other black people doing. He's not afraid of them.

He got a traffic ticket and they got into a big old argument. I was very proud of him because he stood up to the Man. If he thinks he's in the right, he's going to go to jail arguing. (*Laughs.*)

Richard's school burned down when he was in seventh grade. So from a "95 percent Negro" school he was "shipped" to one with only six or eight nonwhites.

Every day at five o'clock, there'd be a big mass of white boys waiting for us. We'd get into a big old fight and after we cleaned the white boys out, the Man'd come and get *us!* And *they're* coming up there and beating us. We were fourteen, fifteen years old and fighting cats from eighteen to twenty-one. No matter what happens, it's always the black kids' fault. You get kicked out of school, the soul brothers get put in juvenile, whitey stays in school, gets his education. No matter *what* happens, like, you're in the gym dressing, and this cat he runs in there and push you up against the locker. You get up enough

nerve to hit this cat, and . . . white boys, they're always innocent. When I
was in the seventh grade, I'd get kicked out of school every two weeks.

A lot of cats dropped out of that school. 'Cause they couldn't stand the
pressure. You don't want to do nothing that's gonna cause you to go to jail.
You're trying to avoid this the best way you can. But pretty soon you just
gonna explode. You gonna do *something* to get that cat off your back! I had to
get out of [high school] 'cause I would've ended up doing something to somebody! They'd call the police and come to your classroom to get you.

They gave me the lowest classes. Everything they supposed to be teaching,
I already knew. Just because I wasn't going to college that didn't mean I want
to be dumb. Doesn't mean I don't want to know as much as the other kids. I
was young then and [wrote down] I wasn't going to college—my father, he
wants you out on your own, making your own money. But supposing I
changed my mind?

I wouldn't salute the American flag, so they would send me to the office.
And the principal, he tells me that he's not prejudiced or nothing. But in my
eyesight, he *is* a prejudiced man. And the vice-principal used to always mix
me up in a fight in the gym or something. The teacher'd *tell* him I was in the
classroom, but they'd say I was out there participating. So they kept on messing with me, trying to get me into some trouble, get me put in jail. Rather
than take all that, I just dropped out, four weeks before graduation.

Some of the teachers [were] pretty groovy, and some, they're just honkies.
If you disagree with them, they'll put you out of the classroom. Like they tell
you the scientific viewpoint on how the world begins. And I go by what the
Bible says. So we argued and argued. He put me and three of the brothers out
of the classroom.

We'd ask him, my history teacher, how come they wouldn't teach more
about black people. How come we wasn't mentioned in the history books as
much as we s'posed to be. They say it *should* be taught. But they wouldn't
teach it. Instead of trying to teach the African culture, they would show a
lot of African movies, to make it a joke or something. Everybody laughed.
You know, big joke. They would show pictures of the Alamo. White prejudiced kids jump and holler, "Remember the Alamo." Making the Mexican
kids feel bad.

*He attends continuation school now and he likes it better than high school be-
cause the principal can't expel him for speaking his mind. It's more adult,
"man to man." He defines a man as someone who organizes other blacks and
"fights for the causes he believes in"—like Malcolm X, who was "with the
brothers," and not like middle-class black leaders who live well outside the
community.*

Nor are the Black Panthers his models of manhood. Richard dismisses their recent march into the State Capitol with shotguns as a big publicity stunt that "played right into whitey's hand. Those tough Panthers." The Sacramento Panthers asked Simmons's youth club (he's president) to join up with them. But the club members voted the idea down because they didn't want to be "guinea pigs for their messes, get busted." He might have respected them "if they woulda showed some kind of actual militancy against the Man instead of just getting their pictures in the paper."

Last summer Richard saw two black police officers apprehend two men for unauthorized parking. When he asked why they were jailing the men, the "Uncle Tom cop" arrested him. Though he didn't resist, four officers grabbed and manhandled him. He was locked in the drunk tank without access to cigarettes or the telephone. At the hearing the policeman testified that Richard had been throwing bottles. "The police system is a dictatorship toward the black people."

That was my first time in jail, you know. It's just terrible, man. I wouldn't eat the food. It's for pigs. You gotta sleep on the floor every night. Little old blanket covering, torn up. And it's cold as hell in there. I'm not planning to go back anymore. Because that twenty days seemed like twenty years to me.

Some of the cats, they talk all big right in front of the Man, start cussing at him and do the stuff that will cause them to get busted. There's ways you can act that shows the Man you hate him but don't give him no reason to actually come up and hurt you. Try to outthink him instead of outfighting him and you won't get put in the jailhouse on false charges. Outsmart him, until we can get ourselves together to fight him with his weapons. But right now the brothers are not together enough to do so. Like some have their own bag and they worry about *their* bag and nobody else's. But they coming out of this. They beginning to think in terms of *group* instead of individual. And that's a step toward getting together.

I feel that some white people is all right, if [he] is willing to help the brothers in some way. But rich white people obviously are dogs. Because they don't care who they hurt to get this thing for theirselves. Just money hungry. Power hungry. And they're killing poor people to get it. And most of the poor people are black brothers and Mexicans.

■ *Do you ever see a peace between the Man and the brothers?*

When they make a whole lot of changes. When they look at brothers as people and not as animals. When they come down and help the brothers to get a halfway decent job [instead of] using them. Help him do something to fix up that ghetto. People want changes! And throwing rocks and bottles and burning down some of the white property *might* get some changes. Might.

The 1981 followup interview is in chapter 10.

Larry Dillard

"I would like to kill a white man, just to put it on the books"

Age seventeen, Larry Dillard has spent half his adolescence in correctional institutions. At the youth authority "camp," fellow inmates initiated him into a brotherhood of blackness, a nationalism of the streets and prison culture based on a strong conviction of black superiority and a corresponding devaluation of whites and their values.

This interview took place in 1967, two weeks after Huey Newton was arrested and charged with the murder of an Oakland police officer. Dillard was working in the kitchen at the Presidio, a military base in San Francisco.

When I was twelve or thirteen I wanted to be in the street. When I ran the street I did what I wanted to. And I was in jail quite a few times, you know. About five times. First time I was about thirteen. I didn't get nothing but half a month. Once I did six months, and last time I did a year.

I liked to be in the streets. I was on my own. I had a pad. All I wanted to do was drink wine and things like that. All my friends would come over. But all I could do was lay around with my girl friend. We would talk about going to a show, but I couldn't take her nowhere. So I kept wanting these things. This last time I was tired of walking, so I stole a car. (*Laughs.*) I couldn't pay for one, so I stole one.

Jail? It was easy, man. 'Cause it was a game, really. Like, uh, the counselors and things. They played very nice, you know. Nobody's prejudiced. But there was prejudice there—five billion. Brothers, they be in they little section, the white dudes in theirs, the S.A.s [Spanish Americans] in theirs—the Mexican-Americans, you know. And you don't come out of your place.

The minority had a lot of drag around the place. The honkies, they don't have no face, no respect for theirself, you know. They didn't have it like the brothers. The brothers stay together and we call that respect. Togetherness. But them honkies . . .

Like, a brother, he don't have no white friends. If he do, you're a dead brother. You a D.B. No more brothers talk to you, you know. White on black, two-tone. You on a side. You have to hang with the honkies. And the honkies don't want you, 'cause you have no respect in your own race.

You know if the honkies be all together, all the brothers show them that we together too. But the honkies not really together. They don't give a shit, man. Them cats, they can *break away*. They don't like each other. You see a dude who's sloppy, man, just won't clean his pad. Everybody sit around and have a discussion. They'll fire on the dude and say, "Look here, man, you better clean your pad up. You the sloppiest dude in the company." And he don't care. But the brother, if he got a low score for room inspection, he going to clean the pad up. He may not have this home training, but he going to clean up 'cause he want to be with his own race.

And you have to be outstanding in sports. Not everybody. If you don't have it, you don't have it. But if you kinda tall, well, you going to play basketball or you a dead brother, you know. You may be clumsy, but you tall. You can do something. You can knock one of them honkies down and send one over him. Put your hand in his face. If you kinda fast, zipping around all day and everything, you gonna run track. You may not beat nobody, but you can run. Now these little ole honkies, they don't even come around the weights—'cause it's too heavy for them. They play that paddle tennis.

One honky in my company, kid named Bob. That's what I call them all now: Bob. They all look like Bob. He was a big honky, too, boy. Big young dumb honky. Everybody—all the brothers like him, but we couldn't take him in the clique. He couldn't be with us all the time, although he could pile irons with us because he was strong. He did all the physical things we did. Talked about the same things we did. Like, there was such a smart honky in the company, you know, he talked about the smart honky: "I'm gonna bust his neck!" You know. He was always with the brothers.

And the rest of the white dudes got on his case. And they was talking about, "You a nigger-lover" and shit like that. And the dude—one time we were at the dinner tables and the dude got up and denounced his race. He said, "I'm not no white boy." Sometime I talk to the dude. He say, "They're pathetic. They ain't shit. They get in jail and snivel. They childish, man." He was raised by brothers all his life and he didn't want to be no sniveling honky all the time.

You could play a game of dominoes with him. And talk to the dude. But we can't have no honky in the clique. (*Getting excited.*) We fighting the honky, man. Couldn't take him in. He was just by hisself. No race.

When I was coming down on the bus, man, I wasn't hip to the thing. Me and this cat named John, this honky—Italian or something—we used to get out and just run around the track. Just for the fun of it. And we were talking about what we were going to do to their track records and things.

Well, we got to camp. A brother came and told me, "Don't you go around talking to a honky, man." And me and him was sitting up having a cigarette and a bunch of brothers came over. Say, "You smoking behind that honky, man?" I said, "Yeah, it's his cigarette, you know. I ain't got none." They say, "Man, you don't smoke behind honkies. Wanna be a D.B., man?" And I didn't smoke behind the honkies. Nor eat behind the honky or nothing.

The S.A.s . . . they have pride about theirself. They stay together too.

I would say the S.A.s stay together, at times, more than the brothers do. They all right. 'Cause they a minority. The brothers is a minority. The white man got his foot on them too, you know. But I'll tell you, I really don't like S.A.s, man.

■ *Why don't you like them?*

I really don't know. I just don't like them. All the S.A.s are little men. There was only one big S.A. in my company. They used to crack me up playing basketball. That straight hair on the top of their heads would be just a-bouncing. (*Laughs.*)

Since I can remember, I always hear about the white man. My father doesn't like the white man. And it's always something, even small, about the white man that wasn't right. Like if we taking a trip to see Grandma, and we go into a gas station, you know. And the white man say something, Dad don't like it.

By the time I got to fifth or sixth grade, I knew what the situation was. I didn't use the term, but I knew the white man was the Man. Like if you looked at TV, wasn't nothing but white people on TV. See? The people who control society are white, the majority of police is white. The people who control society control the police. The government is white.

If I'm going to shoot somebody, it going to be somebody with some money, man. It going to be the Man—the white man. He got the dust. I would like to kill a white man, just to put it on the books, man. I don't believe they're not going to buy it. (*Both laugh.*) I feel that way. So it be on the books that a nigger killed a white man, and I might get away with it and get me some bread.

■ *You hear about Huey? The cat that shot the cop?*

Yeah, I heard about him. I feel that the man didn't want to go to jail, and he got this attitude where he don't like the white man. Why the hell does it have to be the *president*, the highest official, got to go to jail behind killing a white man? What's wrong with the members, man? They not all the way together yet. Shit, they supposed to be a righteous little ole black army.

Police? They bugs me. Like if you standing on a corner, they'll slow down and look at you a long time. I'm not doing a thing. Just standing there. He might hang a U-turn and come back up. It ain't their job to look at me, make me feel like I'm gonna do something.

Like if it's a car full of brothers. The Man'll follow you. Follow you a long ways, man. Stay right behind you. Happened to me a lot of times. They think we doing something wrong, or fixing to do something wrong, or did something wrong. They might read about Negroes always protesting. That might give them a complex. I may have a complex myself, man, 'cause I have done a lot of wrong.

And I have been confronted by police, and doing nothing. I don't like policemen, period. Some of them might be doing their job (*sarcastically*) to protect the society. This is what they call it. I can see like if somebody's shooting somebody, they can swoop in on the thing. That's their job, man, I give it to them. But not just bugging people.

I do realize that some white people are all right. Like when I went to continuation school this year, there's two teachers up there that are some all-right dudes. They try to teach you knowledge. I done had all my credits, all the required subjects, you know. And the dudes, they asked me, "Well, you really don't need this class, why you take it?" I say, "I dig history, I wants to *learn* about Negro history, you know." And I got off in the class, man, talked to the cats. . . . I know a little bit about it. And the cats went down and bought a whole bunch of books about black folks. James Baldwin and Claude Brown's book and Richard Wright. And the large percentage of students up there is Negro. About four honkies in the three classes I had. And *they* even take Negro history. The whole deal is Negro history. These two cats is some all-right dudes, man.

But he's still a honky. I would never say, "Man, I like you. You my friend." I would never tell him that because his brother might shoot me. His brother might be one of them kind of people in the Ku Klux Klan, or his daddy might have been a Wizard. And he lived with this so long he couldn't take it and broke away, he going to teach Negroes, you know. But still his family got this in them. And I don't want to give him the pleasure of knowing he has Negro friends.

Never finished high school. For what I plan to do, the way I plan to live, education is unnecessary. I want to know about *life*. (*Irritated.*) If I did go to school, like if I got twenty-five credits, I'd get a diploma. And know about as much as I know now. If I ever make up my mind to be rich, I'll try to do it the quick way. And if I get caught trying, why then I go to jail.

But he's not overly concerned about money: "That's society. I'm a society reject. I don't dig too many things about society." And he doesn't care about settling down, taking a "slave" (a regular job), or signing a piece of paper that says "I love this woman enough to take care of her."

■ *What do you care about, then?*

Living. Laying around. Like a joke I read, man. This white dude went to Africa. And the black man was laying under a tree. The white man said, "All you do is lay around? Why don't you build factories? And airports. Get an education. Get a good job. So one day you will be happy with money. So you be able to lay around." The black says, "That's what I'm doing now. Laying around." (*Both laugh.*)

■ *Got it all figured out, huh?*

Yeah. Ain't nothing wrong with the way the Negro lives. The white man is always coming down on the Negro. I feel that Negroes should be *happy*, man. That's why they want all these things in the stores that the white man has. They wants to break loose. They don't want to live in West Oakland or no slums. They want to be up with the white man. So the white man can't put their foot on them. This is what I feel is causing all the disturbance.

But I don't believe they should climb up individually. They should pull each other up. Individually, here and there, somebody's making it. Get together and help everybody make it, man. But I can understand once somebody get on his way, he ain't thinking about all those black people. He is with the white man. Middle-class Negroes. I don't like them. They look down on people like me.

My parents are brainwashed by society. And they wouldn't understand if I sat down and told them what I just told you. They feel that a man is a society man. They brainwashed! And the majority of people go along with that too, 'cause society says, "Get an education, go to work, and get a good job." Do this just like society say to do it, well, he's a man.

■ *What stopped you from getting brainwashed?*

I really don't know, man. I guess it's just rebellion. It may be that I'm lazy. And I'm looking for a way out. But jail was part of it. When you're placed in jail you're supposed to be put away from society. Okay. I want to stay away from the society thing. Why should I follow somebody else, man? Follow my father and be a grocer? I have my own ideas. I'm gonna live for myself.

I don't like my job. After I come home I'm still irritated. Kind of grouchy, especially if I'm tired. Like my mother, she seen a lightweight change in me. I come home and say, "Fix my plate." I say this 'cause she does this for me. But she has noticed a different tone to it now. One time she said, "You are getting too big around here." Too bossy. And she can't handle me about it. But it's something that we understand.

At the Presidio, the officers come in and eat and I don't dig them. 'Cause they have bad attitudes, you know. Like if one gets up from the table I have to wipe his spot. And if the rag accidentally hits the fork of one of the three left, he got a bad attitude.

When I first went to work over there, I asked the man to put me in the scullery. 'Cause I can't see them. And they can't see me. They have little slots where they slide the silverware through, and put the cups through, and the trays through. And I notice some white hands come through there and the silverware come *flying* through that little hole. (*Chuckles.*) That's right, it comes flying through that little hole. But the brothers, they hand the silver-

ware. You can see their hands, they can see yours. And I see black hands and
they see mine. And they know I'm a brother and I know they're a brother.

> For Larry Dillard's life and beliefs in 1980 and
> 1986, see chapter 10.

Sarah Williams

"The marching and demonstrations is stupid"

*Sarah Williams, a twenty-two-year-old clerical worker, sees nothing positive in
civil rights marches, Black Power, riots, black culture, or black pride. Police
brutality might exist, she admits, but unless you're there to see it, how can you
be sure? When topics like the police and the Panthers come on the news, she
turns the dial to another station.*

*Williams is skeptical about black culture, as well as all the talk about only
blacks having "soul." She's also very critical of preachers who are "steady hollering about money" while building big churches. But her most serious criticisms
are directed at black men. On the jobs she's had, the Negro women have been
the better workers. Black men, she complains, aren't living up to their responsibilities. Interviewer Sheila Gibson asks what these responsibilities are.*

Getting a job, trying to make a living for his family, and trying to take care
of his home, and don't be going around goofing off. He should treat his girlfriends or his wife with respect, make sure they have everything they supposed
to, [but] not go overboard trying to buy everything that he think the wife want
and don't think about his kids.

Most of 'em these days, they don't want to do for theirselves. But they expect a woman to go out and do for herself. He should do his best and not go
around feeling sorry for hisself, thinking people supposed to give him handouts. Everywhere I go, that's the attitude they have.

When I was in Job Corps, most of the boys, they didn't want jobs. They
might work one day, and the next day they come late and don't want to do
nothing. I don't see no reason why they wouldn't want to work. They *give*
them the jobs, they don't have to take no tests. All they have to do is go put in
an application. Then, like I say, they work one day, then the next day you
might see 'em sitting down, and when they do get fired they holler about
discrimination.

She graduated from high school, but feels that she didn't really learn anything until the Job Corps, where she mastered typing, filing, payroll, and other office skills. Recently she's been seriously ill and unable to work. Reluctantly, she's had to accept help from welfare.

It's a lot of them jiving on the welfare, 'cause some of them could get out and get them a job and go to work. On the welfare you on a strain anyway. You don't know if you gonna have food tomorrow, because they have so many rules you have to abide by. If you working, you ain't got to worry about nobody telling you how to spend your money. If people need it [welfare], it's nice in a way. But I think they should be kicked off to see if they really need it.

Negroes, they go out and try to get the best of everything and they can't afford it. And they holler about what the white man supposed to give them. The white people, they don't look like they go all out trying to dress and the food and the stuff like that. People going around getting these big cars, for instance big Cadillacs, and knowing they can't afford it. First thing you hear a nigger talk about is buying a Cadillac.

When her sister joined the Black Muslims two years ago, Sarah became aware of racial problems. She went to two or three meetings, but was not impressed: "They go around saying, 'Don't go to the white man.' Everybody have to go to the white man, that's how they make their living." As for the civil rights movement, "the marching and demonstrations and stuff is stupid to me. They been doing it for years and still haven't got nowhere." The riots make even less sense.

All they doing is burning up people's homes, tearing up people's property. People [like Stokely Carmichael] they go around talking about what they gonna do and what they gonna get and time they get something stirring in one place, they gone to the next city and talk the same stuff. They ain't doing nothing but hurting their own people, they ain't doing nothing to the white man. If they don't want it to be a long hot summer, make them go to school. All they have to do is get a education, then go out and get a job. 'Cause nobody gonna give them nothing.

Sarah Williams's followup narrative appears in
chapter 10.

Harold Sampson

"Denying you the right to be a man"

Harold Sampson, a thirty-eight-year-old postal worker and part-time graduate student, is a member of the same activist circle as Howard Spence, Florence Grier, and Millie Harding. He spends much of his free time on the Sacramento streets, working to keep demonstrations from becoming violent—for him the distinction between rioting and civil rights demonstrations, so unimportant to Sarah Williams, is vital.

Sampson lived in Memphis until he was nine. In the mid-sixties he was an activist in Cleveland, working with CORE and organizing the block clubs that helped elect Carl Stokes the first black mayor of a large northern city. He was on the streets during the 1966 Cleveland riots.

It's really frightening. It's one thing to be in a demonstration. A demonstration is going to have some outcome. You're gonna make some social change, some pressure is going to be applied, you're gonna awake some consciences. But it's entirely different when you're out there and all hell is breaking loose and you're losing control.

It's just as frightening to a scared policeman to be confronted with an angry, rock-throwing, bottle-throwing mob. This cat, you've got him frightened, and he has a gun. Somebody is *bound* to get hurt. And always, my consuming concern in any demonstration that has the potential of becoming a riot—if you can't control the situation, don't go into it, pull out.

Right now the younger black is equating defiance of authority with a show of masculinity. And the authority is best symbolized by the police. The cat really wants to obey the law. He don't want to get into no difficulty. But if this cat pushes him, he's gonna let him know, "I'm a man." Last July on Thirty-fifth Street there were just as many girls out here as there were guys, pushing them on. And the reason we couldn't stop them was these guys were bent on proving to those girls that "I am a man!" And how do you do it in this context? Shoot down obscenities to whitey, and dare whitey—almost a suicidal kind of a thing. You know. A lot of these cats had jobs, were working, were making it! They weren't what we call hungry . . . oppressed. These were the young bloods out to prove to these young women that they are men!

Now, some of us never would stand up and say the kinds of things that Rap Brown and Stokely Carmichael say. But we identify with them, we're living this through them, because it's the kind of thing that our masculinity needs to feel. Like Adam Powell! When they stripped Adam Powell of his power, his position, they emasculated every black man in America.* I think the system is designed to do this! Why would welfare be so concerned that there's no man in the house that they're gonna hire investigators to run around at night to see if these women have a boyfriend? We're right back to plantation days—I've got to control your masculine, sexual expression.

And why are there so many crimes that are directed to the genitals? I had a cop *nut* me one time. Excuse the expression. We were in Cleveland in City Hall. A sit-in. It was snowing. There were about two hundred demonstrators and four hundred policemen. And they kept moving you into a smaller and smaller circle. And the big burly cop just stepped over the crowd lying down, stepped on me, and said, "You black burrhead son of a bitch . . . I'll have you fixed."

This is what the Man is trying to do—this business of denying you the right to be a man, to dehumanize you in any way possible. He does it economically, he'll do it physically. In Cleveland once, these cats were laying down at the Board of Education. And the policeman walked up and got a handful of this guy's genitals . . . and you know, just squeezed. This to me is brutality.

It's more harassment now than actual brutality. Picking you up on bum raps, stopping you for suspicion. Getting out of your car, hands in the air, and being patted down. Issuing you warning citations. The police have become a great deal more sophisticated in their oppression. They *provoke* a black man so they can use force. You witness a normal routine arrest procedure, how that's handled. I think the police [and the National Guard] are there to maintain you in your place, to dehumanize you in every sense of the word. That's their role.

His own role is as an advocate for other blacks in their conflicts with the law. He finds lawyers, raises money, gets information to the right place. In Cleveland he knew many black policemen who would tell him which white cops had beaten up the black demonstrators.

Sampson first learned how to work the system when he was one of the few handpicked blacks—most of them athletes—admitted to a white Cleveland high school. At East Tech, Negroes weren't allowed on the swimming team or in student government; one of Sampson's best friends, and one of the school's best

---

*As a Congressional representative from Harlem from 1945 to 1971, Adam Clayton Powell, Jr., fought tirelessly (and often alone) against all forms of racial discrimination, including segregation in Washington, D.C., and the halls of Congress. As chair of the House Committee on Education and Labor, he played a key role in passing much progressive legislation, including the first minimum-wage laws. Attacked for his "playboy" life-style and accused of placing his friends on government payrolls, Powell was censured by the House in 1967 for "misuse of public funds" and removed from his leadership posts. He spent much of the late sixties in the West Indies avoiding process servers on other charges; in 1970 he was narrowly defeated in his reelection bid by Representative Charles Rangel.

students, lost his scholarship when they found out he was Negro. And even football star Marion Motley could only work as a mail-truck driver after a career with the Cleveland Browns that put him in the Football Hall of Fame.

My folks were poor. I worked all the way through school. I learned all kinds of hustles, how to shine shoes, how to smile when the man rubbed your head. He gonna rub your head "for good luck" and give you an extra quarter. My racial survival kit! At one time, in the South, this racial survival kit consisted of the ability to know what the rules were, you know, when to smile, the whole bit. How to operate and make it. And of course as you move North, the contents of your survival kit change; you begin to be a little more sophisticated. But the kit is still there. Because as a black man, you've got to discover how the system operates, and how you operate within that system! As a black man, you will have to excel!

We are being emasculated so many ways. The Man does it with the job! He does it with welfare. And we fight a war at home, to be a man right in your own house. And sometimes you're losing on both fronts, because they're interrelated. Sometimes I say to my wife, "You don't equate me as being a man because I'm not bringing home enough money to live like some of your friends think that you ought to be living."

This system measures a man by the size of his bankroll. And he does, too. And I don't think you can be a man unless you have the assurance that the guy can't take it away from you—your economic stability, your ability to provide, your ability to take care of your own. And as long as the Man has the dollar, he's able to control you in that manner.

I remember my mother telling me, "You have to remember your place. I'm gonna save you from getting killed. It's all right to fight your sisters and brothers, but you don't dare fight them white boys across the field over there." And without knowing it, mothers have crippled black men, to a degree. "You don't fool around with no white girls. You don't become arrogant. You don't become uppity." We were conditioned, as boys.

In my own family here, my wife doesn't overtly say so, but she talks about the amount of time you're involved in something—even [graduate] school. "Why do you have to work so hard?" It's hard to make them understand: "Look, it's not enough to just pass. It's not enough just to be there. It's not enough to make it *yourself*. You've got to grab somebody else and bring him along." And sometimes they don't buy that.

Their job is to keep you alive. And you can admire them for that. But you get to a point where you say, "Look, if I haven't discovered something that's really worth dying for . . . and I'm thirty-eight years old, then life isn't worth living." But you talk like that and it upsets them. She says, "Well, I'm afraid you're going to get hurt." Well, that fear is fine. But you can't cripple me with that fear. And I'm gonna set things up, if anything happens to me, you're set, you're not left out here in the cold. "Look, I'm gonna take this policy out." And that sounds cold. But you've got to realize when you're out there in the street, in a situation where you might very well get wasted . . .

Harold Sampson's 1979 and 1986 interviews are in chapter 12.

CHAPTER 6

The Paradox of
Working-Class Racism

During the 1960s middle-class intellectuals and an elite-oriented media placed much of the blame for the white backlash on the blue-collar working class. It was convenient and self-serving to locate racial prejudice in the lower classes and enlightenment in more educated groups. Blue-collar workers' surprisingly strong support for the segregationist George Wallace in the 1964 presidential primaries lent credence to this view. White workers were also sometimes involved in racial disturbances, in part because they were often more directly affected by the gains of minorities. Compared to middle-class whites, blue-collar whites were more likely to work in jobs where blacks were entering, to send their children to schools and to live in neighborhoods that were experiencing integration.

The political economy of the times also exacerbated working-class racism. In a decade rife with government social programs and movements for social change, none spoke to the class needs of white workers. The unemployed and the very poor improved their lot through the expansion of welfare and Johnson's War on Poverty. Racial minorities benefited from integration and the beginnings of affirmative action. The upper middle class and the rich gained from the decade's overall prosperity. Yet the real income of the working class stood still as workers shouldered disproportionately the inflationary cost of the Vietnam war. It was as if the white working class was expected to sacrifice its own precarious security to satisfy the various movements for social change.[1] And even though the position of white workers was insecure, their racial privilege modest, black militants targeted them along with more affluent whites as equally exploitive of racial minorities. Caught in the middle, many workers vented their anger and frustration at blacks, students, and antiwar activists.*

*Of course, blue-collar workers also expressed their own anti-establishment feelings. Some protests were essentially symbolic (growing beards, for example), but young auto workers staged wildcat strikes and slowdowns.

But this is not the whole story. Because white workers are more likely than other Americans to have on-the-job contact with minorities, they also have a certain concrete understanding of racial oppression. In talking to their fellow workers, they've learned how blacks have been denied jobs on racial grounds, or have been beaten up and hassled by the police. Sensitive to injustice, understanding firsthand the meaning of exploitation, and prone to reacting physically to personal insults and life crises, the blue-collar people in our study seemed more able than many of the middle-class whites to empathize with blacks rioting in the street. And because white and black workers share the difficulties of making a living and a better life for their families, they sometimes acknowledge a common class position.

But white workers also often see their interests at variance with those of blacks, and, as the examples of Joe Rypins in chapter 2 and Jim Corey in this chapter suggest, blue-collar workers look at race relations unabashedly in terms of their own interests. In the late sixties many whites felt that their jobs or promotions were threatened by the economic advances of blacks and other minorities. This sense of conflicting interests was magnified when black workers demanded special programs and special treatment to compensate for previous discrimination. Lawrence Adams, whose story opens this chapter, doesn't object to such hiring and training programs. What really incenses him is the perception that a black worker is exploiting his or her color to get ahead at the expense of people who have played by the rules.

Job-oriented as white workers are, they tend to see decent work and fair employment practices as the essence of the more abstract notions of equality, manhood, and dignity. Fair-minded and pragmatic, they also judge black workers by how well they perform their jobs. In the group discussions we taped, white workers eventually got down to cases, enumerating the various "colored" people at their workplaces, and the consensus was that blacks were good workers. Even when these whites didn't like someone, they separated job skills from feelings about personality or politics. Thus an aircraft machinist talked of his problems in getting along with "a Black Power advocate" whom he found something of an agitator, but he carefully noted that the man was a good machinist who got his work done.

Because workers value smooth work relations, they appreciate co-workers who are easy to get along with, who are sociable, and who participate in the back-and-forth joking, the relaxed camaraderie at the heart of the work group. Much of this social banter involves ethnic background, for ethnic identities remain more central in working-class culture than among the more cosmopolitan middle class. In this chapter, Jim Corey explains that his friend Richie is the very model of the "ideal black" because "you can tell Richie Negro jokes, and he'll tell you Negro jokes, and he expects you to take the same thing about a white joke." Like other white workers, Corey (and Lawrence Adams) are fascinated by the nuances that distinguish such terms as *col-*

ored, *Negro*, and *black*, and they puzzle over why blacks seem so "sensitive" about the word *nigger*.* In the late 1960s when white America was reacting to a whole array of changes in the behavior of blacks, blue-collar workers seemed particularly unsettled, even personally affronted, by blacks who would no longer participate in racially loaded ethnic joking. What represented an assertion of human dignity to blacks was experienced by many whites as withdrawal, even rejection.

Also contributing to the blue-collar worker's racist image is the style of working-class speech: no-nonsense straight talk, even exaggeration for effect. Blue-collar people don't apologize for their racial feelings or soften their stereotyped views, unlike middle-class people who often mask theirs, prettying up their prejudices and talking in generalities. Nevertheless, in their on-the-job work relations, blue-collar people are usually fundamentally equalitarian and fair-minded, perhaps *less* racist than many other segments of the population. Black and white workers often work together on jobs requiring extremely close cooperation and contact, without distinction of rank and with an ease across the color line rare in middle-class work environments, where people say "all the right things."

Unfortunately, working-class equalitarianism often ends at the factory gate. As one man we talked to put it, "We go our way and they [the blacks] go their way." In blue-collar life the division between the world of work and the world of neighborhood, home, and the family is particularly marked. Thus white workers are likely to feel very strongly about maintaining white neighborhoods and they often find the idea of intermarriage, particularly with blacks, anathema.

Traditional on cultural matters, with their life-styles revolving around family and neighborhood, and with extended kinship stronger than among the middle class, blue-collar workers seem to perceive this opposition to intermarriage as a way to "draw the line" definitively at one point—reserving at least one sphere of life as an all-white sanctuary. Some are also concerned that mixed-blood offspring would not belong anywhere, would have "no race," would not be accepted by either the white or the black community. Here, the fear seems to be that of a break in the continuity of the generations, an almost existential dread of nothingness.

A worker who has overcome such fears is Dick Cunningham, a printer whose family includes a black son-in-law and a "mixed-blood" grandson. Cunningham is at least as family-oriented as the other workers, but "somewhere along the line" there were influences "that caused me to not go for the idea of color prejudice." For him color blindness is the ultimate solution for

---

*As several machinists told us in a group discussion, "If Tony doesn't mind being kidded about being a wop, and we can call Derrick a dumb Swede, why should blacks be so sensitive when one of us slips and uses the word *nigger*?"

racial problems. Here he deviates from the working-class mentality that tends to be intensely conscious of color (and ethnicity). And yet—and this is part of the paradox of working-class racism—such a pronounced color consciousness has its positive side. Comfortable with their own whiteness, the workers we talked to didn't suffer from the guilt that afflicted some of the hippies and middle-class whites who aspired without success to a color-blind attitude. Because Jim Corey is proud of being white, or as Lawrence Adams puts it, "I'm proud to be me, and I'm white," neither has a problem accepting black people's pride in their blackness, and in the late sixties this was a relatively rare attitude among white Americans.

Lawrence Adams

"They've got the right to have every human dignity that I have"

Lawrence Adams is twenty-six years old and works for the same employer as his father. He became active in the union because his fellow workers challenged him to do something besides "just bitching" about the company's "bullshit." And though he likes his skilled crafts job at the phone company, he feels that the working conditions are terrible and that the company doesn't "give a damn about their employees." He's also upset at how they're handling the government-sponsored affirmative action program. Adams was interviewed in 1969 by Ed Price.

I want to see anybody given the same opportunity, black or white or Mexican-American. I don't mind seeing [minorities] getting, say, six months longer to prove themselves if they have a history of bad performance. But giving him preferential treatment as far as a job, a promotion, a transfer, I disagree with. If he's going to come into the industry and going to work under the contract and become a full-time employee, he'll be on his own, just like you and me. Then, by God, he has to take the same chance as I do. To get the shaft shoved up his ass.

I don't believe that he has the right to demand preferential treatment and then, if he doesn't get exactly what he wants, start screaming racial discrimination. The company backs down. Very scared of it. That's a bunch of bullshit. As far as I'm concerned, if that guy's going to scream racial prejudice, I'm going to walk up and pop him in the nose. And say, "Look, Bud, we got to work side by side. And if you got a better chance of getting a job because you're smarter than me, fine. Or if we're equal, then it's a toss-up. If I'm better than you are, then I get the job. But, by God, you're not going to be absent twenty out of every thirty days. You're not going to come in tardy and nobody say anything, because *I* as a union representative will put a stop to it. It's not racial prejudice, my friend, it's a fact that you have to compete with us, and if you don't like it, then you should go to another job."

I think there're eleven colored people working within our local. One of them screams racial discrimination every time an operator comes up and says, "You made this ticket out wrong." And right off the assistant manager backs up. It's not right. You're not helping her. All you're doing is hurting some poor slob out there whose call didn't go through right.

Adams has also known many blacks more capable than himself, and some companies' refusal to hire black people because of "a history of supposedly poor work performance" makes him "violently" angry. He has no trouble getting along with black co-workers. When a black union steward thought Adams had been badmouthing him, "the guy had enough guts to come up and say to me, 'Did you say this about me?' And I looked him right square in the eye and said, 'No.' A damned good steward, a damned hard worker, got a good head on his shoulders."

His closest black friend is Frank Simpson, a co-worker Adams nudged into union activism. "He's a helluva nice guy, he's a character." And with Frank he's on good enough terms to relax his guard, to bandy about words like nigger—*in jest, of course.*

In grammar school, the area of town I lived in was mixed. There happened to be some Negroes, there happened to be a lot of Mexican-Americans, there were Chinese there, and a lot of white people, a lot of Italians. I played with them. I go to dances, if I didn't have a girlfriend, I danced with people of all different nationalities. I had my head bashed in (*laughs*) in football by people of all different nationalities.

My dealings with [blacks] have not been to that degree. Most of my opinions formed by reading. I have not been in the middle of a race riot. On the East Side of San Jose they do a good job of breaking things up out there, and I can't disagree with it. Some of the houses, I'd burn the son of a bitch down to the ground if I lived there. Some are rat-infested shitholes. Some of them aren't so bad. And they complain about it. But everybody has a right to their standards.

There are many Negroes in my neighborhood with no problem. These are not the militants by any stretch of the—these are more of the Martin Luther Kings and the pacifists. I mean, they mow their lawn, I mow my lawn. And I've been to their house, and they've been to my house. I can't say I'm particularly friendly with them, because they just don't have the same interests that I do. But as far as the human being goes, they're not different than I am, and they don't act any different, and they don't try to be any different.

- *What do you think of the militants?*

I have two main reactions. The first one is complete, *violent* disagreement with the tactics they're using. I can see that for a hundred years since the Emancipation, they haven't gotten diddly-shit, pardon the expression. But I can also see that this type of tactic destroys. If it gets carried on too much, you can literally wipe out everything you've got, which is sometimes, I think, what they're advocating. I don't agree with them in their separationist attitudes at all, because I happen to believe that men are men, and I don't give a damn what color they belong to. If they can perform a job, then I say that they got as much right as I do to it. And if they can perform it better than me, well, either I got to become better or I got to get out, and that's all there is to it.

The second is I can see exactly what they want. And I agree with 'em one hundred percent. They want to be treated like men. They've got the right to have every human dignity that I have because I'm a white man. They get the same pay for doing the same job.

The militants want a black society. They want to buy black, talk black, think black, and I say, fine, you have a right to be completely proud of the fact that you're black. You have the right to be cohesive as being black. You have the right to go back from slavery where families were torn apart and regenerate the idea of a family as a basic unit. Because it should never have happened in the first place. But at the same time I also believe that [you're] like a man standing inside of a phone booth. The black separationists are going to become the greatest authorities on that goddamned phone booth, but when they open up that door, they have to coexist with the world.

I'm proud that I'm white. I do a good job. I try to live my day as I see it. I try to plan for the future, and you have the same right. With the idea that you don't have to be afraid that some son of a bitch is coming to come up and steal what you've got just because you're black, or some cop is going to come along and beat you on the head because you happen to be black. You have the right to the same freedoms from fear and the same freedoms from want and the right to public speaking that I have. Guaranteed to us by a Constitution and a big set of laws.

As a military policeman, I had to break up a couple of good-sized riots. The violence that we met was physical. The violence that they're meeting on the streets today is getting down to the core of a man. Calling him a white racist pig . . . you're insulting him. And I think I have to admire the vast majority of 'em, the gentlemen in blue, because I think that they have taken more of the physical and verbal abuse than they should have. So as far as this police brutality thing is concerned, I take it with a grain of salt.

There are always the bad apples. But in the main, police departments have damn good recruitment programs and are able to weed out the sadistic ass-holes, the ones that want to dominate. I don't agree with rubber-hose tactics. I have my rights when I'm arrested, and I want those rights guaranteed. But, by God, if I catch a son of a bitch robbing a store, and I whack him on the head, and arrest him, and take him downtown, and I don't read him his goddamned rights, and he starts babbling off at the mouth, he ain't got no right to be let go.

■ *You said earlier you were proud to be white.*

Well, I am a white man. I was born that way and I'm proud to be me, and I'm white. Maybe that's a better explanation of it: I'm proud to be me. I'm here on this earth for a while—sixty, seventy, eighty years. Whether I make any world-affecting moves within my lifetime doesn't really bother me. The fact of the matter is that I have my own purpose in mind, and I intend to obtain these goals the best way I know how, so I'm damn proud of what I do. As a human being, as a man, I just happen to be white. Don't make diddly-shit to me whether I was black or not. It might if I were black; I don't know what it is to be black.

Black men today, the militants want to be called black men. The not-so-militants want to be called Negroes. What are you going to do? I'm a white man. Okay, fine, I also happen to be English, Irish, French, and Scotch. I'm four minorities in one. So what the hell do I do? (*Laughs.*)

> See chapter 11 for the 1979 and 1986 interviews
> with Lawrence Adams.

Jim Corey

"If I can help a colored man without hurting myself, I haven't got anything to lose"

Jim Corey, a twenty-six-year-old maintenance machinist, tries to avoid talking about controversial issues in his rural community of Marshall, Nevada: "I tend to be outspoken and this could lead to a lot of trouble." Corey's grandparents were Irish immigrants. Whenever Jim's brothers and sisters made something of a person's race, his parents would say, "Keep your mouth shut . . . the Irish ain't nothing but a nigger turned inside out." Today he reads articles in the Catholic press comparing the Negro riots of the 1960s to the Irish rebellion.

We're just not getting across to them. The minority groups seem to feel we're dictating to them and not going to them with the position of, "What can I do for you? I'd like to help." It's easy for me to sit here and say I agree with what they're trying to achieve, but I don't agree with how they're going about it. This is easy. But if I was in the same position I might want to bust them white guys upside the head, too. Maybe I'd pick up a big Watts walloper that these kids are turning out and lay it on somebody. Maybe this would be a big way to let white power know that I was grossly dissatisfied with the terms they'd offered me, that I want a chance to set my own terms, look at him eye-to-eye and not look up to him continually.

I think dissatisfaction causes the riots. Maybe it's red organizers, maybe it's American Communist party members, maybe it's dissatisfaction with his living conditions, his earning power, and—I have to say this—his *alleged* claim of not getting the full use of his education. Why do I say "alleged"? Because from our area we've had Negro athletes walk away with sports scholarships, scholastic awards, and there hasn't been a Negro denied that has applied himself. I found out at a tender age that you're going to put a hell of a lot more into anything than you'll ever get out of it. Maybe they're impatient about this, or they fail to see it, or they don't understand, but in our [union] local at least, the people who have applied themselves come up. Richie thinks the riots are senseless. He thinks [the goals] can be achieved another way.

I have no objections to them being where I am, as long as my rights aren't restricted guaranteeing theirs. It's a dog-eat-dog world, and each one of us is out for the best we can for our families. If I can help a colored man without hurting myself, I haven't got anything to lose. If they haven't got the hustle to get out and get it, and I have, that's tough.

The war on poverty, that's different. I've got to pay the taxes anyway, man. I rather see them go into an effective training program for the Negroes or any minority group than running that war in Vietnam. That's a drastic drain financially and on our youth.

I think I resent Black Power as much as they resent white power. As Stokely Carmichael presents it, Black Power means let's put the white man down any way we can, get guns and kill the white man in the streets, destroy their government and make it a black nation. From a personal standpoint, I think it's frightening. I hope Carmichael's attitude is not predominant throughout America; I hope he has just a few following him. I think the leaders have enough sense right now—in spite of all their threats—not to start a civil uprising. It wouldn't beget them a thing, they'd split our nation.

For a long time I felt that Martin Luther King was just another rabble-rouser. Let's see if we can't shake the white foundation, and bring something crashing down. But getting the comprehensive coverage after he was assassinated, you know he was trying to do good. At least he was sincere in a peaceful settlement of the problem.

But every time Martin Luther King went someplace, there was violence. Now whether this was something that followed him or if it was his own doing or someone was trying to run his organization, I don't know. King was obviously a master of mob psychology. Not so much actually saying that you advocate bloodshed in the overthrow of the white power structure, but leave these undertones in your speech, in your enthusiasm, and your feelings. Without really coming out and saying that, you can get people out of hand emotionally.

The shooting of King was a rather asinine move. I think if he got out of hand there were other ways to handle him. It was a great loss for both the whites and the Negroes, but it certainly did a lot for his personal image. It made a martyr out of him.

I generally agree with the NAACP chapter in our area. They haven't been the real hard rabble-rousers. When they felt one of their people was getting a wrong deal, and they honestly felt it was from racial discrimination, they went to bat for them, and you can't blame them for this. Any union does this.

Perhaps if they have to wait too long to get this economic and social equality that they're after, they could be panicked into a race war. I hope I wouldn't have to pick up a gun and fight, but I guess to defend my wife I'd shoot. It bothers me to think that I would have to shoot some of the Negroes I work with, because I've established a relationship with them, where at least I can talk to them. And there's some of my neighbors it wouldn't bother me, I guess, if I had to—I hope not—but at least for self-preservation I wouldn't hesitate to shoot them if I figured they'd turn on me. But there are truly some Negro people out there like my white friends that, just now, under no circumstances . . . I'd have to really sit down and feel how I'd feel at the time to pull a trigger on them. It would truly bother me.

A government military base employs most of Marshall's citizens, including Jim and his father. For as long as Jim can remember, blacks and whites have worked at the base, visited in each other's homes, and bowled on the same teams. Hotheaded youths sometimes fight, but these brawls are not racist or racial in origin, Jim says. The high school students dance together at hops and play together on the football team. When an opposing team said, "We don't want black niggers in our league," the Marshall varsity threw them over the bleachers. When the Marshall team was expelled from the conference, the town backed its team all the way.

The talk turns to Richie Ward, Jim's close buddy, a Negro whom many whites in town use "as an example of how they'd even like some of their kids to turn out."

We've got a couple young fellas out there that are as fine a caliber of person regardless of what they are, their race. They're personable, they're easy to get along with, they're sensible, and at the same time they're boys much in the same sense as you and I when we were growing up. They get vicious and ornery if they have a couple of drinks, but I think they're going to make first-class citizens.

Richie and his brother are shining examples of how a Negro can get along in the world. Evidently it's the way Mrs. Ward has brought her kids up, because they're all very easy to get along with. You can stand and tell Richie Negro jokes, and he'll stand and tell you Negro jokes, and he expects you to take the same thing about a white joke. He can put it in a reverse situation where the Negro is making fun of whites, and he expects you to laugh as hard—which is right. He's fun-loving, and he's far from the "dumb nigger" image that Bill Cosby's been talking about on *Black America*. There's no doubt in Richie's mind that he's as good as any white man alive. But he doesn't push it.

Jim's father had close Negro friends; they came to the house for dinner. His older brother joined the NAACP. Jim's scoutmaster was black and an important role model. So when Jim Corey sees a group of Negroes, his impulse is to go up and talk to them, "to make the first move to get them into the group." But his belief in integration stops at intermarriage.

Where I'm from it's not a common thing to see racially mixed couples. I've noticed several down here [in Berkeley]. I haven't been offended and it hasn't bothered me. This is their business, and if they're big enough people to protect their children from the petty prejudice they're going to be subjected to, then more power to them if this is what they want. I personally don't think that I could look past Negroid features, marry a Negro woman, and be a big enough person to protect my children and be nonviolent about it and try to explain to them that I married their mother regardless of the color difference because I loved her, and no doubt they're going to suffer for it. I don't think I'm a big enough person to really overlook the race barrier.

When I first meet a Negro, clarity of speech is the first thing that strikes me. Whether it's easy to understand him, if he's outwardly friendly. Richie has got an awfully clear speech, and so does his mother. There are some Negroes that mumble, it makes it awfully hard for me to understand. And I don't hold anything against them, you know—don't think it's any particular throwback or mutation or anything—it's just a little hard for me to converse with them.

It's been explained to me that when a white man calls a Negro "a nigger" the connotation it carries is in the tone of voice in a particular situation. I try mostly to use the word *Negro*—it's been [in] my experience the least offensive word. I wouldn't use *black* at all. I've heard Negroes referred to as "black bastards," and I try to stay away from this. I just get a funny feeling when I use ["black"], like, you know, they resent it. This might just be my background. Maybe they've accepted this like they've adopted "Afro-American."

Recently Negroes seemed to be better informed—they're paying more attention to the national situation. They've got more to say on it. They don't just seem to sit back and listen. They're more willing to express their feelings whether you agree with it or not. It seems to me that at least for a period of time if they didn't agree with you, they didn't have anything to say. I think maybe the civil rights law has built up the confidence in them.

- *Do you think Negroes are basically the same as white people?*

I think they have the same human needs: the need to be loved, the tendency to group together, sexual drive, hunger, and the social needs, too. The same fight [to get ahead], only on a much larger scale than mine. Better economic situation, better housing, able to afford a car and still save money, able to educate his children without sweating blood and putting his wife to work at a low-paying job. And without having to knock people in the head and drag them through court to get them educated. I'd say the Negro's got a very tough fight on his hands, and I acknowledge it.

I feel tremendously lucky that I don't have this trouble that the Negro has. Being born white means an easier life. In the South even the white trash tend to look down on the Negro. I guess being white to a lot of people means being superior just by the fact that you are white, and I don't hold for this.

We tend to be a racist society. We subjugated and exploit the Negro. Maybe not all of us, but the good pay for the bad. If the few, or the whole, whoever it is, have subjugated the Negro and beat him out of what's his and made him resort to violence—which he feels is necessary—then I guess we could be classified as a racist society. I'm afraid it's a lot more than a few. Because my wife's relatives are all from Oklahoma and they have strong feelings.

I don't consider myself a racist. I think I'm just as prejudiced against some white people, like hippies, as I am against colored people. It doesn't make any difference to me, I'm not really that hard to be friends with.

- *What if a Negro you knew called you a racist?*

He might have a good basis. I'd be willing to sit down and talk about it. If he called me a racist on the decision of one sentence or one action that might not be intended, I feel I would at least be entitled to an explanation as to why he thinks I'm a racist.

I imagine I'm every bit as proud to be white as Negroes are to be Negro. Because I'm proud to be white, I don't blame them a bit for being proud that they're Negro.

For Jim Corey in 1981, see chapter 11.

Dick Cunningham

"My oldest daughter married a black man"

Dick Cunningham is a printing pressman in his early fifties. Interviewer Ed Price met both Cunningham and George Hendrickson (chapter 4) at the same union meeting in 1969.

I don't know whether you recall from the other night or not, my oldest daughter married a black man. Hell of a swell guy. We deliberately raised our kids to be color-blind. In other words, we did our damnedest to raise them without prejudice. Evidently succeeded.

They don't look at a black person and say he's a black. They say he's a man. They don't see color. One of the first things I remember, when the oldest daughter was maybe three, she was playing out front and a black man walked down the street. She said something about there goes a nigger. And she was informed right then (*pounds the table*) that there was no such thing as a nigger. There was a man.

There were strong anti-Catholic feelings in his family; Dick's grandmother thought his uncle would go to hell for marrying a Catholic.

What she would think if she knew that my daughter married a black man! Probably there wouldn't have been a stronger reaction because her family ran a station on the underground railroad during the Civil War. I've never been a formal junior crusader, letters-to-the-editor kind of guy or anything. I never belonged to the NAACP. In my own quiet little way I tried—well, like the other night. The young man was insisting he wasn't prejudiced, but he wasn't renting apartments to a black man. He just don't know what prejudice is. He wasn't only prejudiced, he was a bigot.

Frankly, a lot of this I have learned since my daughter married. We knew she had been seeing Lionel . . . we had no idea they had got anywhere near so serious. I had gone back home to bury my dad, and two weeks after I was back she called up one night, broke the news on the phone to her mother. Then it wasn't no more than about three, four weeks after that my wife had to go back and bury her mother. That was a coincidence, but we were shook.

We had it all pictured as to what would have happened when we were in Pittsburgh, Pennsylvania. It just wasn't done in those days. You'd have been completely ostracized. In those days a black man didn't walk into every restaurant, because he wouldn't have been served.

One person who helped was one of the kids' professors out at the college. He's a black man himself and a damn smart man and a real thinker. He spirited us into a lot of things, and we've attended quite a number of seminars dealing with the race problem. And I worked through the church, and like one evening we had him come over and talk with them of the subtleties of prejudice—the little things that you don't realize in everyday life, but to the blacks they carry a connotation. The biggest thing it has brought to me is a realization that it is probably impossible—if not impossible, very close to impossible—for the average white person, or even a lot of smart white people, to fully understand what the period of slavery and ever since, the effect it has had on the personality, character, makeup—I don't know what you'd want to call it—of the average black. They had a matriarchal society.

Like I said, prejudice is an awfully subtle thing. We'll be sitting around the house, daughter and son-in-law yakking, the TV's on. You start to come out with some remark . . . that's got the color overtone to it. Used to be I used them; there was no intent, it was merely a saying, it was something I grew up with. To me it meant nothing. But to the black it means something. He knows where it came from, and how does he know that what caused it originally is not in your mind?

My daughter's been married a little over five years. My son-in-law and I are close enough now that he kicks things at me which are the black equivalent of these things. And when I kick mine at him, we get a kick out of it. We know each other now well enough to know that there is no real meaning. But like the ones I work with, they don't know me that well. There's a couple of them are gradually getting to know me. You begin to realize just how ingrained some of it is. Same way with the Jews. In your anti-Semitism, there's a lot of it.

Color blindness is the solution. Color blindness. It's going to come to the point where you don't look at a person as a black, green, yellow, polka-dotted, or what—he's a man. One of the men I work with lives in back of Technical High, very nice neighborhood, gradually becoming integrated, a black man lives next door. He doesn't talk about his "neighbor," talks about "the colored guy next door." They're on friendly terms—see the subtlety of prejudice? If you're color-blind this doesn't happen.

The day Martin Luther King was assassinated, fella that runs the press right next to me got on the bus after work, and this was about the time every high school had let out. He was the only white person on the bus. The bus didn't travel three blocks, 'til a big young black comes up—"You're one of those white SOBs" and whap! Mac's only regret is he didn't get in at least one punch. But he doesn't blame the blacks. Here was a man who was a terrific symbol, and to have him cut down and add this to everything that they know has happened—I'm amazed that this country didn't see a bigger explosion than it did. It shows that gradually we are growing up.

People talk up integration. Now, there are plenty of blacks, they're not interested in it. They have their own little social world, and this is what they want. The only thing they really want, the vast majority, they want to be treated as a man. Not "there's a nigger," [but] "there's a man," and treat him like one. He goes to work, he does his job, shows an ability to do a better job, and gets a better job.

And I have had this battle both in the union and in the [apprenticeship] plan. I've had this battle because for years the unions don't "let niggers in here." Didn't have a darn thing to do with the person's ability to do the work or pay dues or anything else. Was purely the color of his skin. Finally, we've got about four or five of them running press, but it took a lot of persuasion and an awful lot of talking and some threatening.

We'd go to the employers, and they'd say, "Well, the union won't let them." So we got the union convinced to let them in. We go back to the employer and say, "Now they're in the union, what are you going to do?" And amazingly enough, they're doing a good job. You see prejudice of their foreman . . . those of us who are interested in this have to kind of pick up and make sure that they get all the information they need. It's surprising that every day there are more and more people getting interested in this sort of thing.

A lot of these militants, I deplore what they're doing, but I can pretty well understand why they're doing it. Take your Black Panthers, here in Oakland—a group of young blacks that got fed up with the police harassing them whether they were doing anything or not.

- *Do you think this really happens?*

I believe that it did. I don't mean to be condemning the entire police department. But we know that there are bigots in everything, so why aren't there bigots in the police department? Having spent three and a half years in Louisiana, where they don't dare come out on the street after dark, you begin to realize this happens, and I think these young fellas just got fed up with it. So they formed a little organization and they started trailing the police. To keep track of when the police were beating some poor black for no good reason at all. Well, naturally the police react, the bigots will react every time. And it gets blown up, here we are, having a shooting war and everything. What's the answer?

One of the biggest ingredients is going to be time. I realize this is an awful tough pill to swallow for people who figure that two, three hundred years is entirely too darn long. But human beings being what human beings are, you're not going to change them very fast. And I think by law you can force them to accept some things much faster than you could any other way.

If I have to spell an answer, the hope is in the young people. Your age group is the beginnings of it. 'Cause more and more of the old bigots are gonna fade out. Oh, sure, some of them are leaving certain marks on their children, 'cause this is where you get it. Prejudice, you're not born with it, a majority of it is acquired in the home. And here I've got to agree with the old Englishman [George Hendrickson]. He said, "Discipline." I wouldn't use the word *discipline*, I'll say home life. A lot of the problem is in the present-day breakdown of the home.

For Cunningham's 1979 and 1986 interviews, see chapter 11.

CHAPTER 7

Black Workers: New Options
and Old Problems

T hroughout the 1960s blacks as a group remained in the lower levels of
the labor force, but opportunities opened for many individuals. Racial
militancy carried over into the workplace: Afro-Americans, especially the
young and the more educated, were less willing to accept inferior work and
job conditions, and they became more vocal in protesting policies and behavior they perceived as racist. In blue-collar industries with large concentrations
of blacks—auto, steel, and rubber manufacturing, for example—black workers formed caucuses that organized militant job actions for more equal treatment and promulgated a revolutionary consciousness among their supporters.

Developments in the national economy and changes in the composition of
the labor force abetted activism in the workplace. The economic prosperity of
the sixties brought millions of unemployed people back to work. In 1968 and
1969 unemployment rates reached their lowest level since the mid-1950s.
And most of the millions of new jobs for young people entering the work force
were in the more desirable white-collar sector.

Black Americans capitalized on this favorable climate to improve their
overall economic position at a rate faster than that of the white population,
thus making modest though significant strides toward equality. Although
black unemployment remained twice as high as the white rate throughout the
decade—there was no *relative* gain here—the number of nonwhites without
work fell sharply in absolute terms. And blacks upgraded their occupational
position more rapidly than whites: the proportion of the black work force in
white-collar jobs almost doubled between 1960 and 1970—from 13 percent
to 24 percent. During these same years the ratio of black median family income to white median family income improved (from 55 percent to 62 percent), and black income in inflation-adjusted dollars increased 58 percent,
compared to 21 percent for whites.

Moreover, a new kind of black worker entered the labor force. The youth who came of age during the 1960s were more educated than any previous generation, and the educational gap between the races was narrowing. In 1960 only 38 percent of blacks in the 25-to-29 age group were high school graduates; by 1970 the figure was 56 percent. The proportion of blacks who went on to college also increased steadily and brought higher aspirations and expectations. Younger workers were unwilling to make the compromises their parents' generation had; they wanted jobs that offered a future, the opportunity to express their abilities and make a contribution to society, and they insisted that they be treated with the same dignity and respect as others.

The narratives in this chapter depict these generational shifts in values. Richard Holmes, a retired farmhand and janitor, represents the traditional worker. He is contemptuous of the "choosiness" of the younger generation. Like Howard Spence in chapter 1, Holmes takes pride in his willingness to work at any job, no matter how lowly in esteem or how rock-bottom the wages.

Richard Holmes

"The Negro don't want to work"

Seventy years old in 1968, Richard Holmes was born in the San Joaquin Valley, where his father was a farm laborer and lumber-mill worker. Holmes quit school in the eighth grade and for eighteen years was a dairy hand.

I was working over in Stockton, milking cows. And I saw this young fellow that I was raised up with, and he was on the bum. He asked what I was doing. He laughed: "Ho, ho, ho, milking cows." There's nothing wrong with milking cows. White men do it. Why can't I? I saw the West Indian Negroes milking cows, but not any American Negroes. The Negro don't want to work.

A lot of Negroes have the feeling that the world owes them a living. (*Angrily.*) The world doesn't owe them nothing. The government should have a place for them people to work. And if they don't work, don't give them no food. No money. And then they'll work. And those men that don't want to work, put them in jail. There's a lot of work. I could always get a job when I wanted one. Pick up junk, I done that. Picked tomatoes. Picked peas. I didn't make a hundred dollars a day, I made fifty cents a day. So what?

Race never bothered me in getting work. I never heard anything about this prejudice business 'til I was an old man.

Richard Holmes passed away in the early 1970s.

LEN DAVIS, who talked about growing up in the South in chapter 1, is thirty years old and stands between the generations: old enough to have had to settle for what was available when he began work in the early sixties, but young enough to feel the new mood, the recent expansion of the limits of the possible for nonwhites. He therefore feels especially deeply the anguish of his blocked potential: Working in the post office . . . "is the best that I can get. . . . And the reason is because I'm a Negro." In contrast, blacks in their early twenties felt freer to quit constrictive jobs and seek new opportunities; in fact, three of the people in this chapter had made such moves in the year or two before the interview.

In the private spheres of life—family, neighborhood, religion, leisure—black people can choose to avoid having to deal with white people and their prejudices. But work usually demands regular contact and, as virtually all the accounts in this chapter indicate, race relations add another dimension of stress to an already stressful activity. In Davis's words, work is the place where "you are being mistreated every day."

Len Davis

"The postal system has become a Negro-type job"

If you be realistic about it, the hell with a job. I got to get up out of the bed every morning and go to work. And do *manual* labor. In the service, man, I did office work. Most of the time I was sitting up behind a typewriter. I didn't call that work. My job now, it makes me kind of depressed, that I can't cope with a lot of people, mostly whites. In the last five years, man, I've learned a lot about being proud. I'm proud of anything I do, no matter what it is. But still, in the back of my mind, this is the best that I can get. (*Sighs.*) Working in the post office, you know.

And the reason is because I'm a Negro. *That* has always been the reason. And work to me is a headache, really. It's not something that—well, you go to law school and become a lawyer or a doctor, that's work to him, you know. But baby, that's nice. And all that bread he's getting? When I'm out here breaking my back and I ain't getting a damn thing.

I think the average guy, he just settles for something. You've got a job making three dollars an hour. He never heard of that down South. He's spending most of it because it costs him more to live in the North than it does in the South. But he's not looking at that. He's looking that he's got this job, and it's better than what I had in the South. It might not be good, you know. You still might—you *are* being mistreated every day. By just the color of your skin. But he can't go on forever thinking, "Well, I'm down here in the mud and I ain't gonna never get out."

You got to settle for something, and that's what they settle for. I got a better job, I can eat in any restaurant I want to. I can send my kids to any school I want to. Things like that. And they don't really look at it. A lot of people, right today, they shut their minds off to the race problem. Even though it's really flared up in the last ten years. "Man, I don't even want to talk about this." And consequently they become Uncle Toms. They're not gonna speak out against anything, you know. Because they have settled for that one little something in their minds. It's different things, but it all mounts up to a better standard of living.

The whole postal system has become a Negro-type job. "There's nothing else you could do, so we'll just let the government take care of you. All you need is high school, and we'll let you work for the post office." And there's not too much damage you can make in the post office. Any work for the federal government is a Negro-type job now. The white man is making it seem like he's doing you a favor. And he want you to think that's great. When, man, that ain't nothing. You got your security and all that, but don't tell me that it's the greatest, you know. It's kind of like the military service—they got it so you think you're being treated up to par, but the Negro gets the worst jobs, really.

Right now I got a Negro supervisor. I think that I would get a much better break working under a white. I'm not too fond of working for a Negro. Because the Negro feels that he can't go off that line too far, because he's got that white downstairs, and they're saying, "You're giving him a break because he's a Negro." And the average supervisor at the post office or any government installation, he has been brainwashed to think that way. Now the younger generation, these young guys are changing everything. If I could get into a position like that, I'd tell you, baby, I'm gonna give you that break. But I'm gonna do it in a way that he can't prove that I did it.

Right now the black woman is more independent than she's ever been. She's making three hundred dollars a month, got a car and apartment. To her boyfriend, coming by to see her, letting him know, "Baby, you don't have to do a damn thing for me." That makes him feel pretty damn low. And the whole system was designed to make him feel that way. She doesn't know it. But she is putting him down. "Man, you can't say anything to me 'cause I make as much money as you do." And if you ever want to get a Negro male's temper up on him, where he start popping off, you mention that. One of my brothers, his wife started making more money than he did. And it started bugging him. So he quit and [took] a much rougher job. To make more money than she did.

I'm going to tell you something, man. I think we have the right to get up every morning and go shoot some white cats. I really do. As far as moral feelings are concerned, I might be wrong. I *know* I'm wrong, but man—if *anybody* has the right, we have. We have the right to be prejudiced. We haven't did anything to him. And they got the audacity to tell us that we're trying to do this and we're trying to do that. We're not trying to do anything. I mean we're asking for our damn rights, man. And they keeping them from you. There's no way in the world a Negro can be raised up in this society and think otherwise. That woman in there (*points to his wife*), she tells me, "I'm not prejudiced." But I can prove it to her every second of the day: "Baby, you prejudiced." Because of what the Man did to you. Now, that's our reason. What the hell is *his?*

> Len Davis was interviewed again in 1981 and 1987; see chapter 13.

ONE WAY of avoiding the resignation and despair expressed by Len Davis is to take the path of the street hustler, a role that has appealed to generations of prideful black men because it allows one to earn a living without compromising one's dignity in humiliating encounters with whites. In fact, hustling often lets minorities reverse the racial order of things by outsmarting and exploiting whites—as well as other blacks.

Mark Anthony Holder explains the logic of hustling through dialectical reasoning. His thesis is the ideal: the job he would like to have is that of a craftsman, "an artist at his trade" who produces precisely the product that he wants and has the time to carefully perfect his work. It is Marx's vision of the nonalienated worker. Holder's antithesis is the real: the jobs that are available to most black men give them no control over the product or the work process; instead they are plagued by the stress and insecurity of working for prejudiced white people. Holder's synthesis, and the path he took as he became disillusioned with straight jobs, is that of the hustler who lives by his wits, running "games" to "psych" people out of their money.

Mark Anthony Holder

"Being a man is being part of the world"

Born in Texas, Mark Anthony Holder came to California while still a baby. After Mark's father left, his mother raised her six children with only a little help from public assistance. In school the other kids were "so down and defrauded in their minds" they would laugh at the Holder children's "raggedy clothes." Mark

*became self-conscious, felt backward, too shy to participate in classroom dis-
cussions. He left school at sixteen and took to the streets, "just getting a dollar
here and a dollar there."*

*After his military service, he got married, had a daughter, tried to settle
down. He was working as a school janitor in Los Angeles when the police
stopped him "for no reason" and kept him in jail for twenty-four hours. He lost
his job and at the age of twenty-four began hustling full time: "working games"
on people to separate them from their money.*

*In 1968, at the age of twenty-nine, he is in a period of transition between
the streets and a more respectable livelihood as a longshoreman. On the waterfront he retains the outlook of a street hustler and still engages in some part-
time illegal and quasi-legal activities; last year he spent sixty days in jail for
fighting with a bartender. But part of him would like to give up the street life
and have the "peace of mind," the "clear conscience" of a more conventional
life-style—that's his definition of "making it."*

*The interviewer, Alex Papillon, a fellow longshoreman, asks him to describe
the straight jobs he's had.*

That made me feel . . . chesty, or like I accomplished something? (*Pauses,
then sighs.*) Nothing really, man. It's all just common labor. I just accept them
all the same way, man. And I know that this Man got it and I got to play a
tool. Because I don't have the education that he prescribed for me. I'd *like* to
be born with a silver spoon in my mouth. Not working, period. Just lay out—
you know, glorious, all [my] life. Work, man? Honestly, it's a slave job.
Whereas if opportunities was open for me to be a salesman, travel from here
to there, trying to sell a product or trying to represent a certain firm, well, I
could dig this. This would be something leisureable to me.

Say, for instance, like a barber. He just stands. He's an artist at his trade.
He likes to do something that he really likes. That's not work, man. Even if
you are a welder, you like to weld things, a type of thing that you're doing the
way that *you* wanted to. Like you going to produce the product that you want
to manufacture yourself. Can you dig it? Which means that you're happy with
your job, man. If I made a mistake I could always go back over it, not feeling
like I'm going to be downed or ridiculed about it. I don't like to go to a job,
man, feeling on pins every day. Feeling insecure, man. Under pressure. Not
be able to express the way that I righteously want to do things.

The job that I got now kind of makes me feel like a man. I'm not kidding. I
dig it. I can kind of express my opinion. I can kind of do the things that I want
to do. Because it's dominated by all black people right now, as you know. Just
because it's 'dominately colored, I don't hide behind that, man. That's a
crutch and I never try to lean.

I don't have to work when I don't want to. I could tell the Man where to go.

This is the way it's supposed to be, but they try to put it like it's a privilege. The Tom say, "Oh man, this cat is giving you this. Why you going to take advantage, man? Why you going to be laying up? Why you ain't going to be doing this here?" Brother, he's cheating you. Why not give it back to him?

- *What would it mean to you to really "make it"?*

When you look at an average person who is doing well, you feel these material things you want. You want a home. You want to live easy. You want to smile. You don't want to be hiding in shadows. Dig it? So to make it, man, you just want to have a clear conscience, that's all. Making it is peace of mind. If I could obtain the things that the normal person has—that whitey has—I'll say that I have made it.

- *What things in particular?*

Security, man. Self being. Left alone. Could venture into any kind of field that I want to. Dig things. *Just knowing the world, man.* I don't even know a fourth of the world. Not me. Or no other black man. You don't even know a fourth of the world. 'Cause we've been denied of it. You couldn't imagine, man, all the beautiful things. It's never been open to us, but you could see it. This keeps you going on all the time, trying to obtain it. They tell you you can make it, but yet you still working. This is a brainwashing in itself, man. The fields are not open to you. When you get up so far, they gonna cut you down, and you know it. Some kind of way. You'll *never* make the million. Those that have . . . you've got to be Tomish to obtain it.

In school, I read the history on this cat, Tom. He was a message for the white man, a spy. The Tom's a man who will sell his soul for his own welfare. Or to get over. Now it's sort of sad, man, because he's gaining for himself, which he got to—the law of nature says survival, you know. But he's hurting so *many*, man. When he goes out and tells on this other brother, somebody he trusted in, telling the Man what he's trying to do. And that way you can never get over. He is a Tom. He is a outcast. He is a dog.

And if you don't be that way, you just got to struggle. And this is why—I'm not afraid to mention it—I rightfully dig the Panthers. I don't say make violence or do violence, but if it's the thing to do, *do* it. I mean you got to make a stand, brother. I'm not downing Martin Luther King, because he's older than we are. When we come through, we in a different era altogether, so our opinion on things is different from him. He may be true at heart, thinking this is right. But he's not right. I don't agree with turning one cheek. Because this Man is a *wrong* man. He's a smart devil, brother. He's constantly thinking. When you think everything is mellow, he done set up a plan already.

I wasn't against school. I would have liked to learn if I would have had the righteous teachers. Someone that understands the way things are, a teacher that be around peoples that's stricken with poverty. She would have known me and given me the righteous special care that I would have tried to seek. She could have rendered me unique knowledge . . . the way my sister or my neighbor would. Not telling me about the things that she's accomplished—material-type things—when I don't have anything.

One day in sixth grade he talked back to a teacher, an "Aunt Jemima" who was following "whitey's program." When she expelled him, his mother had some strong words for the principal.

After that my teachers more or less boosted me through school. "Gee, his mother came, I want to show her that I'm right, so I'll give him good grades." Which I knew I didn't deserve. When I goes to the seventh grade, boom. Nothing, man. Honest to God, I didn't know anything. I'm not lying. All my knowledge that I have learned, all my actions, come from the street—as you can probably dig from my conversation. These are just the words that I rightfully speak. Just a dialect, man.

The society say, "Not having book knowledge, you're dumb." But I don't consider myself a complete numbskull. I just never was part of nothing. This gave me the attitude that I couldn't learn anything from school. So I accepted the life of the streets.

On the streets I was using psych on peoples, man, righteously conning them. For instance, I come up to you in a place—a hamburger place or any sociable place where the public meets. I sit and observe you. See your actions, see your dough. You can tell how a cat's been brought up. If he's had all the things in life, it makes him kind of lame. The cat don't know the grab, you know. So we prey on him. Psych him out. This takes a lot of honest-to-God meditation. But cats out here—none of them even went to school—they got this . . . they call it mother wit. You can't psych them. They may not know how to count, but you can't beat them out of no money.

■ *What's a hustler?*

He's a cat with many games, man. He's a dude that is versatile. Anything for the buck. He knows what he faces. Whereas you take a dude out there, just trying something, and not really thinking about the outcome—then you wouldn't consider him no hustler. Because he's the type of cat that will freeze in situations. He gets caught. He's not a hustler. A hustler is a guy, man, that will take chances. Matter of fact, he's a warrior, a warrior by his natural instincts. In his natural habitat.

And this is [what you do] when you're young and you've been in poverty. You constantly trying to get it. Once you grab some the first time, you're going to grab another thing. This first thing was easy, but you want a bigger thing now. So you got to exercise your mind to make it strong enough to obtain this other thing. Your knowledge expands and it's going to keep expanding. This is where you start getting your wits.

I'm talking about black people. We are warriors, man, because we've been dominated so long. We got to be witty. To obtain anything, man. If you go lame or anything, you just down. You adjusted to society, period.

■ *You run any games on the job?*

Yeah. I try to be always outthinking this man. He's honky. First I look at him, I know he didn't dig me. He wanted to fire me. I wasn't laughing or tee-heeing or mingling with them [whites] or adjusting to their set. Because I'm real. If you notice me on the job, brother, I am myself. And now dig this. (*Points to his hair.*) I could cut all this off, wear my hair short, and just be a plain dude, man. So I keep him off my back. I don't talk too much. And do my job. He's scared of me, and I know he's trying to figure me out, but I've got him psyched. When a person figure you out, they know you, then you just hung up, you been conquered. But long as you stay obvious, they don't know you. You got them. You don't have to do it by words, man. Just nice little natural instincts and signs. *I never took no psychiatry, man, but I can analyze a person.*

Mark Anthony Holder is also an amateur painter. He points to the canvasses that decorate his apartment. Though he's an atheist who sees Christianity as part of the white man's oppressive scheme, many of the portraits are of Jesus. "The reason I paint Jesus, man, is this is a train of life they believe in, so I paint him colored. Nothing in my house, man, is white."

Being a man is being part of the world, man. This is what we're fighting for now. Being a part of the world. That's a man. But we're a man within ourself and we know it. 'Cause we don't take nothing. We don't take no fool-ishness. I'll put it frankly, I think this here Huey Newton, he's a man. He gave up something, brother. He gave up his life for what he actually thought was right. Now me, man? If I had a unity of peoples, a cat would put hisself forward. [But] we have a whole lot of Toms out there. Like Martin Luther King, turning one cheek, then the other, you'll never get nothing over, brother. Because this Man don't care. He's been killing all his life. Killed the Indians, took their land. He's trying to conquer every other land, because he is the *Yahoo.*

■ *What is soul?*

Gee, can't you feel it, man? I feel soul like this. When things are bearing on me so hard, so cold that I could still whimper a tune and kind of laugh and smile and walk around. And soul means like you could feel things and could bear it. You could feel it, man, so hard you won't crack behind it. You won't fade. Your mind is still stable. But the white man, he can't take it. He get red in the face, the beast come out in him. He fall apart. He do drastic things. He even kills. We don't like to kill. We try to be mellow. This is soul, brother. Where you could take something. It's so hurting to the soul, but still you got a soul. But when this white man is hurting, it penetrates right through and he got a hole in his soul, brother.

It's soul when you could walk around raggedy and still smile. Or pick cotton, knowing that this ain't the way it's supposed to do, but you need this here dollar to eat, which they call soul food. He can't get this. He got to have this upper crust which is killing him. He's wondering why we could exist on all this hardship. He say, "I couldn't do it." Because he don't have soul, man.

> Mark Holder's 1980 followup interview appears in
> chapter 11.

WORKING IN a predominantly black industry spares Mark Holder many of the indignities most black men must face in earning a living. The pathos for black men is the belief that to be an adequate provider or breadwinner, one has to sacrifice one's integrity and manhood in the process by acquiescing to belittling treatment and to racist conditions at work. Caught in this bind, many blacks define their masculinity outside of work, in contrast to white men— and in particular, to blue-collar workers—who derive from their jobs or their careers what Andrew Tolson calls a "socially sanctioned masculinity."[1]

Jim Pettit quit a fairly well paying job as a domestic because his Beverly Hills employer made him feel like a boy when she ordered him to scrub the floor on his hands and knees. Since he had a family to support he stayed on that job *one* extra day. Other black men, more practical and less volatile than Pettit, stay on such jobs for years or for their entire lives. The problem, of course, is that if a man refuses work that denigrates his manliness, his sense of masculinity will be even further diminished by the lack of money and capacity to support himself and his loved ones.

Jim Pettit

"These people had been treating me bad all my life,
and I didn't know it"

About the middle of 1966 I really resented white people for the first time. My wife and one of her friends had been talking about honkies. I had been sitting taking in all this information, but it didn't dawn on me until two or three months after. These people had been treating me bad all my life, and I didn't know it.

This revelation changed his attitude toward his fellow workers at Burger House, a fast-food establishment. He started analyzing how people were treating him and several times he let loose hostile outbursts against customers and co-workers. But he kept his job, perhaps because the company was reluctant to fire one of their first black fry cooks in the charged atmosphere of 1967.

Pettit isn't clear how much his difficulties have stemmed from the racial prejudices of those around him and how much his problems are self-created. He had been fired from one job for cursing at a countergirl who was pushing him to work faster. Then he went to work for a rich lady in Beverly Hills.

I had to keep the kitchen area clean and the dining room area clean and polish the silver. The first day it was okay. The next day she wanted me to scrub black marks out of this beet-red linoleum. You know how when you walk across a clean floor, you kind of slide and make a mark? I tried not to get down on my hands and knees, but it was difficult not to. Seemed like I was being a boy—this thought had always run through my mind when I was down on my hands and knees. But I kept the job because of my wife and kids.

And then she wanted me to scrub off a spot on the dining room wall that had been there about two years. I said, "Screw it, I'm going home." I'm a cook, I should be making at least four hundred, five hundred a month.

When I first started Burger House, I thought it was going to be groovy. This friend I kind of liked was white. We talked over problems. He asked me about Negroes, about their education. And he said, "Don't get me wrong, I got all kinds of colored friends." He said, "I ain't prejudiced." I said, "Yes, you are. You a damn liar." I learned after they transferred him that he was the most prejudiced person [at] Burger House. My wife had told me honkies will tell you, "I ain't prejudiced, Negro friends are my best friends."

They brought somebody else there. He tried to get along with me, but he was just the same. One day this black boy was riding his bike across the street, and this white man hit him in a car. I said, "The honky was in the wrong," and we argued all day. He said, "Is there anything that you can think of that you are being deprived of because of your color?" It made me so mad, I couldn't think of anything. How could he deprive me of my own opinion? I wanted to say, "This is what I felt, so you feel how you feel and I feel how I feel."

After that they put me over on MacArthur. I thought I had a friend over there, but he was a honky just like all the rest. He was married to a Japanese or a Chinese, and I felt that he could understand more. I got to telling him all my problems, all my business toward my race and color. I wanted to know how they felt about me. He gave me a few good suggestions. He said it was all in my head—I was exaggerating things too much, I was creating my own problems. He said I think the whole world is against me. I found out later he was like all the rest of the white guys that worked for Burger House. They were always telling lies or telling things on people and going back and saying, "This is my best friend."

After that they put me out on San Pablo. My first day two girls come up and said, "What's that nigger doing in there?" Like I wasn't supposed to hear. I wasn't going to pay any attention because I had got really bad in talking against the white man. If people didn't say thank you, I said, "You're welcome." I had to say something to irritate them.

As time went on I got acquainted with the people and they kind of looked at me with respect. They took a lot of shit off of me while I was working there. I don't think nobody is going to put up with me cursing out the customers, and cursing at the employees, wanting to fight somebody, and telling Mr. Barnes to kiss my ass. Mr. Barnes came in and called me a boy, and I had been telling Ray [the manager] the same day I didn't like to be called a boy. It makes me feel shitty, it really does, because I feel that I am a man.

I kept coming to work late because I couldn't get up and sometimes I couldn't catch a bus. They put me down to five days a week and I was just sick of them. And then my change of life came in. Where you start accepting life the way it is. And I realized my associates actually had been treating me good. I brought all of this on my own self. I still think they prejudiced. But I don't think it was as bad as I did when I was working there.

I brought my problems home and my wife made it badder; I brought my problems to work, back and forth. My wife and I get along very bad. I suppose I bitch at her a lot. I'm trying to get ahead, and it seems like she's holding me down. I tell her when you're not using the light and you're not looking at TV, please turn it off because the light and gas bill is very high in that house. If she could help me, this would make it a lot easier, because it is not too good getting out there working every day and not really seeing anything. You don't have enough to pay this bill, and when your wife gets on you it's bad, because you got all these problems to think about and then here she comes talking about some damn eyeliner shit. I don't buy myself anything. I cook dinner, wash dishes, and clean up the whole house. And she still comes bringing it up in my face that I don't appreciate her.

> Interviews with Jim Pettit in 1979 and 1986
> appear in chapter 10.

THE IMPACT of work on family life and self-esteem is an important theme in the next interview also, as Frank Casey describes how unemployment eroded his ability to be a father to his children and how a fulfilling job restored his sense of self-worth.

Frank Casey

"They call me an instigator"

During the 1960s the Johnson administration's Great Society programs created jobs for low-income and street blacks who lacked educational credentials and conventional work histories. One such project was a New Careers for the Poor program in Richmond, California, which trained low-income minority residents in subprofessional positions with the schools, the police department, and community organizations. The project was based on the premises that "indigenous" members of the community might have a special calling for the human services, because they themselves had experienced poverty and discrimination, and that their life experience, "mother wit," motivation, and ability to communicate would more than compensate for the absence of standard qualifications.

Frank Casey was one of the school-community workers hired to bridge the gap between the predominantly black parents and children and the predominantly white teachers and administrators. When I interviewed him in 1967 he was thirty-one. With a ninth-grade education, he had swept floors for a living, cleaned streets, hustled a little, but never found steady work. Years of irregular employment and welfare had demoralized him.

In this "new career" which he "wouldn't trade for anything," Casey is fired by an intense identification with his clients: low-income parents, the unemployed and underemployed people who didn't get "the break" that he did, and schoolchildren who remind him of his own trials growing up.

There's something about each child—black and white—I don't give a damn who it is—that I have a little bit of me in. A little bit of something in me when I was a little boy. I'm not a bragger, but I feel I'm very settled when I'm working with kids. It comes to me very easily. I can understand them. I can talk with them. They're not going to hold too much back from me; that's girls and boys.

It's all in the way that you talk with the kid. Authority ain't going to get you nowhere. If you're joking with them, pretty soon they'll say, "You know my teacher, I just don't like my teacher." "Aw, no, what do you mean you don't like your teacher? You know you got a good teacher." I'm joking. But the thing about it is, *he's* not joking. He means exactly what he say. And while I'm joking with him and laughing with him, he's going to tell exactly what's on his mind. And when you get to understand what brought him to room 2403, then you can say, "You know, you could be right. Maybe she is a little bit too unjustified to you. Maybe she isn't giving you enough attention. And then maybe there's something you want and she can't come to your aid, by her having so many kids in that classroom."

And then the child can come in and talk to the teacher. And she has another look at this young man or this young girl that have given her so much problem, and she needs to deal with in a different kind of way. And then if you're any kind of a teacher, you gonna find some way to talk to Johnny or Mary and show them why things shouldn't be this way and we can work together.

Frank was the eighth child in a poor family. When he was but two months old, his father died. In school there was prejudice and misunderstanding. In the ninth grade he took a swing at his teacher. He was expelled, and that was the end of his formal education.

I watch him in room 2403, talking to kids who have problems with their teachers. His manner is relaxed and easy as he helps them see the reasons for the school's rules and regulations. Without blaming, he gets them to explore the part that they played in the chain of events that brought them to the school-community worker's office. He is teaching responsibility—if kids learn that at an early age, Frank says, they'll be spared a lot of grief later on.

At first many teachers felt threatened by these new workers and questioned their lack of credentials. Casey himself began with a general distrust of teachers, especially the white ones. But he has seen teachers who once wouldn't even talk with Negro children make great changes. Their sincerity helped restore his faith in people.

Administrators are another matter. All their "doubts, policies, rules, and all that crap" hamstring teachers who would put forward new ideas. "They just keep you from doing what you want to do. I know [policy] is important. But damn, ain't there another way?"

Preparing for a conference on the mentally retarded, with whom he works closely, Casey talked with parents about the shortcomings of the school's program. At the conference he read a list of questions that the parents wanted answered. His supervisors were upset. Though he was authorized to be there, he had not cleared this action in advance. They talked of not rehiring him the following year.

I'm going to say what I believe, and [if] this is what they consist of agitating, troublemaking—I'm going to be one of the biggest damn troublemakers they ever heard.

[They think] I should be grateful that I'm wearing a white shirt and a suit every day. To me that's not it, just wearing a white shirt and suit. That doesn't give me any more dignity than I had before.

- *Where does the dignity come from, the real dignity?*

Of knowing that I can help people, knowing I'm helping myself doing this, not going back because I got me a suit on, and the people I'm working with got some overalls on, and I'm supposed to do them like they have been doing us so many years. Just pushing [them] down, and say, "Looka here. There's nothing I can do for you." I couldn't do this because doing it would hurt his kids later on. Because he will suffer from what has happened to him, and he will be unable to go out to his children to help them, because he's so drowned. Fear that he feel, is just like looking into a mirror. He's there, but there's no reflection.

And this is the way I was. [My own] kids could look up to me, but they wouldn't see anything. They see me in the morning when they left to go to school, they see me when they came from school at two o'clock, they see me on the days the school is not in progress. They knew I wasn't working. They knew I was getting aid from the welfare. They couldn't see me in a role really, like, you know, a father will go out with his lunch bucket and come back all dirty and tired. I wasn't that way, because I didn't have no job. And a whole lot built up within me that made me feel that I wasn't no father no more. I wasn't nothing but an empty shell. And I couldn't throw out to my kids what I wanted to. And I couldn't even help them, even with homework—not that I didn't know how, but inside of me I felt that I couldn't.

And this is the same way that I see other people, other men out here now. Only they didn't get a break like I did. I got a break and I'm working. I'm bringing in money. My kids can begin to identify themself a little bit with me, because I work in the school, and they know I'm helping other kids. So now when they say shut up, what they saying is, "Be glad you working, and don't do nothing to destroy it, or you be right back down there where you was." I'd rather be back down there where I was than to get up here and deny them, the people that's in the community.

- *Suppose you had played the game?*

If I had just stayed quiet and did my work, I'd see the image of that other man when I go to that mirror. The one that is asking me, "What can you do for my family? How can you help us to help ourselves?" See, I'd be lower than a snake to turn my back and say, "There's nothing I can do."

And I'm not hurting the school either. I'm helping the school. They call me an instigator. All right. But I feel I'm instigating for a cause. I see things happen way before they happen, and I'm trying to say, "Let's do something," instead of waiting until it happened and say, "If I had a known that, it might had a worked out different." Let's get all those hard feelings out, and then let's work together.

You only going to climb so high [because] the white man has every way you can think of to push you back down. It might be money. It might be they find something in his past, hold it over him. Might be because he didn't keep himself quiet. The white man's thinking a hundred miles an hour. He's going to find a way. He knows he's got to keep ahead of the black man.

At nineteen Casey was a chauffeur in the air force, driving generals around Europe and Korea, and he had made airman first class. A sergeant from Georgia began calling him "boy."

I told him I stopped sucking lollipops a long time ago, and I stopped wearing short pants, and I'm in what you consist of United States of America Air Force, and I must have been a man or they wouldn't have let me in. He told me I was a smart aleck and stop being insubordination to him. So I lost my stripes, and that meant I was decreased in pay, and set back. But I felt good, real *good*, after I let him know that I was a man, and that if he wanted to give me orders, he'd better begin to treat me like a man.

He doesn't hear so much "boy" or "nigger" talk today.

Now they say, "You're all right." Patting you on the back, laughing and smiling with you, and tearing you up when you gone. See, I don't want nobody patting me on my shoulder, especially the white man. Now don't get me wrong. I'm not down on all white men. Some of them are very dedicated. But I've listened for years and years and years to what happened to my people and what is still happening to me, so instead of me opening up, and say, "God made all of us brothers regardless of what color we are," I can't open up because all this other stuff is on top of it, keeping it down.

Still, Frank Casey is hopeful. If God would let each white person be black for a day, he says, things would be better, whites would understand. He already sees the spirit of teamwork developing in his community: teachers and parents are working together, and black kids and white kids are talking to each other. But to really move forward, the school bureaucracy has to change too: "The world is changing, so they cannot do things like in the older days."

Next fall the demonstration project is ending, and the community workers will be placed on the school's payroll. Frank has already told them he's not going to change, and he expects that within a year they'll have found some way to get rid of him.

When I leave, I'd be willing to bet my life that they are going to be having somebody else doing the same thing that they said I was instigating. Because sooner or later they going to realize when you doing people unjust, it's going to come back on you some kind of way.

> Frank Casey's 1978 followup interview appears in chapter 12.

ALTHOUGH SIX of the seven narratives in this chapter are those of men, black women have always played a crucial economic role, contributing proportionately more than their white female counterparts to the incomes of their families. During the 1960s black female participation in the labor force increased dramatically as hundreds of thousands of women of all races went to work for the first time. But most noteworthy was the historic change in the kind of work black women did. In 1940 fully 60 percent of black women were employed as private household workers; by 1960 domestic work was still the largest single occupational category (46 percent); but by 1970 only 15 percent of black women were still cleaning the homes of whites for a living, and most of these were women in their fifties and sixties who had started out in such work. Women in the younger generation were working in stores and offices as sales and clerical employees, a category of black female employment that increased from 10 percent to 21 percent during the 1960s.[2]

But even with these greater opportunities, black women such as Carleta Reeves, whose story follows, were still likely to be placed in dead-end jobs, tedious or physically demanding work without opportunities for advancement or personal growth.

Carleta Reeves

"I'd come home bitching and yelling"

Anything that we as blacks do is always better than whitey. 'Cause we're for real. We can dance and they can't. (*Guffaws.*) And most anything else! (*A torrent of laughter.*) I think that we appreciate life much more than they do. We know what it is to suffer; we know what it is to want; we know what it is to be abused. And misused. I can't explain it. Black people have soul.

After high school Carleta Reeves worked for the University of California for four years.

The reason there were so many blacks in our department [at the university] was because it was menial labor. Women had to stand on their feet eight hours a day, running the mimeograph machine, running the xerox machine, running the multilith machine—which is very strenuous work. I ran the multilith for a year! And my doctor eventually took me off of it, because of the fact that I have a bad back. And that's the reason that they have so many blacks, because they know we'll work.

There's no opportunity for advancement. I felt I was a valuable asset to the department and I wasn't getting paid for what I was doing at all. Salary for a multilith [operator] starts around four hundred fifty, four hundred ninety dollars [a month]. When I was running the machine, I was making something like three hundred eighty-six dollars, maybe not even that much. They said I couldn't get the multilith title because I hadn't been there long enough. Then they hired a friend of the supervisor. She got the title.

I feel I was resented. Because I was capable of running *all* the machines in the office, whereas the supervisor, she couldn't. And many times I had to fill in for girls that were out. And anything I did, there were no errors, but I was never given priority for raises or advancement. If I went to Personnel for a transfer, they would always say that there were no openings. But many of the whites got transferred.

The supervisor was white. The assistant supervisor was white. And when both of them were out, there was one black lady who usually was in command. And the reason was that she kissed up to whitey. And then, too, she had worked there for years. But as far as her telling me what to do, I didn't pay no attention to her. 'Cause she was just like whitey. And whatever went down, she ran back and told 'em the next day. And I didn't dig that coming from another sister, you know. That department was just *all screwed up!*

I should've been getting a five-percent raise, but I never did. And I never bothered to mention it, because being black there's some things that you just don't say because you're afraid you might lose your job.

■ *Did you feel angry a lot of times?*

Very much so. Angry, disgusted, used. I'd come home bitching and yelling. I'd just blow up every time I'd get home. And every time I'd get ready to go to work in the morning, I'd be sick. It built up to the point where I didn't give a damn whether I had a job or not! My husband had tried to make me see: "Okay, quit, it's better for you." And around the last two months it got to the point where if she said anything to me, I didn't give a damn what I said to her, because I just didn't care anymore. If she didn't respect me, then I didn't feel that I had to respect her. Whereas before I respected her because she's my boss.

When my last raise came up and she gave me that two and a half percent—

I deserved seven percent really—I told her how I felt. Then it was, "Oh, Carleta, why are you leaving?" And I knew it was a front.

Today she's working as a secretary for a black community organization in San Francisco. The job enables her "to do something for my own people."

My husband was off this past week because he was in an accident. And he was saying how bored he was. And I was telling him this is something that you just do every day, you get in the habit of it. Nobody wants to work, if you could have money coming in, you know. But twenty-four hours a day, what would you do with it? I can't even start to think what I'd do with it. I get up, I go to work, I come home, and then I do what I have to when I get home, 'cause going to work sort of makes my day.

For followup interviews with Carleta Reeves in 1978 and 1986, see chapter 12.

THE ALMOST obsessive concern with Uncle Toms in these interviews suggests the depth of the inner conflict between personal integrity and career achievement that so many black workers experience. The fear that acceptance in the white world implies that one has sold out one's race and one's true self has made black people, and possibly black men in particular, ambivalent about success and social mobility. The tendency to dismiss middle-class and professional blacks as Uncle Toms unless the individual has clearly demonstrated militant credentials poses so heavy a psychological burden that many people decide it is better not to aim too high.

Successful achievers like Dr. Henry Smith, whose story closes this chapter, are the most likely to be labeled so disparagingly. And if they have been trained in all-black colleges and professional schools, as Dr. Smith was, they also have to face their own doubts as to whether their preparation has been as good as that of their white colleagues. Henry Smith resolved these self-doubts during his residency at an integrated hospital, and his achievements illustrate another path that minorities have taken in pursuing their personal and vocational aspirations within the context of racial oppression.

Henry Smith

"This was my means of retaliating"

Dr. Henry Smith, a forty-one-year-old surgeon living in Fresno, California, began practicing medicine in 1961. At the time most black doctors received their training in segregated medical schools and hospitals. His experience suggests some of the advantages of the Negro school system. From grammar school on, his teachers were dedicated and instilled in him high levels of motivation, achievement, and racial pride. He grew up in Parkin, Georgia.

My parents operated a shoe shop and a cleaning and pressing establishment. There were six of us in the way of children: four boys, two girls. All of us participated in earning a living. Either help repair shoes or deliver clothes, shoes, or what have you. And one of the earliest experiences that I remember rather vividly was one afternoon, summertime, quite hot, humid heat. I'd made a delivery on my bicycle. As any youngster would be, I was riding, singing, whistling, pumping the bicycle. Passed a service station and was beckoned to come over. He asked me to sit down. And as I sat down, a little button was pressed, sort of a shock device, and I jumped up, more afraid, I think, than hurt. But this was a "big joke," and of course I did not do anything about it. Later, I passed by that store at night. I had my rock and the window was broken. This was a means of retaliation as I knew it.

His teachers instilled in him "the doctrine of being the best that you could be under the circumstances, no matter what you were doing." He gives them part of the credit for his ability to compete with whites "more or less on the same basis" all his life.

The first of each year our teachers would ask, "Whadda you gonna be when you grow up?" And from my mother my first knowledge was, "You're gonna be a doctor; you tell 'em you're gonna be a doctor." So I began saying this every year. And probably by the sixth grade I did like science. And this began to grow on me, so that I felt that I was mentally bound to continue. And I didn't really think anything about how I would fare as a Negro in medicine.

There was only one Negro doctor at home. If there was a patient who was sick enough [to] go to the hospital, then he would have to refer the patient to another doctor. And by the time I got into college, they had finally allowed him to practice in the hospital. And of course he was restricted to the segregated wing. And the delivery room and so forth, these things were completely inadequate for the work that you had to do.

I got into Howard and began rubbing shoulders with students who did go to school in northern or western states. And as you begin comparing grades, and in class your oral pronouncement to instructors, you begin to understand that, well, there's not really a *lot* of difference. There were doubts, you know . . . particularly having come from a high school with only the eleventh grade. And after college, I spent an additional year at Ohio State studying toward a masters in biology. My appraisal of how I did was certainly above average. And these things begin dispelling some of the negative attitudes I had concerning myself.

But after medical school you still don't know how you are going to respond as a finished product. My next level was a segregated hospital in Kansas City. *There* there was no real chance for comparison. But when I got into service, I was placed with doctors, one of whom had finished Harvard, another from University of Pennsylvania, another from the University of Illinois. All of us then were practicing on the same level, and there was no doubt in my mind that I had gotten a good education—comparable to the other fellows.

Why did I go to Howard and not a white medical school? Maybe deep within, there was an inner feeling that I may not be able to make it at Illinois or Michigan. I really don't know. *If* the feeling were present, I think it has been erased, but I was never really aware of this as an intention for going to Howard. I liked the school! The doctor at home was a Howard doctor. And the men who'd come back to visit, they would give us a feeling, well, you're getting a real good education. You've got the same, you know, curriculum as these guys from Oxford. . . .

■ *Is there racism in the medical profession?*

(*Low, subdued voice.*) Well, I think so, yes. I had friends who were looking for specialty residencies, a lot of whom were turned down because they were Negro. Particularly in the field of obstetrics and gynecology. The medical profession as a whole . . . there has been a change, although it's certainly got a long way to go. Four to five years ago at one of the local hospitals a Negro patient would be placed either in a private room or a ward room. This did not give him a free choice. I may not have been able to afford a private room, and I may not have wanted to go in a room with four, five, or six people. I went to the administrator and was told that this was *not* the policy of the hospital. But other people admitted that this *was* the policy. And following this I looked for evidences of racism each day or time I'd go into the hospital. How was this Negro treated compared to another patient?

My own treatment? I think I would disregard the social aspects, because it doesn't pertain to qualifications, it's more of an individual like or dislike. But from the strict medical aspect, I personally feel that my treatment has not been much different. Well, I'm sure that there has been *little* differences that I don't know about. But as far as overt expressions of dislike, I've not felt it. I can go to any of the hospitals in town and in my specialty I can do any of the things that I am qualified to do. I have not been called before any committees of self-discipline within the medical profession. So that I've had no reason to feel that they were checking me out particularly. When I first came, course, I was much more acutely aware of who was gonna make the first move against me, so to speak. And I may have been a bit more cautious than I am now, but I found no real attempts to do this. And Dr. Lawrence and Dr. Wilson [Negro doctors who preceded him in the area] had something to do with it.

When I came here I selected sponsors, white surgeons, based on the other Negro doctors' telling me that this guy's all right, that guy's all right. The first surgical patient that I had was a little white boy, extremely ill. And one of the white doctors who was a sponsor, we went over the patient together and ultimately [I] had to operate on him. And luckily for me, things went extremely well. Things that I heard after that were all complimentary—I've never really heard anyone by word of mouth make any remarks that were derogatory. There are times when you will walk up on a conversation in progression, and the conversation will, you know, cease. Now, these things we know happen, and what they were talking about before you never *really* know.

I was doing a six-months urology residency, and I presented the case of a complicated problem regarding the urinary system, whether it was a stone or what they call nephritis, or whether it was a tumor, now I don't recall. The discussion began, and all of a sudden one of the staff urologists says, "Gee, I don't know, but there's a nigger in the woodpile someplace." When he said that I *stared* directly at him, and his face got real red 'n' everyone else in the room got quiet. And the conversation then went on. Now in a situation like that, I think that they just sort of forget that "this Negro" is here. In other words, he has been—I don't say accepted, but his presence has been forgotten. *Personally* I was treated no different from what I thought the white resident was treated. So once they tend to accept you—whether it's just a superficial acceptance or not—they forget, and things like this are said which I'm sure would not be said if they were constantly aware of my presence.

I was sitting in the doctors' lounge and an ambulance attendant asked me what did I think of this Black Power, that here was a guy on television advocating power and violence and so forth. And to be frank with you, I had not heard the term used. And I told him, I think Black Power is good; for years the power has been white power. You have all the courts, you got all the policemen, you have the so-called power structure. And you've been using it in the wrong manner. I don't look at Black Power as a form of violence. We get together, as a group, so that we can vote for what we want, we can do what the initial economic boycotts were doing—all these things to me, is power.

When Dr. King was assassinated, I actually got—got angry. When I first heard it, of course I didn't believe it. I was here working when my wife called—asked had I heard the news. So I went and turned the radio on. And then a feeling of real *anger* hit me, and I didn't really know where this anger should be pointed. Course, I was quite sorry to see his loss, because I think he was the most influential as far as instilling within the Negro the incentive to push forward. And being in medicine, I got thinking, What certain *type* of person could do this? And then I said, well, it's probably not really his fault— either he's mentally ill, or someone has promised him a certain amount of gain, plus the fact that it's more condoned. Although a lot of people would not do it, I'm sure most . . . not most . . . but a *lot* of the white population would. Or have thought the same thing whether they did it or not.

In that first little experience when I was a boy, I could have kicked the window out or done a lot of things physically. But I knew that I couldn't win, so I didn't do it. Now at the time that I felt I could retaliate, then I did re- taliate. It was in a sneaky manner, so to speak, but I *did* it and I got a self- satisfaction. If I had carried this frustration for a long, long time, I think it would've done much more harm to me. Later, I would do it more or less as the Man is doing it. If I've had contact with a resident and if I heard little remarks that was not complimentary, or something that he said to a patient, and I got to be his chief—he just didn't get the kinda case that he wanted. This was my means of retaliating.

The 1981 and 1986 followup interviews appear in chapter 12.

PART TWO

1978-1987

GROWING OLDER
IN THE SEVENTIES
AND EIGHTIES

The Ambiguities of
Racial Change

Sitting in the park one hot summer afternoon in 1981, Florence Grier pointed to a group of black men, mostly in their early twenties, just standing around. There was no work for them, and the likelihood was small that there ever would be. Until that situation changes, Mrs. Grier told me, she would continue to question how much had been accomplished during the activist sixties, and she would continue to be pessimistic about the future, especially because the schools were not preparing black youngsters to do much more than stand around.

Like many of the people I reinterviewed (black as well as white), Florence Grier experienced measurable improvement in her own circumstances during the 1970s. But she saw herself as the highly unusual exception—as did many of the Afro-Americans I talked to. They reported extremely positive changes in their own lives coupled with a skeptical, even negative, assessment of the progress of black people as a group.[1]

With some exceptions, whites were much more positive about racial change. After the turbulence of the sixties, they were tired of the racial issue and wanted to put it behind them. They were also impressed by the success of integration. They have seen blacks and other minorities come into the places where they work or study, become visible in politics, the media, and the arts. But the relatively few middle-class success stories and "superstars" the whites see don't seem that significant to the blacks, who focus instead on those who are poor, jobless, in jail, or on drugs—struggling folks rarely seen by whites in the course of their daily lives, but whom successful blacks know as friends, neighbors, or even relatives.

Blacks are inevitably more sensitive than whites to the nuances of racism. They are alert to its various and varying forms and make more distinctions as

163

to what has changed and what has not. In their view, today's racism is more subtle, and therefore harder to fight, than the overt discrimination of earlier times. When they were excluded from a school or a job or from political par-ticipation, they could fight to open the doors, to become part of "the system." Today, people are in those doors, or halfway in, or at least a few have entered. But once inside, they still encounter barriers. They feel that the deck is stacked, and not in their favor.

There is truth to both the black and the white perspectives on contemporary racism: they focus on different aspects of a complex picture of two decades of uneven racial change. The black perspective, I believe, reflects more of a long-term historical outlook and a deeper and more comprehensive understanding of the ambiguities of progress and stagnation. In the last two decades we have seen both a greater acceptance of people of color and a disquieting return of bigotry and racial hatred. The situation is further complicated because the degree of change varies markedly from city to city and by social institution, and because black America itself is so split between those who are "making it" and those who have been left behind. One of the few sure generalizations is that the South has changed more profoundly than the North or the West.

North and South

During the 1970s and 1980s race relations in the South have varied by county and city, as the vastly different experiences of Florence Grier and Howard Spence on returning to their hometowns suggest (see chapter 8). Nonetheless, and despite an increase in Klan activity in the 1980s, there will be no return to the traditional forms of racial segregation in the southern states. While neither the "slavemaster" nor the "slave" mentality is dead, black southerners will no longer be intimidated from voting, exerting political influence, or defending themselves against racial attacks.

Southern blacks still lag behind whites economically, educationally, and politically. But school desegregation is more advanced in the South than in the North (despite the private academies whites use to circumvent it), and southern cities have made more progress than northern ones in reducing the still prevalent residential segregation.[2] Most scholars agree that the South's superior performance reflects a stronger commitment to change, though in part the region simply had further to go because of its segregationist and discriminatory patterns. In southern cities especially, the northern pattern of black bifurcation—a growing middle class *and* a growing underclass—is replacing the more cohesive community of the past. Too, an old-fashioned racism remains entrenched in many places. At the University of Mississippi and other southern colleges, white students flaunt the Confederate flag as the number of blacks on campus increases.[3]

Despite the virtual elimination of Jim Crow practices, segregation and even resegregation continue on a de facto basis, both in the South and in the North. More blacks now live in suburban and better urban neighborhoods, but metropolitan areas are increasingly divided into predominantly white suburbs and central cities that are becoming more black, more brown, and more Asian (with the arrival of new immigrants). Despite some improvements during the 1970s, Reynolds Farley's observation holds for southern cities as well: "Chicago, St. Louis, and Cleveland were almost as segregated as they would have been if a law mandated that all blacks must live in exclusively black blocks and whites in exclusively white ones"; and in many cities "black and white students go to separate schools, just as they did when 'separate but equal' was the guiding principle."[4]

Another measure of change during the 1970s and 1980s is the success of blacks in electoral politics. In June 1988 black mayors were leading most of our largest cities and were presiding over many medium-sized cities as well. Although in some cases this has meant administering the almost unsolvable urban problems of economically depressed, largely minority central cities for a larger white power structure, this new political influence has democratized access to municipal and public service jobs and has helped consolidate the economic position of the black middle class.

At the local level, the rise in black elected officials has been spectacular, particularly in the South, where their number quadrupled between 1969 and 1979.[5] The tenure of blacks on school boards, city councils, and in state legislatures and the election of black sheriffs and police chiefs have made a real difference in many communities.

Yet the degree of underrepresentation remains as impressive as the gains. Although 12 percent of the voting-age population is black, fewer than 1.5 percent of political officeholders are black.[6] Parity would call for twelve blacks in the U.S. Senate—there are none. Even in Mississippi, where blacks constitute 37 percent of the population, only 10 percent of the state representatives are black.[7] Gerrymandering and devices such as runoff elections continue to limit black political power, especially in the South.

Moreover, this new political influence often benefits middle-class blacks more than the poor and the working class. In Oakland, California, where blacks dominate city politics, police officers typically treat middle-class blacks courteously, while in poor neighborhoods reports of continuing harassment have prompted lawsuits against the city.[8] And the ability of mayors to respond to the urban poor has diminished as the federal government has reduced its financial support and revenue-sharing programs.

Finally, the continuing importance of race in the political arena is suggested by the growing polarization in the 1984 and 1986 elections. Middle-class and working-class blacks vote overwhelmingly Democratic, whereas whites have been moving toward Republican candidates.[9]

The Black Middle Class

Discrimination in hiring and in training programs has lessened significantly over the past two decades, and affirmative action has had an effect in public-sector jobs and in the larger private companies. But small businesses (the fastest-growing segment of the economy) are not governed by the same equal opportunity standards, and expanding companies of all sizes can ensure a predominantly white work force by locating new plants and offices in areas where few blacks live.[10]

On-the-job discrimination persists. It is usually subtle, but not always so. A sociological study of members of the black elite has found that "racism remains a major obstacle in their mobility and in interaction with whites" because whites, in particular white males, feel threatened by upwardly mobile blacks, particularly black men.[11]

But the striking growth of the black middle class is one of the most significant legacies of the civil rights movement. Almost one-quarter of all black families had incomes of more than $25,000 (in constant dollars) in 1982, compared to only 8.7 percent in 1960. Among employed blacks the proportion who hold middle-class jobs increased from 13.4 percent in 1960 to 37.8 percent in 1981.[12] The proportion is even higher for women, whose rapid movement into the white-collar ranks accounted for much of the growth in the black middle class during the 1970s: by 1980 almost half of all employed black women (49.3 percent) were working in clerical, sales, professional, or managerial positions.[13]

This occupational mobility is a product of affirmative action, the expansion of public-sector employment, and, especially, higher levels of education. The number of black college students increased from 340,000 to more than a million between 1966 and 1982. In 1980 some 80 percent of black college students were attending predominantly white institutions, rather than the traditional Negro colleges.[14] However, black dropout rates have been extremely high at the mainstream schools, and since the economic downturn in the early 1980s fewer black high school graduates have been going on to college. From 1980 to 1984 black college enrollment dropped 3 percent nationwide,[15] a decline that has deepened even during the improved economic conditions of the middle and late eighties.

Overall, a much smaller proportion of blacks than of whites has arrived in the middle class, and blacks are more concentrated in the lower middle class.[16] Compared to whites, employment in the public sector accounts for a much higher (and increasing) proportion of the black middle class. Even in professional occupations, blacks tend to be in the lower-paying, lower-prestige fields, though there have been impressive increases in law and medicine since 1978. Among black middle-class families, even more so than among whites, two paychecks are the norm; indeed, a middle-class income is often the result of two working-class wages. A higher proportion of married black women work than married white women, and their average earnings more nearly equal their husbands', since black women have reached parity with white women in occupations and earnings, whereas the gap between black men and white men remains extremely wide.[17]

With a more precarious economic status, the black middle class is highly vulnerable to economic recession, government budget cuts, and even changes in affirmative action policy.[18] Thus the black middle class still lags behind its white counterpart in its ability to transmit its favored class position to its children. Part of this situation is financial: in Bart Landry's 1976 survey, the wealth of middle-class whites was almost two and a half times that of middle-class blacks.[19] But part of it is situational: despite the exodus from the ghetto, many middle-class blacks remain there, and even in partly integrated neighborhoods they cannot always protect their children from the atmosphere of the streets, the pressure of peers, and the inadequacies of the schools.

Even with its newfound purchasing power, the black middle class has no significant influence on the nation's economy or on corporate decision making. In the nation's one thousand largest companies there were only three black senior executives in 1979, four in 1985. There are no black-owned firms in *Fortune*'s list of the five hundred largest corporations, and none of these corporations has a black chief executive officer.[20]

Yet the new black middle class is not a transitory phenomenon; it is not a minuscule stratum; and it is not composed only of marginally middle-class aspirants. In cities such as Atlanta, Philadelphia, New York, Los Angeles, Chicago, Oakland, and Washington, significant numbers of blacks are entering the upper-middle-class ranks. Despite the problems, the upward mobility of many Afro-Americans during the past three decades has been unprecedented in American history.

The Black Underclass

But these gains have had little meaning for poor blacks still trapped in deteriorating ghettos. Members of this underclass have less hope for the future today than they did in the sixties. Traditionally, the ghettos were the meeting ground for both poor and more successful blacks, the site of a shared identity and sense of community, because racism and discrimination limited the possibilities of life for all black people. But the very successes of the middle class have created a class polarization that has weakened this sense of unity. When middle-class blacks find better housing and schools in integrated or previously white neighborhoods, the ghetto is deprived of their economic contributions and their influence as models of success.

Between 1959 and 1970 the percentage of blacks classed as poor fell sharply, from 55 percent to 34 percent. But since then there has been little progress: in 1979 the black poverty rate was 33 percent; in 1986 it was 31 per-cent. Worse yet, the number of poor blacks increased from 7.1 million in 1970 to 9.7 million in 1982. Although the majority of poor people are white, the proportion who are black rose during the sixties and seventies, from 25 percent to 31 percent.[21] The situation has worsened in the eighties: the lowest-earning quintile of black families had 22 percent less purchasing power in 1984 than they did in 1980.[22] Half of all black children are growing up in poverty today.

The seventies and eighties have been particularly difficult for urban black teenagers and young adults as jobs have continued to move to suburbs, rural areas, and the predominantly white areas of the sunbelt. Blue-collar manu-facturing work is disappearing, and young blacks who do not finish high school and college cannot compete for the new jobs in the white-collar, ser-vice, and high-tech industries. Between 1949 and 1979 the proportion of black eighteen- and nineteen-year-olds not in school and neither employed nor looking for work increased from 22 percent to 42 percent.[23] And from 1971 to 1980 unemployment among those teenagers *in* the labor force (work-ing or actively looking for work) increased from 26 percent to 40 percent in New York, from 36 percent to 55 percent in Chicago, to name two cities.[24]

Unsuccessful in school and unable to find legitimate work, many young black males turn to hustling and crime. National statistics for 1980 attribute 51 percent of all violent juvenile crime to black youths. More than 90 percent of the victims of these crimes were other blacks; homicide has become the leading cause of death for young black males *and* females. In 1979 alone, 15 percent of blacks aged sixteen to nineteen were arrested. Today, black men constitute 46 percent of the prison population, and blacks are jailed at a rate eight times higher than that of whites.[25]

Traditionally, black men were more likely than white men to be either working or looking for work. But today fewer than two-thirds of black men participate in the labor force, and about half of them are either unemployed or employed only part time.[26] During the early seventies the official black unem-ployment rate was twice the white rate; today it is almost three times as high.

Although black women in the labor force made impressive gains in the 1970s, they have been hard hit by the "feminization of poverty." More un-married black women are having children, and fewer black men have the steady incomes needed to marry and support a family. Separation and divorce rates are rising. In the mid-eighties 43 percent of all black families were headed by a single parent, and one-parent families accounted for 73 percent of black families below the poverty line. Single-parent families are increasing in the middle class as well. More than half of all black children live with one parent—almost always the mother.[27]

All these developments have seriously undermined the integrity and the unity of the black community. Joblessness and single-parent households have weakened the inner-city nuclear family, and extended families are not as strong as they once were. Even in street life there is less solidarity than in the sixties, as drugs and crime divide the community and create a climate of fear. The increasing distance between the classes makes it harder for Afro-Americans to speak with a unified voice. And an unwelcome by-product of integration has been the weakening of the traditional institutions of the black community. Black businesses, black colleges, and even the black church now compete with white and integrated institutions.

The Racial Climate

In the 1960s, despite the backlash, many white people tended to be sympathetic to black demands for equal opportunity and integration and to feel that black poverty and suffering were the result of objective structures of racial discrimination. But beginning in the seventies and intensifying in the eighties, a conservative zeitgeist has brought forth a very different attitude. No longer are centuries of slavery and racism, or even present-day lack of opportunities, used to explain black disadvantage. Pointing to state and federal civil rights laws, whites presuppose that blacks now have a fair chance to succeed and that affirmative action even gives them an unfair advantage. So, these whites argue, if blacks remain poor and unemployed, it's nobody's fault but their own—especially considering how well Asian-Americans are progressing.* As sociologist Troy Duster puts it: "Blacks have lost the moral advantage."

At the same time, individual blacks are more likely to be welcomed into formerly white worlds—if they meet white middle-class standards of acceptability. Integration and incorporation have taken place even in strategic aspects of culture and national symbolism: black history has become part of the curriculum in many high schools and colleges, and Martin Luther King's birthday is a national holiday in all but eleven states. On television, the Ed Bradleys report the news to nationwide audiences, the Dennis Richmonds (of

---

*Viewing Asian-Americans as a "model minority" and using their successes to denigrate Afro-Americans has become a commonplace argument of the neoconservatives, a group of scholars and social commentators who have achieved considerable influence in political and intellectual circles in the seventies and eighties.

Oakland's Channel 2) anchor local broadcasts, and in white households Bill Cosby's show is the most popular program, with white teenagers voting him their number one hero.[28]

Yet whites also made Bernhard Goetz a folk hero, identifying with his 1984 shooting of four black youths on a New York subway.[29] Black teenagers are viewed with fear and suspicion; welfare mothers, with anger and moral contempt. Thus public race relations, especially between strangers, remain tense. Racial friction is endemic in integrated schools, and incidents of racial conflict have been increasing throughout the eighties. But in situations where people know one another personally—at work, in neighborhood life—interracial contacts have improved markedly.

Whites are less likely today to see people of color in the global, undifferentiated mode of the classical racist tradition. Instead they view blacks more often in terms of class, reserving most of their animus for the poor and protesting too much that blacks similar to themselves would be welcome in their neighborhoods. Because class prejudice is the more acceptable attitude, it is sometimes used to conceal racial feelings.

William J. Wilson, in his very important sociological study *The Declining Significance of Race*, argued that since the late 1960s the "life chances" of black youths have been determined by their class position, not by the color of their skin.[30] Wilson is correct to emphasize the growing importance of class divisions in the black community. But class and race are not antithetical, nor are they reciprocals in a zero-sum relationship where "more class" must mean "less race." Race and class have always been closely connected in American life, and their separate influences cannot be easily unraveled. The black underclass is not simply a product of shifts in the economy and changes in the type and location of available jobs, as Wilson has argued. That blacks without marketable skills live in inner-city ghettos is also the result of centuries of overt discrimination and today's more subtle institutional racism.* Social class does loom more fateful in racial stratification, but the significance of race has not declined correspondingly. Despite the dismantling of discriminatory barriers and some improvement in white attitudes and in day-to-day relations between the races, the separation between blacks and whites, and the racism that feeds on this division, remains a powerful force in American life.

What has declined dramatically since the 1960s is *racial consciousness* and awareness. As Alice Kahn, a Bay Area columnist, capsulizes it: "The problems between black people and white people never got solved. We just stopped talking about them."[31]

---

*Wilson has moved closer to this position in his more recent works; see especially his *The Truly Disadvantaged: The Inner City, the Underclass, and Public Policy* (Chicago: University of Chicago Press, 1987).

I began this chapter by noting the differences between black and white respondents during the second round of interviews in 1978–79. By the third round of interviews in 1986, the two perspectives were somewhat closer. The whites were not quite as positive as they had been in the late seventies, largely, I think, because during the eighties the mass media have focused more on black *problems*, especially the plight of the underclass, than they did in the seventies. Here I discount the whites' personal experiences with blacks as a key factor, for most whites were still leading predominantly white lives. And the blacks I interviewed were less likely to focus only on negative trends. The passage of time has convinced them that at least some of the changes produced by the sixties are real and permanent, whereas eight years earlier they were much more skeptical. Too, over time, their intense initial disappointment in the failure of the sixties' promise of a fundamental, radical social transformation has softened such that they view more objectively the changes that have taken place.

Yet the differences in outlook persist. Whites remain more optimistic overall, more likely to believe that race relations and attitudes have continued to improve through the eighties. Blacks tend to be more fearful that opportunities are tightening up, that during the Reagan years progress has halted and gains have been lost. They are also much more likely to be seriously worried about their children's and grandchildren's futures.

CHAPTER 8

"Still in the Struggle":
Black Activists Ten Years Later

Despite the decline of the national civil rights movement in the 1970s, the three Sacramento activists introduced in Part One—Howard Spence, Florence Grier, and Millie Harding—are still working politically in their communities. But, like other former sixties' activists of all races, they are trying to effect change from within the system. Each has been elected or appointed to influential positions within their communities.

Disappointed with the degree of racial progress and disturbed that the situation of the poor is worsening as the gains of the 1960s are chipped away, these activists continue to protest racial injustice in all its forms. But now they are more concerned with the internal problems of the black community and are more critical of black people themselves for not having taken sufficient advantage of the opportunities that have opened up. Like other Americans in the seventies and eighties, they want a return to traditional values—family, work, responsibility—what Howard Spence calls "the basics." This emphasis on traditional values, however, does not mark a retreat to conservatism. Rather, it reflects their sense of what is needed to rebuild the texture of the black community, whose cohesiveness has been gravely weakened by economic depression, class division, and integration.

The personal lives of these activists have also changed, both materially—new jobs, better homes, greater economic and personal security—and internally. Some, like Florence Grier, downplay the degree of their personal changes, identifying change with inconstancy and a failure to remain true to oneself. Howard Spence, in contrast, views the changes in his attitudes and values positively, as signs of personal deepening and growth. He said that he had changed more during his sixties and seventies than at any other time in his life, and he attributed this to the powerful, often painful, experiences of the 1950s and 1960s. His story makes especially clear the interplay of history and life course, of social change and personal change.

Howard Spence

"I'm going to protect this land"

1979. Though Howard Spence was forced to flee Mississippi in the mid-1950s (see chapter 1), he did not cut off all ties with his native state. Like other southern-born blacks in our study, he made frequent trips south to visit his relatives. In the early 1970s he noticed that people were beginning to view him differently: "I could go in the bank, I could go in the back of the bank and talk to the man about a home." Blacks begged him to return; even whites wanted him to come back. With nothing holding him in California any longer, he returned to the South at the age of seventy-two.

In August 1979 I visited the home in Verian, Mississippi, where he and his wife had settled four years earlier. He is still pessimistic about race in America, for many reasons: black people, at least the poor, are worse off than they were in the sixties; in the South blacks are losing their land to whites; political consciousness has fallen; the old slave mentality is making a comeback; welfare is ruining the black family. And he remains disappointed in the youth—for their unwillingness to work as hard as he did, for their lack of appreciation of his generation's struggle. Foreseeing another upsurge in racial hatred, he wouldn't want to be reborn into today's world.

But personally he feels transformed. He feels free—for the first time in his life—to go wherever he wants, talk to whomever he pleases, pursue his goals. Asked by local whites to run for office, he was elected the town's first black alderman. He is also the building inspector and the food inspector. He was a leading figure in Verian's Bicentennial celebration. He's active in the Emergency Land Service, a southern regional organization started by former sixties' activists, dedicated to saving black people's land. And despite his continuing disdain for organized religion, he built the local black church and taught Sunday School there. In his garage workshop he has more tools than anyone for miles, so he's the local jack-of-all-trades, the man to whom people come to get handles fitted on their axes and hoes. He has two other businesses, a restaurant and an automobile service station, and two future ones that are on the drawing board.

His home adjoins the white cemetery, the only still segregated facility in town except for the new private school "academies." Buried in that cemetery are the very whites who drove him away in the mid-1950s. He feels a sense of vindication in this irony. The boy who was never taught anything in school about government and politics, the man who was almost shot for organizing his people to vote, is Verian's foremost citizen, white or black.

I'm part of the pilgrimage back South. Whether you want to accept it or not. Look at what *Roots* done. I got the book in there. And I looked at it on TV until I couldn't stand it. But the thing about it, people naturally go back to their habitat. I hardly miss a week somebody don't call me from Detroit, Chicago, Rockford—that's where all our people live—and ask, "Can you find me some land?"

You couldn't *give* me a place in Chicago. You couldn't *give* me a place in Detroit or New York or Philadelphia. My wife just come back Monday from Chicago. I got people up there. If they die, well, if they don't bring them home I don't go to the funeral. See, I was there when you could sleep in the park all night and nobody wouldn't bother your pocketbook. I was there when you could sleep with your door open and nobody would bother you. Now my sister's house is barred up like a jail. You go through about three iron doors before you can get inside the house. And they still come in. She put fifteen hundred dollars' worth of bars around her room—these are wrought-iron bars—and she's still afraid to stay at home. And you mean to tell me I want my last days to be like that? When I can sleep with my doors wide open and the birds wake me in the morning and [I can] smell the flowers?

Howard Spence is a quiet-mannered man, benevolent-looking in his old-fashioned spectacles, and well over six feet tall. When I ask him how it felt to come back and build his house on the very spot where the town's mayor had threatened twenty years earlier to burn him out, there is a tone of triumph in his slow, deliberate reply.

I may not have won the whole war, but I won a victory. Because I had it dug out here and had it leveled off for my home, paid a bulldozer twenty-four dollars an hour, and they said you can't build. Now twenty years later, here I am living in the same spot. The people that objected to me being here is buried up here in this cemetery.

If I had a shot those people that night and been killed, I wouldn't have lived to see myself win this victory. Now it may not be a victory for some people. But if I come through all I did and they had everything they had, and I'm living here and they're up there pushing up daisies, I wonder if it isn't better to try to do what's right.

He shows me a hole in an old cedar chest. Twenty-five years ago, the night he saw two Klansmen placing the cross on his lawn, he had picked up his rifle, deciding to shoot them and be killed himself. In a terrible state of mind, he rushed toward the door and somehow the gun went off in the house. At first he was afraid he had shot his wife. Instead the bullet went through the cedar chest, pulling the silks stored inside right up through the hole. By the time he sorted out what had happened, the men were turning the corner.

I'm not afraid about anything happening now. When I was here before, I was afraid. The big difference is I feel free. I'm much more in control. I can make a decision without being afraid. I can go downtown, anywhere I want to, I can talk to anybody.

My mayor, I can call her up tonight, she can come here, talk to me. She's a white woman. And I see a time when she wouldn't come in this house. They walk in there, there's children and grown people say "yes, sir" to me. They don't call me Uncle Howard, Preacher, or boy no more.

The mayor who drove him out of town lies in the cemetery. But the mayor's widow still lives in Verian. The day Mr. Spence moved back, she invited him to park his trailer on her property. The next night she called to offer him a place to stay until his home was built.

I was the first black man that ever lived up there. And when I left out of that place, I put bannisters on the steps, pipe bannisters. I cleaned it from front to back, perfectly. And she said, "I've had a lot of people living up there, but nobody has left it clean like you've left it." Wouldn't I rather have that kind of a compliment than for her to say she don't want no niggers up there? We that *know* better, don't we have to make more of a sacrifice than those that don't know?

The sixties gave us people in higher places. But the rank and file is worse off than they was then. They're on a destruction course. We have more killing, more murder. We have dropouts. Our schools is gone. Our churches is gone. And our business is gone. I'm going to say this—you don't have to accept it—if we could do it over again, I don't think I would suggest integration as what we want. It didn't work. What we should have done was sue for separate but equal.

Our progress shouldn't have been the privilege to eat in a restaurant. What the heck's the difference? Our progress shouldn't be the privilege to ride in a Pullman car, or sit on the same seat of a bus, or stay in a motel. What the heck's the difference? I don't know who's in the next room no way.

They had a trick up their sleeves. Satisfy them. Let 'em stay in a motel, give 'em these automobiles, let 'em be on welfare. Get him complacent so he don't want nothing. *That's why we're losing our land here.* I'm only concerned now—I could give you less than a hoot about anything else—the *land* that we're losing. Black people in America, in Alabama, Georgia, Florida, in Louisiana, Tennessee, South and North Carolina, Arkansas, we're losing land with oil in it. Losing land with timbers on it. They're *taking* it away from us. And we're so busy living, we're so busy enjoying . . . the newfound freedom—which was a newfound confusion . . . we got out of one kind of a confusion and got into a more complicated kind.

I wish I could take you through Starkweather farms. It was *hundreds* of Negroes that had land in there. And they come down from the North—Weyerhauser Lumber Company or Georgia Pacific . . . they bought everything. Price, that ain't no problem. "Would you sell it?" "Yes, I'll sell it." "Okay, here's your money." Now you can drive eight miles through there. And all you see is the land that's been leveled and fertilized.

I sit in a meeting in Belzoni, a big luncheon by one of the lending agencies here. And somehow I got in a conversation with this man. He had one hundred eighty acres in there, sandwiched in between two hostile white farmers. And they were pressing him for lines and margins. This is in the Delta, in Sharkey County. I say, "Have you got a will made for this land?" "No, sir," and he got fifteen children. "What would happen if you die?" I say. "Even your wife living, it wouldn't be long before the whites have that land back in their hands." You don't have no will, they would have to have a partition sale.

Working with the Emergency Land Service (ELS), he encourages people to make wills, to get their land surveyed. He raises money, which the federal government matches, dollar for dollar. ELS uses money to buy land that whites would otherwise gobble up; later ELS sells the land back to blacks. For example, blacks who migrate to the cities often don't keep up their property taxes. Under Mississippi law, whites can pay the taxes for two years and claim the land. But now ELS pays the defaulted taxes. It's an uphill battle: blacks are losing their land at the rate of three hundred thousand acres a year.[1]

When men are in the condition we black men are in and then he don't know no better [than] to have fifteen or twenty children . . . what kind of courage does he have to even try to stay there and feed 'em? They're poor people. Yes, there's something nice about a big family. When they can get along. But it's the worst hellhole in the world when that daddy walk off and leave this woman with all those children. Then you wonder *why* we kill, we murder one another. And the society has gotten so smart on indoctrinating peoples . . . working with their minds that what they have done makes these people become angry because I am black. "I don't want to be black. There's nothing that black people can do." If this kind of a mentality come up in a family of fifteen children, what do you expect that they come out to be? Dope addicts, streetwalkers, what-have-you. Whenever you block a person's future, whenever you make their future look impossible, what kind of a person do you expect to come out of that? A monster or something?

They cut this place up down there in Harms County, in thirty-five-acre plots, and built beautiful homes on it. And people could pay a *minimum* amount to stay in there. And you could raise cotton like mad, you could raise hogs, cows, chickens, everything. A lot of those people could never adjust to having a place where they could be independent. They give it back, and now those people are down there working for the people that got that land. If you keep a person, a dog, or a cat, a slave for two hundred years, what make you think you can free him overnight and he become equal with you? I don't think you can motivate a person that's been on welfare for thirty years. Because the best way to destroy a man is to break his spirit.

So . . . frankly speaking, without a whole lot of rigamarole and a whole lot of talking, we're going to have to educate our people. And our people is got to learn this: responsibility and privilege goes together. If a man don't accept his family and be responsible for his family, he's got no business having any privileges.

I have no hopes for us until each black man get up, and by his ways, by his behavior, by his life, be a better image than just a hand-me-down. We need a *black* image. I'm not talking about somebody to go around and brag about Martin Luther King. Martin Luther King is dead. I'm not discrediting Martin Luther King. You know yourself there wasn't no replacement for Martin Luther King (*sadly*). I have often wondered if he was the Booker T. Washington of this century. But he played his role. And that's no reason why everybody should give us all the privileges and we do nothing—because Martin Luther King was on the scene.

Like those Black Panthers in Sacramento. They were going to rebuild Oak Park. But they never were able to finish anything. The buildings that they had wrecked, they were unable to rebuild those buildings. Therefore we that *lived in the community* suffered. Because we had to go to the outlying shopping districts, which was miles away. I asked them, "Suppose they turn Oak Park over to you. What would you do about the sewage, the lights, the streets?"

■ *How did they answer?*

Wasn't no answer. (*Mockingly.*) "We want to change things." A lot of empty talk and a lot of rhetoric, and a lot of lies. 'Cause you couldn't, you just couldn't *talk* things into existence. You couldn't talk one of these buildings with a new front on it when you done bust out all the glass.

The racial situation is going to get worse. There're more white people beginning to hate us now than ever before. And there's a couple of reasons for it.

One is that the whites are afraid to let the blacks live on the same level with them. It's all right if we can just be a little below him. [And] he don't want to be our father anymore. He don't want that responsibility anymore. And some of *us* don't want to give up that, because it relieve us of having to be responsible. The other reason they are afraid is because they cannot assimilate us. You marry freely into every race but us.

Legislation and political movements are no longer the answer—if they ever were, he says. If black Americans are going to get anywhere, it must be by their own efforts, by going back to "the basics": family, education, traditional skills, and in the South, of course, land.

At the corner of his property line stand two colorful eighteenth-century wagons. He bought them for Verian's Bicentennial and spent a month restoring them. He reveled in the Bicentennial, because "it gave us a chance to go back." With his wife, he helped write up the history of the town.* His home is filled with antique furniture, and everywhere there are signs of his deep attachment to the past. He points to a wild herb, the one his mother treated his cuts with when he was a child, and regrets that today's young people aren't interested in such things.

In 1920 I was working in Jackson, Tennessee. Haul wood, sell wood, one dollar a load . . . I'd go by a land [grant] college. Nothing would have pleased me [more] than to have been able to be in there with them beautiful boys and girls, could have went to school with them, and they had their books and looked like such clean-cut. . . . Here I am, full of soot and dust, driving a wagon and unloading coal—couldn't get nothing else. I didn't even have a grammar school education then. There wasn't nothing—no *hope* for me. My father had all these children. That's the reason I sent my boy to Tuskegee, because my daddy wanted to send me. But he didn't have the money and he was going to work my sisters to death—I didn't have nothing but sisters. So I went to work and I sent my sisters to school, used to help my mother with them. 'Cause they separated.

When I was twenty-five and at the height of my manhood, strengthwise, I wouldn't have a job unless it was hard work. Proving that I'm a man. (*Mimics deep macho voice.*) "I'm strong, I've got everything you need." We got young men that way now. But when you get my age, you going to be saying, "Well, I wish I hadn't a done it." 'Cause his legs going to tell him and his arms going to tell him. . . . Until now I didn't know how wonderful and how fearful the

---

*Verian's Bicentennial events were thoroughly integrated, except for the time capsules buried under the library cornerstone, which are to be opened in 2076. Mr. Spence filled the black capsule; though he had a richer collection, there was little difference in cultural content between the white and black capsules.

body was. There's nothing man will ever come up with that will even emulate this beautiful body of ours.

God didn't make nothing ugly. The most ugliest creature you can find—I got some toad frogs around here, I can't hardly cut grass for killing them. And it breaks my heart to see the blade chop 'em up. Because in his awkward, bumpy self, he's just as beautiful to me as any flower out there in that yard. Because God made him. Whoever made us, made him. These birds that you and I looked at today, they know I'm their friend. They come to this window and sings. I buy sunflower seeds and feed them. So on a cold morning when snow is on the ground and these birds are peeping around that window, they gets food from me until that snow's gone.

I made a birdhouse. I made half a dozen, give 'em to people. I say, "Put 'em up." If God made this bird to like a house and he didn't make him so he could build a house, why don't you build it for him? He put you over everything. It makes as much sense to me as building one for myself. This is God's *creation*. Take care of his creation, don't destroy it.

So many people see what I'm doing—you'd be surprised at the little boys that will think about me. Where I got my ideas was from old men—they'd be a hundred fifty years old probably now, if they'd a been living. And I saw that man when I was a child—he made baskets—and he left an impression on me.

Ideas or seeds, he's "a great hand" for planting them, and whether or not he'll be around to see them, he knows they'll grow. Like the pine trees, like the ideas of which he's had "just a gander" all his life and only now, home in Mississippi in his last years, is able to put into practice. Hold on to your idea, keep it until the time is ripe, the soil favorable, he counsels. And you need time and space, physical space and spiritual elbowroom. This gives courage.

One such idea is his restaurant, which he opened two months ago. He started it, not for profit, but to fill a need in Verian and to create jobs for blacks. He has three employees and business is pretty good, with more than half of his trade coming from whites. We're sitting there, eating the superb soul food, and an attractive white woman comes in. I look to see if Spence's nephew Jack, reputed to be quite a "lady's man," is looking at the woman as intently as I am, but he seems to be keeping his eyes to himself. Later, back at the house, I ask if it's still dangerous for a black man to "look over" a white woman. Spence scoffs at the notion: Jack doesn't like light women, period! Every day in Verian, black men, usually from the North, bring their white women into the stores. And nobody cares anymore, he tells me, although he doesn't like to see mixed couples flaunt themselves. The upsurge in intermarriage he calls "a terrible situation" that makes race relations worse.

It's hardest on the children, he continues, and only after a while blurts out:

*"I might as well tell you the truth about it. My grandbaby is whiter than you
are." His son's second wife is white, and it was a* "terrible *blow"* to him. *Although he's now very close to his daughter-in-law and thirteen-year-old grandchild, he's not comfortable with the situation. He gets embarrassed in public
places when his white kin call him Dad or Granddad, or when his "gritty"
daughter-in-law takes on narrow-minded store clerks. And when his son's family is entertaining friends and business associates, he worries that his presence
might cause them embarrassment. At heart, he still doesn't want to be "mixed
up with them, no more than they want to be mixed up with me. I was born in
the wrong age, in the wrong circumstances."*

In the last ten years I have felt I can do anything I want to do bad enough.
The greatest changes in my life come in the last ten years. Those changes
come after being able to *survive* the sixties. As many times as I could have
been destroyed in the sixties, and wasn't, it made me feel that something
somewhere, greater than me, was sparing me for something.

The police in the streets and the dogs, and like they bombed the church in
Birmingham and killed these little girls. And when I went there, I said, "I
wonder why it wasn't me." It could have happened to me. They could have
bombed my [service] station over there and blowed my brains out.

You know what I'm trying to keep from doing . . . If I spent forty years
hoping and trusting that this would come about and then it comes, and then
we muffed it . . . we bungled it? If we have to relive history and go through
with the struggle that we've had because we didn't take advantage of our opportunities, who's going to survive that? Not me. I can't sit up all night watching over my family with a rifle or something like this. That's over with. But we
better be very careful about what we do in the future. 'Cause if they ever get
us back into that place again, we'll die slaves. We'll *never* get out of it again.
The Ku Klux Klan has promised that, "If we can get all the land away from
these niggers—give 'em whatever they want, give it to 'em. But get the land."
And when they get that land, there's a sign go up: "No hunting, no fishing,
and no trespassing."

See, as long as I got land, I can stay here. I had a surveyor here the other
day. The surveyor guaranteed me within five inches this land was mine, according to the books in Riverton, and he's drawing me a map now. That's
costing me two hundred twenty-five dollars, but that's *my* land. I'm going
to protect this land as long as I can. I'm going to protect this land. This is
my home.

August and September 1986. *Howard Spence and I have two phone conversations. Mrs. Spence had died a year earlier. At eighty-three, he's working less
than before, but remains very active, involved with a newly opened museum*

*for black history and culture in Jackson—he's probably its largest contribu-
tor—and doing volunteer work in a nearby hospital.*

*In Verian, blacks and whites are getting along fine, working together, living
together. There's still plenty of "submerged prejudice," but "there is no discrimination at all." Everything is integrated except for the private schools, whose
high tuitions keep blacks out. "Quite a few" blacks hold responsible positions,
in the banks, the post office, the county clerk's office, and there are black lawyers, doctors, and dentists.*

*In 1980 the mayor of Verian was elected to the Statehouse, and she encour-
aged Howard Spence to run for mayor himself. He was elected by one vote. At
first "it was kinda rough," but his careful diplomacy enabled him to gain the
town's cooperation. During his term, Verian got new paved streets, an improved water system, and a brand new post office. More businesses have
opened, and "you'd hardly recognize the town," he told me.*

Crime and dope, they're really sweeping this country, ruining this country.
First the dope was on the black side of town, now it's all over, in the schools
and everything else. And they're growing it in every bog or swamp place they
can find. That's where your marijuana's coming from. They're turning con-
victs loose here. It puts everybody on guard. People carry guns and their
houses [are] barred up with iron. We used to didn't do it. These are changing
times. I'm afraid. Before it's over, it's going to be something that none of us
have seen before. I don't know what will happen.

Millie Harding

"Dealing with the human issues"

*1979. During the civil rights and black power movements, black women and
their needs were sometimes shunted to the sidelines. By the 1970s, however,
more black women began to publicly question this strategy. At the same time,
the women's movement provoked much criticism in the black community, especially among activists. One objection was that it was a white middle-class
movement, many of whose members had racist or patronizing attitudes toward
minorities and seemed uninterested in the problems of poor women. Second,
increased opportunities for white women, especially at the workplace, could be
expected to come at the expense of blacks, who were just beginning to gain entry into new jobs. Finally, feminism threatened to further strain relations between black men and black women.*

Though most black women chose to "do their politics" within the framework of black community movements, rather than as feminists working with white women on women's issues, the women's movement has had an important impact on the black community. Most of the black women I talked with in the late 1970s seemed more explicitly feminist than ten years earlier—including Millie Harding.

In 1979 Millie Harding turned forty-four. She has raised five daughters and five sons and now works in a community project teaching young people skills to qualify for apprentice programs in the building trades. As part of the training, they paint houses, fix fences, and repair roofs for community people who can't pay for the labor.

I supervise fifteen young people, and I'm the person that makes sure they stucco the wall right or that they put the paneling up properly. I've always been good with a screwdriver and hammer. I never was a knitter or embroiderer. As a young child, my godfather, who sort of raised me, was an auto mechanic, so I found I can put lawnmowers together and take irons and fix them and fix cars. [But] I had to grab me a few books, and a few carpenters and a few painters give me a crash course in how you do this.

The best-qualified kid in this whole project [is a] very attractive, tall, stately black girl. The next-best guy feels very threatened by her. He and that girl vies all the time. Sometimes she lets him make mistakes, because, "If I say he's wrong, he would have jumped all over me, so I just decided to let him go ahead and do it." That cost me an eighteen-dollar piece of paneling.

I think women are beginning to reach the point—I look at my twenty-eight-year-old daughter—of saying, "I don't want to play the role you played with my dad. I don't want to have to not admit that I can play a game better, whether it's a Scrabble game or anything else, because it makes him feel better to win."

■ *Is women's liberation affecting young black females?*

It is affecting young black females and maybe that's because of an influence from older black females like myself. I think black women now are farther from their males than they've been since the fifties. At one time, no matter what the problem was during the day, in the evenings all was resolved because that man and that woman came together—not only in terms of physical being together but spiritually and emotionally. I think the pressures in the later years, because of lack of employment, upward mobility—every time a new movement come into place, wanting to be recognized—the gay movement, the women's movement, and everybody else—means the black movement, who started all of this, has to take a backseat row.

Our men couldn't deal with our dreams and what we want and wish for. They don't want to come home from work and deal with me and what happened at home with the children and why the washer doesn't work. And he has a competition kind of thing when he comes home, rather than resolving and salving and healing so you can go into the next day's battle.

In the black community, our men still see us as sort of an enemy. We've had to become aggressive to do things that our men couldn't do in the South, at a time they could not have stood up and still be alive. It has made our men—shall I say the older guys above forty-five, forty-year-bracket—very sensitive to the fact we are a threat to them. They feel that there ought to be something that we can do "by acclamation" that will put them into a role they feel they rightfully belong in. They also resent us in that they feel the white males have used us to keep black males down.

Black men are finding that white women are more willing [than] black women to be told what to do and when to do it and how to do it. They find them less threatening. They find them more submissive and they're intrigued. So now there are more black males going to white women. I think they are doing a payback kind of thing. This [white] man has violated my women, he's kept me a slave. Here's his woman, so I'll take her.

We've lost so many men in wars and in the street battles of the sixties, and when you start sharing him with a white sister, then that means you've got nothing. White women and I talk about this. [I tell them:] "You're trying to use me and my man to shake or jolt your man into saying you are an individual and you have a mind, you're separate and you're total. You're trying to be an individual. We've been an individual. We're trying to be a unit. And so we can't be sisters at this point because you're winning off the only thing I had to perpetuate my race. You're taking my man. That's all I got left."

There's gonna be a lot of very shook-up black males. So [I] say to my five daughters, "Oh, don't get panic-stricken that you don't have a male now. You have to get ready so that when he comes back with his tail tucked, and needs his wounds healed . . . start from there, that's what you're gonna have to do."

I am a political person. The [white] lady in Alabama that we worked for [as domestics] was very, very political. I watched her wield power in that town and I guess I learned my basics of politics from her. When I came to this town, it had been about fifty-seven years since a black had held any kind of office. So I set as my goal we were gonna put somebody on the city council. I spent my time getting to know supervisors, council people, what kinds of decisions they make, what were their biases. At one time people would tell you I was the best authority on the council. I could walk in the room, look at an issue, and tell how you would get a vote out of that.

Seven of the nine council members were from the same rich neighborhood, because they were elected at-large, not by district. Harding and her friends campaigned to change that, and soon after elected a young black minister. The

minister died of a heart attack, and in the next election eight black candidates
canceled each other out and a white man won. When he resigned, the black
community supported Millie Harding over sixteen other aspirants to replace
him, and the council named her to the open seat.

She moved her office from City Hall to skid row, continued to spend most of
her time on the street, and at meetings would insist that the attorneys on the
council talk in simple language that ordinary people could understand. At first
this offended people, but within two years her expertise and effectiveness had
impressed the council members; seven of the eight endorsed her bid for re-
election. But the local Republicans wanted to get rid of her. They chose a
young black man who had been her protégé, whom she had groomed politically
and taught "street smarts"; he had been like a son to her. People knew that she
would not attack him—"People in this town know how I feel about black
males." But when he waged a very personal campaign against her, she was
caught in a bind between the urge to come out swinging and the ideal she had
always worked for: "the business of creating young black males, not killing
them off." She decided not to attack him, and though she carried the minority
community, she lost by seventeen votes. Afterward, a number of male politicos
apologized to her, acknowledging that she was the better candidate, but that
they had voted against her because they wanted to place a black man in office.

Like Howard Spence, Millie Harding is disappointed that black people failed
to take full advantage of the unique possibilities for racial change in the 1960s.

Blacks, we just run out there and act on an impulse. Nobody thinks it out,
nobody sits down and makes a plan. And because of that, young people have
killed themselves off and produced very little. [The sixties] didn't produce
what it should have. We didn't put the right combination together. It's one
thing to have a lot of energy and a lot of guts, but it's something else to have
some experience to go along with it. Panthers forgot to get their experience
and the expertise to go along with their energy. They ran out there and got the
system's attention for a minute. Then the system said, "We can't have folks
running around saying 'We ain't gonna be pushed around no more.'" So they
took the most vicious way to rid this system of the Panthers.

Look what happened in Watts. Watts is worse off today than it was before
they burnt the first building. They never replaced one house in Watts. The
businesses they burned out are no longer there. Yes, one or two opportunists
made a killing. They got some federal money and they set up their own ge-
stapo rules and a few people got some benefits from it. But the overall black
community of Watts didn't get anything but a hard way to go and a very cold
last winter. Didn't get any more young people any more jobs, any better education, or anything else than they had before.

All of that dying and destruction bred the Office of Economic Opportunity. The president was too busy with Vietnam; he didn't want to deal with niggers in this country then. "Pacify them folks so they'd get off our backs." So they gave some money. I knew that money was short-lived. As soon as they got that thing resolved with the upper-middle-class white America, they were gonna come home and kick niggers' butts for running out and get somebody's attention. And we as black women decided to take in all the training and expertise we could gather, so they can't take what I got up here when the money ran out. There's some very capable women, not only in Sacramento, but all over this country. Most of us are products of that OEO money.

Our young people are off into a self-destruct right now: "I don't care about politics. Who needs to vote? They gonna do what they want to do anyway." There's never gonna be another rioting like you saw in the sixties. This system will not tolerate it. There will be genocide and there will be concentration camps like they did the Asians, but there will be no more street riots as we knew them.

September 1986. *Millie Harding is now directing a civic organization that has been owned and operated by black women for more than fifty years. When the center was faltering, she was asked to "get it back into shape for the community," and she has done just that, supervising a staff of eighty. Low-income people, especially men without jobs, are already lining up for the free noontime meal. The center provides all kinds of services for blacks and the growing number of Asian immigrants and refugees who have moved to Oak Park.*

Vietnamese, Thailanders, Koreans, they're as illiterate as any black you would find. They had washers and dryers [in] this building where they put all the refugees, but nobody dealt with the fact that they couldn't read or write. So when they washed their clothes, they hung them over people's cars. The brothers spend their last dime and hustle every girl they could to buy this little old raggedy car. They went ape down there [when] they came out in the morning and they've got all this crap over their wax job.

What black people see is that a lot of their stores are going to Vietnamese who are getting welfare. The system sets up conflicts and confrontations. Minorities on general assistance don't get medical cards anymore to go to doctors. We have to go to the county clinic. A refugee gets a medical card and can go anywhere. For the people here, that's a slap in the face.

Since the crank [crack cocaine] came out, you walk out of here to the corner and you'll probably run into five, six kids that want to sell you some. The drugs are the only place our folk can get jobs or earn money. The other is to rob, steal, knock open heads. Which is the lesser of the evils, the drugs which is burning their brains out [or] knocking little old ladies in the head with their handbags? I'll say to you what I said to the police: "I'm not going out here and tell no kid on this street, 'Don't go and make fifty dollars for that man delivering no drugs' if I don't have nothing to put in the place of it." How can I do that? I cannot say to a lady, "Don't be on the corner and be a prostitute" [if she] can't get a job or pass a test.

You look at time and then you start saying, "Okay, lady, what's your good-by going to be like?" It's curtain time coming. I got very sick during the late sixties, and I really didn't think I was going to come out of that hospital. And I prayed, "Lord, the only thing I've done since I've been in this world is have a bunch of babies. If you let me out of here, I know I can do more than that." I have stayed in the political arena because I truly like it. I don't like some of the viciousness, but I [made] a difference, dealing with the human issues. I don't think there was a person anywhere in this town that did not feel I did that well.

Florence Grier

"I haven't changed that much"

1979. *During the 1970s, the center of gravity of black politics was shifting from the national level, where male leaders and symbols had predominated, to the local community, where black women continued to play an important, if not leading, role. As Millie Harding said, many of the new women organizers were trained in various programs of the war on poverty during the late sixties and early seventies. Such a government program also provided a job for Florence Grier, who at age fifty-five was getting paid to do the same kind of things she had done on her own in the sixties: community organizing, advocacy, and general social work.*

When a housing office opened in 1973, Oak Park citizens insisted that Florence be hired as a community services specialist. People come into her office with all sorts of problems and grievances: "plumbing, wiring, police problems, eviction notices" or personal needs—a new mother has no money to buy milk for her baby. Mrs. Grier also remains involved in local politics, with the schools, and especially the police.

In the early 1970s a new chief made important reforms in the Sacramento Police Department: officers were to address citizens with respect and were to use physical force or weapons only as a last resort. At least one white officer, the notorious Lieutenant Rivers (see chapter 3), was demoted. The force remains predominantly white, but racial tensions have been reduced. The department is "more answerable" to the black community, and blacks are not as frightened of the police.

Florence expresses little personal satisfaction and refuses to take any credit for her contribution to these changes: "It was the community as a whole. People were doing that all over the country." The county sheriff's department, however, acknowledged her role by appointing her to the board that approves the hiring and promotion of law enforcement officers. She has been "very vociferous" in pointing out the racism of the correction personnel, and her colleagues have learned to respect her forthrightness.

To tell you the truth, I'm not hopeful that we're going to progress in the eighties as fast as we progressed from the sixties to the seventies. Because it's a different struggle now, and those people who have a little bit of a job are not going to be as honest, and they're not going to be as dedicated as people who really didn't have anything.

She lists some accomplishments of the sixties—black students going to college, black history courses, the decline in police brutality—but "the struggle" is never won; it's constant, it goes on. As for herself, "I haven't changed that much. Only difference is that I have a job now."

The people she feels closest to are fellow Christian Scientists in her church, most of whom are white. Christian Science is a way of life: "You live it every single day."

[The Christian Science] concept is the law of love and it says that there is no race of man. There's one race. That there are only ideas and that all you have to do is change things into thoughts.

From the first Sunday that I sat in that church, I've changed my whole sphere of thinking. I honestly have to say to myself that I'm black and you're white. I know that—my color is that. But I don't go into any place and I'm sitting there—these are white people and I'm black. It's tremendous [not] to have that feeling anymore. That's how I'm able to get out there on the street and fight the police department. Because they have no right to do anything but love.

Florence is not at all impressed with the general progress of black people in America. With the new influx of Asian immigrants, she fears that blacks, especially the young men without jobs or hope, will end up at the bottom. And while the sixties did create opportunities, she estimates that only 3 percent of nonwhites were able to take advantage of them. The rest were not prepared, and they've been left behind. As for talk of the new black middle class:

I always say *pseudo*–middle class, I refuse to call it anything else. Because as long as you're aspiring to a place of comfort, and if you have a catastrophe in your life and you're right back where you started, I wouldn't really call you middle class.

Sacramento has more pseudo-middle-class blacks than any other city in this state. Yet Sacramento doesn't have anything blacks put up on their own. Like businesses—well, just the fishmarkets. We have one person out in Del Paso Heights who has a drugstore. We have some doctors.

Places like Chicago and New York City and California, a lot of the governmental places, you've got some blacks with some money. What could be done when you put those salaries together among those people who have been able to move up—there's a twelve-thousand-dollar building sitting there going to ruin, and all you need is, say, three thousand dollars as a down payment. If four or five black men get together, businessmen, doctors, attorneys . . . you don't have to go begging for CETA regulations, and everybody else to put [up] a youth center.

We have not outgrown the slave mentality—that you have to depend on the white man to breathe and to think and to do what you need to do. I'm tired of begging. I'm tired of the rhetoric. Until we find out that we have the power ourselves to do some of the things we're waiting for the Man to do, until that time, we're going to be sort of stuck. Self-help—I think I was influenced by Elijah Muhammad.

So I think a lot of things will have to be changed within the community, within the black community. I think we have a responsibility to produce, and I don't think we can hold the white man responsible at this time. During the struggle we couldn't even get the doors open. But once you're in the doors, sit on the boards, help to make some of the decisions—get some of the information back to the community. If you get in a position, and then you allow yourself to sit there behind a desk and do nothing as a puppet in order to get your money—so, I haven't changed as far as the black elite is concerned. They're not any better. (*Laughs.*)

Although the doors were open in the sixties, Mrs. Grier believes they began closing once whites realized that affirmative action costs them. And she regrets that blacks didn't fully capitalize on that special moment in history, brought about by white guilt and the black movement. A case in point: college special admissions programs. Her son Will went to the university on such a program, and her youngest daughter qualified for regular admission but received special financial aid. Yet along with her children and her friends' children, all of whom had middle-class values and aspirations, another group of students also enrolled:

When the doors were opened, we had whores, we had pimps, you had thieves, robbers, murderers—all kinds of people were able to go into the colleges. So a lot of our young daughters, a lot of young men, when they hit the campuses, they were not able to distinguish between well-experienced prostitutes, pimps, and all the others. Some of the young men fell in love with prostitutes. Some of the girls met guys who were well seasoned in all kinds of . . . shady kinds of work. My daughter was one.

My son got disillusioned over there. He put in about two years. Some of them went on and got their degrees, but others—some of the brightest ones— got caught in the struggle. In the black student unions, they got caught up in a lot of the rhetoric and lost the sense of proportion that they should have had. And those are the people who are the most frustrated of all. Because they didn't make anything for themselves out of it.

- *Was the idea of special admissions a mistake?*

No! You got hundreds and hundreds of kids who went to college that would never have gotten an opportunity. It still should be pushed. The parents would know what they're doing now. The young people who will come on after this will know how to protect themselves.

- *Compared to when you talked to Hardy in 1968, you seem so calm today.*

At the time I made that tape I was in the street almost every single night, keeping the police from beating or killing some youngster. There was just really not a night that I didn't have to leave home at a moment's notice. The police department was carrying guns on top of the car. It was just a battlefield. . . . You couldn't go to Oakland, or you couldn't go to San Francisco, or you couldn't leave here unless you were under a cloud of guns. Kids were afraid to go to school. This whole area was just completely surrounded all the time.

The FBI was causing a lot of the problems. We have the proof now that they went into Black Panther headquarters and they set one civil rights group against the other. I knew all of those guys that were active in the Panther organization. And they weren't no thugs. Those were college guys that were out there on the campus with me. All they were doing at the time [the police] broke into that place, they had all kinds of Post Toasties and things in there, to feed kids breakfast.

She gets tired from carrying on the struggle without any respite. Yet even if she had the money, she wouldn't take off much time—there are just too many people in the community who need her help. But trying to do everything at once, with only a few others helping, is stretching her thin. She would like to reach a wider public with her ideas for building the community, to have a daily TV or radio show, if she could find someone to sponsor her.

She feels her job hasn't changed her except that she was able to buy a nicer home. The real value of her job is that it puts her in a better position to communicate with people in power, people who can get things done. As for status or recognition, she shrugs them off. The community tries to recognize her, but she won't let them. More than once there's been a dinner in her honor or a plaque or other token of recognition presented for her contributions. She just doesn't show up.

Summer 1981. *To my surprise, Florence tells me that the new president's cuts in social programs for the poor may be a "blessing in disguise."*

The welfare system has been taking the creativity away from us. I feel that with Ronald Reagan pulling back some of the funds, somebody will have to think. You can't go to a methadone clinic, because we're going to take the methadone clinics away. You can't go to an alcoholic clinic—there's no place to go and get some extra food. Then the blacks will have to start thinking, and the whites will start thinking. We need some roominghouses. Single men need places to stay. Anybody, right in this community, who's got enough guts to get off welfare can get a great big house with six or seven rooms to it and put you a bed and a dresser into each room. I'm talking about these ideas coming out of your own head instead of going down to the city or the county and saying, "We want sixty thousand dollars to get that house." You understand what I'm saying?

My father couldn't go down to the white man and say, "I need some help with these kids." He had to go pick grapes. He had to sweep, wash windows, work in pool halls, steal, do whatever he could . . . to, to make a living. Plus get out in the backyard and plant some onions and green beans, try to raise a hog. You saw over in my office—we have a garden over behind that center. And you would be surprised at the people who are sitting around, people who have got families who should be in there teaching those kids how to plant turnips and greens. The stuff is not being used.

Maybe Ronald Reagan is saying that some of the things that the government is doing for the people, they need to do for themselves. Even though I've lived on welfare myself, I see a complete "gimme" concept now that robs kids of any will to wash windows, to mow lawns, to wash dishes. Some of it stems from the fact that if this youngster gets out and makes enough money, the welfare department takes some of the money away from them.

And you look on TV, they show you a bunch of little thugs knocking somebody in the head, and that looks smart. Standing around, think you can afford to smoke cigarettes, you can afford to drink beer, you can afford to have everything you want to, and if you don't get it, you kill for it. Or you go rob some old person. I was going to have us eat right across the street [from her office] at the Country Bumpkin. They got robbed last night.

We're eating instead in McClatchy Park, where she and Hardy Frye confronted the police thirteen years ago. She points to where an $880,000 swimming pool is going to be built, shows me the new community center, with its meeting rooms and facilities for senior citizens. Across the street three-bedroom townhouses, each with its own yard, are to be erected for poor families.

You should have heard the clamor from the people that didn't want low-income people. "They're trashy, they deteriorate the property, they cause the children's education to be lowered." [Even Oak Park blacks] went down to the city council and opposed low-income housing in Thirty-fifth Street. As I told them at the county supervisors, out in Oak Park ninety percent of the homes are fifty years old, it's a rundown area. They were clamoring not to have low-income housing in a low-income area. This is what I mean by pseudo–middle class.

It's not really a racial thing, it's getting to be a class kind of struggle. Between the upper blacks . . . Once you move on the scale and your belly gets full, you tend to lose your empathy for the underdog. A lot of blacks have lost their altruism. Once he gets a salary, a couple of cars, and a down payment, and a bunch of credit cards in his purse—he's not any different than anybody else.

MacGeorge [Law School] is buying up everything between here and the freeway. They're going to make it so uncomfortable that you won't want to come in here. And the Oak Park Library that you see there (*pointing*), as soon as MacGeorge gets the people in the community conditioned, MacGeorge is going to take that. Remember I told you that, okay? Now unless the community sets up a howl, I strongly suspect in five years we will probably have to start fighting the police again. If I had enough energy I would alert all the women—and I have to say *women* because in our race usually women have to get up and do it if it gets done.

A police car rides over the curb and circles the park, driving across the grass. "Wonder why he's driving all through there like that?" I sense that her attitude toward the police has hardened since two years ago.

Deep down in my gut I resent what the police do to black men. Because when they emasculate the black man, they emasculate the black woman. As long as you stay on his neck all the time, that real man can't come out and he's still a boy. If he lets it out, if he stands up, he has to leave this country, just like Eldridge Cleaver left, and when he comes back he's just a big whipped dog.

It's worse now than it was then [in the sixties]. "You've had enough and you've been given a chance." It's okay for the police to go in and mow you down now. It wasn't okay at that time because we were clamoring about that. The struggle now has fallen back to the NAACP and the Urban League, [but] they're not doing anything but talking.

Kids today, Florence complains, don't understand that with freedom goes responsibility: "You have responsibility to go to school, you have responsibility to be courteous and to be nice—nobody owes you anything." True, black mothers are no longer beating the rebellion out of their sons, but the sons are not being well disciplined—they lack the courtesy and manners that once made blacks "the most gracious people."

Ten years ago we had a [junior high] school in this community. Today we don't. It was a desegregation attempt. [We] didn't have any say-so. I'm so frustrated and disillusioned with the whole integration bit. A lot of mothers are beginning to complain. Because what are the kids getting? They can't read. I have people coming to me saying, "Let's organize and bring our kids back here and demand quality education. Quality teachers."

See those guys standing over there in the street right now? Those are young men—they don't have any jobs. Young people should be able to get jobs, young people need to be given an opportunity not to become animals. With all the CETA programs and everything, we have not raised the level of ninety percent of the young blacks out there. Blacks now are beginning to go into the banks and rob. And that's not all drug money—that's desperation for food money. And the sad part about it is that they are breaking into blacks' homes. We had less of that kind of thing than we have now.

My kids are doing okay. One daughter works for Sacramento City Unified. My youngest son [Will], he's working as a plumbing contractor. He sort of wandered for a while. The oldest son works for the city, he's not having any problems. Another daughter works at the telephone company, for eight or nine years.

Her youngest daughter is a college student in history. That she is also doing "day work" doesn't bother Florence. The five dollars an hour her daughter earns is at least ten times more than what she herself used to make. Florence is more concerned about her oldest daughter, who has recently separated from her husband.

My daughter's going to have a struggle every day to handle her job. And to pick her babies up and put them in a nursery school, and go back in the evening and pick them up, and feed the children, and she's tired herself. You don't have enough time to sit down and listen to them read, there's no time to listen to them whine. . . . You have to have some time to sit down, to learn who they are. My little grandson is five, so in ten years he'll be fifteen, and she might not even know him. Because the teachers will have him. And what they're learning now at school and on TV . . . It'll take every bit of Saturday and Sunday that she has, and that means fixing your hair, it means cleaning up the house, going to the store and doing the shopping. . . . There's just so many little kinds of things that make up an everyday life.

They'll grow up just like all the rest of the little black kids. And I don't have two little dull-headed grandkids. They're two little smart pieces of flesh that if they don't have some help they'll be just like all the rest of them. So if you ask me what hopes do I have for them—the schools are worse than they were before . . . and they're just brilliant little boys.

If I could just stop working and take them over for the next ten years. With what I know now. I'd like to send those kids to private schools. I'd like to have them educated. That's one of the reasons I'm going to get out and fight for bringing the school back here. At least you'll have them close to home, where they can walk to school and then you can communicate with the teachers and you can communicate with the principal, and the community can throw out the teachers if they don't act right. You know, we used to communicate with the teachers. The teachers could almost tell you what your youngster was going to be because he had him every day and he had the brothers and sisters. And the teachers came to my house and found out that I needed a chance. I can remember Mrs. Axton in the eighth grade, she said, "Florence, I want to do something for you. I don't want you to read these detectives and I don't want you to read these *True Stories*. Here's a list of books I want you to read." And those books included Shakespeare and Longfellow's poems and *Huck Finn* and Stevenson and George Washington Carver. So it's the teacher, teachers who are dedicated and understand.

That was an all-black school back in Oklahoma, just one school for grades 1 through 12. Five years ago, in 1976, the school held a reunion, and Florence returned home for the first time in almost thirty years.

There was not a street changed, there was not a house repainted. I rented a little Mercury and rode up and down every street. And I knew every house. The city was just the way I had left it. No progress whatsoever. The same old dusty streets. There were no lights, no gutters, nothing had changed whatsoever. Only difference that I saw was a so-called integrated school on Highway 66 leading into Tulsa. And the blacks were on one side, and the whites were on the other. If you have enough people—blacks—in a city to have a Baptist, two Methodist churches, a Seventh Day Adventist, a Jehovah's Witness, and two Pentecostal churches, you have enough blacks in that community to have gotten some streetlights, there should have been some hardtop put [down].

There was not even a hotel that we could all stay in. The man said, "Well, the coloreds live on that side of town." And I just looked at him. In the era of television, you mean to tell me . . . there's just that one paved street that the upper coloreds lived on. Seven or eight hundred people had to go to a park about thirty miles way out on [Highway] 99.

And I went to Tulsa. And the cafeteria and things that we had not been able to eat in . . . you could go in there and they said to you, "I'll be with you in just a minute." They were sort of bending over backwards to see that they were taking good care of you. But to go back to that little town just fifteen miles away and not have people change. When I got on the airplane in Tulsa, the tears just came. Nothing, you know, nothing changed for the better. What had been the ball diamond for the blacks, the weeds are growing up there.

The police car no longer in sight, I ask her how she's changed personally in the last ten, fifteen years.

I don't like the justice system any better than I liked it before. I think we have driven the police department under cover. They don't come out blatantly and pull the stunts that they pulled. If they shoot somebody in the back now, they have to make a big lie. If they arrest people they have to say—

■ (Interrupting.) *You don't like to talk about yourself, do you?*

Well, let me tell you about that. Blacks have not got a pot to pee in, in this community. And until such time as some of us can get together a ten-thousand-dollar building over here—we need two thousand dollars to make a down payment on it, and then we need about ten or fifteen other people to sustain a donation to keep this going—I don't really see anything to brag about. Do you understand what I'm saying?

■ *Maybe you haven't changed much.*

I'm still hostile to the police. I still would like to go into the police system and change a lot of things that I see there. I can't say that I've changed. I'm older, and what I have been able to see—but I've been knowing that all my life—that all people are really basically the same. If given some money, your outlook changes. If given enough money, you're not as hassled as you were.

I've got a house over there. That's all I need, I've got three bedrooms. I don't need any more. I need fifty, sixty people that can sustain the community, fifty or sixty good fighting people that can keep MacGeorge from taking over this park. I need fifty or sixty people that we had before in this community that would stay alert on every problem that we have here. . . . It was called Oak Park Action and Service Group. I don't want any more than that. I'd like to be known for the struggle that I've been able to help accomplish.

■ *Don't you think people appreciate you for what you're trying to accomplish?*

I know they do. But it's not like having a place where I can see five or six carpenters out there, they came to this school and I know that they're certified. It's not like five or six plumbers in this city that have black faces, and I know that they're certified because I helped create it. It's not like blacks getting together, owning a radio station or a television station. I don't really think that I'm accomplishing anything, to tell you the truth about it. I'm struggling like all the rest of the people. Maybe my mouth is bigger.

I'm older. . . . I'm changed in that I used to walk this park from Monday morning until . . . I didn't ride everywhere I wanted to. I don't know all the kids in the park now. I'm older, I'm a grandmother. But other than that I haven't changed. I could say that maybe I'm a little bit more critical of blacks than I was in the past.

■ *You seem to think that change is bad, that it means giving up the struggle, your values.*

I don't know. A lot of things I feel now, I felt them years ago. When I was a girl I always would say to God, "I don't want to know this much." Because if you know so much and you can't do anything about it, it's very, very hard for you. It's better to not understand. But to know it all your life and then to live with it all your life . . . it's close to putting you in the booby hatch. It can be overwhelming.

And I have a pretty good idea of the reason that some people are walking around [like they're crazy] in the community now is because they're aware of what happens and nobody seems to be able to help. Where do you go to get something done? And a lot of people are not aware. You can't be aware when you're hungry all the time . . . you can't think past survival. In order to be creative you have to have the time to sit down and look back.

I am kind of tired, weary of having to struggle so much all the time. I've gotten to the point where I don't know if I have the energy to do some of the things that need to be done—time is slipping away from me. Maybe I should put them down on tape and leave them for my daughter or for somebody else to do. . . . So if you hear I'm gone in the next two or three months, you'll know I was pretty close on it. (*Laughs.*)

■ *I don't think so.*

You don't think so? . . . I'm trying to figure out, there was an ordinance that stopped the police department from riding over here. . . . He rode over in on the grass. Now if anybody else rides in here on this grass like that—what gives him the privilege of riding on the grass? In the cool over on the grass and other people couldn't do it. I don't exactly understand it. Well, I guess I'm a grumble. If I was closer to him, I'd get his badge number and his car number and call down . . .

Florence Grier died four years later. Millie Harding told me, "This year I've really missed her. There's so few of us working for change, when one person drops off the scene . . . nobody can fill Florence's place."

CHAPTER 9

White Lives and the
Limits of Integration

Except for Bill Harcliff, the whites in this chapter are very impressed with the scale of integration that has taken place since the 1960s. At Virginia Lawrence's school the number of black teachers has increased from three to one-third of the faculty. George Hendrickson sees "big changes" in the growing ranks of middle-class blacks, and he has more contact with them than he did in the sixties. Maude Wiley reports that homeowners in her all-white Sacramento suburb are now ready to accept blacks as neighbors.

While these changes are real, they are also very limited. Only a handful of blacks have broken the color bar in Hendrickson's union. His garden club and William Singer's Elks and Rotary societies remain predominantly white, despite their efforts to find minority members. The one black family that moved into Mrs. Wiley's suburb in the 1980s has already moved away. Family life, friendship circles, civic organizations, and leisure time tend to be shared primarily with white people like themselves. They once met people of color at work or at PTA meetings, but now many have retired and their children have grown up, so that—with the exception of Virginia Lawrence—these whites continue to lead essentially "white lives." Indeed, Harcliff, who now works with the physically disabled, is today even further away, physically and emotionally, from blacks and their situation.

In feeling good about the 1970s, whites typically focus on the climate of race relations and the easing of tensions between blacks and whites, rather than on the structure of disadvantage that Florence Grier and other blacks emphasize. The late seventies was a relatively benign period: the Carter administration reaffirmed the national commitment to civil rights, and whites and blacks alike were more concerned with the shared problems of inflation and other economic woes than with racial grievances.

In the second round of interviews I heard none of the blatantly racist remarks that were common in 1968. Perhaps white people have simply learned what is appropriate to say publicly about race and what is not. Perhaps whites have learned to veil their biases in the more acceptable language of class prejudice, all the while implicitly identifying "the poor" with "nonwhites." There are hints of such euphemizing in George Hendrickson's interview and, like other whites who were strongly opposed to intermarriage, he hasn't changed these views one whit. And yet it is equally significant that Hendrickson no longer talks about Congos and Zulus, placing less emphasis on the biology of race and more on the sociology of inequality than he did ten years earlier.

George Hendrickson

"The man is a damn fool who won't change his mind"

1979. *Ten years ago property taxes were so high that George Hendrickson was afraid he and his wife would have to leave their small, comfortable two-bed-room house. But California voters approved a measure to cut property taxes substantially, so they were able to stay, even after he retired six years ago. He speaks of his house the way his contemporary Howard Spence speaks about land: it is the key to independence, the central value of his life.*

George Hendrickson is a small, wiry man, very alert, with a twinkle in his eye, and quick, almost birdlike movements. At seventy-eight, he's in great health, except for a pair of crutches he can't wait to throw away—the result of an automobile accident six months ago. He's eager to be able to again take care of his house. Before the accident, he did it all: minor repairs and painting, as well as any major construction projects. "Maybe in another ten years I'll have to back off on such things as going up a ladder," he says. But until the day he's "bedridden on [his] backside," he's going to take care of himself.

George is enjoying his retirement, but when he goes into a print shop, "right away I start smelling the ink, and I want to get my hands onto a machine. It's instinct." And he still goes down to the union hall to help with the bookkeeping and other problems, including internal politics. There are more blacks in print-ing than ten years ago, but still relatively few, "the literate ones . . . on a par with us. You can't put a man to setting type if he can't spell, if he doesn't know punctuation, grammar." And he mentions another problem: blacks are more often red-green color-blind than whites. A pressman, he explains, needs to be able to distinguish colors.

■ *How are blacks doing overall?*

There's been some big changes. We find a certain number of those people that move amongst us . . . they're very proud, they're very proud of their accomplishments, and I think rightly so. They are advancing, but there's a lot of them yet who haven't developed the abilities to compete. They say they can't get a job, but they don't go down and try.

Let's face another fact here. All men are born equal. Trouble is, they don't stay that way. Even your universities, you'll find that your Japanese, your Chinese, and your whites are all intermingled up at the head of the class as the grades go out, and then about the middle of the class you'd come in with your best blacks and then from there on down, the lower end of the class is loaded with them. But it's because these people haven't been given a chance. After all, what kind of a person can you get who is raised—born and raised in a pigsty? If you want to look at it that way. He doesn't have the chance.

- *Is it more environmental or is it heredity?*

A lot of it is environmental. I would say more of it is environmental. Probably because we have held them down, and it may be our fault. And it's going to take several generations for them to come up out of this. There are the few exceptions that can be born in the slums and become a judge and the mayor of a city and so on and so forth, but those are the exceptions.

- *People like William Shockley say that blacks have lower IQs inherently.*

He's taking an average in a class of people and he does find this, but the problem is environmental. It is not because they themselves are not intelligent, but they have no help with their homework when they go home from school. If you see the way some of them, here in the park, throw the dirt around and the garbage after their picnic, they do the same at home. They're not encouraged to do what man has done, what man can do.

- *Ten years ago you seemed to believe that they were inferior biologically.*

(*Pauses.*) The man is a damn fool that won't change his mind about things as you go along. But basic policies, there are things that you can't change.

I listened to a woman last night on TV and I can't give you her name, it was—Jordan?

- *Barbara Jordan?*

Yeah, on "60 Minutes." Boy, I'm telling you, there is an intelligent woman. That gal *knows* what she is talking about.* But she's an example that is the exception. But I feel sorry for the poor kid that comes out of a slummy area. Because he's not going to get the chances. And many of them because of their

---

*In 1979 Barbara Jordan was completing her third term in the U.S. House of Representatives. During the Watergate hearings she received national attention for her work on the House Judiciary Committee.

belligerent attitude, their lack of desire, their feeling that, "No matter how hard I try, I can't make it anyway," they stay down.

I don't think you can judge a race of people by those that live in the ghetto, or those who have a full education and a good life. The top ones are so different from those that live in the ghetto. So you can't say blacks are bad and you can't say they're all good.

George now has a lot more contact with those "top ones," the successful blacks, than he had in the 1960s. One of his garden clubs is made up of rose fanciers, and because the rose garden is a public park, he has been trying to locate similar clubs and rose enthusiasts in the black community to involve in their activities. He mentions several local black leaders by name, "good men . . . equal to me," people whose hands he shakes.

[The successful black has] advanced himself by his bootstraps and he's accredited with accomplishments today. But I wouldn't want to see him walk in with a white wife. Intermarriage, I disapprove of. I disapprove of it because the educated black doesn't want to accept the white wife or the white husband of a colored person any more than . . . tea and coffee don't mix.

I can't help but slightly grit my teeth when I walk down the street and see a real nice-looking blonde coming along with a black man or something like that. And yet it's none of my business too. But it's—to me it's a . . . I can't get over . . . I can't accept it.

■ *How do you feel about whites and Asians marrying?*

I don't find it as offensive as the black, I suppose. I don't know why. There isn't the instinctive . . . there's too much of a difference between black and white.

It's a hard thing to assimilate, particularly for the older people. A lot of it is tradition. My mother and my dad were [in India] as young adults and they developed the philosophies and the psychologies of the whites that were there, because that's who they lived with and were amongst. And the rest were, well, they were fine, good Hindus in those days, people that were educated in Oxford and Cambridge and all of that. You met them on a level, socially, but you would never think of marrying one.

GRACE [his wife]: I think they're trying to make their way in life and [intermarriage] is one way of doing it. The other way was that every colored gal had to have ten to fifteen children—they didn't have to have them by the same man—in order to bring up their population so they could demonstrate.

Grace made only brief asides during the 1969 interview; now she's much more assertive. The Hendricksons see eye to eye on most issues, though she disagrees with his opinion that women can't do physically demanding or dangerous work—firefighting, police work, working on ships at sea. Some women can handle these jobs, she contends, and she dismisses certain stereotypes as "brainwashing." George thinks that women are fine in managerial roles, but it comes down to the fact that for 100,000 years the man has been "bringing home the bacon and the woman cooking it." He doesn't approve of the women's movement or gay liberation.

A man's sexual preferences are his own private business. And I think he should keep it that way. When I see them appear on TV and when I see them proudly going down the street, and announcing what they are, I want to go over there and shut the TV off. I look upon these people with a great deal of contempt. Not because of what they do, but because they haven't got the brains enough to keep it to themselves. Now this Dan White trial over in San Francisco was a horrible miscarriage of justice. Dan White should be put away for the rest of his life. But what occurred after it was equally horrible.*

I think these demonstrations are directed by a hard core who hope that they can go home and catch their picture on TV. The same way with atomic power. Dealing with the atom and with radiation is a dangerous thing, but nevertheless the people that demonstrate against it . . . you can find five thousand of them and you won't find five of them that are engineers—atomic engineers that know what the hell they're talking about. The rest of them are just steaming off.

I think that nuclear power's in its infancy and I think there's going to be mistakes made. But I think we need it. Again I blame the news media. They're always talking about something that causes cancer. Well, hell, I suppose if I went in there and drank too much water, I could develop a cancer of the stomach. If I kept drinking and drinking and drinking and there were things in the water. They spread fear. They slant the news and they do it deliberately. This affair in Guyana, the terrible thing that happened down there, it was a news item of great importance and it could have been talked about and discussed one, two, maybe three evenings.† After that, I say they are squeezing the last drop out of it.

---

*In November 1978 Dan White murdered San Francisco Mayor George Moscone and Supervisor Harvey Milk; Milk was the city's first openly announced gay to be elected to office. When White was convicted on the lesser charges of voluntary manslaughter in May 1979, an angry demonstration outside City Hall by gays and others turned into a violent confrontation with the police.

†A week before Moscone and Milk were killed, more than nine hundred members of Jim Jones's Peoples Temple, many of them black Californians, died in a mass suicide in Jonestown, Guyana. Congressman Leo Ryan was one of five Americans ambushed and killed by Jones's associates as his fact-finding party was leaving the country.

I'm going to tell you a little thing I saw on TV not so long ago. It was about the Klamath Indians and how they were wanting help, and they interviewed this squaw in her little shack home; it was definitely falling apart. She was a woman in her fifties and she was wanting this and wanting that. She had a carton of cigarettes on the table in front of her. There was a carton of beer on the kitchen sink, the sink was full of dirty dishes and she was sitting there begging for somebody to do something for her. And *hell*, she wasn't even apparently capable of cleaning up her own place. She was capable, but she was too damn lazy. They can afford to go out and buy liquor, but they can't afford to buy a pair of shoes for their little kid that's running around barefoot. I says damn 'em, let 'em go hungry.

I don't think you change an awful lot throughout your life. I don't change. I would much sooner work for a hundred dollars than get it free. I'll go hungry before I'll apply for any welfare. And I think that there's an awful lot of people that can get along without it that are taking it. I think there's a lot of people on state unemployment that never needed it. People I knew of, they worked for six months and then took six months of the year off to draw their unemployment. Connived to do it. *Deliberately.*

■ *How do you feel about your life, at age seventy-eight?*

Well, I could have done better and could have done a hell of a lot worse! But I've done one thing in the course of my life and that is maintain my independence. I went through the Depression of the thirties and never asked anything of anybody. I never went on welfare and I was pretty hungry at times. I've seen the time when I put my dime with the wife's nickel and we went to the store and got a can of beans for dinner that night. And I've seen the time when I almost lost my home and shirt and everything else. I worked whenever I could, *at* anything I could, and never was too proud to wash dishes in a restaurant, or pick and shovel, or whatever I could scrounge. And I want to maintain my independence 'til the day I die. And I shall be very, very put out with myself if I don't.

What I have acquired, a few bucks in the bank, and we have our little pensions, and we have our social securities, and we own this place, and the only bills that we owe are the monthly bills, our living expenses—and I want to maintain this as long as I can. And I guard what I have like a hawk, or an eagle, and I'm not about to let anybody take anything away from me.

I offer him the small payment—Ford Foundation money—I've been giving people for their time and energy in talking to me. But, independent to the last, George Hendrickson refuses it.

Summer 1986. *Eighty-five now, George Hendrickson is recovering from major surgery, and his doctors can't believe how well he has been responding to the* *chemotherapy treatments, the way he has bounced back physically, and his very positive frame of mind. Next spring he expects to be out working in his garden.*

Lately he has been thinking a lot about historical greatness. He wouldn't classify Ronald Reagan as a "great man"; neither was Martin Luther King. In his view, Caesar, Cromwell, and Napoleon were great men. For the twentieth century, he lists Churchill, Franklin D. Roosevelt, Hitler, and Lenin, with Harry Truman coming close.

We talk about South Africa:

I am as opposed to apartheid as I am opposed to slavery. I don't know whether you know it or not, but [of the] forty-eight or forty-nine countries in Africa, there are ten of them that still have actual slavery today. I am also opposed to the methods being used to fight [apartheid]. You've heard talks, you've seen demonstrations. Have you ever heard anybody mention education? And education is the way out. I think that sanctions will hurt the people over there and they will hurt us. South Africa is one of the richest little countries in the world in natural resources. South Africa mines sixty-five percent of the gold in the whole world. They also have tremendous deposits of silver and magnesium, copper, iron ore, industrial diamonds used for drilling, cutting, shaping. [It would] hurt our industry if we ceased to have that.

Being attached to U.C. [the University of California], you're probably interested in divestment. They want to sell their stock that they hold in retirement funds and so forth. Who's going to buy it? I'm not. You're not. So the stock goes down in price. So divestment is not the way either. This has to be handled very slowly, over a *long* period of time. Maybe fifty years from now—and I'll be long gone—apartheid will cease to exist.

Maude Wiley

"That was such a strong time of change"

1979. Now in her early sixties, Maude Wiley, who was quite worried ten years ago about blacks gaining the upper hand, says she is not as aware of race and black people's problems as she was in the sixties. It's not in the news these days, she adds. Even more important, her children were in college then, and because they were active and concerned, they kept her involved and interested. Today she and her retired husband are in their "own little sheltered world," living in the kind of white middle-class suburb she's known all her life. Her interest in race relations has also declined because she no longer feels as threatened by black people.

We may have been torn between the feeling that the blacks have been discriminated against and it's terrible what they have lived through, and yet deep down we were fearful of the blacks getting too strong and perhaps reversing the situation. And maybe we don't have that fear as much now.

That was such a strong time of change. We've kind of lost our frenzy that we had during those years. And we're drifting back. . . . I don't feel that people should be complacent, not trying to fight it anymore. I felt it was a good thing that people were protesting ten, fifteen years ago. In the beginning stages. I could never go along with bombings or any of those things.

There have been changes. I think people look back and respect Martin Luther King's work. During the time he was on his sit-down strikes and whatnot, people felt very strongly against him. I was so upset when Mr. King was assassinated. I came in and told my husband, and he made some remark [like] "They ought to shoot more of them." I think he would deny that he had ever said that now, because he would no longer feel that way. He still has some prejudices—I cringe when he says *nigger*, you know. But I think he's mellowed to the blacks.

We have gradually learned to accept the black people. We're not even as shocked when we see the mixed races in our marriages now. I think many people might invite people into their homes where they have a mixed marriage, while they wouldn't have ten, fifteen years ago.

■ *What if your daughter were to bring home a young black man?*

I've thought about it. It's more or less what I say with everything she does: she has to make her own decision. I wish she wouldn't, because it might add problems—outside prejudices interfering with happiness. But I think I could love a little black grandchild as much as I love my other little grandchildren.

■ *Would you have felt the same way ten years ago or twenty years ago?*

Possibly not, because of peer pressure. It would be so unacceptable. You'd be so aware of what your neighbors or your friends think—"They have a black person in their family." *Now* it wouldn't be so shocking. If I was going to a party, I would invite my black son-in-law and introduce him to my friends. I wouldn't quaver about it like I might have done.

■ *You seem very responsive to what other people think.*

Aren't we all? We all are. I mean, we live in a society and we want to be accepted. I think that's the whole thing, people want to be accepted. Don't we?

Maude Wiley is a housewife and a writer. She has been publishing in magazines since her youth, and her big ambition is "to have a book—with my name on it." There aren't any black characters in her novel: she doesn't know the group well enough to create characters who wouldn't be stereotypes. I ask her if she thinks blacks are any different from whites.

They have certain ethnic traits just as [all people do]. Their singing voices are great—they're so rich—and the same with their dancing. I'm sure they're very fun-loving, from what I've seen. And warm, friendly people.

They're handicapped by their beginnings—improper food and improper care, the matriarchal families that they are living in—and it takes years ahead of us to bring them to where they can fit into the same level of society that we have, because of our advantages.

The job situation is the big problem with them. The fact that they cannot step into the same jobs that the whites [have] because they haven't had the advantages. They shouldn't have special preference to jobs if they're not qualified. I can understand why an employer doesn't want to risk his profit bringing in an unskilled person simply because that person is black.

July 1986. We don't get all paranoid if we see a black family moving in our neighborhood. A few years ago one family moved in, and the people, the children, were accepted just like anyone else. They moved, though, and it's strictly a white neighborhood now.

I think the black people themselves are still in desperate shape, because they're not getting enough education, and too many of them are dropping out of school. Their financial situation hasn't bettered a great deal. Look how many blacks are out of work, it's terrible. How can they ever pull themselves up when the situation is still like that? There're still too many on welfare, and I think that's the really critical situation.

I don't go along with many of [Reagan's] policies. In South Africa, if we're going to put emphasis on humanitarianism, we'd have to cut more of our relations with the government. We still have too many money interests there.

Some years ago her husband died after a long bout with cancer. Her own health is good, though she's "getting up there" in years. "The wonderful thing about being a writer [is that] you don't really retire, you still always work at it."

Virginia Lawrence

"The world changed exactly the way I was going"

1978. *Now in her mid-fifties, Virginia Lawrence, her school's liberal maverick in 1968, still teaches students with learning difficulties and still lives in an* *integrated neighborhood of Berkeley. The living room of her shingled house is furnished with oak and old Japanese prints and artifacts; growth-movement books sit on the coffee table. She's small and slight, with dark graying hair. She gives off intensity, highly concentrated energy.*

I find that I am frequently making comparisons between what *now* feels like to me and what it was like in the sixties. I feel that era had a particularness about it that separates it from other periods of time. I'm a visual person, and I can almost see with my eye a wave rising which involved all kinds of people and expressed itself most particularly in rebellion against authority and against institutions. And I just see that wave rising and just crashing against the rocks of authority and the rocks of the institutions. It was a very much more dramatic thing than anything I've experienced at any other time. It was just an enormous challenge to middle-class values or traditional values . . . to the concept that certain things are good and certain things are bad in the moral sense.

[Today] I feel the wave is receding. It's been three or four years since a kid has tried on me some kind of serious racial challenge. Now they may say "white bitch" under their breath, but that's routine, that ain't nothing racial. [Even] during the very late sixties and early seventies, I always felt the problem was rebellion against authority, and they couldn't have cared less what color I was. [Race] was a big fat issue. It was usable. You could really freak a lot of people out, especially a guilty white person, with all this shit you threw at them.

- *You never fell for that?*

Oh, I must have at some times. But not very much, because I really didn't feel that guilty. I don't see any way that whites in this country can avoid carrying something of our history. But to let that control you is to do a real injustice to personally relating. It leads to really inappropriate indulgences of people that ultimately are an enormous racial put-down. You know, if some kid is screwing up and because he's black, I don't say, "Hey, you're screwing up," when that's what I ought to say.

For a while, the emphasis on black identity and Black Power was painful for her. The separatists didn't take into account color-blind whites like herself. But eventually, with the help of her students and Martin, a black Latino man with whom she was romantically involved, she realized that there was no hope for real integration until the hostility, as well as the self-affirmation, was voiced.

[Around 1970] we had this great student uprising among the black kids, for a black student union. Let me tell you, half the faculty was absolutely outraged the principal would even consider it. Just totally outraged. She called me in and [because] we just didn't have the kind of black leadership on the faculty to handle it, I as a white woman was responsible for helping to establish a black student group.

It produced an interesting conflict in me because I'm an integrationist. And I had to really think hard to realize that security in one's identity has to precede integration. And those kids and I met for hours. I was determined, man, it was gonna be done right, so we were totally unassailable. I reached back into everything I ever used—I was program director for the Y—and I taught them everything I could think of about leadership. So we created a constitution, by-laws, all that stuff. And it was gonna come up for a vote of the student body—could the black student union be included as one of the clubs in the school? God, they were great kids. In the spring they were all elected into office because they were such good leaders and they were so well known.

You know what they did? [They graduate and] go on to Oakland High and were the greatest integrationists you've ever seen. They were all elected into office, part of a group in which some were black and some were white. And they'd come back and see me, this black kid and this white kid working together. You know what happened? Having fought and bled and died and threatened to strike until the principal was gonna let them have this . . . the next year nobody wanted it.

Johnson School has been totally transformed from the "absolute desert island of WASPish conformity" it was in the early sixties. The teachers who used to make disparaging remarks about black students have left or have learned to keep quiet. A third of the teachers and many of the administrators are black. Lawrence gives the major credit for these changes to Marcus Foster, the progressive black superintendent of schools who was assassinated by the Symbionese Liberation Army (SLA) in 1974, and to her school's new principal, who is white, but "without a prejudiced bone in her body."

People used to be so totally unaware. I look back on our funny ole faculty human relations committee. Damn it, we did do some good education. We caught the people who were teetering and we brought a lot of 'em along with us. And they had social experiences that they just never had before. And some of them began to realize, you know, you can't generalize. And "maybe a few of 'em are good." (*Chuckles.*) And you think of the movies and the TV specials and stuff that have happened in a ten-year period. People are better educated about all this and they're more exposed. And so some people who would've said things out of ignorance *don't* say them anymore. It's also true that it's terribly unfashionable and it isn't *in* at all. People who thought I was an absolute nut ten years ago have noticed that the world changed exactly the way I was going.

The people who were really hard-core racists and hard-core conservatives are long gone. But the teachers I came in with, the generation that was scared to talk, we're the old guard now. And the *young* teachers were teenagers ten years ago.

■ *So there's no more fuss about the way the black students dance?*

What can you say if the teachers are doing it? The class that graduated three years ago had the most beautiful graduation dance. It was totally integrated. The teachers and the kids were all "bumping" with each other and, by God, it did not matter what color you were, you bumped with whoever was beside you.

But integration has fallen short in other areas. Black teachers tend to sit together, apart from the whites, in the lunchroom. And the grouping together of the "bad" black kids—she gestures to emphasize the quotation marks around bad—reinforces their disruptive behavior as well as reinforcing stereotypes. Then she mentions affirmative action.

One of the bad things we've done is hire ill-equipped people, which just exacerbates racial prejudice because then you see the guy behind the counter who can't even write, and you think all blacks are like that. In the great panic to promote integration, one of the things that was done by Oakland administrators was take buses into the South and hire practically anybody who would submit to coming North. And now competent people are having to stand on their heads trying to contain bosses who are incredibly incompetent.

■ *Is this a criticism of affirmative action or just a misuse of it?*

It's a terrible misuse of it. And I think anything like affirmative action is a mixed bag. It's necessitated by our history and by our prejudice, and I just feel that the script we wrote a few centuries ago had that in it then. But in some way it works against the very causes some of us care about. If I had a vote as to whether it would exist or not, I would undoubtedly vote for it, and then I'd say, "Yeah, I'm voting for it, but look, this, this, and this are the problems it creates."

■ *Remember that faculty party where no one would talk to you and your black "date"?*

It would never happen today. The younger black faculty members move with a kind of ease and a kind of comfort and a kind of sense that they belong there. There are still some problems and this weird in-fighting that goes on, but it isn't over race as an issue.

People are *very* much more comfortable about acknowledging racial differences. And race itself. There was a period when you never identified anybody as "the black kid." You went six days around Sunday not to mention race. That doesn't prevail at all anymore.

When I got my hair cut and got a natural, the kids just went ga-ga over that. They came back from high school to compare notes and "Do I set mine?" "Do they set theirs?"—just really natural, comfortable conversation about the ordinary events that surround our particular physical characteristics.

A [black] kid came up to me today who just had his hair done with the "wet look." And he said, "Hey, Mrs. Lawrence, you got some scissors? I got to cut this straight piece." And I said, "Sure, here, let me fix it for you." And it was just the most natural thing in the world for him to lean forward and me to find that piece of hair and cut it. And I said, "You really ought to take the kleenex and wipe the grease off your face." My God, that never would have happened ten years ago.

Blacks have come a very long way, as a political force, as an economic force. I look at the number of blacks on the roster of Oakland public schools. They're getting money in their pockets from jobs that they didn't have before. And they're feeding their kids adequately, and they're living in nice houses— all over the place—and buying their clothes at Magnin's, and some are paying to send their kids to private schools. Those kids are growing up as middle-class kids. My kids can meet middle-class blacks any time they want, on the job, in the neighborhood. In my mother's generation—she has said this to me many times—there weren't middle-class blacks available for her to meet.

A new student started at Johnson this fall. She's half black. Her name is Mary, and she is Virginia's first grandchild.

It's such a turn-on for me to think that I have been able to contribute to that child's life a school which receives her well, an administration which will absolutely knock themselves out to [provide] a really comfortable social situation for her. It's really neat. She pops in my room and says "hi."

She's noticeably pleased about how her four children have turned out. They have all carried on Virginia's commitment to "an integrated life," identifying themselves as black or marrying or living with a black person. It's as if interraciality has become family tradition, her great-great-grandmother's warning heeded.

Donna, Mary's mother, lives with a man who comes from an interracial family. He's militantly "prejudiced" against whites, but Virginia is hopeful that they can work it out. Her next oldest, Paul, was "extremely prejudiced" against black women back in 1968. But now he's living with a woman who's part black and part three other minorities. Virginia is especially proud that Paul and Arthur, her youngest, were conscientious objectors during the Vietnam era.

My third child identified totally black all the way through Berkeley High. She was the one white girl in a black sorority. And the kids had parties here just over and over and over. She has gradually returned to her white identity and married an absolutely neat guy who himself has led a very integrated life.

Arthur led an integrated existence from thing one. He just had a real interesting mixture of friends. And a very comfortable experience racially. Took a lot of black history and took a black jazz course and a lot of stuff like that, but also quite a few quote-unquote "white things," whatever they may be. And then a black friend of his introduced him to Lita, whom he eventually married.

The man I'm living with now happens to be white. Jim's much younger than I am, by the way, he's really a redneck in his point of view. When I became involved with Jim, to my utter surprise, I was v-e-r-y aware of Jim's whiteness. I think that for a long time I relied on the interraciality of my closest relationships to carry something in myself that maybe I was unwilling to carry alone. It was as though I had lost something, something about an identity having to do with a way of looking at things from the inside. And it drives me crazy that Jim looks at things from the outside that I look at from the inside, racially. I view minority-group experience from identification. So I can even say critical things from the inside, that I don't want somebody saying from the outside. But it's very interesting to be involved with a man who makes really negative comments.

She explains that she no longer feels the need to make "the kind of public statement" that going with a man of color implies, but "it's nothing like I've graduated from interracial dating." She's still very close to many black people, but she no longer thinks race is that important. When her former lover, who was black and Latino, made a big issue of her leaving him for a white man:

I did not go under in the face of that. I would have been much more vulnerable to those accusations twenty years before. I knew I was not involved with him to crown blackness. I was involved with him because I really cared about the man Martin, and I didn't have to go to another black man simply to prove that.

Now in retrospect I realize he just pulled anything out of the bag that he could use. . . . He really wanted me to come back. He was slamming me with all this white stuff, and certainly my mind knows plenty of black stuff I could say, but I could not bring up a racial thing to retort to him. It wasn't a factor for me.

■ *You're not at all racially conscious, yet so much of your life has been oriented around color!*

Isn't that funny? How do you explain that?

■ *Don't look at me. How do you explain it?*

It's not the color, it's the marginality my life is organized around. It's just color shows.

- *But there are a lot of different ways people are marginal. You could have a thing about gay men or Asian men, for example.*

I have a lot of close friendships with gays. Black men seem more the same culture to me than Asian men. My close relationships are essentially with middle-class blacks in terms of drinking orange juice and being relatively responsible and having some intellectual competence and not living in outright poverty. I find it hard to relate to people who have totally different values. So what's left? Religious differences. I've done that, too.

I'm not sure I have a thing about race as much as I'm simply in touch with my collective unconscious and I bear that out in the way I live my life. The collective unconscious of people in the United States centers around the black-white drama.

July 1986. *Virginia is very close once again to her friend Harold, in part because "I feel isolated when I am in a world in which I look around and don't see anything but white faces." But the new man in her life is white. He's very supportive of her integrated family, though some of his friends are highly prejudiced: "So I always have the dilemma of shall I educate [them], shall I speak to this, or shall I not?"*

During the 1980s racial integration has proceeded well at her school, with kids of all races working together. But the "misuses" of affirmative action still disturb her.

Recently I had a very unsavory experience as a consequence of being a white woman in Oakland schools. I was encouraged to apply for a job. A woman who was *infinitely* less qualified was hired. Fortunately, I didn't want the job very much. But I look at it as real unfortunate because Oakland lost a person who was extremely prepared to do the job. That's happening a very great deal in Oakland. And as a consequence a lot of good black leadership has left, because they were at the mercy of unable black leadership.

It's also true that unable white people hold down jobs. White nepotism is rampant throughout corporations and institutions. So when minorities get in and have the opportunity to practice minority nepotism, why the hell shouldn't they?

In 1984 she took an early retirement. Funding cuts indiscriminately eliminated her successful individualized teaching program along with ineffectual holdover programs from the sixties and seventies. Now she's using her methods and program in a special youth employment project that teaches mostly black students and high school dropouts about work by training them to trim trees and clear trails. They're experiencing success for the first time in their lives, and Virginia calls it the most exciting job she's ever had.

William Singer

"We've turned life itself into a quota business"

1978. William Singer, now in his mid-fifties, had recently returned from the hospital when I talked to him. His first heart attack, five years earlier, had forced him to stop working. He misses the job, but he still keeps up with current issues, especially in Berkeley, where he lives.

You have a few here in town that consider themselves militants, but they're really not militant anymore. They found they could accomplish more by working within the establishment than by running through town and throwing rocks and breaking windows and waving banners. I think a good case in point is Tom Hayden. When he was a part of the Red Mountain tribe down here on Regent Street, there wasn't anything that was right with the world and he was up here every day raising hell. Today he's still going around for causes, but I think they're causes of the times and not necessarily the cause of militancy. Our times have changed and there's a greater sense of awareness today of certain things that are going on. The establishment itself has changed in a little way.

The [sixties] made us aware that a large segment of the community wasn't getting any attention at all, that there were unmet needs, that there were other people, a world, outside their own house. I'm trying to think about how to word this. Influence was really being exerted through association, cronyism. If you had a good friend, he represented you, your point of view. But there were a lot of people that weren't being represented at all. And the disturbances made the representatives aware. And the public, some of them rallied around these causes.

I think a lot of them were phony causes. Here at the university the third-world programs got so screwed up that they were wiped out. Then we went back to the more traditional approach to education. But a lot of this is a lasting effect. People became aware there were health problems, that there was a large segment of the United States that was not only impoverished—they didn't have medical care, nutrition, and a lot of other things. And programs were developed through the U.S. Public Health Service, which is a typical bureaucratic sort of organization, but they do some good. It was an educational experience for America as a whole, whether they agreed with it or not.

I think it's a credit to the student today that goes to U.C. that he pretty much doesn't get involved in those sorts of things. He's more interested in a learning process than pounding the streets and waving banners. For a while all you had to have was three units to be enrolled. Your militant group picked up a lot of hangers-on that didn't have any direction at all but they wanted to be part of the action.

The poverty programs didn't benefit the people intended to be the benefici-aries. What it did was set up a new structure of administration and it benefited the audit groups that were established to monitor those programs. [Congress-man Ron] Dellums was a part of Social Dynamics, a group that was black-owned and audited all the OEO [Office of Economic Opportunity] programs along the West Coast. The poor people themselves, they were just a part of the scene. It didn't really improve their lot very much. It gave them a little stature, but it didn't help them economically.

Despite his health, Singer keeps up his memberships in civic organizations. Ten years ago these groups were all-white; today some have a few nonwhite mem-bers. Some members quit the Elks to protest the lack of minorities, but Singer believes it's better to work inside the group to make changes. He and his friends made a serious effort to bring blacks into Rotary, but there are few black businessmen in Berkeley, so they had to turn to managers in the banks and government agencies.

Now whenever you get in a group, you count the number of this or the number of that. When we gathered before, we gathered in common, it was an association, and before the awareness wasn't there. This great awareness that we have to meet quotas, it holds back the whole thing. There's the initial feel-ing of uneasiness. You can communicate a lot better when you don't have this uneasiness. So we've turned it, life itself, into a quota business.

[In Berkeley] we were aware of black opportunities even in the early fifties. We didn't need the Civil Rights Act of '64. And when we hired in the parking division, the meter maids and so forth, they were almost all blacks, but they had the qualifications. They came through the regular civil service proce-dures, they got it competitively, they didn't get it on the basis of color, or race, or national origin. We couldn't ask on their application what race they were, and we couldn't even give out figures on the racial composition of our work force because it was forbidden under the FEPC [Fair Employment Practices Commission] rules. And so they were hired and they were retained strictly on the basis of merit.

Singer finds Asians to be the most productive race. The Japanese, especially, "were our very good friends . . . and still are." The internment of Japanese Americans during World War II was unfair, he says, providing a field day for opportunists to buy up their property—homes, land, farms—for almost noth-ing. Most of them were loyal to the United States—Tokyo Rose was the great exception—and they just wanted to preserve their culture and have their chil-dren study their own language after school. As for Hispanics, Singer feels they'd progress more if they'd learn English and not demand the teaching of Spanish in the schools. But they're also hampered by the competition be-tween minorities in this country: "There's only one minority; the blacks have the clout."

There's been a tremendous change in the employment structure. They fig-ure that industry is bad for the community: it creates noise, dust, fumes and brings in parking [problems] and congestion. So Berkeley, San Francisco, Oakland drove the industries out and there's very little opportunity for un-skilled workers. And who were the beneficiaries? San Leandro, Fremont, Modesto, Fresno. Fresno's the fastest-growing city in northern California.

In the last five years we've had nothing but federal programs. You have the CETA program coming in here, you have 'em at the university, every struc-ture of government has CETA. They look upon that as the great savior. But really what is it? It's a one-year contract or a six-month contract. You ar-tificially create jobs. You train 'em to be street sweepers. This is Comprehen-sive Employment Training? Where in the hell are they gonna get jobs as a street sweeper unless they work for a city that has hand-swept streets? It's a WPA all over again, except there's nothing productive. [In the thirties] you had state emergency relief programs, federal emergency relief programs, WPA programs, CCC programs, and what have you, but they were constructive programs. The big cut outside Vallejo as you go up the hill over toward Fair-field, the original two-lane highway was done with pick and shovel and wheel-barrow. They worked all during the Depression on that, but they did it, the unemployed people. Today you hand out money for meaningless tasks. Things that don't produce anything.

Mr. Singer passed away before I could speak with him again.

Bill Harcliff

"What I really do is live in a white neighborhood"

1981. *In 1968 Bill and Diane Harcliff were planning to move to Berkeley from San Francisco because of all the racial hassles in Haight-Ashbury. They* *did move, but they also split up. In 1981, though Bill is only thirty-one, he resembles an agrarian patriarch with his farmer's coveralls, long hair, and a wispy beard that reaches almost to his waist. House plants fill the living room of the Berkeley home he shares with his new wife, Lynn, their young child, and Bill's pre-teen son; they've only recently moved back from Chico.*

I feel kind of smug about the fact that I think I've changed less than most. Same beard. That's nothing, but I believe the same stuff. I've kept the faith and I'm proud of it. In other senses I've changed. I've gotten older, calmed down a lot. My idealism has gotten a little more realistic. I'm less strident. In those days I was more likely to shake my fist at authority figures and the like. So, like the mellowness of thirteen years maybe is the biggest change. But basically the same values. I think I'm a hard-core bohemian in the sense I don't think I've changed very much at all.

Most hippies were rebelling against something. It was something they had to get out of their system, and they did, and then they went back to what their parents had taught them to do. They're probably what we'd call liberals now, a bad word. They send their dues to the ACLU. Probably got a job at the university. And their attitudes went, too.

In my case it wasn't rebelling. I got a little farther out than they might have liked, but my mother was an old anarchist from way back and my father was quite a lefty. The word *conventional* in my family was synonymous with the word *mediocre*. That sort of says it right there. I can go back to my roots and stay crazy. I was wild and fast-talking and they were my authority figures, so like any other kid I bitched and hollered at them. But as I look back, we've been quite close. And I feel these days very much a part of a tradition—continuing what they did. From my mother I learned about things like yoga, vegetarianism, utopian communities. A lot of those things which became new-left ideas, I first learned from her.

I live a contemplative life devoted mostly to thinking, meditating, and not too much to acquiring skills or acquiring security or acquiring money. The way I conceive myself is very hard to explain to an average person. Go through the world and people ask, "What is it that you do? Explain yourself." And you have to do that thousands and thousands of times in your life. I guess that's the microway in which society is asking you, "Where is it that you fit in? Are you a part of us or what?" We all want to fit in. I remember for several months being depressed, being discouraged, and being very sensitive to what other people thought I was doing. Twice I tried junior colleges as a way to define or focus what the hell I was doing. I thought, this is the conduit to come in from the cold, this is the amnesty program. It didn't work.

I work with the disabled. In Berkeley there's probably about ten thousand disabled people and a support community of people who take care of them. That's people who get them out of bed in the morning and wipe their ass and put their clothes on them. I do a whole lot of that. I'm into "crip politics," lobbying for rights, going down to the welfare office with someone who can't, representing people.

I think of myself in a tradition of monks: hermit monks, wandering monks, the religious contemplatives. That's what feels like my vocation. I spend a lot of time meditating. A lot of time. But there's an active side to it. A lot of my Zen friends, the people who are into Eastern religions are too quietistic for my taste. From my background I have this very strong sense of social justice and a sense of the maldistribution of wealth and the sense of the stupidity of war—they're very much in my bones. That's why I like Ho Chi Minh. He was a contemplative, a poetic mind, who had as deep an insight into things as any monk, but obviously he was very concerned with social justice.

What I really do every day is live in a white neighborhood. I don't mix much with black people, and it just seems real sad. I grew up liberal and I was taught that Negroes are nice people and we should be their friends. At school I would always rush to be the first guy to sit next to the Negro and all this. I had an important experience before the Haight-Ashbury, about '66 when I was in jail. Was that in the interview? ("Yes.") I think that effect has largely worn off, but I feel separate. I feel threatened. I'm very conscious that as communities we don't get along, we hate each other, we threaten each other. When I was house hunting in Berkeley I had my own kind of red lines. I'd rather not live in the Berkeley ghetto if I can help it. And why? Because I know damn well that I won't talk as freely and openly with my neighbors as I would if they were white or I were black. And I'll have to protect myself more, worry more about whether my stereo is going to get ripped off, stuff like that. I have that kind of paranoia—it's not really paranoia, it's a social fear. And I feel very sad about it, because it seems we've been battering away at that one for—what?—four hundred years. And it hasn't gotten an inch [better]. Maybe one inch.

We raised a girl who was nine months older than Jerry [his son] for several years. She's family, I think of her as a daughter. She's with her mother in El Cerrito now, they're white flight, white and/or drug flight, call it what you will, but consciously so—they'll admit it. The mother is a battered-down liberal who really believed in integration and ended up out of the frying pan and into the fire. In El Cerrito the black and white kids are thrown together at the last minute, in the ninth grade. One day her mother brought her over, she'd been beaten up by twelve, thirteen, twenty black kids. What was coming out of her mouth was like straight out of the KKK: "jungle bunnies," "send them back to the jungle," "we should all have guns so we can shoot those damn niggers." I know she knows better, but then again she doesn't know better. I just felt real sad. Lots and lots of white kids are growing up this way still. Nothing much has changed. In Berkeley it's a little better, but only a little better. We ain't integrated. We're not even close.

I have a lot of trouble with ghetto blacks. They're as paranoid of me as I am of them, and that's going to make it hard for both of us. But the other reason is just style. The extreme outgoing quality of it, the extreme aggressiveness, the extreme "if you want it, you take it, or you say it," the loud talking, fast walking—that's what I think of as a ghetto black style which is roughly what I would call "pushy." I can cope with it pretty much of the time if they're not beating me up. A lot of the time I'm thinking inside, "Lighten up, talk slower, talk quieter, come on."

One of the guys I work for is black and we know each other very well. So we can speak our minds, and we can kid around a lot. He wanted me to comb his afro, and I said, "Come on, I grew up on the wrong side of the tracks. I have blue eyes, I don't know from an afro." And he wants me to make breakfast, he says, "Cook some of those grits." I say, "That's all you niggers eat is grits, that's why you're so dumb." It's fun. It's okay. I think at its best, racial discrimination, if I can turn the word on its head, is appreciating each other's music and food, dialect. That would be my optimistic hope for America, that we could be that kind of melting pot.

Every now and again I go to a black church. I have gospel records, there's a mixture of reverence and lustiness which is just right. Why is gospel music so good and soul music so bad? Soul music usually comes out of gospel. It's that quality of pushiness, I think. Christianity as a whole to me is kind of disgusting. Any school of thought that's based on prohibitions, that's based on denying, is always going to make you sick, going to make you tight-assed. Black people, it's the other way around. They use it to express and it's great, it's sexy, it's sweaty, it's exalting. It's probably one of the best supports of the black community.

Another quality I like about the black world is the same thing I like about the redneck world. It's not so cerebral. It's much more hearty. In the ghetto, cars frequently stop next to each other and talk. You notice it? I think, "Oh, fuck, come on, this is a street." But when I really sit back and think about it, that's a real good quality. They're saying it's not so important to get there, but it's very important to stop and say hello. Here people even walking on the sidewalk don't stop. And certainly not in their BMW cars.

In Berkeley, he has found, "it's a miracle for a couple to stay together for two years," but he cites "feminism" as the cause of his divorce.* Diane had been "peddled a bill of goods," an "us-against-them vision" that made her see him as an oppressor. Bill draws a distinction: he deplores "competitive machismo and

*Diane's version of their break-up differs. Although she doesn't minimize her own role, she says that the marriage just didn't give her enough scope "to be a person" and that many of the problems came from Bill's instability and his compulsive need to constantly get involved in new romantic relationships. (Shortly after our interview he moved away from Lynn to live with someone else.)

Diane, who has gone on to graduate school and is in a longstanding, "very satisfying relationship," remains much more of a racial liberal than Bill, strongly supporting affirmative action.

the whole narrow male role" (as a father he's "goopy" and loves to change dia-
pers), but men and women are inherently different. Women are intuitive,
gentle and nurturing, into magic and mystery, while men are naturally hard
and tough. But the industrial revolution "mangled families and individuals"
by making men weak. In America today most work is meaningless, Bill feels,
and that leaves men in a "tremendous confusion" that shatters their self-
esteem. Men can't "hold up our end of things," and when a woman tries to
lean on a man, she falls over because he's "a skeleton." One of Bill's missions in
life is "to do something about the breakdown of the family."

Growing up in the sixties was pretty fortunate. The stuff I would have done anyway happened to be in style. There was tremendous peer support to be wild during those hard years—hardest at growing up. I'm glad they happened to coincide with a time when my idiosyncrasies were fashionable. In the seventies there [was] more peer pressure to get safe, get a career and go to college and become a computer programmer.

I think in the eighties there's going to be lots and lots of crazies. As things unravel further, as things look more and more absurd to kids—either because of nuclear bombs or because of so much wealth or whatever, the problem of freedom is really going to be overwhelming. (*To his son who has been listening:*) You'll do okay. When you have crazy stuff going on, you've got people around you who can say, "That's just such and such, don't worry about that. Just take a deep breath." But when a kid's having fantastic visionary experiences and his father is an engineer who never saw any of this stuff in his life, that kid's in trouble.

Our institutions were affected by all that ferment. Like Silicon Valley and the work style there. Splitting job times, having a gymnasium in your factory . . . these are maybe consolation prizes for the great hippy hopes. The environmental movement has survived. That may be the main remnant of the hippies' political thought.

November 1986. *Bill's major activity is his Zen practice. His new mission is to inject happiness, warmth, and joy into an overly puritanical Japanese Buddhism, something like the Hasidim did for Orthodox Judaism in the eighteenth century. Bill meditates at least four hours a day. Meditation is a "human birthright"; people "need to find a way to be quiet and reflect, to get to this larger religious sense of being in the world."*

Race continues to be fateful in his life. A black man murdered Lynn, his second wife, a few years ago. For much of her life she had been very close to black people and "race was a significant issue in that [murder]." He has remarried and his family has moved to a small rural town. In part the move was a "basic back-to-the-land impulse"—he never did like Berkeley—at bottom it

was "white flight," an "apartheid move to a peaceful little white community"
that gives him "a certain feeling of abdicating some social responsibilities."

A lot of the tensions that we wanted to get away from were in fact race tensions. There's just a level of stress that's part of the background noise. White people are very tense about black people, and black people are very tense about white people. White people feel guilty because they don't know how to redistribute their wealth. There's guilt and there's fear, and then we put up walls and get more cops to keep them away from us.

In no other place do I feel race prejudice as personally as when I go to a black bureaucrat to get welfare. Ooooh, do I feel it. "What the hell are you doing here?" They never say that, but when they nitpick me about filling out a form—I know what the issue is: "This money's for us." There's a very strong disapproval that they should divide *their* dollars with a white middle-class kid.

In general I don't go around worrying about crime, but I certainly feel the tension in the air. People say, "In Berkeley you can't leave your car unlocked; in Berkeley somebody's going to mug you; in Berkeley there's a lot of crime." People say "crime"—what they *mean* is "black." They never say black people will attack you, take some of your money away. It doesn't mean white-collar crime and it doesn't mean people breaking laws. It means the race war.

CHAPTER 10

Black Youth:
The Worsening Crisis

With the nationwide decline in economic prosperity in the early 1970s, employment prospects worsened for black youths who dropped out of school and had no marketable skills. For many of these teenagers, hustling on the ghetto streets became a way of life. In this chapter, for example, Richard Simmons and Larry Dillard describe how they became firmly entrenched in the street milieu. Other young blacks outgrow the street. But age is only a predisposing factor. The specific avenues out of the street culture and into the mainstream economy are simply not available to most poor ghetto youth.

Because of the scarcity of entry-level jobs for nonskilled workers (other than minimum-wage fast-food jobs) and the soaring profits to be made in selling illegal drugs, during the 1970s the drug trade became the biggest business in the inner cities. Today, dealing drugs or serving as a courier or lookout for dealers is a major source of employment for disadvantaged ghetto youths.

The drug boom has sparked an increase in urban burglaries and muggings, as users try to finance their habits, and wars between competing dealers make the streets more dangerous than ever. Although some inner-city communities have organized to reclaim their streets by driving out the dealers, other blacks and Hispanics openly admire the flamboyance and wealth of such narcotics czars as Felix Mitchell, whose funeral in Oakland in August 1987 was a major community event.[1]

In the late sixties black activists talked about gaining community control by restraining or driving out predominantly white police forces. Today's campaigns are directed instead at demanding a stronger police presence to control nonwhite drug dealers. This change may be a metaphor for a shift in the spirit of the times, but it also reflects a measure of improvement in police-minority relations in many cities. Though racial discrimination, harassment, and brutality have by no means disappeared,[2] many police departments have added more black and Hispanic officers, implemented policies to limit their officers' use of guns and life-threatening chokeholds, and trained their officers to be more sensitive and courteous in their dealings with minority citizens.

All four of the narratives in this chapter suggest how difficult it was to be young, poor, and black during the 1970s. These life stories include prison terms, welfare dependency, unemployment, and drug addiction. The last two voices in this chapter, Sarah Williams and Jim Pettit, suggest how particularly vulnerable minority youths are to the psychological and emotional problems that all young adults must face. For that, their struggles to achieve greater self-understanding and self-acceptance are all the more impressive.

Richard Simmons

"The American black man is a dying species"

1981. Racial pressures at his Sacramento high school led Richard Simmons to drop out of school in 1968. By 1972 he seemed headed for state prison. While on probation for burglary and resisting arrest, he was picked up and charged with selling heroin, possessing a variety of other drugs, and having a sawed-off shotgun. The judge refused to set bail, but the sheriff's office mistakenly released him after he pled guilty to one of the charges. Simmons seized the opportunity to skip town and adopted a new identity.

He remained free for five years, until the police stopped him one day because his car resembled a vehicle used in an armed robbery. Cleared of the robbery, he and his companion were charged with possessing a gun, a number of misdemeanors, and "flight from justice." But because he had gotten into only minor difficulties during his years as a fugitive, a sympathetic judge placed him on five years' probation with the stipulation that he serve one year in jail and stay away from guns, drugs, and drug users. "One slip and you're on your way to state prison," the judge warned.

Simmons served his sentence, and his probation period is almost over. He's now thirty-one, unemployed, and the father of seven children.

I don't have the time now to go to the pen and get out and still be a young man. Then I was young, I was eighteen, nineteen. I go to the pen now, I can just about kiss it good-by. And I just struggled back to where I might be able to get a job and really advance myself, push myself to maybe work out some kinda way in this society.

I'm walking a thin line. Because they know me and, you know, any black man got to walk a thin line. These is troubled times and no one's trusting anyone any more. They got me in a state where I wanna be armed, at all times . . . because everyone else is armed. Brothers wiping out brothers. Mexicans wiping out brothers. Whites is wiping out brothers. (*Laughs.*) The American black man is a dying species. We're extinct. Our women out-number us, too.

From the time of that interview to this time right now, we lost that whole generation to drugs. They poison the black people's minds with drugs. The streets right now, drugs is everywhere. You can buy drugs before you can find some types of whiskey. Heroin is selling faster than penny candy. White America, was nobody hollering until it started reaching their sons and daughters. Because the heroin, the cocaine, the reds and all—it's all been in the ghetto.

■ *Are the streets changed from the sixties?*

Yeah. There's no togetherness. In the sixties you went out and felt like you had a certain amount of power. Because everyone knew everybody. When I come home I might bring twelve people with me. We'd eat, share bread, get loaded, smoke weed, or whatever. We all have problems, we all get together and discussed these problems, trying to do something about it. Now it's dog eat dog. I'm out in the world by myself. If I'm not with my brothers—my *blood* brothers, you know where I'm coming from, my momma and daddy's stock—I feel alone. Which I am alone.

They think I got a dollar now. In the sixties they might ask me for that dollar, but now they'll figure a way to take that dollar from me. If I got enough dollars, they might kill me.

It's way harder to survive. It's way less money. They're laying people off. In the sixties if you wanted a job, you could find a job. Now there's no jobs, the people are running around here going crazy. And now they cutting these people off welfare, and just turning us right back out into the streets. So it's either we get drafted, go fighting again, or come back here and deal drugs or pimp out women, go to jail for robbery . . . we got to do something to make money.

The younger generation is going to have it twice, three or four times as hard as I had it. And I had it hard! (*Laughs.*) Nowadays no one cares about the kids on the streets. Fourteen, thirteen, twelve—they don't be going to school, no one cares. When I was going to school, they had truant officers. They see us on the street, they would take us back to school. I don't think the black youth see any future in the country. Like I said, we lost a whole generation to drugs.

We gonna have to start preaching togetherness, 'cause our numbers is dwindling. Very few of us is making it in the world. What few that survive this genocide with these pills and this abortion . . .

- *Do you really see the birth control pill and abortion as a plot against black survival?*

It's statistically showing it every day. The white population's growth jumped. The Mexican-American population's growth jumped. Our population is the only one that declined. Since birth control hit the ghetto, our population has been decreasing and dwindling. And we getting murdered here. Financially, they're killing us.

- *But homicide, that's blacks killing blacks.*

Because if you trying to make a dollar to come home and feed yourself and your family and pay your rent, you can't go over to the white community to do anything, because when you seen over there, you're already stopped on suspicion. So you got to prey in your den, because you're less noticeable over here. You got to burglarize your own people.

Even the blacks that kill blacks, they don't go to jail for it anymore. Shit, a friend of mine I grew up with, he killed two brothers. And he did, what? Three months? He's back on the street. I know of other incidents, whites killed the black man. Automatically back on the street. Where if I killed a white man, I would go to the chair maybe. I'm not gonna be right back on the street.

They're getting rid of us, man. They're killing us with the pills. And making us kill each other. Making our women see where it's really more profitable to be by theirself than to be with a black man. Or marry a white man. For money. You know we can't support ourselves, so how can we support them and a family?

Over half your prison population is black. You go in there, you a gladiator. It's a way of fighting back. The people out there on the streets, the drugs got 'em. I know dudes been in jail for nine, ten years. Come out and stay six months. Because they got power in there. They can pull strings. A lot of people make more money in there than they do on the streets. That's why the penitentiaries be so full. They don't have to get out and hustle for that dollar every day. They get up, they got breakfast. It's more danger there, but you can work if you want to.

- *What's happened to the people you grew up with?*

Most of them is in the pen. Doing stretches. Leading the Black Guerrilla [Family]. When they hit the pens, they don't even be let out into the population. They lock them down in the hole, bam, bam. They're generals and they call the shots. Send an order out for you to get hit, you *hit*. They tell *you*, go kill a white guy. You gotta do it or die.

They got a Mexican Mafia and a Familia. I've seen an instance where a Mexican dude hang around with nothing but blacks on the streets. And when they sent to the pen they had to be Mexicans or die. Even a mixed breed, they have to choose one way or the other.

I think I would rather die on the streets than go to the pen. I was lucky to be able to escape. And that I had a judge that gave me a choice. Because if I would've went to the pen, I would've been dead.

As a teenager he was the president of a black social club. Then he became director of a young adult organization under the auspices of Sacramento's poverty program.

We was running programs to get black youths into jobs. We built that park in Oak Park, on Fourth Avenue. Every Sunday we would be there, there would be thousands of people there. So when the riots and stuff jumped off, we got the blame for it. I think they wanted anyone that had any kind of leadership ability or could generate the people into a mass—they wanted them out of town, or in jail, or did away with. 'Cause we had people motivated about the black movement. And they didn't want that. The police chief, he wanted us out of there real bad. Anything got committed: "Was it any of these guys?" And they got rid of us, everybody that was involved with us. And that was the end of the movement here, really. There haven't been any kind of movements since. We got black history in schools and Mexican-American history, but black people are in worse—way worse—condition now than then.

The people are too passive. They've been literally *beat* into [passivity] because any black man that tries to lead anything is killed. Martin Luther King, who believe in peace. They shot and killed him. Malcolm X, he's dead. People that even stuck up for black people gets killed.

In the sixties, people kept you conscious. Because everything was vivid, loud. People was hollering it. Now a few dudes might sit back and kick about what we gonna do here, but as far as getting out to really generate the people, everyone's afraid. Because you don't want to go to jail. You don't wanna be killed.

So what can we do? If we pick up arms, we're dead. If we sit here, we're dead. What I'm saying is it's going to take a hell of a jolt to make black people come together under some common cause. There's gonna be riots. Like it was in England this year. There's gonna be an all-out race war! White people killing blacks, blacks killing Mexicans, and vice versa.

■ *Lot of people say people aren't as race-conscious as they used to be.*

Anybody that's saying that is not even looking. . . . He's dreaming. His eyes must be closed to the world. The whole world struggle is a race struggle. You got Libya, we got trouble with Iran. These Chinese people, they're already fighting Russia. All the dark-skin nations of the world. They literally beat us out of Vietnam. That was what all these other people are saying: "Just get your foot off us, man." And that's the way they're treating our minorities here. They got their foot on our necks.

In this country our main problem is racism. Every time you turn on the
TV, the Klan this, the Klan that. I truly believe that most of these people in
the sheriff's department is Ku Klux Klan. You is like subhuman to them. In
the county jail, if you say anything, if you stand up like a man, you gonna get
beat up.

People saying, "Let's get a group together to fight the Klan." Well, you can
fight 'em, but not in the streets physically. That's just adding fuel to the fire
where it's gonna be an all-out race war. Then we're all doomed. We have to
figure out some kind of way to make it in this country together. Once we get
all this racism off the face of the earth, we all be a much better people.

*Extremist solutions don't appeal to him. He was involved with the Black Libera-
tion Army while in jail, but "it was a little too strong for my blood." And he
doesn't agree with the communists, a prominent force at the college he attended, because "it wouldn't work here at all. That's not where the people are.
I want to do something here, within the frame of our own government."*

So we been talking about reorganizing, trying to get back out in the neighborhood and get some of these younger people aware of what's happening
around us, what's happening in the world, and what we got to do as a race and
as a people to survive. This is the thing I'm planning on doing. How far they
gonna let me go, I don't know—I'm talking about the system, the police here
in Sacramento. And I'm really afraid to get up and speak or even try to organize on the public scale because I'm afraid of what the consequences gonna
be. Like, one move, I'm in the pen! One little sneeze.

*When he was apprehended four years earlier, the local press had quoted a pro-
bation officer as saying that Simmons had been "irresponsible in his life-style,
fathering one child by his wife and five others by three different women, including a known prostitute with whom he was arrested here, and not contributing
to the children's support."*

All of my kids are here. That's one reason I'm still here. I love my kids.
They're all sons, that's what's really kind of bad. It's not bad, but if they was
girls . . . a woman can make it. Where dudes are more hard. They gonna be
on those streets. And I'm afraid. I want them to be strong. I want them to be
ready. I want them to be aware. I try to get behind them and push 'em to do
the right thing.

I contribute as much as I can. If I get a dollar, they get fifty cents. Mostly
it's just hustling. I do odd jobs here and there. I help people move. Tomorrow
I might help somebody put up a door or something. I got people in the streets.
But the main thing, if you do something, don't do felonies. I get a misde-

meanor, it scare me to death. 'Cause if they drive it up to a felony, I'm gone. So if I have to do something illegal, which I don't say I'm just straight Honest John, I'm not gonna hurt anyone. I'm not gonna rob nobody or do nothing to physically harm anyone that ain't doing nothing to me. But if something come by where I think I can make a buck off it, I'll make a buck off it.

I haven't been on welfare, 'cause that's not me. I don't want no handouts. I don't like the changes they take you through. I'm healthy. I'm a black man. I wouldn't feel comfortable accepting that money.

■ *So you agree with Reagan that welfare's a bad system?*

No, we don't agree. I think the welfare is doing a lot of people a lotta good. Like most of my kids on welfare. He's taking food out of my kids' mouths. But if someone is able-bodied, I think they should try to work. A lot of these people on welfare, they would be better off in the streets trying to do something for theirself. You being a man about it, anyway. I'm not depending on anyone but me. I pay rent here, light, gas, you know. I keep food here. If my kids don't have anything to eat at home, I got a place for 'em to stay. If I'm getting the check, if they cut that check off, where they gonna run to? You see where I'm coming from? I got to be as much of a man as I can, to survive, for my kids to survive, for my kids to look up to me as being a man, as being their father. I got to try to be independent.

■ *Sounds like it's not getting any easier to be a man.*

No, man, it's not. They're paying you not to be. (*Laughs.*) You can just let your woman get on welfare and live. You can't live with your family. But you can live with another man's family. And this is the way they seem like they want us situated. They won't give a woman welfare if they with their [children's] natural fathers. That's really crazy to me.

When I returned the newspaper clipping he had given me describing his arrest, my letter came back stamped "Moved, left no address." Millie Harding told me in 1986 and 1987 that Simmons visits from time to time. But I kept missing him, and he never called me back.

Larry Dillard

"Without [the Black Panthers], my generation would be a different generation"

1980. It took me almost a year and a half to locate Larry Dillard. When I finally reached him on the phone, he was outraged that I knew his real name.

But he agreed to meet to discuss the possibility of an interview. I opened my office door to a suspicious, guarded, very tall and very imposing man. After a shaky, uncomfortable start, the interview finds its rhythm. Dillard, now almost thirty, draws out his words unhurriedly, laughing frequently, with his whole body and much gusto.

I don't think I was ever a revolutionary. (*Laughs.*) I never wanted to be in no organization or anything like that. Like the Panther Party, I could respect Huey Newton and couldn't respect nobody else, you know. All the rest of the cats wasn't nothing but followers, and a lot of them I know and went to school together, hung out on the streets together. And it takes something like a damn organization for them to stand up and be men, see. And I know at heart, they ain't nothing but some poop-butts anyway, man to man.

There was a lot of resentment toward me in the Panther Party. They wanted me to join. I was with my partner, Harold, and we were all sitting together over here on Telegraph—Bobby [Seale] and Newton—and he told me, "You don't want to be in this poop-butt, jive-ass party." I shared those feelings, even before I met him, but I wasn't able to talk to them like that. There ain't no telling what I'd ended up, talking to them cats like that. He told them, "If you want my friend in the party, you have to make him a goddamn minister." (*Laughs.*)

At eighteen, Dillard "graduated" from juvenile jail to adult prison. Even though prison was much more brutal and he had his "ass whipped" regularly by the guards, he felt "more like a man" to be treated "like an animal" than "like a child" by the youth authority. In prison he met a "heavy cat," Harold Cowell, who became the most important influence on his life. Considerably older, a college graduate, a theorist of the black revolution: "Huey and Bobby, they knew him, they respected him. He was in the joint with Eldridge. He knew James Baldwin." Harold became his mentor, took him under his wing, introduced him as his protégé when he read his poetry to college audiences; they ran the street together.

I'd accept what he'd say, you know. Most of what he said, anyway. Because I really think that he cared about me, and he wouldn't try and tell me nothing wrong. He told me that it wasn't cool to be racist. "Okay, the honky dogs you around, fucks you over and everything, the honky hates you—why are you going to be like the honky?" And really I couldn't understand him, because I actually put 'em both together, you know, being a revolutionary and a racist. He couldn't tell it to me overnight, but over a period of time, I think it kind of sunk in. Race hatred and everything, that's what I call it now, bullshit talk. Ain't anything but bullshit. I try and deal with people as people.

The Panthers have no more power. The pigs is back to normal. You know.

They back to shooting brothers down on the street and everything. But there had been a time when they stopped pulling that shit, and it was due to the Black Panther Party. Like I said, the Party itself ain't nothing. There was a few people that was down people and believed in what they was saying and would hold their own and back their shit up. Huey—I always did think he was down—he would die for what he believed, you know, but a bunch of his popcorn-ass followers, they were shit snitches, informers. Even for them people that I'm down on, it did them a lot of good, man. Made them think that they was strong and part of something, you know. I mean those cats would end up standing on the goddamn corner selling newspapers and shit, a little old newsboy position, but they felt better doing it.

When I was eighteen to twenty-three, I was having some good days in and out of the jailhouse. I was doing plenty wrong, and I was getting ahold to a lot of money. But ever since then, the whole shit done slack up. There used to be money. It was circulating, it was going around. And there ain't no money like that no more.

Like, say, in the sixties and early seventies, on the streets, you could find a whole bunch of cats that call theirselves pimps—you know—have a brand new Cadillac and things, diamond rings, nice clothes and shit—you know, penthouses and things. No more. You don't see them no more. (*Laughs.*) I swear to God. I haven't seen a pimp—a real pimp—since I don't know when. I know some guys that got girls . . . turning tricks and things. He's a pimp, know what I mean, he's a construction worker digging a fucking hole down there on Sacramento [Street]. I don't know who the pimps are.

■ *So what happened to the pimps?*

I don't know, man. What happened to the 'ho's? What happened to the fucking tricks? They put a lot of pressure in Oakland, man. When the tricks started getting busted and shit, that knocked out a lot of action. The guys that have the money are—drugs, that's what we call [the] "big boys." And there's no more big boy pimps. 'Cause I would know who's pimping and who's not pimping.

My little brother, he's twenty-two years old. There's a thing they got where everybody walks fast, like whirlwinds, man. And they talk crazy, man. They have their hair done in some certain way—they call it "jerry curl," their hair—and they be talking some old strange-ass shit, the bitch this, the bitch that. Maybe I did the same thing, but it was a different thing. And I don't even know where they get it from, because like I say, ain't nobody pimping. Maybe it's the drug thing. Like they call my little brother "nut." 'Cause he acts like a nut. And this is cool, acting crazy. To go around talking real loud and vulgar, with disrespect for everybody and anybody. Whereas like in '68, it was better to be low-keyed, you understand what I mean, and cool. Real cool. Quiet. That's what the word *cool* is about. But these cats is nuts. (*Laughs.*)

My older brother and them, all them cats, they was good General Motors workers and shit, man, and good family boys or men. (*Laughs.*) But like in my generation, a lot more cats didn't even necessarily want to participate in the mainstream. And that's come about through organizations such as the Black Panther Party. I think it was a hell of an influence. Without it, my generation would be a different generation. It even opened up shit to my generation—higher educational institutions and things—not necessarily the Black Panther Party, but the total civil rights movement.

He pauses to take a sip of his Budweiser. When I brought out the Bud in that first tense moment, he said, "That's my brand." I breathed a sigh of relief.

You're bringing out thoughts in me now, man. It's hard to be thinking of all this shit right off the top, man, because I ain't been thinking of this kind of stuff. My mind been way off on other things.

Like this here free-basing. You hip to it? Smoking cocaine—or washing it—what they call cooking it back to the raw and smoking it in the toker. The first time I was aware of it was like in '69. I just saw it then, it wasn't really even no word for it then. I think it done hit the scene in the last couple of years. I know some cats claim they was basing three years [before], but that's about the earliest I ever heard.

Heroin has kind of quieted down. People that have shot heroin say that this free-basing makes a ass out of heroin. I ain't never liked heroin—I'm scared of that shit. I don't want to fuck with nothing that's going to take me over. Heroin, it really makes dogs out of people.

I wouldn't even use [cocaine] for about six months. I watched these cats, I be around them all the time, day and night. "Come on, Larry, come on, try it, try it." I said, "Nooo, I don't want to fuck with it." And I said, "Well, ain't nobody going crazy." (*Laughs.*) That's what I was checking out. There ain't nobody jumping off no roof or nothing. So I told myself, "What in the hell can you lose? You ain't got a damn thing anyway. So you might as well have your little fun." (*Laughs.*)

■ *Is it addictive like heroin?*

No, but it's a heavy mind thing. It's hard to quit. You want more and more. It seems like you ain't never satisfied with that shit, man. You just have to run out of money. And go through a fit of depression and go home.

It's a beautiful high. Oh yeah, it's a right-on high. It's better than shooting cocaine; it's better than tooting cocaine—this is the righteous high on the cocaine thing. It make you feel real good. It don't last a minute though, boy. You get a nice hit on the pipe, and it's gone. It's nothing like smoking hash or weed or anything where the high hang with you. It goes. You got to get you another hit.

Two hits apiece for two people cost fifty dollars, five minutes of "that righteous feeling." He sighs heavily: the expense of free-basing has already broken some big dope dealers, and it's going to more and more "fuck up the church's money." To finance his own hits, he does little jobs "here and there." At the night spot where he tends bar, he serves also as the bouncer and sometimes does "little enforcement things" for his boss. "There ain't no job that he can't give me that I won't take care of for him." It bothers Dillard that his boss—and others as well—are afraid of him. Despite his reputation, he's "no mad dog," but people hear things and "get it all off and twisted."

He works closely with the police maintaining order at the club. The heavy criminals, the really dangerous people, they're never a problem. But there's always a few young kids, "poop-butt fools," who are out to terrorize the place—just like he did when he was their age. But he could hold his own; that's the difference. Since most of the time the white cop on the beat doesn't want to be bothered, Larry has the green light to handle these situations himself. The cop once said, "How come you didn't take that little knife from the dude and shove it up his goddamn ass, and then call me?"

So I practice a few of my little old things on people down there, you know, the foolie-rulies, I'm having fun with them. I give them all the chance in the world to be good and go on about their business, but of course they don't want to. Like I had to shoot a dude one night down there. He was the lucky one; he got off light—I shot him in the leg. But the ones that I whupped, they were in big trouble. They wished they had of got shot.

He's never married and doesn't plan to. When he was young, "too young," he became the father of two children. They were supposedly accidents, but he suspects "the mamas were doing a little planning on my ass." At any rate, he didn't want the responsibility, and though he sees them occasionally— tomorrow he's supposed to buy his son shoes—he doesn't find his kids easy to be with. "I don't take a whole lot of time with them," he says very softly, an uncharacteristic edge of sadness in his voice. I ask him how he's changed in the last dozen years.

Things that used to make me mad don't make me mad no more. I used to be kind of hotheaded, you know. Fly off the handle. I used to get mad if a person called me out of my name. I used to do shit like *demand* respect from people.

I used to be what they call a tender-dick youngster. (*Chuckles.*) You know what I mean. I just had to have me some pussy. And I used to think you ain't cool if you ain't got a steady girlfriend, man, you're missing something in life. I got girlfriends now, but I don't have none that I would really care about or something. I just knock out a shot every now and then and that's cool. A lot of times, I don't even know what the hell to say to one of them, you know, a young lady be up in my face, I'll be down there bartending, we've always got action, one right there in my face, pretty little thing and everything, and (*poignantly, wistfully*) there ain't nothing I can even say. Whereas there was a time, oooh, would I tell something, you know, I'd go to rapping on. And catch fish. I'm not trying to make you think I'm no punk or nothing. (*Laughs.*) You understand me.

■ *Is it like slowing down?*

I don't like to put it like that—slowing down. I'm a little too *vain* for that. (*Very hearty laugh.*) Slowing down. It's kind of like, lost interest a little bit. It's not important to me.

He hasn't been in prison for eight years. He won't take the same chances he did when he was younger: "At one time I didn't give a damn if I went to jail or not—it wasn't no big thing." But today he cares, he doesn't want to be in "those asshole places" anymore. Not that he's becoming "a straight-up-all-the-way-legit dude." If he had a chance to get rich quick, he'd take that chance, even if it meant ending up in jail.

In some ways Dillard is more of an outsider than he was in 1967; but there's also a part of him that fits in better. He's no longer actively "against society": the problems of survival, like the price of gas, don't give him time to think about social issues. But he's furious about the profits of "the goddamn oil companies": "If I can see it, if the whole society can see it, how come there ain't something done about it?" And when Iran took American hostages a month ago, he got angry and discovered that he still had feelings of patriotism.

He likes the changes he sees in race relations. Today blacks and whites are associating more naturally, in work or play, out of necessity or true friendliness. Without any of "that pretentious shit," when whites used to hang out with blacks because it was fashionable. But all in all Larry rarely thinks about race any more.

I would like to think that black people are superior to whites. I used to maintain that and really believe it too. But I can't no more. Don't have no help. Ain't nobody else feeling like that. There ain't no black leaders going around preaching no shit like that no more.

I used to have a theory that black people were born rich, just naturally rich in nature, you know, and white people weren't. That white people created false riches, like money and things, and created a society where everybody had to strive to achieve these false riches and in doing so, they never feel their true riches.

Now the same theory can be applied to everybody, every human. That you're born lords of the land, king and queen of the earth. But you don't never know it because you're not allowed to know it. Man has taken himself out of harmony with nature. You can never feel yourself, your true self. Instead of striving to really feel the natural things that are *here* on the world to feel—you know, sometime I can look at the damn stars like I ain't never seen them before. Because I haven't seen them. I haven't even looked up and paid any attention to them. Sometimes I can look out on the world in amazement, and say, ooh, this is really pretty. Like I never seen the trees and [the] rolling hills and shit, how green they are, how pretty they are. And that's really out of touch, man. I'm not talking about tripping or being on no drugs or nothing. And I think this is where man is cheating himself. He's not really feeling the true riches of being man.

From a bookshelf he picks up a copy of the American Sociological Review. *"This is what you do?" he asks me. And sensing some wistfulness in his question, I ask whether he ever regrets not having gone to college, considering his obvious intelligence.*

No. It isn't something I want to do. I'm very comfortable with myself. I just have to face the fact that I'm standing on shaky ground because I'm not securing no future or anything of that sort. But I actually believe the whole goddamn country is on shaky ground, and for me to be securing shit for the future might not do me a damn bit of good.

I was thinking about getting up there to thirty. And I asked myself, "Boy, you're thinking about you're going to change?" And I said, "Hell, no, I'm not going to change. Not now, not when I'm thirty, not when I'm after thirty." Just gon' keep on until the whole goddamn bottom fall out. And when it does, there ain't going to be a big drop. It's just going to be a little drop because I'm sitting on the bottom now.

Afterwards he tells me he had intended to fire a whole bunch of questions at me, "to mess me up." He never got around to it. Not so much because he decided to trust me. Rather, I think, he was just having too good a time, enjoying his memories, laughing heartily at himself and the old times. All this made him nostalgic for jail. In fact, he wouldn't mind being back there a couple of years, just to have that quiet, the time to think about these larger questions, to figure out who he really is.

November 1986. Nobody believes me when I tell them this guy I know, he's been interviewing me for fifteen years. "Are you really going to be in the book, Larry?" I say yes. They say, "Oh man, you've got to be jiving." (*Laughs uproariously.*)

His two teenage children—"I've been 'Pops' all their lives"—are living with him. But all his attention is focused on free-basing cocaine. He doesn't like the example he's setting: his son has already shown interest in dealing. "I told him I would break his neck if I hear about him trying to sell it or use." Larry's not worried about his daughter, because she keeps after him to get clean.

A lot of people think this is a brand new drug situation, but it's not. Crack is just another word for *free-base* or for *rock*. Out here we call it a *pop* or a *rock*. On the East Coast they call it *crack* or *crank*. It was here around 1975. It's a media twist, a media scare that say they was running with this new form of cocaine called crack. Crack is not a killer, it's just free-basing.

I be selling drugs to support my habit. And in doing that I make a little living too. I could be rich if I didn't have a habit.

- *Would you like to be rich?*

It don't look like it. (*Laughs.*) 'Cause I swear I could be. It's a lot of money went through my hands. Then again I might be in the penitentiary too. 'Cause the bigger you get, the closer you get to going to jail. Just supporting your habit like I do, you don't draw a lot of heat on yourself.

It's a new generation of dealers coming through, young black guys. They don't use the drug, they're stacking it up big. Me being in the first generation of free-basers, dealers and users, I'm a failure. (*Laughs.*) But the younger guys, they've seen us going before them, and they not coming behind us with the same mistake. It's straight up for them, a lot of money. They're buying homes and things, fast cars, they're getting into property.

- *Do you think cocaine should be legalized?*

No, *shit* no. Cocaine, shit, attacks the central nervous system. It's mind altering, it's psychologically very addictive. It's very rare that a person kicks this drug, very rare. I've seen a lot of tragedy surrounding free-basing. I don't mean death-related use of it—I can't imagine *free-basing* killed Len Bias, it had to be something else—I just mean the tragedy of people losing families and their homes and jobs and things of that nature. Their fucking mind, you know. No, I don't think it should be legalized.

- *You'd be angry as hell if your own kids became users and yet you're part of the apparatus that gets other people's kids into it.*

I don't have any conflicts about that. Not right on the surface. I don't even look at it in those terms, other people's kids and things. If there's any conflict it would be in my own personal use of it, what it does to me, why I want to get out of it.

As for black people in Oakland, he feels they are "prospering very nicely," politically and economically. He's very impressed by the number of black-owned businesses in construction and in retail sales. The prosperity of the middle class and government programs have raised the standard of lower-class people too. In the late sixties he viewed the black bourgeoisie as "traitors" because they had left the community. But today he sees them in the community, providing goods, services, and jobs.

The 1960s pride of race had a lasting impact, Dillard feels.

But I don't think it's "Black is beautiful" [anymore]. It's "I am beautiful and I'm black." First the black is beautiful had to come, so you can know you're beautiful and you're black. It's not the symbolic thing, the afro, power sign, it's not something that has to be taught or shouted or something people had to unite together to feel. That phase is over and it succeeded. My children feel better about theirselves and they know that they're black.

For the most part Larry is enjoying life, but not as much as before he became a single parent. Then he was able to stay for weeks at a time at expensive hotels, "just fucking up money," at places like Reno, Tahoe, Las Vegas, Palm Springs. Has he noticed any change in the way white people act toward him in those places?

The change was in me. I don't look for racial attitudes anymore. I don't even think about it. I would know if it had hit me in the face. It hasn't. I've had more exposure dealing with white people than when I was younger. When I was younger it was more racism involved. But with the more being exposed [today], there's nothing to give an attitude to be guarded against. So I guess there is a change, not only in me, but in the white people in my community.

Did you hear me say "and the *white* people in my community"? I used to wouldn't refer to being in the same community. Years ago I would have been talking about North Oakland [a predominantly black area]. [Today] I'm talking about the [whole] East Bay.

Sarah Williams

"I had him and everything just changed"

1979. *In 1968 Sarah Williams was turned off by the black movement, a lack of interest that seemed to reflect a personal despair. Ten years later, now thirty-*

three, she feels more connected to the world. Her overall outlook is more positive, and her beliefs seem to flow naturally from her personal life. At the center of her life is her seven-year-old son.

Since I have grown older and see what it is to raise a child and all the ups and downs and the way that the times is changing—I have changed a lot. I have matured. Because if I would have been like I was ten years ago, I would have been in the nuthouse.

I don't know what I would have done if he wouldn't have come when he did. I didn't care what happened to me. I would get so depressed sometime that I wouldn't go anywhere. I was just content in being within the house, and it'd seem like the walls, you know, be closing in on me. Then all of a sudden, I got pregnant with him. And I had him and then everything just changed.

Back then, people could bring me down just by saying things—the least little thing. And they might not be true, but the way it come across and it seem like it go in my mind and locks there. And I get all down and depressed and I'll be wondering is it really like what they say?

The crisis came in 1970. One morning she couldn't get out of bed: there was no feeling in her legs. Told that the problem was emotional, she was sent to the psychiatric ward. After she left the hospital, a psychiatrist helped her come to terms with her feelings about her mother. Her mother had objected to her boyfriend, but Sarah kept seeing him. A year later she was pregnant with Arthur.

He'll be seven years old this year, and so far it's been a joy raising the child and seeing what motherhood is all about. When I had him, my mother'd say, "I didn't tell you it was going to be easy." Plus doing it all by yourself. It's really hard. He would ask me different things about why me and his father is not together. I don't think he still understand that. We haven't seen his father in three years.

There's different things that he wants explained to him about what's going on in the world, and you have to know exactly. I try to answer to the best of my ability. He'll think over the answer, then he'll come back with another question. He rolls them off so fast, he really keep you on your toes.

Before I had surgery, I been getting a kick of going into his classroom and volunteer time just to keep up-to-date with what's going on. You have to keep up with everything to keep up with him.

Ten years ago she wasn't even registered to vote. Today she's active in community groups: "Since I had him everything has come open for me. I got it in my mind that I was a part of the world and society."

The jobs she's had—government personnel clerk, real estate sales—didn't leave her enough time to be with Arthur. Now she has applied to work in the schools as a Headstart assistant. She receives no financial support from Arthur's father.

What rankles Arthur is certain kids that have a mother and father in the home, they seem to dwell on this. And when they start dwelling on it, he don't have anything to say. Whenever I go into the classroom, "Does Arthur have a father?" I'll say, "Yeah, how do you think he got here?" "Oh, well, where's his father at?" They want to know every little detail. I can understand what he's going through. I'll say, "Well, you have a father, he might not be in the house with you, but you always know you have a father." Most kids, when a man come into the house, they call him Daddy. It might not be the child's father. So I try to explain, "Whenever you see me with a friend, that don't mean he's your father." One guy I was dating, he would call him Daddy, and I would say, "That's not your father." The guy got kinda upset. "Why don't you want him to call me that?" "Because he knows who his father is, and I don't want him growing up mixed up."

I've tried to bring him up where he have a sense of value. Whenever my boyfriend spend the night or something, my son is usually away from home. My mother raised us without a father, too. And I thought it was awful, like she had a man come over her childrens. I tried hard not to let that happen with him.

He going to be a man some day—I hope to live to see it. He's got to grow up and find out what he's going to come up against in the world and all the changes that the world is going through. I'm going to try to teach him that a man has certain responsibilities.

■ *Ten years ago you talked about how black men didn't take responsibility, they expected a handout.*

They did. Some of them still do. It's getting worse. They see a woman alone—see her doing so much and accomplishing so much, they figure, "Well, this is what I need. She can provide for me." My sister say, "Well, you know it's so many womens to every man." And I say, "I ain't got nothing to do with that."

Maybe I got the wrong philosophy of life when it comes to dealing with men. Because I don't feel that a man has to have more than one woman. When I get involved with somebody I go into it with my whole heart. But a man, I guess he feels somebody going to run over him if he really shows his true feeling. He won't tell me how he feels. I let him know at all times how I feel about him.

I don't want to be equal to no man. I always did like for a man to wait on me and open the door for me. I ain't never wanted to be treated as if I was the same. A man was put here for a purpose, and with all this women's liberation, it just took the purpose out of what he was put here for.

Arthur is staying with his grandmother while Sarah recuperates from surgery.

He was at the top of the class. He'd come home and would drive me crazy: "You got to help me read this book or help me spell these words." And he had made it a point of learning ten words a day. Then all of a sudden he stopped reading like he used to. And then his teacher told him, he can play, he can jump, he can swing from the chandelier as long as he had his pencil in his hand ready to work. [Now] she's off on maternity leave. The substitute, she wants him to sit: you can't be flipping and flopping. Since he's not able to express himself, he rebels.

In St. Ignatius, there wasn't that many blacks in his classroom. When he was in child care it was a mixture. Then when he got out of St. Ignatius, it was all black. He thought it was kinda odd that there wasn't any white kids. He say, "Mama, you know there ain't no white people." It's kinda hard on a black child if it ain't a mixture.

■ *How do you see the progress of racial minorities?*

It look like it's getting worse to me. Because, you go down to the welfare, you see all these people sitting in the waiting room. Now, I don't know why . . . they got to go every day. Seven days a week. You see four waiting rooms full of people. And I think that's awful that they have to take these people through all these changes. The red tape and stuff, one year they wouldn't send no check. They didn't send no food stamps or nothing.

It got to the point where they would hate to see me coming. Because I know how to go through channels. If I had a problem and it didn't look like they was going to settle it down there, I'd get on the phone and call a county supervisor. They'd wonder how you get their phone number—how you do this and how you do that. I wouldn't go down there, standing in no line and sitting in no waiting room. They take forever to come out, and when they come out they talk to you like you're an animal or something. It's not only blacks. It's whites. (*Very upset.*) They do everybody.

■ *How about racial prejudice? Have you experienced any?*

Never. I've seen it done. But I have never experienced it myself. 'Cause, Norma used to say it's something about me that draws people to me, whether they're white or black. I can talk to a white person just as I was talking to a black person. It doesn't make any difference, and I want Arthur to be the same way.

■ *Is there more or less racism than ten years ago?*

I think it's more. You can see it out there. Like when I go to the employment office. You can just look at the expression on some people's faces when they interviewing. Like one time, she said, "I don't know if you can do this job." I say, "You're not looking at my experience. There might be jobs that don't look [like] I might be able to do. And then after a week or so I master the job." "In that neighborhood they don't cater to blacks. He might not even want to interview you." She didn't even want to say the address. It was a card store in the MacArthur-Broadway shopping center. I got on the phone and made an appointment.

I don't go to church as much as I should, but I really believe in God. I believe strongly. 'Cause there's nobody else helping me through all these hard times. When I think I'm on my last leg, I might go out there tomorrow and some money I didn't even know I was going to have would be in my mailbox. With my name on it. This is the way it's been. So I know He's there.

I look at the news every day. It's really depressing, you know. They talk about the gas. You're going to have to ration your gas. Only time I use my car is when I'm going to a meeting or to his school. I don't mind using my gas for something like that, because it's meaningful to me and it's something that he look forward to. 'Cause I did him all the good in the world when I was going to his classroom. "My mother's going to come to school today."

1986. Sarah has recently moved to Las Vegas, where she's wanted to live for a long time. Within a week she found a job as a cashier in a department store. She lives in an integrated neighborhood. It feels safe and peaceful. Already she likes it better than Oakland.

Her son hasn't joined her yet; he's staying with his godparents. He was doing very well in school until two years ago. But with the coming of the teenage years, he's succumbed to peer pressure and his schoolwork has suffered.

As for the future of black people in this country:

I'm optimistic. I always have been optimistic. We can't expect anybody to give us anything. You have to get up and go out there and get it. So if they don't have, it's nobody's fault but their own.

Jim Pettit

"Two counts against me: I'm black and I'm gay"

1979. At his Oakland home, I'm interviewing Jim Pettit, the fry cook who was so upset by the racial prejudice of his co-workers at Burger House. I admire one of the original oil paintings on the wall. Jim painted those birds himself, as part of his therapy after a "nervous breakdown." He discovered a talent, and now at age thirty-three he sees art as a serious calling, his future career.

Back in 1968, the black movement was going on and I had just been learning about being black. I just started blurting everything out. I was very anti-white . . . or maybe I wasn't and I was just trying to be. But I think I was resentful. And it was hard. It was hard for me to make that transition from liking whites in my childhood, then not liking whites, then liking whites again. So I guess change is hard. My biggest problem is, I don't know if you know it, but I'm gay now, I'm a homosexual, and I worry too much about what people are thinking about me.

■ *Were you aware of your gayness in '68?*

Kind of. I used to have gay, homosexual activities at that time. I guess I didn't want to believe it, but it was there, you know, and I think that was the biggest part in my nervous breakdown. Being married and having kids and then having the gay activities.

I'm still going to a therapist and we're working on my accepting it. I still don't feel very comfortable about being a homosexual, but I don't think I would feel comfortable with being a heterosexual either. I think that just my being, you know, my living, is difficult.

I have lots of complexes. Like when I get on the bus, I think everybody's looking at me, and if I make one move, they'll see it. [Like] when you're in a crowd of people and you have a hole in your pants or something, you feel very self-conscious.

When I first left my wife, it was hard because I guess I was still in love with her. And I hated leaving my kids. I was very confused. That's another thing that probably prompted the breakdown, my getting married so young, and having all that responsibility, not living my full life as a teenager, as a young adult. I was seventeen, still in high school when I got married. It was dumb of me. I wish I had it to do all over again.

I'm still on disability from the breakdown. Once I start working I'll get more responsibility and I'm looking toward being independent. And my lover is always stressing me to do that. He doesn't want to play daddy with me.

■ *How about your kids?*

I just had them over last weekend. There's four of them, but it's the two youngest that usually come over. The girl's one of the oldest, and there's a boy that's sixteen. He's working now, so he doesn't come over. I told him I was gay, and he went to his mother and said, "Why does my father have to be gay?" And that's all that was said about it. I wish that we could sit down and talk about it, but he never comes over.

I guess I was a lonely kid. I stayed off to myself a lot. I didn't want to stay around my sisters and brothers too much because I didn't want them to figure out that I was gay. I didn't know if I was gay myself. But see, people would come up and call me names, and in school they would call me a "bootie giver." In the eighth grade, I didn't even know what that was.

I had a job at Macy's last year. There were all these young kids working there, you know, nineteen or twenty, eighteen, sixteen. I kept that job two months and quit because the kids were talking about me. It got so bad, when I'd ride home on the bus, I would feel like I was having a stroke. I'd take it home with me, go to sleep with it, every day it got worse and worse. And these were black kids, most of them.

I guess that's what my world is, people being nice. And I know that's not good for me, because people aren't nice (*greatly anguished*). And I don't know how to overcome that. On a job, I start trying to be nice and they just roll all over you, you know. I'm so timid that if I say something to somebody in a bad way, I just get afraid, of either hostility or somebody calling me a punk in front of a crowd.

Martin, Jim's lover, is forty-eight and white. He owns the house where they live. It's a pleasant working-class neighborhood, predominantly black. Their neighbors are hostile, Jim says, especially the kids, and they've been burglarized three times.

The kid next door, he wouldn't ask me to cut the lawn. He would always ask Martin. Whenever something needs to be done, they come and ask Martin. They're thinking that because he's white, he owns the house, and because I'm black I don't. Like when we go out to dinner, they usually set the check by Martin.

Once we were in Canada, in Medicine Hat. It's a *very, very* racial town. We went into this restaurant, and I just felt that I wanted to choke, because I-I-I, I just felt so, so—what do you call it, I don't know the word for it. ("*Exposed?*") No, I felt I was being looked at, I felt terrible.

■ *Did Martin feel the same way?*

No, he usually doesn't. Because he's white and because he's less sensitive. I guess that's why I'm so sensitive, because I'm black. We were going camping up in Mendocino; we both love camping. And I was saying, "I have two counts against me: I'm black and I'm gay." And he says, "These people don't give a damn about that. Besides I'm with you." He's never had to go through those changes. It's hard both ways, being black and being gay.

- *Which is harder in this day and age?*

I think being gay is. I can't explain it. I lived in Montclair—that's a rich neighborhood, you know. There are homosexuals all around in that area. They wouldn't like us because I was black. But down here I think people want us out because we're gay.

I think being black has been accepted more than being gay. Because they have the black movement for such a long time and the gay movement just started recently. Look at the Catholics. They really despise gay people. And there are a lot of other religious groups that are against gays. I guess most religions are.

Jim feels that while blacks don't accept homosexuality, they're more comfortable around gays than whites are. "A lot of [straight] blacks just love gay people." Jim's father and his sisters and brothers accept Martin "as one of the family." In contrast, whites are more tolerant of homosexuality as a general principle, but they have more trouble accepting gays as people. Of Martin's relatives, his sister is the only one who accepts Jim.

My parents, they didn't have much of an education, and we never talked about blacks and whites. School was predominantly white. I had good times with the white kids, I didn't have any conflicts with them. The black movement made me change. It kind of opened my eyes to the world. I was growing up, I wasn't so naive. It scared the shit out of me, and as I said, it made me feel resentful.

- *And now?*

I feel good being black. I don't think I want to be anything else. You know, every time I permanent my hair I take on the attitude of being white because I'm so light. And then my hair was down to my shoulders practically and I could shake it and it would blow in the wind and I just loved that. I like the corn-row now.

I like being black. But I don't think I'm a strong enough black. I should take some more black studies courses. And I want to go into African art. That's where my head is right now.

If I had a black lover I would probably have more insight into being black. There was this one guy I had sex with, and he told me if you had a black lover you would probably want to play the female part instead of the male part. If you know what I mean.

- *How does that relate to being black?*

Because blacks like to play a male role. There are some white people, white gays that just don't like blacks. At S.F. State, they just turn off to blacks.

And over in the Castro area. I hate going over there. All of them are so stereo-typed. The beards and mustaches and the tight pants, they try to act so prissy or cute or whatever.

Some white people, I think they have changed. They don't say, "Black people are some of my best friends." I haven't heard that in a long time. But there's still some overtones of prejudice. They're slyer with it. They've got some kind of code going on. And they seem to give the impression that "well, we really do like blacks," but I don't think they really do. So I don't think that they've changed that much. And I don't think they ever will until there's one big hell of a revolution in this country. I mean something like bombs and shooting and all kinds of stuff.

- *Who's going to bring it about?*

Probably blacks and the minor—, I mean the liberal whites and Mexicans, the third world. I think it's going to come to that, if this world doesn't get blown up first. Nothing has really changed other than money getting scarcer and people are getting poorer.

They pacify people into little programs like CETA, and then maybe four or five years later they take the money back and the people are right into the same ditch that they were in. The government's just letting people freeze to death, like in New York, because they don't have any heat and they don't have any money to buy heaters. This country is wealthy enough to give people money to make them real comfortable.

I hate this country. I would like to live in Canada. Either in Montreal or Vancouver. Montreal has more blacks. The French people up there, they seem to like me. We went to a bar and the guys were just all over me. I've been to Mexico. Holland was very nice. They take care of their old, and the streets were clean and I didn't see hardly any kind of poverty-stricken areas. So I've really been doing a lot with my life since '68. I guess I've grown, in the sense that I've gotten my head together a little bit. At that time I was a naive child and *very* paranoid.

I'm basically pretty happy, but if I got up against the world again, I proba-bly wouldn't be. That's why I'm going back to school. To face the world. I've been in and out of school for a long time. I wanted to be a psychiatric social worker once. I wanted to be a cook. I wanted to be an English teacher. Now I'm going for art and I think this is the thing for me. Lately my paintings have really come to say a lot more. Painting makes me feel that I have something to live for.

1986. *Jim and Martin now own a house in San Francisco, and Jim has deco-rated it with antique furniture and his paintings. No longer estranged from his* *children, he advises them on their futures; he is concerned that one son and one daughter are already single parents. He's been working as a gourmet cook in a private home and getting lots of recognition. It's made him feel more independent and self-confident, and he seems much more settled, much less nervous, than when I last saw him.*

I think black people are doing bad. I don't think Reagan gives a shit about anyone. There are more people on welfare, more people on drugs. They tell themselves, "Hey, man, it's your fault that I'm here hung up in the ghetto, so I'm going to blow my head up with drugs so I can escape."

And there are the older people that should be working that have never really worked and don't want to work. That's where I came from. Somehow I struggled out of that cesspool of not wanting to work. I was afraid to work, just like most young people are afraid to work. It was a struggle for me to get off disability and it still is a struggle to stay there and say I'm independent.

I think that jobs are out there for young people—busing dishes, washing dishes, there are always jobs. For older blacks, say, thirty-five, thirty and up, I don't know if there's that many. I don't think older blacks—I'm speaking mainly about men—really want to work. If you really want to work, you'll go out and find a job.

Black women have carried black men for an awful long time. I think it's getting better in the middle class, but in the poorer class it's getting worse. The man is saying, "There's no hope for me," and he drinks and loses his job. And the woman is carrying the family. . . . His balls have been cut off.

The middle class are turning their backs on poor blacks and they're saying, "We don't want anything to do with them," just like middle-class whites. "I got what I got and I'm not going to help anybody get any more." The middle class are the worst kind of blacks. When a person is successful, you should give back to the community that you took away from.

When I walk past the projects, it's very frightful. I guess I'm afraid of the violence and the drugs, afraid that someone's going to come up. . . . I feel embarrassed about myself that I don't fit into the norm. Because I once came from that type of environment where we sometimes didn't have anything to eat, where we sometimes didn't have money enough to wash clothes.

When I was growing up people were more gregarious, more understanding. Bring some flour or bring some sugar over—I don't think that happens anymore because people are so afraid. It's a worse type of ghetto than when I grew up, because of the drugs and the alcohol. The communication is through drugs and through loud music and through violence, as opposed to having fun and being loving and caring.

I still don't accept being gay. I don't know if most gay people accept totally their gayhood. I identify myself as a human being first. I don't think of myself as being gay, I don't think of myself as being straight. Maybe I'm bisexual. I was at a dance, a straight dance, and I found myself being very attracted to a woman. If I could meet the right woman, her having to be gentle and understanding of gay life, I could possibly get into that again.

CHAPTER 11

Blue-Collar Men
in a Tight Economy

During the 1970s and 1980s the long-term shift from a manufacturing to a service economy has accelerated and the traditional blue-collar working class has shrunk. Jobs have been lost in the industrial sector as imports of manufactured goods have risen, capital investment has shifted from older smokestack industries to new high-tech fields, and the drive for cost efficiency has led management to deploy fewer workers and to introduce labor-saving methods of production.

These trends have not spared the men in this study: Dick Cunningham's printing firm closed down in order to relocate in an area with lower labor costs. On the waterfront automated containerization has reduced the membership of San Francisco's Longshoremen's Local 10 from 10,000 in 1959 to 1,600 in 1988. Joe Rypins and Mark Holder remain protected by the union's agreement with management to secure the jobs of its older members, but the union has not opened up its register since 1969.

Since the first interview, Rypins has risen from the blue-collar ranks into a low-level supervisorial position, as have Jim Corey and Lawrence Adams. Since Adams is no longer a union member, he's no longer as interested in political issues, including race. Indeed, all the blue-collar workers in this chapter are less interested in the social and political issues that dominated public life in the 1960s; aside from questions of economic survival, their concerns have shifted to a more personal sphere, particularly family life.

Like other whites, the workers point to examples of racial progress: the many prominent black mayors, racially integrated neighborhoods and workplaces, and a general decline in prejudice and racial militancy. This optimism has led to a certain complacency: racial inequalities no longer seem to be pressing issues—with the exception of affirmative action. The slow-growth economy and intense competition for jobs and promotions have made affirmative action extremely controversial. Some workers argue that it's "reverse racism," while others complain that it propels incompetent or unprepared minorities into jobs they cannot handle. Almost everyone, including the liberal Dick Cunningham, has stories to tell about incompetent blacks who expect to get ahead just because they're black and who cry "racism" when their performance is assessed by prevailing standards.

There were such stories in the late sixties, too, but the emphasis then was on the fact that blacks, still new to many industrial jobs, were good workers. Perhaps this shift in perception reflects the progress black workers have made: that their numbers and their abilities make them a more serious competitive threat to whites. Yet it would be a mistake to dismiss these perceptions as simply racist, for many blacks have similar qualms about the promotion of inadequately prepared minorities into positions of authority and responsibility. And the white workers themselves are not of one mind on affirmative action; Joe Rypins, though he calls it "a general screw-up," understands its rationale, and Lawrence Adams, despite all his griping, wants the federal program continued at his company.

White workers have learned a lot about race since the 1960s. They no longer hold many of the old stereotypes. They're clear today what race words mean and why certain epithets are offensive. All in all they're much more sophisticated, but many still draw the line at intermarriage, an issue that has become even more salient for Jim Corey, now that he has a daughter of his own.

Jim Corey

"He's just a boy, Daddy"

1981. Jim Corey is thirty-eight now and his small Nevada town has grown: he no longer knows everyone as well as he used to. But he still enjoys the serenity, the home life it provides, the safety. "If my daughter wants to go bicycle riding at this time of night, I tell her, 'Go ahead.'"

Jim Corey likes his lower-management job, though he wishes it drew on more of his abilities and paid better. He's thought about transferring "back East," where there are high-level openings. Not long ago he believed he was in line for the next promotion in the department where "I've busted my ass for seventeen years." But a twenty-two-year-old woman without any experience got the job instead and became his boss. Angry and frustrated, he "pouted" for days. He had disliked the women supervisors he'd had and had said, "I'd quit before I ever work for another." But in time she won him over, and today they're working well together.

The government has invested a lot of money in the federal woman's program and equal employment opportunities. I think it's an expensive hype. They say it's not a quota system. Well, it is, when you tell somebody that a minimum of ten percent of his staff is going to be such and such a race, color, creed, or religion. I thoroughly agreed with Bakke, on the medical school.* I guess that's Archie Bunker coming out in me. That's prejudice and I admit it.

In the early seventies he went back to school at a local community college.

We had a young black guy in class and the kid flat sat there and told the political science teacher, "You owe me a passing grade because I'm black." And I came uncorked. I said, "I can accept the fact that perhaps we owe you an advantage over somebody else getting into school because you came from an inner-city school that was predominantly black, had teachers that were not of the best quality. But sucker, once you're in the race, you got to run as hard as the next guy. Once you get in, you're on your own." I honestly thought the guy was going to whip me. And that's what I get upset with EEO [equal employment opportunity] and the federal woman's program: "You owe me the whole nine yards because of what I am."

- Are racial minorities being hired or promoted ahead of more qualified whites?

I don't think it's happening. There was a foreman's job opening up and a black fellow that lives around the corner, I felt he had a real good shot at it. He's an intelligent fellow, he was capable of doing the job well. He come up to me and says, "I don't think they want another black out there." I was shocked that he felt he was being discriminated against.

I went to Virginia for a five-week class. I was flabbergasted at the free association of both male and female between the races. Dancing, social interaction, congeniality. I found out that I was a hell of a bigger bigot than the people from Petersburg, Virginia. The South [has changed] much more drastically than we have out here. I was just stunned that they were so much more progressive in this area. I would actively, possibly even physically, retaliate if my daughter walked through the door with a black boyfriend.

---

*In June 1978 the U.S. Supreme Court upheld Allan Bakke's contention that the admissions policy of the University of California at Davis had wrongly discriminated against white applicants. The Court held that affirmative action plans could not mandate racial quotas, as the university had when it reserved 16 percent of the places in its entering class for nonwhites. Archie Bunker, to whom Corey compares himself in the next sentence, was the white, blue-collar Everyman in "All in the Family," one of the most popular TV programs in the 1970s.

■ *Your feelings seem even stronger than before.*

Yeah. It's more of a threat to me now, because I have a daughter. I see it as a real possibility. Because no matter what I do to raise my daughter—it took me a long time to admit this—when she's out of my sight, or she's out of her mother's sight, she becomes her own person. I've tried to do the best job I can in raising my near-eleven-year-old. And you have to hope to hope. Even if I want to instill that prejudice in my daughter that I don't want her to marry a black, that she's going to react just as she would if I was around—I know better because I didn't when I was out of my mother's sight.

When I started on Jennifer, she was about seven. I don't think she perceived them as any different, outside of color. Other than as human beings. And I guess I haven't been fair to her, but that's my prerogative, she's my daughter. It's fair from my point of view. (*Sighs, with a pained expression.*) I've tried to tell Jennifer that they were no less of a human being, they had the same feelings, they had the same reactions—not identical, you know—I told her they get hurt when you put fire to them, they get just as hurt when you say something bad about them, whether it's color or something they did. They're every bit as much of a human being as you are. And they're entitled to every bit as much of human dignity as you're entitled to. But they're not entitled to be my son-in-law.

■ *Did that make sense to her?*

It startled her. It startled her that I perceived them as human beings different than I would perceive her. Don't get me wrong. One of the finest guys I know in my life lives behind me and he's a black fellow. His name is B. D. Wilson. He's quiet, he's mild, he's unassuming, he's purposeful. In a lot of ways I envy B. for the kind of person he is. One of the heroes of my life was a black scout leader. He taught me how to fish, how to set up a tent, he taught me first aid. I think fondly of John. And I think fondly of B. If B. had a son that wanted to marry my daughter, that'd be a tough proposition. I'd really be between a rock and a hard spot. B. is fiercely proud of being black. But he's not pushy with it.

■ *What is it about intermarriage that puts you off so?*

I don't know. I don't know. (*Sighs.*) I just don't find the black people an attractive people. Okay? Physically attractive from the classic lines of beauty, the Greek sense of beauty. I've known a *lot* of very personable black people that were fun to be with and had good personalities, and yet in the sense of physical beauty, I don't find them attractive. As I would a good-looking white man, [with] a straight nose, a narrow chin, thin lips.

I have a friend, she's got three black children. She's not suffering. It's the kids that pay the price. I've gone to school with mulattos—the blacks don't want 'em and the whites don't want 'em. They really can't find a comfortable social niche. Because of the rednecks like me and the rednecks like them—there's blacks that are just as redneck as I am.

Jennifer goes to school with a boy her age. She knows Craig has a white mother, but she doesn't perceive Craig as anything but a black because his father's black. She asked me about it, and I told her that was his parents' choice. And I asked her how she felt about Craig. And she said, "He's just a boy, Daddy, he's a classmate. I like him as a classmate."

It was a lot easier for the Irish to be sucked up into the system because they were white. Once the guy gets rid of his brogue and changes his name, it's hard to tell whether he's a native-born or he's an Irishman or he's a Swede. A black man can't do that. He can't just change his name and get lost in the system. Physiologically he stands out. They have a disadvantage that the Irish didn't have, once the heat got off the Irish. You know, the Irish didn't come as slaves, but they suffered social prejudice. They were ostracized the same as the blacks.

I think we're further down the road to racial equality, but I don't know that there's ever going to be total racial equality. I'm not going to get upset if my daughter brings a Jewish boy home and says, "This is Herby Goldstein." I'm going to get upset if she walks in the door and says, "Daddy, this is Herby Goldstein," and Herby Goldstein looks like Sammy Davis, Jr.

Atlanta really amazes me. I expected Atlanta to blow up.* If this had happened back in the late sixties, it might well have erupted in riots. I'm not going to say that [Mayor] Maynard Jackson is the sole reason that Atlanta hasn't erupted into an L.A.–type situation. The special task force has well-spoken blacks that are answering the charges and the questions. It's not the white people that are doing all the answering.

The race riots in '65 were because there weren't enough blacks who had become proficient at working within the system enough to alleviate the social pressures. And it boiled over. There were not black mayors of major cities around that the blacks could turn to. It was literally the blacks trying to survive under a white regime. Many of them still perceive it that way. But there are Jesse Jacksons and Maynard Jacksons and the Tom Bradleys that at least they can look to. Through the efforts of people like Maynard Jackson, the blacks have become a hell of a lot more sophisticated politically. I don't say they're getting all their satisfaction, nobody is. (*Laughs.*)

I enjoyed the sixties. They were good years in my life, they were a learning period. I still enjoy the music of the Beach Boys. In the early sixties I got out of the navy, I got to Alaska and found out that I wouldn't live in Alaska for all the damn Yukon gold! I come down here and got a job, I met my wife, I got to

*Between 1979 and 1981 twenty-eight black children, teenagers, and young adults were murdered in Atlanta. In July 1981 Wayne Williams, a twenty-three-year-old black man, was charged with two of the murders.

know her, I was married, in '67, I guess it was. The sixties was not a bad time for me; it was a good time, and at the end of it my daughter was born.

I didn't like Berkeley. *That* was a shock. The mode of dress, the casualness. The bralessness was the big thing down there, and it didn't happen up here. We took a stroll through the campus one evening and we found people in some rather heavy petting. Totally oblivious to what was going on around them. I found it highly offensive. I thought it was the epitome of moral degradation. (*Laughs.*) I would still resent it today.

That was the year of our great hippies, wasn't it? I think I saw them as a threat to the American moral fiber, God help me. I just couldn't comprehend their life-style. It seemed they just weren't trying to chew on the hand that was feeding 'em, they were trying to bite the sucker off. I felt a lot of them were down there just wasting dad's money, taking up good space in the university for people who really wanted to learn. I perceived it as sacrilege—affronting the authority of the university officials, tearing down the university buildings. Not that they weren't entitled to be heard. But destroying property, I couldn't condone that today. Our taxes helped build it. It's nice to note that a lot of them have joined the establishment. (*Laughs.*)

When Jim returned to school, the hippies of Berkeley and San Francisco were in his classes; they had established rural communes not far from his town. He had several confrontations with them, particularly with those whose standards of cleanliness he found offensive. But he also met hippies who didn't fit the stereotype of "the old worn-out levis, unwashed, barefooted, pot-smoking, the scroungy hair that looked like it hadn't been washed for ten years." They helped him see that "underneath all of it they were people," just like everyone else.

I didn't agree with the anti-Vietnam demonstrations. I really used to think that the guys that run up to Canada ought to have been shot. But I did a lot of thinking about it. (*Pauses.*) A whole lot of thinking. I really talked with my brother-in-law—Billy went willingly—I can't honestly say that the people that went to Canada are wrong. They're wrong in my sense. But based on their perceptions, and the things that come out, I'm willing to give them the benefit of the doubt. In 1968 I wasn't. We didn't prove a damn thing by going. All we did was kill a bunch of kids. It was just a political sham.

■ *How do you feel about Reagan's defense policy?*

I'm really for it. Our preparedness was undermined, aggressively undermined. A lot of the young people see the armed forces as a nine-to-five job. I never really had to experience any battle situations, but there was no doubt in my mind why I was there. I believe in my country. I'm not saying it can't be wrong. But it's mine, and I think it's the best going in the world.

When I first started to work I thought that I would be one of those people that would have twenty or twenty-five grand in the bank and some T-bills floating around. And God, if I got tired of my car, let me go get a new one. Well, the worst-looking car you see out there is the only new one I've ever owned in my life—it's that blue Chevy. I figured that when I was forty [he's almost thirty-nine] I'd be a hell of a lot better off economically. When my wife and I got married I was making two dollars and ten cents an hour, always had more loose pennies than I've got now. I'm making ten dollars twenty-three cents an hour now, seventeen years later, working for the same employer, and it just doesn't seem like there's enough. Don't get me wrong, I've got a lot more assets. At two-ten an hour, we didn't have our own home, we didn't have two cars, we didn't each have a ten-speed bicycle, nobody was taking ballet lessons. I'm not poor. Don't get me wrong. I'm [just] upset that it takes damn near all my income every month to survive.

Today there just doesn't seem to be pride in workmanship, the sense of responsibility. Discipline and responsibility, that's what I want to try to teach my daughter. That's [what] I find missing in even my nieces and nephews and the teenagers of friends. It's not, "I want to mow the lawn the best I can because my dad asked me." [It's] "I want to mow the sucker and get him off my butt."

- *You haven't mentioned Richie Ward today.*

Richie Ward? I hadn't even remembered Richie—I kind of put Richie aside. Richie was a disappointment to me personally. I still like his mother. He left here and he went to Reno and got a job. He got hooked up in drugs and got busted for pushing. And this was the kid I thought was really going to go places. He was the one who used to tell all the funny jokes about being black and laugh and carry on. And yet he was really an intelligent guy. I haven't see Richie in (*long pause*) ten years.

Jim Corey eventually did move across the country, to another small town, for a better job. When I tried to contact him in 1986, he did not reply to my phone messages and letters.

Dick Cunningham

"Even Walnut Creek, it's integrating"

1979. At sixty-three, Dick Cunningham is the oldest male in his family and says he's "getting closer to heaven every day." He is happy with his life, especially his close family, even though he hasn't gotten ahead materially. And his

grandson Jason, the child of his daughter's interracial marriage, has been grow-
ing up without any special problems.

I think our society is far more tolerant today than it used to be. Like right in
my own family. The oldest daughter's husband is a black man. Prior to the
sixties, as a couple they would have had an *awful rough* row to hoe. They live
in Lafayette. It's a pretty posh neighborhood. And they have no problems.
They pretty much go anywhere, do anything they want to. Occasionally
they might go to a restaurant and get seated behind a pillar, this sort of
thing. They just don't bother to go there anymore, because there's too many
other places that don't treat them that way. When the kids first got married,
the wife and I were kind of shook up because we figured they're gonna have a
pretty rough row to hoe. I am very happy to say I've been proven wrong.

Ten years ago the printing plant he worked at closed.

At the time I was kinda bitter. But it's probably the best thing that ever
happened to me, 'cause it was the kind of job you'd never *quit*. Now if I had
been younger, with a family still to educate and everything, I would have
moved and stayed on in the industry. A lot of the guys, the younger guys, did.
But at my age I couldn't see selling my home and starting all over. Both of our
kids live in this area. So we pulled in our horns and I started driving a school
bus, and then the kids got this business of theirs started. It grew, and they
asked me to come in 'cause it got too much for the daughter to run.

"The business," the only full-scale hockey store in the Bay Area, started when
Jason became a hockey fanatic and his parents discovered there was no place to
buy or rent top-flight equipment. Now Cunningham handles all the mechani-
cal tasks: sharpening skates, mounting blades, packing and shipping merchan-
dise. "The strong back and the weak mind," he jokes. He enjoys the job im-
mensely—working with so many kids keeps him young, he says—and he
doesn't miss the pressure of production schedules at the printing plant.
  The hockey team Jason plays on is half white, half black. They spend every
summer at hockey schools in Canada, and everyone mixes very well. Jason,
who thinks of himself as "just a person," rather than in terms of a particular
color, is equally comfortable with white and black teammates.

You can't legislate the attitudes that lead to racism. It takes education. As
my grandchildren get older, you're going to see a whole lot less of it. You're
still going to see some, because a certain number of rednecks are going to raise
a certain number of rednecks. But I'd have to say things are progressing,
they're improving *slowly*. Some aspects too darn slowly.

Now take my own little area—what is known as Valley Homes. We have Orientals, blacks, Chicanos, all within the last ten years. Ten years ago was strictly WASP. Fifth house down the street from us, a black family bought about three years ago. Been accepted—as good friends, PTA and all, no problem. Kids play with the rest of the kids. Round the corner is a Chicano family—no sweat. Our own church is more integrated. Where there have been minorities come into the area, they have been welcomed.

Even Walnut Creek, it's integrating. Not on a large scale. What integration there is isn't causing any panic, either, the way it has in some areas, where the minute a black moved into the block, every other house went up for sale.

I think housing-wise a lot of your minorities don't necessarily want to get out of their "ghetto." They're more comfortable with their own. Now some of them want to and can't, for economic reasons.

The racial situation today is not perfect by a damn sight. Your minorities have made progress. They haven't made the progress that they *should* have. Part of it is the resistance that the establishment has put up. Racial discrimination, it's still there.

And part of it is their own fault. Too many of them are approaching the whole thing with the idea that just 'cause they're black you should give it to them. Or just 'cause they're brown or whatever color, be it yellow, blue, pink, or polka dot. I say give them the opportunity. If they're not willing to work once they have the opportunity then you cease to owe them anything. And the son-in-law freely admits that he has progressed very well because he was black. But he has maintained his position only because he was willing to work. He runs into too many that think all they have to do is show up every day and they done their bit. They thought they had it made and started goofing off. He's had to fire 'em.

- *Do you find this attitude to be more common among minorities than among whites?*

No, not necessarily. Many of your whites are in the same category. But most of your whites don't get quite so vociferous about it.

I stood in the unemployment line for a while, never drawn unemployment in my life . . . and I've been paying into it ever since it was originated, and the woman did her damnedest to make me take an inferior job rather than pay me the unemployment. But you see them driving up in new big automobiles, they got more angles to continue [getting compensation] once their twenty-six weeks is up, and they get away with it. There's something wrong with the system.

When it comes to foreign policy, I don't think very much of it. This country has gone too long on the premise "you have to do it our way because we say it's the best." They're talking about sending troops to Nicaragua. It wouldn't be the first time. I think it's entirely up to the Nicaraguans. Too long we have supported dictatorships, here, there, and the other place. And claimed out of one side of our mouths one thing and done the exact opposite.

My forebears were, I regret to say, very anti-Semitic. I deplored it, I still deplore it. Any anti-feeling, be it religion, race, sexual orientation, or whatever. I think that was pretty much ingrained in me by a couple of my aunts when I was a kid. Anything that anybody does that doesn't hurt anybody else . . . fine. Like this Nazi party group that wants to hold some kind of a rally in Walnut Creek. I deplore the fact that the outfit exists, but I'll defend their right to have their rally.

1986. *Dick Cunningham is retired now and still in good health. Jason played on a semi-pro hockey team for a while; now twenty-one, he works in a department store in San Francisco. The family store went out of business in 1982, a casualty of the bust in the hockey boom (energy prices made freezing and heating costs prohibitive) and the divorce of his daughter and son-in-law. Cunningham doesn't think that racial factors caused their marital difficulties; their problems were just people problems.*

There's been a lot of yack lately in the media about race problems in this area, in view of this Timmy Lee's hanging.* Well, I haven't seen it. Our family right down here, no problem. They've got teenage kids and no sweat. I ran into a little bit of reverse discrimination when I was driving the school bus. The blacks resented me.

■ *The NAACP had this whole weekend of hearings about racism in your area.*

I haven't seen it. Of course, I'm white. Now if I were black and trying to rent an apartment or buy a house—I'm not saying it doesn't exist. But I can't quite feel it is as horrendous as the NAACP wanted to picture it.

■ *Over the past five years you haven't noticed any more prejudiced attitudes?*

If anything, it's less. Among my age group we've become more tolerant as we've gotten older. Because you don't have the conflicts that you used to have.

An awful lot of them . . . well, some of them . . . are never going to improve themselves because they don't want to. It's too easy to stay on welfare, have illegitimate children, and get that much more. They don't want to improve themselves. And the opportunity for an education, they're throwing it down the drain. In the sixties a lot of people thought I was much too liberal. Today they think I'm more conservative. But I think my thinking and my feeling is the same, it's merely a difference in the times.

---

*Timmy Lee was a young gay black whose body was found hanging from a tree outside the Walnut Creek train station. At the time police said the evidence suggested suicide; Lee's family and the NAACP claimed it had to have been murder.

Lawrence Adams

"The federal government and AT&T screwed up"

1979. A union activist in the late 1960s, Lawrence Adams had his eyes set on a career as a union or a Democratic party official. But a few years ago he lost a key union election, even though his group had effectively represented the members: "We wouldn't bullshit and say we'll go after the moon, so people got angry with us." He dropped out of labor and party politics and no longer keeps "up-to-date [on] civil rights and human rights." "Interest just went the other way," to his family and getting ahead at the phone company.

Once he quit union politics, he found his craft job less fulfilling. So he's become a first-line supervisor of a technical unit, and at age thirty-seven he's looking to a career in management. Recalling some of his anti-management statements ten years earlier, I express my surprise.

There are things I can do as a manager to see that the things that I griped about don't happen to my people. If they do a good job, I make sure they know about it, and if it's really something to crow about, I put it in their file. When they do something bad, I take 'em in the back room and chew their ass off. Most of the stuff is done by committee—the boss is just one input.

At the executive level the company is [now] more people-oriented, but too many of the middle-level managers are the old school. They're assholes. They were hard-knocking assholes when they came up, and that's the way they run the company: "*I am the fourth line.* Do it my way whether you like it or not." I don't have to do that. If my second line is giving me that kind of irrational crap, I can take it, absorb it, and put it back out the way it should be. I want people who are motivated. If you take care of the people who do your work for you, they will take care of business for you. So that's what I try. I don't always succeed. But I outproduce anybody in our district.

Everything about his office demeanor is informal. He isn't wearing a tie, and his sport shirt hangs out over his belt. There is no door to his cubicle office; subordinates walk in freely, interrupting with questions and comments, and there's much back-and-forth kidding. He's still a temporary supervisor.

If they don't promote me permanently or give me another temporary title, I'll be back as a craftsman after a full year as a manager. Right now one out of every twenty-three slots that are promoted is a white male. When you have a hundred eighty-five white males sitting in temporary titles, you see how many other people of different sexes and races have to get promoted [first] in order to satisfy affirmative action.

You going to ask me if that makes me feel good? Hell, no, it doesn't make me feel good. It pisses the hell out of me. I believe the federal government and the American Telephone and Telegraph Company and its subsidiaries *screwed up.* I believe that they overreacted in trying to solve a hundred years, two hundred years, of discrimination by saying we will legally discriminate. The quality of the people has gone down the tubes. They have promoted people who couldn't do the job just for the sake of numbers.

Now don't get me wrong. There are people—black people, Asians, lot of women—who are very capable people and who are going to progress up the line. The fact that they would be able to progress faster than I would because of affirmative action is not the part that bothers me. The part that bothers me, I can name you as many of them who are an incompetent bunch of bastards who have no right being there, but are only there because their last name is Hispanic or black or they are females—and that's wrong.

The gal that just walked in here, Jane Wiggins, got her permanent title because of the numbers game under affirmative action. I got my temporary title first, but if they would make her my boss right now, it would be the greatest thing in the world. Because she's a very capable woman, a very capable person. She just happens to be female.

What the hell good does prejudice do you? Are you mad at somebody because he's black or because he's a son of a bitch? Now if you're mad at him because he's black, you're all screwed up; but if you're mad at him because he's a son of a bitch, that's fine.

But how about the backlash, the other guy? Why can you legally discriminate against him? I'm one of the guys that gets to pay for it. And I struggled. I've struggled for a year under these conditions. I think it's wrong, but I live with it. What does that make me? *Am I giving up?* Am I kowtowing? I don't miss an opportunity to scream about it, but a lot of people would say that I'm bending my own moral concepts and precepts. I don't know if I am or not.

It's hard for me to conceive somebody really being happy who sits on his ass all day long and draws his pay just because he happens to be a minority. Now if that person doesn't cut the mustard because they lack the skills, it's my job to see that they get the necessary training. If he's a person that can't learn at all or his attitude is "I don't give a shit," that guy ought to be fired. I don't believe in sending him next door and letting that guy worry about it.

To fire a minority person can invite a bureaucratic and legal nightmare, he says. In one current case, lawyers, doctors, the benefits committee, the union, and many levels of management had to be consulted. Some employees try to take advantage, saying in effect, "You can't fire me, I'm black." Twice Adams has tried to fire someone; twice he's been overturned by higher management.

People like myself who are getting stymied because of it have a tendency to be critical of racial minority people. We have Chinese here, we have Japanese, Mexican-Americans, females, blacks, and by and large they're a very competent group. I don't really see that much of a problem because of race. The new generations coming into this outfit have forced a definite change. They're not as willing to accept the prejudices of their dads and mothers and grandfathers and grandmothers.

You know, there are good guys and there are bad guys, and it doesn't make no difference what color they are. People will steal from people or people will help people, no matter what color they are. The fact that a person's of a different race is becoming less important.

Don't ask me about busing. That pisses me off. We don't have it here because everything is so integrated. Almost every district around here is made up of all different kinds of races. The East Side is not predominantly black and Mexican-American. Baloney! It's predominantly poor. It's the poor against the rich, not the blacks against the whites. The ethnic problem is still a problem. There are a lot of Archie Bunkers running around in all different races, people who don't like you because you're black or green or white. [But] I think economic situations are becoming damned important; everybody is involved with it.

You see a lot more involvement in political activity of Mexican-Americans and blacks. People are getting into the mainstream that weren't there before. They're being accepted because they are people and not because they happen to be Mexican-American.

In contrast to 1969, today Adams makes no references to particular black friends and associates. His main source of new acquaintances is the YMCA, where he has been very active in father-son and father-daughter programs. Unlike the union, his Y branch is predominantly white. The black man he had once pushed into union work and with whom he had exchanged racial jokes, he couldn't recall at all. But, he responds, the extent of his interracial activity has never been important to him: "I never kept statistics on it. I can't say that I take a black to lunch on Fridays, you know, it don't work that way with me."

The individual person, I think they are much more aware now of what's going on than they were before. They're much more willing to make up their own minds about things whether it's politics, human rights, consumer rights. You're almost forced to have opinions on gay rights or anything else. So I think opinions have liberalized. I happen to believe that what a person does in his bedroom is his own damn fault. *Fault's* the wrong word. If he wants to make love to another man, fine. If he wants to make love to a woman or a cow, I don't think anybody should give a shit. One of my high school instructors was gay. They fired him. That really pissed me off. I said, "Where you going to find another math teacher like this turkey?'"

Adams sees today's emphasis on human rights, the quality of life, the "self-actualized man" as a positive legacy of the 1960s. "It started with the pot-smokers and the dope-shooters. All of a sudden people said, 'I have a right to do certain things. I have a right to swear. I have a right to tell you to get bent. You can't take that from me.'" But it went too far: until the Symbionese Liberation Army appeared, "the radicals thought it was charming to blow up the Bank of America." After that, people began to work within the system.

People change. Tom Hayden changed. This is your SDS. He's just as much an advocate of that opinion as before, but not the violent end of it. Why? Because it didn't work. So it's all changing and (*sighs*), hell, I don't know if it's changing far enough, fast enough, or good enough.

You cannot change whole vast societies at one shot, overnight. In their wisdom our forefathers built the process to be slow. Things that we do in haste have a tendency to be wrong. And the things that take time and stand the test of time are the things that seem to be worthwhile. All of this came out of the sixties. All this self-awareness, political activity, Ralph Nader.

As I pack up my recording gear, Adams tells me his company's affirmative action program has only one year left to go to fulfill its five-year obligation to "the feds." No one knows if they'll continue the program after that. When I suggest that his own future might be brighter if they drop the program, he says: "Shit, I hope they renew it. I gripe like hell about it all the time, I need to let off steam. But those other guys need the help. I can always get by, somehow."

July 1986. *Not too long after we last spoke, Lawrence Adams got his permanent title as a first-line supervisor. Now he has a new job with the same company. The work involves traveling, some teaching, a great deal of independence, and a lot less pressure. He loves it.*

Affirmative action, I don't see too much of it anymore. You won't necessarily get passed up just because your number doesn't sit right. It's a lot better now if you happen to be a white male Caucasian. They may be short of females or minorities, but if I'm qualified for the job—or more qualified—I'm likely to get it irregardless of the affirmative action goals.

Inside the company, the different races are getting along quite well, he feels, and life has improved for minorities in the society at large. But he's not sure the underlying causes have been dealt with, although "both sides have learned to talk a lot better." He's angry about Reagan cutting social programs while increasing the defense budget.

I don't think we have any business doing business with South Africa. I've always thought that South Africa is an asshole place. Botha's not going to quit, so I think it's not going to be long before it explodes into a full-scale civil war, or somebody on the white side assassinates him.

Joe Rypins

"Smelling like a rose"

1979. I never knew much about black people until I went on the waterfront. I just was never around them. The first black people that I ever had anything to do with in my life beat the hell out of me. In boot camp. I'll never forget that as long as I live. But when I got on the waterfront that was my first opportunity to work with black guys who were like me, you know, my age, as smart as me, as physical as I am. Another Joe Rypins but a different color.

Black people used to scare me. 'Cause I didn't know anything about 'em. You know, I never even heard of greens. It's just like anything else, if you don't understand it, you're suspicious and you're off it. I guess I came to understand the different ways of talking, [their] language. People are people. Shit, they're all the same, you know. There are good ones and there're bad ones and there's average ones. And black people are just people of a different color and they stayed in the toaster longer than I did or something.

I remember Jackson used to tell me that on the farm in Louisiana, he didn't know there was a difference until he was damn near seven or eight years old. And all of a sudden he's in the service and he's a nigger. You know, "What's a nigger, man?" He didn't know. I guess I encountered things I didn't understand as I came into their world. [Like] the things that used to happen to them when they was kids back in Texas or Louisiana. "So why did you put up with that shit? Why don't you get a baseball bat . . ." They say, "You don't do that." I still don't understand that. If somebody treats me like that, he's got a whole lot of lumps coming and he's gonna get 'em as quick as I can find something to give 'em with. These guys are as big or bigger than Alex and they says, "No, you don't do that."

Three years ago Joe Rypins became a "walking boss." Before, he did the longshore work; now he directs it. It's the highest-paying position on the waterfront:

he makes more than $60,000 a year, up from $20,000. So he feels "pretty well set" for the rest of his life. Not yet forty when he was promoted, he says it's no wonder that "the young guys are jealous, the old guys are jealous. The black guys are jealous, the white guys are jealous. You see?"

I'm very comfortable now. I do exactly what I want to do, almost exactly when I want to. I have no financial problems, I live in a fairly nice house, and I have all the vehicles I want. You know, all my life I've thought, Jesus, I really want to build a jeep like I want because I've been in the woods many times and I don't like the jeeps I see. It's sitting right out there and, hell, it's exactly what I've always dreamed of. I've got four-wheel-drive pickups out there and campers. I've always dreamed of having different rifles. They're in there in the gun cabinet. What do I need that I don't have? If that's not successful, I guess I don't care to be successful beyond that.

Joe Rypins is big, good-looking, and he's enjoying himself as we sit around the kitchen table in his new ranch house in a fairly expensive suburb. Joe believes that it's class and not race that determines where a man lives: he doesn't know of any place that keeps people out just because they're the wrong color.

He muses on how far he's come in the past ten years. He gives himself some credit—he was blessed with a few natural skills and "the ability to think a little bit"—but when he thinks back on how he messed up when he was younger, it's almost like he "fell into shit and came up smelling like a rose!" And his job requires him to work only two nights one week and one night the next—unless "Greedy here," as he addresses his wife, pushes him to take additional shifts so that they can buy things faster or accelerate their savings–early retirement timetable. "And every time the dispatcher calls, she says, 'Are you going to work tonight?' I say, 'Oh no, I ain't going to work tonight!'"

Instead, he gets up well before dawn to go fishing for shad in Sacramento, or to go duck or pheasant hunting, depending on the season. I ask him how he's changed personally in the past ten years.

That's hard for me to say. I don't keep track of how I am as a person. [But] I'm not quite so eager to jump out of the car and snatch somebody that's made me mad and smack them in the face. Not because I no longer think that's the right thing to do. I'm over forty now, and you just can't get away with that stuff.

Two years ago he was beaten up in a car incident; that was his last fight. It's too risky when "kids got guns and knives and they're so paranoid and afraid of everything and they want to kill." When he was growing up, two kids would fight one day and the next day they'd be eating ice cream together.

Learning to control himself on the job wasn't easy. At first he would get tight enough to burst.

One of the first things I found when they made me a walking boss is I'm not just responsible for me. I'm handling millions of dollars' worth of somebody else's equipment and I'm responsible for that almost solely. And so when some smart guy, knows his way around a little bit, starts saying, "You son of a bitch, I'll get your ass," I just tell him, "You're fired," and walk away. You can't take the personal insults and the ego-tramping thing he's doing to you, and grab him, and say, "No, you won't," because then he's *got* you. I've fired him for a direct violation and [if] he can get me to commit something, then he's off the hook. Don't ever think they don't know that. Everybody on the waterfront knows Joe Rypins's subject to grabbing somebody.

The first time he fired someone, he was accused of racial prejudice. That was hard to swallow, but he's learned to deal with it, to play a few games himself. He tells me about Timmy, whom he fired one afternoon for being late. The next day Timmy was picked up for a burglary that had taken place the night before. Timmy claimed that he'd been working, but Joe wouldn't confirm the alibi. And when Timmy was released from jail, Joe wouldn't hire him back. "'You just don't like blacks, man, you keep pickin' on us,' [Timmy said]. 'No, I don't like niggers at all, motherfucker, get out of here.' And he didn't know what to say." (Laughs.) Though Joe still considers himself lazy, "I got an awful lot of devotion on my job. I can't stand anybody who gets in the way of my doing a good job. In fact, I fire them immediately."

Ego in a *male* animal, anyway, to my knowledge and to my experience, is the biggest single factor in *everything*. Whatever feeds ego is good, whatever tears down ego is bad. And that applies to me. I like it when somebody tells me, "You did a hell of a good job." I'm considered a pretty good walking boss. Everybody knows I don't have to work, but they still call, "Would you come in and take our shift, it's a tough one." And a lot of times because "Bank of America" here says, "Hey, go to work," I'll go ahead and do it. And the next time I see 'em, "Thanks a lot, Joe. That was a hell of a job, and we didn't think you were going to make it." Shit! I feel good. I mean I feel *super*. I get ten feet tall, man.

Most guys that work for me, I'm talking about three or four hundred different guys, I'd say eight-five or ninety percent of them are damned good men. Just good men, good workers. A lot of them I got no use for and they know it, but I just could not stand to give this guy a good job 'cause I like him and this guy a lousy job 'cause I don't like him. That's out. Favoritism—I used to hate that. . . . Guys come on a job and you'd see them fifteen minutes and they'd be gone and get paid all night and I'm there doing his work. I don't let that happen now. Everybody knows they don't have to kiss my ass to get a good job.

Longshoring in the Bay Area is a predominantly black industry, yet the bosses are overwhelmingly white. When the union of the rank and file, the ILWU, put enough pressure on the union of the walking bosses so that two of the four current openings will be filled by blacks, Joe was upset. He understands that for years blacks were not allowed to become walking bosses, and he agrees that management should make a serious effort to create a racial balance. But he doesn't like the government and the ILWU shoving affirmative action down his union's throat: "Why can't they say you have to hire four good, competent men?"

He understands the logic of affirmative action—"whites were never slaves in this country"—but it still doesn't make sense to him: "If somebody hired me 'cause I have to be white, I wouldn't take the goddamn job." And lots of blacks, he is sure, feel this way too: they want to be promoted because they can do the job. Blacks are as competent as whites, Joe emphasizes, but affirmative action has produced some incompetent black bosses—and yet, Joe adds, being fair, there are some no-good whites too.

I don't think I have any feeling about a guy strictly because he's a different color. As a matter of fact, I know I don't. There's black guys I can't stand, there's white guys I can't stand, there's Chinamen that I'll get at the drop of a hat. If I'm prejudiced against somebody it hurts everybody concerned. It hurts me, it hurts the guy I'm prejudiced against. I'm teaching my wife and I'm teaching my kids that that guy's no good because he's a Chinaman or a nigger or a spick or whatever, and kids grow with that. You know, they keep that. My kids like fishing because I fish. And it perpetuates the situation. I only hope that because more people are getting a better attitude about that, that the better understanding will multiply.

■ *How do you feel today about Stokely Carmichael and Martin Luther King?*

Just like any other politician, just full of shit and in a position. Nixon, Reagan, Johnson, Carmichael, Huey Newton, this is something for ego, for money, for power—whatever it is that drives people to do things.

■ *King's been made into a national hero, hasn't he?*

By who and for what? The guy took a lot of brave steps, there's no doubt about that. But you can bet your last nickel that he didn't do it strictly out of the goodness of his heart. Nobody goes that far out on a personal limb, physically puts himself in a lot of danger, in fact ends up getting killed, just because they think it's the "right thing to do."

- *You're saying that people don't do things for ideals or values—*

  Bullshit. No way!

- *Or to make it a better country or help their people?*

  No, they don't. There something there for 'em.

- *That makes you sound kind of cynical.*

  Oh, yes, oh yes, indeed. Although I don't call it cynical. I call it realistic, realistically cynical. Nobody does something for nothing. Not even priests or preachers. Okay, a friendly favor. You need my ashtray at your house, then take the goddamn thing. You need a ride, I'll give you a ride. That don't cost me, it don't hurt me.

Referring to the intense racial feelings of the sixties, Joe says, "You don't hear that kind of stuff anymore." Then it was new, like the gay movement today, he reasons, and people were for the blacks because they needed a cause, just like today there are people supporting gays "who don't give a shit about gays one way or the other." Joe considers himself anti-gay; he's not comfortable with the subject or the people. There are no openly gay people on the waterfront, he is certain.

Women, too, are still out of place on the docks, but when the longshore local runs short of hands, sometimes they call for help from "sister" locals. So how do these women do?

Terrible! It's just too physical a job. There's exceptions. Little black lady well over sixty, not as big as Norma [Joe's wife]. I've seen her pack cane. She come on the job I had one night to lash some heavy equipment, and I said, "Hon, you better replace yourself now, 'cause when you can't handle this I'm gonna fire you, and I can just about tell you can't handle it." "Well, if I can't do my job, you just fire me." She did a hell of a job. Which makes me mad. Not because she did a hell of a job. But what the hell is a goddamn woman sixty-plus years old doing working like that? Where the hell's her kids at? (*Passionately, very excited.*) They should see to it that she don't have to do that kind of stuff.

I have one saying that I abide by almost strictly. If you want to act like a woman, you get treated like a woman. If you want to act like a man, you get treated like a man.

I don't know if I want to see a woman walking boss. I'd have to compete with that, and I don't feel there's one woman in the world that can do my job like I do. Not too many men, either . . . Dummy up, daughter.

Most of his daughter Julie's boyfriends are Asians. "Funny-looking guys, all little bastards," Joe comments. Not true, says Julie. Her special friend, a Filipino, is tall, with blond hair and blue eyes. Joe guesses it would be all right if she married an Asian, but not just to make a point of it. His prime consideration would be the type of person he was: "What he's doing, where he's going, where he's been. No bums. And I'd expect her to explain that decision, to try to help me understand it. And if I could understand it, I'd accept it." But he clearly doesn't want her to marry a black.

I don't know why—the darker the color, the worse it would be for me. It's kind of a mysterious thing. I hope it's as tough a question for everybody else as it is for me.

If I told you what I did two years ago, you'd never believe me. I ran for city council. (*Laughs.*) I was sick and tired of the goddamn politics, doing things to please somebody, instead of doing it because it's right. I actively campaigned. I made speeches and I was on TV and all that bullshit. As it started getting closer, I got scared to death I'd win. If I go for something, I'd do the job right, which would mean I wouldn't put as many hours in on the pheasants as I do now. (*Laughs.*) I didn't get elected. Thank God.

The phone rings. It's the dispatcher asking if he wants to work a special shift tonight. "Nothing doing," he tells his wife.

June 1987. *Not long after our interview, Joe and his wife moved to another city, to be closer to his children in college and the wilderness he loves. His new home is in a major port city, and Joe remains a walking boss. He is pleased that almost all the workers, including racial minorities and white ethnics, take great pride in their work. And he's impressed with how many women are now working on the waterfront. At first there was a lot of resentment; but since most of them do a good job, there are no problems anymore.*

He feels "mellower" than in his youth: "I'm kind of just enjoying life now." His grown kids have exciting, challenging careers, and he spends even more time fishing and hunting. What disturbs him is the way the lumber companies are cutting down the forests, shrinking the habitat of moose and other animals. "They've raped a lot of the country. The logging areas are just a disaster." He doesn't criticize radical environmentalists who put spikes in trees to discourage logging: "How else are you going to stop the big lumber companies? They just don't care. I see what they're doing to the woods. I think conservation is one of the most pressing, important issues of this entire universe."

He had much less to say about racial issues. "I just don't keep up with it." Two days earlier a New York jury had handed down its verdict in the Bernhard Goetz case.

I think it probably came out as good as it could. They got what they deserved. (*"The four black youths?"*) Black had nothing to do with it, punks like that come in all colors. They're animals. It may not be their fault, but that's the way they were brought up.

I'VE INCLUDED Mark Holder in this otherwise all-white chapter to suggest some of the convergences in outlook between white and black workers during the 1970s: the shift from politics to personal life, the emphasis on economic issues, and the attitude that, with color becoming secondary, "people are people."

Mark Anthony Holder

"Peoples of forty, they're no longer thinking about a race thing"

1980. Like his fellow longshoreman Joe Rypins, Mark Holder says he has outgrown his youthful rebellion and he is optimistic about his future. His paragon of manhood is no longer the streetwise hustler-warrior, but the family-oriented, economically responsible adult. His views on the extent of racial change are more positive than those of most of the other blacks I talked to, perhaps because of the unique race relations in the longshore industry and the success of integration in Oakland, where he lives.

Holder has been saving money from his job and buying old buildings to fix them up. He is enjoying the chance to express his creativity and to see his ideas materialize in the finished product. But right now he's cautious: "People aren't buying, money's short, everything's in a Jimmy Carter uproar. The Iran crisis, it's affecting a lot of peoples." The economic situation is a lot tighter than it was in 1968, when he had just gotten his first well-paid job.

I was young and I used the money foolishly. But as years went by, I got more responsible with myself, and I see now that I have to put that money in a situation where I know I'm going to receive something back from it. A cousin inspired me to get into the building thing. He's younger than I am and he was always productive. He had a better chance than I did. His father and his mother never separated, there was only two [children], and they gave him the best of things. And he bought all these little houses, and I felt that I was just lagging.

I'm looking at my future now. I'm forty-one. I have about twenty—about fifteen—more good years, of working and good health. And in my older years I want to be responsible for myself. I'm afraid to be needy. I don't want to be leaning on anyone, so I make preparations now.

I've always—not *feared* getting old or anything, but it was strange and foreign to me when I was coming on, looking at an older person. I looked at guys that was forty, and I had never took it serious. "Well, hey, I'll be forty," but I was inside still feeling like I'm thirty. But now I feel myself getting older, I see wrinkles, I could never be again like thirty. At thirty I could go out, last, drink with the best of them. I'm feeling jolly, I can approach the opposite sex and be liked.

I still feel good, but I respect my age. I no longer can be with [younger] people, because they're not thinking positive. I have to be around peoples of my age. Now that I have reached forty, I see how they act. I see what they've accomplished. And if I'm to be forty, well, I expect to have this too. Or what was my years worth?

At forty I feel that I'm a part of the system. I didn't have the opportunity as a twenty-nine-year-old to go and sit and converse with forty-year-old peoples or fifty, that makes rules. But at forty I'm very responsible and I'm supposed to make sound decisions and to be followed by youth. Hey, take some advice if I've got it to give. Right now I'm in the realm of where a forty-year-old person is supposed to be.

I had a divorce, which was a hard battle for three years. I still got my documents and everything—I keep all of that. My lawyer told me, "It's very unusual for a man to gain custody of a daughter." I'm not that religious but I really prayed that if I ever got my daughter, I'd go all out. And I've been all out for her and, well, she's [the] one really that prompted me to getting off into real estate and cutting things in my past life that I was living loose. And just making a forty-year-old family life, you know.

■ *In '68 you seemed to feel that the system was stacked against you.*

Right. I felt that the world was closing in on me. You had a lot of racial things at that time. You had the FBI . . . infiltrating everybody's business, preferably blacks that they thought would interfere with the system. Now it's a little more slack. Peoples of forty, they're no longer thinking about a race thing.

I had to be on the offensive because I was into things that was, you know, possibly wrong and against the law. Now I have established myself where I don't have to be off into any crime. But then I thought it was possible to exist and just never really allow that person to get that close to me so that he would know what I was doing. Using the knowledge that I have learned from people that I was around to exist in the street life.

■ *Are you feeling now that it was wrong, that part of your life?*

It wasn't hurting anyone. To me, it wasn't [wrong]—it was a way of surviving, making it, you know. As I worked and money was plentiful and as years went, times changed, situations changed. So I felt, hey, I don't have to do that no more. I have enough knowledge now. I'm getting older and I have a daughter that I'm interested in seeing through college. I'm her only support, I can't let her down. So I don't take chances anymore. I'll just be whatever they call the common guy. Because I've had my fun. And at forty everything is serious. It's no more play. It's time to live for someone.

This business venture I'm in now, it's easy. The people that I'm dealing with is peoples my age. They recognize a forty-year-old man as being established. So I been getting this consideration. Before I had slangs. I would talk with different slangs because I wasn't mature enough to know how to correct my speech or try to conversate on different subjects. I would always go into the street thing, still keeping offensive, you know.

Like if I'm talking with a guy that I want to buy a house from, he's going to look at me, "Is this guy serious?" If I'm talking the way he's talking, I'm serious. But if I'm talking, "Hey, daddy, looka here, wow, like man," he wouldn't take me serious at all. So that language just disappeared from my vocabulary as being older.

- *Are you talking differently because I'm white?*

These words then was just a quick way to eliminate a whole sentence. So now in speaking with you, not because you're white or anything, I'm looking at you as a man of my age that we are understanding each other. And I couldn't talk to you with "dig" because that doesn't mean anything now.

The white man? They have changed. Now whether they finally realized that, hey, this man is a human being, walks and breathes just as I—who's to say if they felt that inside? Or is it they've changed because they were forced to by law? Okay. I see a slackness in the white man now. He's more concerned, he's willing to listen at what you're saying, before he would just ignore you altogether. He's not as hard as he was. But it still exists there. Because I guess it's just human nature. I can't condemn this man because he has this mental thought about the race thing. Me, myself, I have even this little thing in me where I may look at the white man . . . you may feel a little hatred come in you. I can't explain it. It was probably inherited or just the thing that a black person or a white person grew up to feel. Superiority, it's just a lingering thing from the past.

He feels threatened in some ways. He fears maybe that this black guy's got a tail. It starts from childhood—embedded in your mind. You can't figure it out. But all you know is you know it, and as you grow older, it's just there. It's hard to explain. I can't say that he looks at me as being masculine 'cause I'm black. It's not the fact that they're afraid of what you could do physically to him. It's not that kind of afraid. It's afraid of what your ability is, the possibility that I may go beyond him as far as progress. He may feel that his job is to keep me back. Because he may feel that if everybody get these opportunities, it may knock him back. Or his youngster.

I used to think it was a color factor. He's white, he's this way. But as years went by, I seen white guys that think just like I do and they don't look at no color barrier. They say, man, come on over, let's indulge in this, let's do this together. On the waterfront, they got the same type job I have. So they acts just like I do. And I found some that thought just like I did. They're non-religious as far as being a Protestant or a Catholic or whatever. They're realist. I don't look at it as a race thing anymore, because I got a little more knowledge on it. I look at it now as a man, now that I'm working over here with them and everything.

■ *When that started happening, did it threaten your preconceptions?*

Yeah, because what I've always believed then was beginning to turn false. I thought all whites was against me. Because all my dealings with them was trying to get out of this situation, or I owe a bill to 'em, and it was always *on* me. But after being there, he's looking at me as a man and asking me, "Hey, man, what have you got to say about what you think?" and I could ask him. It's no black thing where your idea is null, because, you know, you don't have no thoughts. It's not like that there. I'm working with this guy and I say, "Hey, it would be a better idea, man, if we take this and position it this way." "Hey, I agree." So we together.

The Caucasians, they don't have time to think about no hatred because they're busy trying to think about the dollar, which has declined so. It don't give 'em that much time to try to hate this man. Because this man is doing what *he's* trying to do, trying to survive. Now there may be some hostility when you go up and try to get this job that this guy is trying to apply for—there may be an exception there, but there's a law to make that all go even.

[Racism] still exists. But it's not that visible. You know what I'm saying? It's still going on, but they set out laws which like say: hey, you got to have a certain amount of blacks in this job, you know. So that eased the pressure, you know—the race thing, a little bit. It's easier now for the black man 'cause he got a little more ground, a little more opportunity, so he goes forward. It's a little slack now. He don't have to confront this guy saying, "To heck with you, I'm going to give you the ax." He can't do that. It's the law.

Like this statement on the news where Reagan's wife made sort of a racial slur. (*"All those beautiful white people?"*) Yeah, but check this out—blacks didn't care about it. It just was, "Oh really?" It didn't even faze me. I always had this on Reagan when he was over here cutting the welfare. He was so *American*, he was strictly one hundred percent blue blood, see. So right then,

I formed an opinion about him. Everybody knew what he was, what he stood for.

Holder's only regret is that he isn't educated enough to help his daughter with her studies. But he had her transfer to one of the best college preparatory schools in the area.

When I was that age, money was short and we were poverty. So there wasn't really no one preparing me. I was just making it through school best I could. And if somebody would have given me a thought like, "Hey, I'm behind you," I think I'd a went for it all the way. I wanted to be a musician. My father never bought me a horn, which I used to constantly draw. I used to draw things that I wanted and just look at it and, you know, get off into it. I wanted to play a sax—real bad.

Today he paints as a way to relax when stresses pile up. Sometimes he'll take his sketch pad, go up to the regional park, just to "walk through those woods" and be "enchanted by the forest." "I like nature, I like insects, butterflies, trees, anything of beauty—now this is a joy to me. It's a spiritual type thing."

- How do you feel today about Martin Luther King?

He was ahead of his time, he really was. If he would have been able to carry on his plan, things today would be so different. You'd a had more blacks in the White House—I mean with jobs, like Andrew Young. They would have started a machine, which could have been so advanced. But since he was killed, it never did come to pass.

Martin Luther King today would have been another Marcus Garvey. Martin Luther King's philosophy was equal rights for all people, and Marcus Garvey's was, "Okay, since you don't like us here in the States, give us the money and the ship and we'll go back to Africa."

- In '68 you were down on King. You almost called him an Uncle Tom.

True, true. I really did and I'm still against his tactics. He had to come on nonviolent because he's speaking for everyone, not just blacks. He had this mass media followers. But I don't think he ever could have achieved what he was going to do by being nonviolent. He had to be more like a militant, like Huey [Newton].

If [King] appeared to be Tom, it was because he was trying to last as long as he could, so he could push this over. I didn't want any hardship coming on him. He was being jailed, he had to take the kicks and blows. But now I see why he did. To get a chance to get out there and be heard. And he wasn't so Uncle Tomish over the years.

He drew a lot of peoples with him on that nonviolence. Peoples looking at blacks as being crazy and want to fight, then he showed you: Hey, we are nonviolent peoples. All we want is justice, a break. And he sounded meek and crying and pitiful. When they show these pictures of them slapping him, they look real *ancient*. Because that was way back, and people today look at that and feel ashamed.

■ *We've talked about just everything except soul.*

It's just a feeling anyway. Anybody could have it. It's just something that agony brings about in a deprived person. You could feel agony and you could divert agony into something, to forget it, so you smile with it. It's universal.

It was a cliché or it was a slang to say "soul." That meant, "Hey, you're black, we can relate to you now, you're a soul brother." I'm not going to hurt your building or tear it up. You can trust me. It was just a fad, a word. We could even put it into a rhythm factor. I got rhythm. That's the same as soul. [Today] I feel a little more self-confident and secure. When I didn't have anything, naturally, I'm going to think about agony and all the hardships. So things are peaceful now, so I'm not mad (*laughs*) and I have peace of mind. See, that was more or less a pass-type word to assure you, "I'm all right, man." Hey, man, we feel good because we share the same thing. We've been through the forefather things, the four hundred, three hundred years, and so we feel this. But another race of people, what if they want to relate their sorrows to their cultural thing? For instance, when the Jews went through this Holocaust, over there in Germany, they had this feeling that no other nation would have, of agony. They could have termed this feeling as *something . . .*

■ *A monopoly on suffering?*

Right, right! And then only *them* could have it. Can you see what I'm saying? Because they're the onliest ones that went through it. So other peoples try to say, well, I got this. "How could you, if you've never been there?" See, the onliest things which blacks have on the Caucasians was, "Hey, we got soul because we went through the cotton fields and went through this agony." Awwww.

■ *So blacks don't need that as much anymore?*

No, because opportunities now is more open.

1986. *Mark Holder is still working on the waterfront. He didn't answer my requests for another interview and told Alex Papillon that the project had begun to feel "old" to him.*

CHAPTER 12

Men, Women, and Opportunity

During the height of the black culture movement in the sixties and early seventies, black nationalists often viewed single-parent families and unmarried mothers as a cultural variant of the traditional mainstream family, even as an ethnic strength. During the seventies and eighties, our interviews document a growing concern about the Afro-American family. No one I interviewed in 1979 or 1986 repeated the argument in defense of mother-led families. Particularly troubled were people watching their own grandchildren grow up without fathers in the home.

The special problems of black men are seen as the gist of the family crisis. Several people I spoke with felt that black men had made important gains since the sixties: the civil rights and Black Power movements gave them more confidence, and the opening of opportunity structures provided educational and occupational skills. But most would agree with Harold Sampson that "black men don't have it together like black women do." Nevertheless, most of the blacks in this book don't agree with the arguments of media analysts such as Bill Moyers (in his CBS Report on "The Vanishing Family: Crisis in Black America") that the heart of the issue is the irresponsibility and other character flaws of the Afro-American male. Instead, they blame the rise in single-parent families on the economy: high unemployment and underemployment prevent black men from fulfilling the role of breadwinner.

That black women improved their earnings and occupational status at a rate faster than black men from the 1960s through the 1980s, achieving virtual parity in earnings and education with white women, speaks well for their energy and initiative. But structural trends in the job market may have been the critical factor. Most new jobs have been in the white-collar, service, and professional occupations, where women predominate. Concurrently, there has been a devastating net loss of jobs requiring little education or formal training, a sector that once provided employment for many black males.

In addition, affirmative action programs sometimes give black women another advantage: by hiring a black female, a company at once improves the racial and sexual balance of its work force. But probably even more significant, black women have been accepted more readily than black men in many work situations because their presence is less threatening to white male co-workers and supervisors.

Although the situation has improved since the sixties, in most workplaces blacks are not permitted the same latitude as whites to be assertive, aggressive, ambitious, or angry. Competent, assertive black men are still perceived by some whites as a threat, particularly at middle and high levels of corporations and government bureaucracies and in blue-collar jobs, such as firefighting, that require co-workers to live together. In the interview that follows, Harold Sampson talks about how he was subjected to special scrutiny and how whites were always surprised when he showed real competence.

Harold Sampson

"I have not been able to achieve selfhood through the civil rights movement"

1979. Ten years ago Harold Sampson spent every night on the streets, trying to prevent race riots, and every day working in the post office. He says he'd still be carrying mail now, at age forty-nine, if it hadn't been for the sixties. Instead, Sampson completed a doctoral degree in education and is a dean of community-based education at a small community college near Sacramento. It was a drastic change, "like coming out of the street-fighter image, putting on a shirt and tie, and getting on the board [of directors.]"

When he went back to college in the mid-sixties, his night-school instructors were not helpful: "It's almost as if there was a mindset: 'Okay, it's politically wise for us to let these guys and gals in now, but don't challenge them, don't make them think, don't help them.'" The two skills that were to prove indispensable in his career, writing grant proposals and preparing budgets, he learned on his own.

Since the 1950s, Martin Luther King had been a major influence on Dr. Sampson—spiritually as well as politically—and King's assassination (just weeks after the 1968 interview) was a major turning point in his life. He was already beginning to question the confrontational strategies of the late 1960s,

*when a friendly police officer warned him, "If you don't stop making the state-
ments you're making, there's nothing we can do to protect you or your family."
Nine years of that kind of pressure was enough. It was time for change, political as well as personal.*

*A deliberate man who makes "six- or eight-year plans," he quit the post
office, left his directorship at the Urban League, began work on a master's degree, and took a position as an administrator at the state university. A few
years later, he was thinking about a doctorate, and the Ford Foundation was
looking for someone to direct a major project. He accepted the job, and the
project became his dissertation research. I ask him how much of his success was
due to opportunities created by the 1960s, how much to his own special talents.*

Let me answer it this way. The sixties opened doors for both the competent
and the incompetent. The competent survived. You had to have enough ability to recognize what needed to be done, an ability to survive and perform,
okay? You had to have some competency. People, some of whom I dearly
love, had no perception of what was going on. They still attempted the strategies they used in the sixties, and they just fell off the crack.

[White] people were surprised when you showed some kind of competence. Very surprised. You were expected not to be able to think and to man-
age yourself and to be ethical and moral. And you were constantly tested.
First, can you handle money? The second, white women. And it was applied
over and over and over again. It was almost the rite of passage. If you demonstrated an ability to handle that, you were allowed to move on.

The door, a lot of people—I'm speaking nationally now—were able to
swing in there. But an interesting thing happened. Blacks—you've gotten
yours. So now we bring in a wave of browns. The piece of the pie didn't get
bigger, just divided up more. Cesar Chavez had been marching up and down
this San Joaquin Valley for ten, twelve years, in the grape fields and the let-
tuce. And even though we were supportive of the browns, the Dick Gregorys
and all the movement, suddenly we were enemies. Fighting each other, and
that's still going on.

For years Mexicans counted themselves white. There never was an alle-
giance to the blacks. I think blacks are surprised when they encounter anti-
black feelings coming from Chicanos. Surprised, hurt, and then angered. I
just wish my Chicano brothers and sisters would understand that it doesn't
have to be this way.

That decision—in academia, in the corporate structure, in government—
that we're only going to concede a certain percentage of jobs, a certain percentage of incomes, a certain percentage of opportunities to these groups—it's
not an accident. So that in order for me to get a larger piece, I've got to take it
from you, my Chicano brother, or you, my white sister. That door, it closed

a little bit more because of women. It closed a little more because of handicapped.

■ *Is that door still open or are we back to square one?*

No, no, the opportunities are continuing. Historically, blacks have their greatest opportunity [today]. You can go to school, get into Ph.D. programs. But you're not going to be given any preferential treatment.

When we were marching, that was effective because we were able to prick the conscience of people. You know, as the Bible says, the conscience has become so seared, you can't prick that anymore. After I see a Buddhist priest set himself on fire in Vietnam—a bunch of people marching around the State Capitol, that's nothing. After the assassinations, the disruptions, the social, economic, political decisions that've been made, it's very difficult to raise issues about human rights—I have no faith in these mass kinds of things happening [again].

There's just so many things that impact on our lives that transcend race and culture. I don't think you can ride a black banner any longer. It had its time and place. *Prolonging* [it] was divisive. Because the coalition, that strong third-world coalition, hasn't occurred.

He foresees that the struggles coming in the eighties and the nineties will be over ethical and moral issues, and the arena will be religion. Sampson is a devout Christian, and the black church has always been an anchor and a political power base for him. It provides him with the "loving, protective spiritual community" that gives his life meaning and without which his worldly accomplishments signify nothing. But today the church meets such needs for fewer and fewer people because of its mistakes and "aberrations." And despite white liberal support of civil rights, "Sunday morning nine to twelve is still the most segregated hour of the week." He is not surprised that so many blacks were attracted to the Peoples Temple and, more important, to a wide variety of new religions that offer spiritual community in a nondenominational and racially integrated setting.

We are better able to look at that spiritual side of us now and, almost out of a desperation, see that the other has not worked. I have not been able to achieve a sense of selfhood by going through the civil rights movement and all that. In my neighborhood I'm still a nigger that lives on that street who happens to have a Ph.D. and is making enough money to live here. Okay? And I drive across town to my black church every Sunday morning and I have friends who come in and we talk, but there's no . . . You know what I'm saying?

■ *That selfhood depends on some kind of community, and people find that community in religious or spiritual groups?*

Exactly. And it's not new or unique. In Old Testament times when the Jew was converted to Christianity, he had no family, no community. So the Jewish-Christians had to come together for survival, creating that communal living that's spoken of in the first four chapters of the Book of Acts.

My wife and I had been looking for a house for five years, and wanted an older home, trees, formal living room, dining room, no swimming pool. And we had worked with three or four real estate people, and we told them exactly what kind of a home we wanted and what area we wanted it in. Well, no one would show us any houses. One day just for a lark we started driving, the real estate person—a white woman—and myself. I said, "Turn here." There was a house [with] a sign lying in some bushes and I spotted it. The house was not in the multiple listing and the lockbox was hidden. (*He spotted that also.*) The key did not open the front door. She said, "Let's go." Obviously she didn't want to show me the house. I took the key and unlocked the kitchen door. Beautiful house.

The owner was out of state, and they had to send my offer in with the others—they couldn't identify me by race. The owner accepts our deal. The real estate salesman was upset because his company gets labeled as the company that puts a black in this all-white neighborhood. [He tells us,] "The bank said it can't finance your loan because there's an easement on your property." So they canceled my deal. This is the neighborhood where the neighbors circulate an announcement saying, "1325 is up for sale, let your white friends know."

Sampson pointedly mentioned to his agent that he was a personal and professional acquaintance of the owner of the realty company. The next morning she called to say that the bank had approved his loan.

Something happened between six o'clock Tuesday evening and seven o'clock Wednesday morning. Now is that racism? Is that classism? What is that? I experienced some things here in Sacramento in 1977 that I thought were *over* with. Bigotry and racism. It's still there.

It's a nice neighborhood. It's called Devon Park. People say, "*You* live in Devon Park?" They don't believe you. Because Devon Park is noted for not having any minorities. I mean *none*. No Asians, no Chicanos, no blacks. We don't socialize. My wife isn't part of the bridge club and the Tuesday . . . all that business. We don't drink. But we're good neighbors. We don't bother anybody. And my son is as big as I am. So he doesn't have any problems. But if he were younger . . . Minority kids are acceptable up to about age nine. Then parents begin getting concerned about dating and sexual activity. I didn't want my kids subjected to that.

My concern is what is happening to my sons. I use them symbolically. It's almost as if that period [the sixties] was completely erased by something which said, "You as a black man in America need to be taking care of your own needs because nobody else is going to do it. And if you have to do it at the expense of your brothers, and sisters, then do it. Be successful quick." You know, the superfly and all that crap.

Somebody decided to market everything that we could use. Our hair styles then were natural, we prided ourselves on that. Every other indicator, every other moral, ethical kind of thing that came up, including the music—you know, the blues and soul and spirituals—it became so commercial and so caught up with everyone else. Trying to hold on to some sense of identity became well-nigh impossible. I have a son who lives in San Francisco and I call him my black hippy. His sense of black identity is just lost.

It scares me that our black youth have lost the ability to hustle, that is, to "make it." They think of themselves as streetwise, but they only think street-wise means being some kind of a pimp. Now white youth out of the "hippy" [culture] know how to hustle and live off the street, doing something to survive. Blacks somehow felt that they had to go to school, get a degree, wear a white shirt, and go to work for IBM. They got coopted. The strategy was "get some niggers off the street corner, put 'em in school, give 'em EOP [Equal Opportunity Program] and everything else."

One time [at the state university], a group of students—black girls—came to me and said, "We're concerned that the guys on campus are being unfair to us." And I confronted them, these guys walking across campus with the big natural and a dashiki with a white girl swinging on his arm. A guy said to me, "Well, the sisters won't come across. What do you expect us to do?" I said, "Don't you realize you're making a political statement? You're walking around, talking about how African you are, and this is what you're doing."

They're being coopted away from a stance that says, "Hey, I'm a black man and this is what I stand for." Okay? "As a black man, there's some things that I won't do." There was nothing unusual that in the heat of all the civil rights struggles that relationships—genuine, sincere kinds of [interracial] relations—developed. That was cool. But there was also a whole lot of superficial, one-night stands. Well, some people got caught up on the one-night-stand level, and that's where they stay. So establishing firm family kinds of relationships is very, very difficult. When you look at all of that, I don't know that black man-hood has gained a great deal by what we've experienced.

I don't think black women are addressing the feminist movement in large numbers, but I think their sense of womanhood is more now. Don't have to apologize for some success. It's all right to be married and to treat your man okay, but if you're not, don't feel that you're less than a person. And [the feminist movement] saying that, making it okay, means it's okay now. So you find black women who aren't going to waste too much time with guys who don't have it together. And it's taking longer for the brothers to get it together. Think about it, if you tell someone that it's just enough to be black—you don't really have to be competent. And you use that as some sort of a hustle. And you find out that it's not enough, that you really don't have it together, it's a devastating realization. You came from the street corner and you went to school because someone says you ought to get that B.A. and you thought that B.A. was a conveyor belt to a job and when you got there, it wasn't. But now you got the B.A., but you really don't know how to write and here you are with a major in journalism. You present yourself to the newspaper, they won't hire you, and you know deep inside that you can't write, so what do you do? You've gotten married and your wife is working at the telephone company waiting for you to get through so you can support the family. And she's haranguing you because she's making more money than you're making. So that sense of the black female being able to do more with the opportunities is still there. Even more so now.

At the same time this other thing was saying, "Hey, you're too good to carry mail, to be a garbage man, to do work with your hands. This is the era for you to be doing professional things." And what happened? While we were talking that crap, those long-haired kids had cut their hair. Because the garbage men were making eighteen thousand dollars. They were starting teachers at ten thousand, the janitor in the school made seventeen thousand.

- *And the political consciousness of black youth, like your sons . . .*

It's nil. It's nil. And part of that loss was a turning away from the black church. So that element that was there for us wasn't there for them.

All my life I've been hearing that if blacks could just get it together, how much power we would have. I think that there's less potential for coming together in what a real coming together means. What I call healing. Dr. King with his style, and also Malcolm X, was able to provide that. Now that's not taking place. We can't talk to one another to really communicate how we are feeling, without placing blame or putting one another down. Obviously we're not a tribe, we all think differently, and to a degree America has done that, and that's something that was unexpected.

If I were where I am [today] in the sixties, Hardy would be attacking me as the middle-class black who's made it, who's insensitive. You know, the successful Ph.D. living in an all-white neighborhood and not over with the blacks "helping them." But if I had a chance, the decisions and the route would be exactly the same. You go where you can influence the lives of the greatest number of people, preferably poor people—irregardless of race.

Dr. Sampson feels that blacks need to develop their "sense of paranoia" once again. It's the first thing he'd add to bring his "survival kit" for dealing with racism up to date.

Nobody's going to walk up to you and insult you to your face. It's a lot more subtle. And your survival kit needs to include the fact that that degree doesn't mean a thing if you're not competent. And finally, your own supportive network, which would include some blacks and some whites. That supportive network can't be just the black church or the NAACP. My network would include some folks who would let me know what's really going on. Honest, upfront feedback, not a lot of . . .

■ *Are whites more able to give you honest feedback today?*

No question in my mind. We've gone beyond that race-racism thing. Way beyond. We can sit right down and deal man-to-man or woman-to-woman.

In 1968 Hardy, Len Davis, Florence Grier, Millie Harding, and a dozen or so other people felt the need to pull together those diverse elements [in the black community] that sometimes fought against one another. OPAS, Oak Park Action and Service, was one of the most significant things that's happened in Sacramento. OPAS had an impact on a lot of sectors. The police, after the Oak Park Four incident. Employment. The people in the core of OPAS, they couldn't brand us as fly-by-night. Various BSU [Black Student Union] types on the campus who were identified as the wild-eyed militants aren't around. The people who were solid are still here. Who stayed and who said, "Hey, you're important. I'm not going to use you."

September 1986. *Recently returned from a trip to the South, Harold Sampson finds genuine racial change much more impressive there, "in California, still superficial." Over the past five years, he says, whites in California have pulled back.*

There's a regression. Positions become hardened, and "it's now time for us white males to get some of what we've lost," [for] white females to take back the advantages that have been going to other minorities. There isn't a need for people to be courteous anymore; it can be blatant. I don't think it's coming from Reagan. Reagan's smart, he has taken the pulse of the population and . . . there's a widespread attitudinal change out there.

Affirmative action—I think that window is closed. What we're experiencing now is, "We're all on equal footing, baby. If you don't cut it, don't come crying to me about slavery or any of those things. Because I'm going to get mine, and you had better get yours." There's nothing to appeal to now, no fairness.

Progress for black people is "a mixed picture." Sampson sees improvement in housing—"If you've got the money you can buy a house anywhere you can afford to"—and also in better police-community relations. But education has worsened, unemployment and underemployment have risen, and drugs and teenage pregnancies are "just staggering."

What's happening to the black family, the single-parent household, is "one of the tragedies in our generation." And it's not, Sampson explains, that black men are deserters or "not caring"—the tough economic reality prevents them from being able to support a family. Even his three sons haven't married yet because "they simply can't put the economics together." With the shortage of successful black males, he notices that more black women are now dating white men.

Harold Sampson no longer makes that Sunday morning trip back to his old church. Like many other black professionals, he and his wife have joined an integrated congregation: Hispanics, Asians, whites. They're the only black members so far, and it's working out "just great."

He feels much more positive today about his neighborhood, though they're still the only black family. When a racial incident happened a few years back:

The neighbors were more indignant about it than I was. They nurtured me and cared for me, it's been genuine. Dinner parties, barbeques in the back-yard, that kind of thing. It's been more than comfortable; ideal, really.

Frank Casey

"If they had gave me the green light"

1978. Frank Casey's "second chance," the opportunity to break out of the cycle of poverty and discrimination, was a special product of the 1960s. He was hired as a school-community worker on the basis of his "mother wit," interpersonal skills, and life experience. But ten years later formal credentials were again the measuring stick, and Casey's direct, confrontational manner was out of style. As Frank put it, in that black working-class speech which must have made him appear to the bureaucracy as hopelessly unpolished, never to be assimilated: "They couldn't determinize distinctions from hostile to speaking their mind, because if you speak loud, you hostile."

He was fired a year ago. After "almost eleven years, they gonna tell me I don't have no seniority!" While he and his lawyer prepare a case to win him back his job, he has been working as a housing specialist on a temporary CETA job, helping to stop evictions and foreclosures. But at a salary so low that "I don't even care to talk about it."

At age forty-two, he's much thinner, his natural hair is longer, and there's a smoother, more sophisticated air to him. He's dressed fashionably and looks even better than he did in the sixties. But he has suffered a great deal. Once the most gregarious of persons, he now talks to almost no one. He is separated from his wife, drinking too much, staggering under economic burdens. Strikingly absent is his buoyant optimism: the idealistic belief that he could reach out and help people change.

I think everyone feels that he or she was put on this earth for some reason or another. I honestly believed and felt that I was put on this earth to help to work with kids, I really did. And I was good, I was damn good at my job to have, let's say, less education than probably anybody at that school. But the determination and the will and the common sense and putting all that together I was able to promote the kinds of communication, the kinds of liaison [that] goes into bringing about a working relationship, an understanding relationship with those kids. If they had gave me the green light . . . now don't get me wrong, I don't think no man is an island . . . but I feel with the help of others, who was somewhat scared, our job as school-community worker would have been so worldwide known it would have been pathetic.

You know, Bob, I *am* angry. I'm very angry. Because what they did, they didn't do because I was not performing my job. They did [it] because I was a black man and I spoke out on what I believe and felt. If I hadda been one of their little henchmen to say "yes, no" "yes, no," . . . "go do this," went and did that, and went and did this, I would still be there. I know this.

I sit up nighttimes sometimes and really think of demolishing them because they don't know what the hell they have put me through. I know I could have a job if it wasn't for them folks down there. They have shut off my livelihood. They don't know the suffering, not that I am absorbing, but my kids. Why, their kids, going on to school (*he's had to take his own daughter out of college*), got a place to live, don't have to worry about whether the man's going to walk to your door to serve you a notice or not. . . . I don't know how many times I didn't have the money to pay the rent. They got food on their table when they come in, in the evening. Sometimes I don't have food here on my table for my kids.

A plaque on the wall reads "Father of the Year, 1975—Frank Casey." It is signed by four of his children. The fifth, his youngest son, was killed in 1972. Frank didn't want to talk about that. But he kept mentioning 1972, instead of 1969, when he was telling me about the first time the school fired the school-community workers, accusing them of stirring up the community against the school district.

Specifically, the school charged that the five liaison workers had been involving themselves in school-board politics, campaigning for and against candi-

dates in elections and lobbying for funding proposals. On one occasion the chairman of the school board made some uninformed comments about the school-community workers at a meeting. Frank challenged him. "He had never visited our office or come down to talk in terms of what we do." When Frank wouldn't leave the podium, they cut off the mike, ended the meeting, even called the police. Casey feels the main problem was that the school expected him to bring its viewpoint to the community but didn't want him to bring the community's ideas to the school.

I wasn't there just to satisfy them. I was there because I wanted to bring unity within the community and schools. To have parents be able to walk in and talk to a principal about a kid's problem without having to be scared . . . be ready to get talked down to: "I only have a few minutes." I wanted the principal and teachers to not have to put that professional etiquette on parents, that they can get across what they need to say to the parents just by being what they are. But I struck out there too, and that's because they felt that I had just too much association with the community. Because everyone knew me and I knew them, and I think that's one reason why I was able to do a good job. I lived with 'em, I went to the bathroom with 'em, I went to wash my socks with 'em, I went to the joints with 'em, you know, I *live* there.

When the five liaison workers were fired, the community responded with letters, petitions, and pickets. They went to court and won their jobs back. The district appealed.

I didn't work very much with kids after the suit. I was doing merely janitor work . . . staying on the yard, you know, watching the kids, being in the lunchroom, make sure it was orderly, taking them home when they got bad. That was part of my duty. But that was the *only* duty I was supplying. It got to the place where I wasn't allowed to leave the school ground, you know, to talk to parents. There had been days and weeks that I have sat down in my office and I didn't see *a* kid.

He was transferred to another school, then shunted to yet another.

Wherever school I went they was ready and prepared for me. It's like a kid having [a] behavioral problem, if he acting up at one school, before he get to the next school he's known. It's not where they would let this kid come in a classroom and decide on their own what kind of behavior this child is having. He's already marked. And this is the same what's happening to me. No matter what school they put me at, I was already marked 'cause I was known to speak very bluntly out against whatever I thought was wrong.

At his last school the principal ordered weekly evaluations of his work. He was required to check in and out whenever he went from one place to another. There were clicks on his telephone, and things he said at meetings got back to head-quarters—usually distorted. To protect himself, he began tape recording every-thing he said. He was sick more in that last year than in all the rest of his years on the job. His "whole innerside" was upset.

Frank Casey no longer believes that social progress is inevitable. Once the urgency of the 1960s was over, social programs were cut, budgets reduced, and innovative projects coopted and reabsorbed into the establishment. Now changes will be hard to come by, "because of the way society is . . . the politicking, the backstabbing." Frank has also learned some hard lessons about power: "There's a little Watergate in every [establishment] and a lot of Watergate in the school system."

The students he had been working with, especially those with behavioral problems, are in worse shape than kids were ten years ago. Classes have gotten larger, while the support staff has shrunk.

Are we supposed to leave those kids out because they have a problem or because they come on to the point where "Motherfuck, you go to hell, kiss my ass," or "You white honky, you can't tell me shit"? Because the kids say that, what we suppose to do, write 'em off? Seems to me those are the kids that need our help the most.

Yet Frank feels positive about the general state of race relations. Race and color are less of an issue, and he sees more closeness, especially in intermarriage. In the long run, he believes, more kids will say: "I'm black, I'm white. I got a little blackness in me, I got a little whiteness in me. Hey, I'm American. I don't want to hear that [racial] shit."

Three years ago, Frank returned to the church and there he's found "a sense of great quietness." And "a little confidence in knowing that if you believe in the Lord and you pray, that he will help you out of your troubles." He's president of his choir, but he wonders how he can be an example to others if he's not following the right path himself. Still, the church has been his mainstay through his great trials. Without it he might have done something he would now regret.

When I ask him what happened to the sixties, all that ferment and consciousness, he points to people getting better jobs and then leaving their communities, forgetting their identity and their original goals. Black men have more opportunities today, "but they're up to the top in survival . . . survival and that greenback." And he points to fear and how it makes people go along with the establishment. "Fear is a son of a gun."

When money wasn't coming in and I can wonder where I was going to get my rent, my food, sometime I stand here and say, "Well, damn, Frank, you a stupid ass. Fuck it, nobody cares, why didn't you just go sit down behind the desk, do whatever you suppose to do, from eight-thirty to four or four-thirty, make a showing. Shit, you'd be right there drawing down the money. You stuck your goddamn head out there and you got the son of a bitch chopped off." And then I look at a lot of little kids running around and I say to myself, whatever happens was worth it. Sure, I probably would still have my job, but do I have to climb over the others to achieve what I want to have? At least I have the pleasure of knowing that I wasn't in that establishment doing what has been done to our childrens. And when I say children now I'm not just only talking about black children. All the children is getting ripped off, the poor whites, the Mexicans, the Orientals, blacks, all of 'em. A lot of those kids remind me of me when I was coming up. They need help. So I just says to myself: "Well, fuck it, Frank, you go for broke."

1988. In 1986 and 1987 no one could tell me how to reach Frank Casey. Those who had seen him last said he looked "down and out." In 1988 Frank called just as this book was off to the printer. Politically involved again, he had applied to be a member of a community commission, but he had been passed over for a white man. He is considering suing the county for racial discrimination. He drives a bus for his church part-time. He spends much of his time with a woman friend, and he's been painting her house. In what may be another indication that life is looking up for him, he not only has a phone again, but he also has an answering machine. His recorded message ends: "Remember, Jesus loves you."

Carleta Reeves

"To grow and develop with the times"

1978. In 1968 Carleta Reeves had talked mostly about the problems she encountered as an office worker at the university. The politics of the time didn't interest her. In the past few years she's become more political and has succeeded in integrating her personal concerns with her political outlook. She attributes some of her expanded awareness to the shock of events in the late sixties— King's assassination, Berkeley's third-world strike—and the rest to growing older. At thirty-three, she is more able today to connect her life to society and its problems.

From twenty-one to thirty, those years flew by so fast. I was into so much, I don't know that I had any concept of the fact I was getting older. But boy, when I looked up and "Hey, like next year you'll be thirty years old," then I had to look and see, "What have you done, what have you accomplished?" I don't think any other age will be that significant to me. America says if you're under thirty you're young, over thirty you're old. I feel younger than I did when I was nineteen. I really feel good about myself, totally.

In the sixties I was ignorant of a lot of things. Because my parents were very religious and I was raised with that kind of background. I was pretty passive. I just sort of took things for granted. Whereas now I will question what's happening to me.

King's assassination really opened my eyes to myself, what I was about, what I was doing. I began to reassess who I was, what commitment did I have about any and everything. I became more aware of myself as an individual, as a person, and that I *could* determine my own destiny. That I did not have to just sort of flow along with what was happening to me. I feel I have more control over my life than I did at that time.

That was a time when a lot of people really had to look at what was happening in this country. Black as well as white. You got to the point where you had to say, "Well, where am I in all of this?" And if you ask yourself that question and pursued it, then you moved to another level. But if you asked that question and didn't do anything about it, then maybe people are still where they were in the sixties. I'm trying to pinpoint what really made me see that I wanted to be *about something*. Okay?

To grow and develop with the times, that's very important to me. I think it's important that people participate in their destiny. I really think that people should be much more involved than they are and make this government get off their butts and do something. I think the government needs to play a much larger role. I'm very concerned about the unemployment situation, particularly for the youth.

She's tall, dark, and very good looking. Her hair is natural now, though in '68 she thought the natural was just a fad. As she talks, her face and eyes become very expressive.

The Black Panther Party was the only thing that I considered joining back in the sixties, and that was just a thought. (*Chuckles.*) I personally do not like joining groups, but I am very concerned about issues. So when it comes time for the march on whatever, I march. I guess one could say that the groups didn't accomplish much. I think people've been disillusioned by group efforts and are trying much more to do their own individual thing. They're more career-oriented. And they have a reason to be, given where our country seems to be moving.

Working at the university, I am obviously caught up in the whole system. It took me a long time to come to grips with that. In order for me to survive, I have to be a part of the system—make it work for me. I do not agree with the system. There are a lot of things that could be changed.

It was being a divorced mother that brought her back into "the system." To raise her daughter alone, she needed more job security than the community organization she was working for could provide. So she returned to the institution that had once caused her so much anguish. By this time the university was interested in affirmative action, and she was hired as a secretary in a major department. She's now an administrative assistant, a first-line supervisor with considerable responsibility. But she's not impressed with her advancement, or with her future prospects. She has found that the university has few minorities or women in the middle-management position she aspires to.

In terms of the working situation, racial minorities are still at the bottom. Not that much has changed. Of course, there are more black students on the campus than there were ten years ago, but in terms of numbers I doubt if it's been that significant. And not only the blacks but the whites are more passive than they were in the sixties. They're going back into the traditional thing— you join the sorority, you go to the Big Game.

I feel race is even more of an issue now. Because if nothing has changed in the ten years that have passed, and the problem is still here, then it's a bigger problem than it was. I'm [still] conscious that America's a black-and-white country. I am very conscious of that.

You do see more interracial couples, children, that whole thing. There's a new generation, my generation, rearing children now. And parents are much more open, more honest, and the children are beginning to accept each other much more for what they are.

There's more interracial contact. I see high school kids, from Berkeley High, outside of the BART station, and they're all together, gaming and funning around. You do see blacks in one group and whites in another, but you also see them together, almost as equals . . . a sense that there are just two people as opposed to a black-white situation. But that doesn't say those prejudices don't still exist.

Black women have a big part in the women's movement because the black woman is the last person on the ladder. Anything that affects women is going to affect black women even more so . . . inequities, you know, in terms of employment, in terms of salary, in terms of everything. Women are discriminated against on so many levels—credit, you name it. For me, though, I'm more concerned about my own ethnicity.

Summer 1986. *Carleta Reeves still works at the university, in a different department, and she administers the work of more than fifty faculty and staff members.*

The university is a very positive environment, working with very brilliant people who are movers and shakers in the country. And the campus is beautiful. [But] I don't think the system is fair. It's not based on what you do—I still think that there is discrimination. When people have the same level of responsibility, and they can be promoted, and you can't . . .

I enjoy working in the department, true, but I am always aware by the way people relate to me that I'm black and I'm a woman. There are times you can go along with it. But there are other times when you get very, very angry. Because you know it's because [of] the color of my skin.

I think there's a stigma attached to people who come because of affirmative action. "You don't meet the standard because you're a minority. That's how you got in." You're always questioned about what you do, and whether you did it right. You're the reason why this didn't happen or why the problem came up. Even the staff have been able to see the discrimination; they comment to me about it.

Henry Smith

"If I were a white guy . . ."

1981. *Now in his mid-fifties, Dr. Henry Smith splits his surgical practice between Fresno and Gunderson, an outlying valley town. When the older black doctors, a chief source of his referrals, retired and his caseload dropped off, a white physician invited him to take the Gunderson position. Ironically, this was the same white doctor who had once made the "nigger in the woodpile" remark: "I don't think he was as prejudiced as his talk was. I could have bristled and called him a racist and knocked off the relationship." But over the years this white doctor has turned out to be the most generous of Dr. Smith's colleagues, black or white, providing the most referrals, favors, and jobs for black medical students. And through this doctor's circle of friends, Smith has made real estate investments that have helped put his four children through college.*

And helped put them through medical school. All four of his children, including three daughters, are following in his footsteps. The oldest daughter went to the same university and medical school he did. The second went to a private Catholic university and then to Meharry, one of the top black med schools. His son is halfway through Howard's med school, and his youngest is an undergraduate contemplating a career in medicine.

I tell my wife—she's a nurse—if she were growing up now, she would have been a doctor. That's my personal feeling. She has enough smarts and enough drive and enough discipline. She helped direct them toward medicine, maybe even more [than I did].

The oldest girl slept next to the room where we were and she'd hear the telephone ring at night, and I'd get up and I'm talking: "This wasn't carried out right or done like you wanted." And when I found she had some interest, then I'd bring her in here and have her do some typing and learn to file. And there would be times I would have her make out the bank statements—most of my money comes in by check—so she can see without my telling her what the benefits were from that standpoint. She could hear the patients thanking me, and all those things helped to get her continued motivation. And, of course once she did it, it was a lot easier for the others to follow.

- *How do you feel about the increase of women in medicine?*

Sort of ambivalent, really. If they're going to go to medical school, get the training, and then utilize it to the point where it's their profession . . . But if it's, "I've finished and I've practiced at it and I don't like it as well, so I think I'll just stay home and let my husband . . ."—if that's the case, that gets more difficult for me to handle.

Personally, I have no real complaints. I've done sufficiently well. I've had a lot of personal fulfillments—work and family and whatever's related to those things. And there's been a certain amount of economic security.

My practice has been pretty much general surgery ever since I've been in Fresno. It's a referral-type practice. And my practice has been reasonably good. It certainly could have been a lot, lot better. You know, if I had, if I were different from the way I am.

- *How do you mean?*

I guess if I were a white guy I would have had a better practice, more local. I got a fairly good start, a lot of the early referrals were from the black doctors, some of whom I did not know. You cultivate referrals by personal contact, and then they hear about your proficiency or like your demeanor or your work. Or the patients go back and say, "I like him."

Now I go out to Gunderson, which is older. It's conservative, and basically more hillbilly, you know. I may lose two or three patients because I'm black. The guys who send them to me say, "I'm going to send you to a black surgeon, you're not prejudiced, are you?" And most often it would be "no." Occasionally it would be "yes." [If] it's a lady, the man frequently would say, "No, we'll go somewhere else." The man tends to be more threatened when their wives are involved. But that's not a frequent occurrence.

Sometimes a patient will tell me, "Doc, if I have cancer, don't tell me. I don't want to know." I'm not very good with people who are dying. I'm too sentimental. When I talk to them, I get all choked in my voice, and tears come to my eyes. So whenever possible with my cancer patients, I send them to the chemotherapists. The chemotherapists seem to know how to handle this. They can cover over everything really well; they're good at it, it's like you have to have a . . . ("A *thick skin?*") . . . Yeah.

The telephone rings and I turn off the tape recorder. When Dr. Smith returns, I hit the play button instead of record. What follows is my best reconstruction of what he said.

Over the years his white patients have become more relaxed with him. "The patient learns that his mythical concepts about me or the black doctors are wrong, that we're as competent as the next fellow. And in the hospital they find out that we really don't have tails."

At least half of Dr. Smith's patients are white, a figure slightly higher now that so much of his practice has shifted out of town. He gets along well with all of them, approaching them individually, taking time to talk about family, work, and hobbies. I ask whether he thinks being black has anything to do with this personal approach. No, race doesn't have anything to do with it, he says, but he has seen studies that confirm his own experience that black doctors tend to communicate more with their patients. Which may explain, he suggests, why they are sued less often for malpractice.

In 1968 there were eight to ten black doctors in Fresno; today there are about fifteen. Not a huge increase, he says, but the range of specializations is broader. For example, at one time blacks were not assigned to an obstetrics-gynecology residency because it involved the intimate treatment of white women. This taboo has been lifted. Radiology, however, remains closed: it requires a huge investment in equipment, so doctors group together in large practices that, like the big law partnerships, tend to be all-white. The trend toward large group practices and health maintenance organizations doesn't bode well for the coming generation of black doctors, he adds.

Otherwise he feels most of the overt discrimination in medicine is a thing of the past. He is welcome to perform surgery at every hospital in town, and black patients are treated equally, no longer assigned to special rooms. "Of course I'm not on top of it today as much as I used to be. I used to snoop around in the wards, the back rooms, to see what was happening to black patients. After a while I just stopped checking up." "Why?" I ask. "Because I could see it wasn't necessary, that there wasn't the bad treatment anymore." But he has also become less interested in racial issues. [Mistake discovered, the tape is recording now.]

I'm sure I could do more. I have gone and talked to groups and done medical-career awareness. It probably is true [that] I was a lot more tuned to the racial issue then. I don't think I'm quite as sensitive now. Most of what I do now is [with] young kids coming through the office. I'll discuss school and grades and how they're doing.

I think I'm more conservative in a lot of ways. My feelings about the country have been fairly consistently positive. I'm still the underdog-type person, but I'm more conservative from a racial power standpoint, especially since I've been involved with the [real estate firm]. I'm not going to as many NAACP meetings, attending rallies, as I previously did. I don't think I'm as participatory as . . . I would probably tend to lean toward the Urban League in approach now. Whether that's more conservative or not . . .

I think [Reagan's] program is going to hurt people, black and white, old— for sure. Definitely it is going to push them into inferior care. It has to be harmful. I think affirmative action is still necessary. It may not be starting early enough. Because if the kid is not motivated, you get delayed reactions, too much anger sometimes, and too much fault-pointing.

Affirmative action was not a factor in his own children's careers.

My kids went to schools that were not "ghetto," and the economic status was not poverty level, and they spoke reasonably good English. So when my kids were going for their interview, I would say, "Now put on your facade, so to speak. If you want to wear your natural wig there, do so. You don't have to be real gung-ho [black], but you want to get in." "Well, I'm going to go like I am." Which was the right answer.

I would have liked them to have more exposure. My oldest daughter went to a black college, so that helped. The area that we moved to was a white area, basically. I couldn't get my lot until I had somebody go out and buy it.

■ *That kind of thing still happens?*

Not to my knowledge. The price will change, whether it's a house or an apartment.

I guess most people would call me a workaholic because I take very little time off. But I enjoy the way my practice is set up and I enjoy my patients well enough and I enjoy the hospital environment. And I get an automatic high when I go into surgery, and if the patient has done well, and they leave, you get that reinforcement of thinking you've done this. Those things kind of keep you going.

Summer 1986. *Henry Smith estimates that there are twenty black doctors practicing in town, up from fifteen in the past five years. He's hoping that his son, who is completing a surgery residency, will decide to become the twenty-first. Dr. Smith has offered him a partnership to help him get established, and* *in time the son could slowly take over his practice. It would be "an ego trip," but he's not sure his son wants to return to Fresno.*

Otherwise, Smith will work till he's eighty. He is even more positive about medicine than he was five years ago. Every once in a while he thinks about going back to Parkin, Georgia, where his father, now remarried, is still working at age eighty-eight. But the town is too small to support a surgeon and family practice doesn't appeal to him, even though a black doctor in Parkin today would probably have as high a proportion of white patients as in California.

Visiting Parkin every year, he sees how the town has changed since the 1960s "from the standpoint of where you can go and where you can eat, where you can stay." And there are more jobs now for blacks, in both the public and the private sectors, though they're mostly at entry level. Black business is down, however, and when the white high school was integrated, his alma mater, the black school, was closed, so that black students have lost some of their most important role models, the black teachers. "Until the time that that took place, most of the kids went away to college—like some of the prep schools here where they get ninety-nine, ninety-five percent college entry—sixty to seventy-five percent finishing. I'm sure they don't get anywhere near that now."

CHAPTER 13

Keeping the Spirit of
the Sixties Alive

he privatized mood of the 1970s is often contrasted with the social consciousness of the 1960s. But the decline in the most dramatic manifestations of social activism, the nationwide movements for change, has mis-
led many into exaggerating the retreat from politics. Civil rights and other
activists have continued to organize on the local community level and, as
Arthur Stein has convincingly documented, many of the locally based self-
help and life-style movements that emerged in the seventies were a continuation—not a negation—of the sixties' ethos of self-determination.[1] In this
sense the two decades are not as starkly discontinuous as they are typically
portrayed.

Yet the sixties was certainly a special era, a time of unusual political ferment whose values and themes continue to influence many of the people who
came of age during the decade. For Vera Brooke the sixties' social ethic has
remained central to her consciousness and commitment, to her inner sense of
who she is in the world. The fading of that ethos, the shift to a more individualistic zeitgeist in the 1970s has been difficult and disorienting to her. She resents
the tendency of old college friends to see sixties' activism as ancient history
and to regard her as an anachronism: "God, Vera, are you still doing *that?*"

The four people in this chapter feel a special responsibility to keep the
spirit of the sixties alive. Though each has "kept the faith" in his or her own
way, they have moved in different directions. After an initial radicalization in
the seventies, Joan Keres gave up activist politics during the 1980s to pursue a
more spiritual path. Len Davis returned to his post office job after achieving
success in a much better-paying and higher-status position; at the same time
he has become somewhat more conservative politically. Elena Albert, who is
particularly discouraged by the seventies' neglect of social problems and the
excessive self-absorption of the young black generation, has become more

internationalist and class conscious. Vera Brooke also identifies "far more with the working class" than she did during the 1960s. But she notices that when she talks about socialism, "people get twitchy," and she adds, regretfully, that "racism is [still] the major umbrella, because the initial factor by which people decide if they are 'fer you or agin you' is what you look like."

Vera Brooke

"The caring factor"

1978. One of my favorite pastimes in the whole wide world is to drive around looking at *us* 'cause we look so damn good. There are just a lot of black people who by their attitudes and their personal/physical bearing [are] much more self-confident than ten years ago. I see more black fathers with their kids, I see more young people who will get it together to get the suit for the interview, I see the young women more and more on top of getting services in a bank or how they handle their kids in a hospital. I ask people, "Is that your little girl?" and tell her, "She's very well mannered for being so small." Those kinds of strokes I see us giving each other more overtly than we used to. And where our office is located in downtown Oakland, the people going by talk about their work and what they do, and they want to know what I do. There is a sharing. Black people are visible, you know, we're just out there.

Since graduating from college, Vera Brooke has had a series of jobs in which she's worked with poor or underprivileged blacks—the kind of people she feared as a young teenager. First she taught basic skills to minority people so they could qualify for work at the phone company. When that program ended, she taught students with learning and attendance problems in a high school enrichment program: "It was fantastic to be that close with the kids over a three-year span and see them grow and blossom." As only the second black administrator at a Marin County hospital, she gave special attention to non-English-speaking people, made a point of referring nonwhite job applicants to department supervisors, and informally counseled minority applicants about the problems of working in a white environment: "There are people here who are going to talk to you like you just fell out of a tree." After two years at the hospital she was overworked, "a basket case." Now, at age thirty-two, she's a receptionist in a small law firm in downtown Oakland.

I've had people call up, basically from insurance companies or doctors' offices, and say: "I'm calling up on the Jefferson case. . . . Gee, if these people would just get a job—civil rights really gave *them* a gravy train." "Oh, you think so?" "Yeah, I mean, look at the average black person." And I say, "You're talking to one of them." Silence. "Er, can I put you on hold for a second?" They never come back on again. And I'm thinking this is nineteen-seventy-fucking-eight, *where are we going?* (*Slowly and deliberately.*) It has not changed in a lot of ways. *It has not changed.*

I don't think that racially the climate in the U.S. is any better. It's just that there are more placebos out there. As a minority person you got a checklist before you get hot. You can't just say, well, nobody black works here. If somebody black does work there, then you gotta find out where they're coming from, have they been coopted, are they a rabble-rouser, are they whatever? There was a time, you know, when you could sit at Auto Row and you knew. There was nobody there who looked like you. Now you got people like that black principal at the high school who wasn't gonna let girls who had been pregnant run for student body office. He is as much of a hassle as the white supervisor who hired me because the personnel office at Kaiser [Hospital] is two-thirds glass and everybody coming in saw a black woman sitting in personnel. They're the same people. One of them's poor-white Vallejo, the other one's from Little Rock, Arkansas. They are my problem, you know. And they are my problem because they grab the brass ring and they're going with it, and they don't particularly care that the ride on the merry-go-round is bullshit. Better to ride than not to ride at all, even if it's a humbug trip that has you trouncing on somebody else's life. I can't do that.

There should not be the coopting that has gone down. There are more black salesmen and service people working for IBM, you see them running around in their little suits carrying their attaché cases. And Yvonne Braithewaite Burke is running for office, and we did have Fannie Lou Hamer, and we've still got Barbara Jordan and Shirley Chisholm. The visibility that used to get us lynched is now at least soothing some quotas, and salving some egos, but I don't know that it's getting a lot done. I do not say that black kids need black teachers. Black kids need good teachers. If they're black, wonderful. If they're not, dear God, make them good teachers, you know.

There are middle-class black people that I am uncomfortable with because they are only going after the bucks. And I am not a member of any black organization because I don't like the basically *bourgie* activity that goes on. Or I am not particularly interested in changing my name to something in Swahili and doing a modified hate-whitey trip, you know. That still isn't gonna get the public health information to the masses. I periodically think, "Now, Vera, what you ought to be doing is find yourself a group. You can't do this whole trip by yourself." And the times that we live in, the proliferation of data and the speed with which things happen . . . I get overloaded real easy.

I need to work in a desegregated environment. Working in lily-white San Rafael just about drove me crazy. It felt real cold and real weird because I just couldn't see the right kind of look in somebody's eyes to know that you understood who I was. And I didn't like having to stop and buy a pack of cigarettes, or ask anybody directions. And it was not the kind of fear thing that I had ten years ago. Have you ever been in a situation where nobody really gives a damn who you are? I'd almost rather be in a situation where somebody made it real clear that I'm gonna try and get you because there's some kind of psychological energy being devoted to my existence. A lot of people still consider third world, especially blacks, to be irrelevant to their lives, and they're gonna be real sorry.

I thought about this this morning: those of us that would like to improve and sustain a better quality of life, we have got to unify our effort a whole lot better. The dollar just speaks too loud and too long. As a friend of mine once tearfully related to me—she's a teacher, one of the people who's been prop-thirteened,* so she's running all over the place teaching a class here and a class there—she said: "I did a seminar of black poetry, and I mentioned civil rights. And do you know, there was a woman in that class that asked, 'Oh, yes, civil rights, when *was* that?'" [My friend said to me,] "Vera, what happened? What in God's name made all the work that we did in the sixties become a chapter in the textbook somewhere, or a *phase* that *happened*?"

There are a whole lot of people who do not understand that the nuclear plants, the ecologically sound housing and living arrangements, the quality of health care, what happens to women, Chicanos, to gays, et cetera, really is, goddammit, rooted in the sixties. And the attempt to make that just a chronically black-and-white confrontation is *bullshit* and it pisses (*snaps fingers*) me off, because it's a rip-off. "Let me see if I can quickly categorize and narrow what you all did back then (*very angry now*) and then we can put it over here"—so that really the hippest thing going is a 240-Z and John Travolta.

You know we still have kids dying of malnutrition. I think we are just doing a very benign kind of genocide with older people in this country. The violence on the streets—I am flat uncomfortable living in Oakland. I don't like the fact that something could happen to me and a whole lot of people won't give a damn. And the only reason that I am more comfortable in Berkeley is there are enough of us still around from the sixties that you turn your head when you hear somebody scream.

---

*In June 1978 California voters overwhelmingly approved Proposition 13, an amendment to the state constitution that cut property-tax rates by roughly 60 percent and made it harder for counties to raise those rates. The resulting drop in revenues forced all counties to curtail services. Because school districts were highly dependent on county funding, many districts consolidated schools, laid off teachers, and reduced "nonessential" programs.

The other night I went to Cody's [bookstore] to hear a black woman read some poetry, Ntozake Shange, who wrote *For Colored Girls*, and the place was jammed. My nose was pressed against somebody's shoulder blades, and we were talking about how hot it was, and this guy standing next to me, white, he said, "Remember how we used to sit down?" And I said, "No shit, we really did." And we started talking about Sproul, Auto Row, third-world liberation, et cetera, et cetera, and I said in a louder than normal talking voice: "If we all decide to sit down, we will see and hear better and be a lot more comfortable." Do you know, half the crowd sat, and half absolutely refused? They were in front, and they were not going to cooperate.

But as soon as I feel myself getting really soured about the whole trip, something will happen, and I will get into a delightful rap with some little ole lady who wants to talk about recipes, food, or clothes. Or when I'm jogging around the lake, meet some old guy who's been walking the lake for years and can tell me how the houses have changed. And these people are not always black, they are not always women.

There was a time when, sitting here talking to you, I would have been happier if you had been a black person, because then you and I are talking about what ought to be happening. I am at a point now where I am happy there is another person who cares.

The caring factor. That is how we taught those ladies to work at the phone company. That's how I got the kid that walked into my [high school] classroom in 1970 reading at third-grade level [to] graduate at grade level three years later. And I didn't have any special books and I didn't just work with him. But I was interested in his progress, interested in his difficulties, and when he bullshitted me, I told him, and when I was bullshitting him, he told me. That kind of dealing is real important. I think that violence on the streets, where somebody just as soon sets fire to your car, cuts your purse off your shoulders and hits you on the back of head . . . a lot of people don't have anything to do that makes him feel good. I think that's why we have punk rock. If it can't sound good, let's see how *bad* we can get it to sound.

- *What happened to the distrust of whites you picked up at college?*

That was based upon the fact that I felt myself to be in a dependent relationship with them. That if they didn't say I was okay, then I wasn't, and it was them I had to impress or make friends with to get through the maze of whatever I wanted to do. There was a time when I wouldn't go to an opening of Chagall prints at the Legion of Honor 'cause somebody might want to talk about art. I don't know anything about art, and I wouldn't have the right clothes, or I didn't know what was happening. And I didn't want to go and be *the* or one of the few black people there and not have someone speak to me intelligibly about what was going on.

Okay. I think the distrust has been modified to a sort of a general "on guard." If it looks like you're going to jump weird, I don't need ya. Or I can play your game. But I am not on the short end of the stick.

I am now in a position where I pretty much go and do what I want to do, and if that bothers the white people that are there, tough beans. You know I read the book or I didn't read the book. I can talk to you about burn-out, I can talk to you about sickle cell, I can talk to you about Andy Young, I can talk to you about whatever you want to talk about. But an awful lot of white people, their savvy over ten years has not increased. And I know *exactly* how to impress you and please, and have you smiling and delighted and I also got what I wanted.

■ *You mean they haven't learned . . .*

No, haven't learned *shit*, haven't learned a *goddamn* thing. If you need me to cakewalk and tell you how I eat corn bread and greens with my hands, depending upon whether I want to do it, I might. Otherwise, I can slide into French and we can discuss ballet and fine wine. You name it. I control what's happening. I'm not afraid anymore as I was of white people. I still won't go to a Johnny Cash concert. All those pickup trucks and rifles scare me, you know. But I'm also not intimidated walking past Blake's and seeing a bunch of jocks pour out of the beer cellar and cross the street, and I used to [be].

■ *Ten years ago a lot of whites viewed you as a sociological phenomenon.*

Sure. Still happens, not as often. And I can still encounter a fair number of white people who have had more than a cursory contact with blacks, so that what I get from them is very real. And not (*mimicking tone*) "I read *Soul on Ice.*" And I say, "I didn't (*very abrupt*). Sorry, Cleaver's a rapist and I'm not interested in anything he has to say. I got a real problem with somebody who experiments on one color of women in order to get the other. That tells me something about how you feel about women, and as a woman, damn your book."

One of the standard responses on the part of a lot of black women is that women's lib is for white women, not for black women. Now, I understand all that. But I don't have to eat it, and I'm not particularly concerned about standing behind or subsuming my needs to a black man because we as a people must be more cohesive. I'm more inclined to subscribe to the idea that sex should not define a person's role, or limit or extend their rights, responsibilities, obligations. All of the jobs I have willingly gone into have made a great deal of demand on my patience, my compassion, my expertise. When I get home from work I don't want to keep it up. I want someone there to listen to how I feel, ask me how my day has been, and not ask me, "When is supper ready?"

Vera talks to her mother more these days, and it's exciting for her when they discuss the kinds of black and women's issues that "I was jumping up and down about as a college student." Then *she thought her mother was just giving lip service to the right attitudes. But nowadays her mother can surprise her, as when she told Vera's father he couldn't ask a woman he was interviewing for a secretary's job whether she had adequate child care: " 'It's none of your business, and if she is under the least bit of impression that her answer has an effect on the result of her interview, you're violating fair employment practice.' "*

If I had come of age in the fifties—or the seventies—I would still be married, I would have had one if not two children by now, I would be taking dance classes to keep my weight down. I might belong to something like Dings for Dellums, or Bells for Brazil, or whatever. I think I would have accepted a certain kind of benumbedness. When you maintain your antenna and your nerves so that you are still responding to stimuli, you get tired. I could still be at Kaiser. I could have gotten a promotion to work in downtown Oakland if I had done the right cakewalk. But I don't give ground easily. Long, long, long ago I read somewhere that the first person you live with is yourself. I couldn't live with myself making so many compromises that would make my life easier.

There are peers of mine who saw a lot of the things that they did when they were in college as part of being in college, not part of living. Who want to know, "God, are you *still* doing that?" Yeah, I still am, 'cause I'm still alive. I am still black, I am still a female, and it's still real important to me that if I tell you who I am, you don't have to say, "hey, you" anymore. And yet I know that I do things and am interested in things that a whole lot of black people, a whole lot of poor people, could care less than shit about. They don't want to go down to the Point and see the whales migrate. I do. I like whales. I happen to like whales 'cause I got exposed to people who did and thought it was a nice thing. I'm a bit of a wine connoisseur; it's important to me what I drink. It can be elitist, but I will not keep a job that keeps down other people just so that I can sit at a teak table and drink, you know, 1974 Parducci Pinot Chardonnay.

Summer 1986. *Vera Brooke is now forty and the mother of a young daughter.*

I'm a single parent by choice. At thirty-five I checked through all my psychic and social resources and said, "Vera, you can do this. It will be difficult." The only thing I didn't calculate well was cost. Children just turn out to be a bit more expensive than anticipated. But Linda's a great kid, and we're having a really good time.

Most of the women I've encountered in my age group, they're single parents by default. They are divorced or left in some way. I haven't encountered that many black women that are single parents by choice. I know lots of white women are—attorneys, nurses, nurse practitioners. Every once in a while I run into little pockets of traditional thinking where people assume I must be divorced. You know, nobody in their right mind at thirty-five would get knocked up and keep the kid. Different strokes! I did. It's now "cool" with my mother, though initially she had some serious misgivings. I don't think I could have done this in any other part of the country. It helps a lot to be in the Oakland-Berkeley area.

I'm involved with a man now that I will probably marry once we sort out a few things.

Linda's quite comfortable not having a daddy because I don't have one (*Vera's father died a few years back*) and neither does grandma. She's aware Daniel has a daddy, all the other kids in her class. Initially I had some real anxieties—I've got to get my kid a father. Linda's father has a drug problem; I have not seen much of [him] since we got pregnant. Her father's mother finally contacted me and said, "She is the only grandchild I will probably ever have. Come for dinner, let me get her stuff for her birthday, we'll go to the park." And Linda calls her Aunt Audrey because it's another female relative, no heavy-duty Grandma stuff.

My daughter says things to me that I said to my mother, but they don't freak me out—like "I want to be white." "I'm sorry you can't be. You're born brown and that's the color you are." She wants to be white. No biggie. Two weeks later she wanted to be Japanese because there was a new teacher at school.

Vera is active in her daughter's school, in theater groups, and in a women's group (three black women, three white). She's working at a medical research project but thinking about returning to teaching, her first love: it would pay more money and, more important, she could make a difference in the lives of black kids who "don't have anybody there for them," who are not getting the support they need from their parents. She is extremely concerned about what's happening to the black family.

I know many young women who are more inclined now to have an abortion or totally eschew sex: "It'll just get you in trouble and you know no nigger's going to take care of you no way. I'm going to learn to type, I'm going to learn computers, I'm going to have something out there for me when I graduate." Far more able to plan long distance than your black men. I don't think we teach young men as well as we teach young women. The thing young men liked about my classes was that I was not particularly interested in breaking them psychologically. It wasn't a contest to see who could be in charge. "I would rather you take your hat off, but I certainly ain't gonna go to the Supreme Court about your goddamn hat."

Overall she's quite impressed with the economic gains black people have made: "a definite economic leg up since you and I last talked." In Oakland "the black middle class is a serious phenomenon, a large group." She sees blacks moving into middle- and upper-management positions, and financial planners are seeking black clients with money to invest. It's still the women who seem to be doing better, "driving BMWs, checking into the Hyatt." But she is dismayed by the lack of political consciousness; even South Africa doesn't evoke that much interest. There's too much "just go for yourself." She's not active in any organized political group, but last month:

I did go storming up to the counter of Ross's Dress Best for Less in Alameda and tell them that every single parka in the children's section was made in South Africa, and I wasn't buying any of them. I wanted that shop person to know how I felt about it, and I explained it to my daughter because she wanted the jacket. We were on our way to pay for it, a twenty-seven-dollar jacket for nine bucks. I said, "Made in South Africa, are you *kidding*?"

Joan Keres

"The way that you view humanity and the earth, those are the main things"

1978. In 1968 Joan Keres was a San Francisco hippy who admired Huey Newton and the Black Panthers and sometimes wished she were black. For Joan the transition from the sixties to the seventies was less disruptive than it was for Vera Brooke. Now twenty-eight, Joan describes her passage from her younger hippy beliefs to her present radical politics as an evolution.

She earns her living as an artist's model. For now the job is all right: the art schools are creative environments, and there's good communication between the students and the models. She also teaches movement and deep relaxation to senior citizens, and works one night at a natural foods restaurant. Three part-time jobs give her a certain freedom; sometimes "job-jobs" where you "don't have to think or put out" are easier.

The tones of a saxophone playing in the next room almost drown out her soft-spoken voice, as we talk in a walk-up apartment above a Chinese laundry.

I'm not free. When you read the newspapers, you realize people aren't free because of the society. Understanding the realities, you don't feel free. You feel bogged down.

But there's times, there's moments when I feel very free. I'm sitting in the park and I'm just breathing air and I'm just quiet and tranquil. There's times when I'm dancing. Things are just moving ahead and I'm improvising and I feel free. You're at the ocean, and you're with someone, and you're having a lot of fun, you're communicating and it's joyful and you feel free then. But in the overall, I don't think you could ever really feel free as long as you know there's so many problems in the world. 'Cause I think it'll always be gnawing at you. Listen, how can I feel free when there's asbestos in the water system, or how can I feel free when there's people being slaughtered or people suffering so, so bad? But I do feel free to actively change it. And you do have a *certain* freedom to speak out.

■ *Do you feel more in control of your life than ten years ago?*

Yeah, 'cause then I was still trying to figure out who I was, or what I could do, or what I could give. Now I have things a little more under my belt. I feel like I have more power to do what I want to do.

I've become more of an internationalist. In 1970 I was in Cuba for a couple of months on the Venceremos Brigade. That really changed me. One day we cut sugar cane together with people from Vietnam and Africa and South America and Korea. People from all over the world working together with the Cubans to help pull themselves up out of underdevelopment. And just that experience, like we can be a united world, we can work together, it can be better for everyone.

I guess one of the hippy things was love, which I believe in. (*Laughs.*) I think that was a real positive thought. You have to see it on a personal level. But you have to see it in a broader sense too. It means having an understanding that there's people all over the world that want the same thing and that if something heavy is going down somewhere, to be able to feel for these people. And to take some responsibility: how I can plug in to make it a better world from where I am in the U.S.? Part of that probably came from the hippy philosophy: "love and harmony and peace" (*a touch of self-mockery*).

It's so demanding. You see the earth crumble, it's in all aspects, you know. . . . The earth dying, the pollution level being so high, and just, ah, so much genocide happening, and you just feel like if you're not full-time . . . I mean, I could just easily live my life, and there's all this happening and I should be working harder. It's so easy in San Francisco just to live from day to day—because the repression isn't as severe. Repression breeds resistance, and unless you have this broad consciousness, you could slide by like so many people do, especially in fantasyland Bay Area. But I'm going to continue to do political work.

I really get depressed sometimes. Like when that Nicaraguan thing was happening, I was on the bus, and I picked up the newspaper and started crying. 'Cause it was like they were committing genocide on the Nicaraguan people. Like it's happening again. And you hear the kids on the bus ("*Nicaraguan kids?*") . . . Yeah, and they haven't heard from their family, they don't know if they're dead or alive.

Her first love is dance. She studied dance for ten years and works at it every day, hoping to make it her livelihood.

I want to be able to integrate the politics and the dance. So I can feel like a cultural worker. And use the dance so it's not so abstract and alienated from what's going on in the world. 'Cause like a lot of the art world is oblivious to the outside world. So I'm always pulled, I'm always pulled in political directions, and I want to combine the two, by being able to make statements, have your dance have social and political content.

Joan also appreciates nonpolitical and abstract art: it's important to say things in new ways. She sees the role of art and aesthetics in her life as another link with her hippy past. She also credits the hippy movement for her concern with health, good diet, and above all her spiritual awareness. Meditation gives her "clearness of mind," a center within herself; "you feel grounded with the earth."

The spiritual movement has really grown a lot. In both the political and the spiritual movements, the way that you view humanity and the earth, those are the main things. The political and the spiritual, they need each other. Because political people that don't have any spirituality—the love and the concern and the compassion—then politics can just turn into something else. It can become a power trip, you know. And if the spiritual people don't have politics and aren't working concretely in the real world to make it a better life, then they're lacking too. In Zen they have a lot of selflessness, there's a lot of bowing. You bow to the Buddha in other people and the Buddha in yourself and to the Buddha consciousness. The selflessness, I think, is really important in making revolutionaries. For they have to be able to sacrifice certain things for the whole of humanity and not just be only concerned with your own self. If people were more selfless then you wouldn't have all that greed out there.

■ *Marxists say that it's the capitalist system that makes us greedy.*

That's part of it. But even the Cubans say, the hard part starts after they made the revolution. It's building the new man and woman, and what is that? That's changing your ideas and changing your way of life. It's not just changing the economic system.

She has become much closer with her parents, appreciating her mother for having raised five children and realizing that her father, an old Wobbly and socialist, had some "positive influence" on her.

The women's movement gave me a keener insight into male chauvinism. It helped me to recognize it and be strong enough to deal with it. I enjoy men, they're people. But they're still indoctrinated with these chauvinistic tendencies, and then you deal with that, struggle with people to make them change.

- *Have you seen some men change?*

Yeah, after many battles, some of them have grown a half-inch. (*Laughs.*) Well, that's not fair. A lot of them have moved right along, men that are consciously working on not being sexist.

Growing up, the commercials and all the way that women are supposed to be, that all has an effect. But then you become aware and you realize that it's a bunch of bullshit. And you realize that you have endless potential and you're not these little roles, whatever society wants to set you up as. That you're a full human being that can grow and grow and grow.

I just didn't want to get caught up in that role of mother-housewife, instead of developing my potential, building a stronger sense of self, and being able to link up with the world, not just through my man, you know. Being a whole complete person. And I think I'm doing that. I know I'm doing that.

- *What about race in America today?*

No way does racial equality exist. No way. You just have to go from neighborhood to neighborhood, from city to city, and see who lives better. Black people are still highly unemployed. I think the schools have gotten worse. A kid who lives across the street was saying they just railroaded him through school: "I didn't learn anything, I don't know anything, I'm unskilled." But he got his diploma. Racism isn't something that people wash out of their minds, especially when you're older and it's more indoctrinated.

- *Do you consider yourself a racist today?*

Now? No. Because I'm actively participating in trying to smash imperialism, and because I feel a love for humanity and I just don't judge people by their race, you know. If they're brown, yellow, red, white, green, I mean, if somebody's funky, they're funky. I may not like them, but I don't not like somebody because they're such a given race. And I'm actively trying to fight against the institution of race: colonialism.

In my older interview I didn't realize the power of nonviolent civil disobedience. The power of all those masses of people and consciousness. That's a very strong force. That's the *power* of the people. But it needs to be linked up with armed struggle too. The Panther Party, they're working more through the electoral process. But I don't know how influential the Panthers are right now. I don't think they're exactly in the vanguard. You know a lot of the strongest revolutionaries got jailed or killed, which stifled the movement.

The police, they're still pulling a lot of shit. They're really mistreating a lot of people. Me being a white woman, a white attractive woman, I don't mean any ego trip, but they don't harass me. But if I were a person of color on the wrong street at the wrong time I would be stopped, thrown in jail, you know. They're still the same.

The hippy movement, it had a good effect. But the negative side is drugs.

And a lot of people dying and being jailed and mental hospitals. And the drugs are still happening. Not in my life so much. There's been a lot cooptation. Everybody smokes dope and snorts coke, no matter what class. The clothes were coopted. The music became more commercial.

- *Do you ever feel nostalgia for those times?*

Nostalgia for those times? Yeah (*great surprise*), it was a lot of fun in a way. 'Cause I was still a kid, I was still a teenager, and it was just a ball, you know. But life is good now.

After I turned off the tape recorder, she talked about how much more confident she feels today. She used to have trouble talking to people, and at political meetings she would feel intimidated. But now she speaks up, although at several points in our interview she felt stuck. That her words might be published in a book flustered her a bit: "Now I feel like I have to say something that really means something, to put out the correct line. Ten years ago I just said what I felt."

July 1986. *Eight years later Joan talks with complete confidence and clarity, without pauses or hesitations. She attributes this sureness to Buddhist chanting and her four years of involvement in an international Zen society. Buddhism and the goal of building world peace through individual enlightenment have totally transformed her life.*

It's a very joyful practice. Whatever you chant for eventually comes to be. I want to meet someone who will meet my physical, mental, emotional, financial, and spiritual needs—chant every day for that, I meet someone. I've been with him a year.

Through chanting she's cured her allergies and achieved "radiant health." She has also discovered a new career, massage: "I really like the work, the contact with people, and the healing aspect of it. It's real human and it's ancient and future. And I have a lot of control over the hours."

Her new boyfriend is black, as was the previous one, and he also practices Buddhism. The Buddhist movement is very integrated, she notes, and many of her leaders are black. Overall, she feels that there's much more integration these days, more acceptance of black people. The negative attitudes she hears from her massage clients are directed at the new immigrants and not at blacks.

Though she retains some of her left political attitudes, she's no longer politically active.

There's only so much time and I'm working in my avenue, on a grass-roots level [to] bring hope back to people so that they're not so beaten down. People don't have to be victims, tossed around by their environments. You can get strong inside and affect your environment. Everybody has the potential to be happy, to have that fulfilled life.

People are trapped by their own minds, by their own little cage they've built around them. If you want to build an everlasting peace, people have to change inside, to deal with their negativity. Changing the economic or the political system isn't going to alleviate the core of human nature.

Len Davis

"My whole damn culture's gone"

1981. My mother died in 1970. And I went home, spent almost two months taking care of business and stuff—I was kind of voted the spokesman for the family. And I saw some things that almost brought tears to my eyes. Really did. All that I believed then, all that molded me into the person that I am, it's gone. Or going. The whole black culture. I don't think there is any black culture *here* to speak of. It was in the South, and now we're losing that because of integration. You know, the old thing they used to say about [being] black on a Saturday night. That was part of our culture, to work hard all week out in the damn fields and on Saturday night, then you had a ball. There'd be some fights and so forth, but that was part of our culture.

Every little town in the South had one little area that all the blacks hung out in. Man, that area is dead now in my hometown. Because they can go into the white restaurant and into the white bars or nightclubs. So who the hell is going to go there now? God, that hurts me. (*Sighs.*) My whole damn culture's gone. What I believe in, down the tubes. Another damn California.

I never went to an integrated school. It was all black teachers. And until I was in junior high school, I didn't realize the education I was getting. They were saying it was a low-quality education, and academically maybe it was. But, man, the other education that we got. Those old girls, they were mostly women teachers, they taught us how to survive, man, in a white man's world. I don't know of a guy that was brought up in the South that hasn't heard over and over, "Boy, you're going to have to be twice as good as the white boy to make it in this world." Now, that was something that was just pounded into us, you know. Now the black kid down there isn't getting that, but the black kid has still got to be twice as good as the white kid to make it. I don't think a damn thing has changed. We're still getting the hind teat.

You won't believe this, but the black family was very typical in [the old] days. Eighty percent of the women did not work. The father was out working, the mother stays home, raises those kids—they had big families then—took care of the house. Before my daddy left, my mother didn't work. Both parents working, that was the greatest contributor to the disintegration of the family.

Man, I had a hell of a childhood. We were dirt poor, but God, we had a ball. My mother raised seven of us by herself, but we were one hell of a *family*. We took care of one another, and when we were old enough we worked and helped Mama pay the bills. *That's family*, man. You never find that anymore. My specialty was delinquent kids. And I haven't seen a delinquent kid yet that come from a stable family, not a single damn one.

We weren't only raised by mother and my grandmother. We were raised by anyone that saw us doing anything wrong. We were supervised by all the people in that little town. And would really put a strap on your tail if they saw you doing something wrong. So what kind of pressure do you think that put on a kid to go straight and try and get his head together?

When my mother died, there must have been at least ten different insurance agents come by. And each one of them walked in and he'd start talking to one of my sisters. And my sister would say, "Hey, my brother Leonard is handling all the business." And he *refused* to sit down and talk to a black man that's got some sense.

The strength of the black community really needs to be developed around the black male. Because that was the key to slavery and oppression—you control the male. My mother was strong, but she was sensitive to the boys—she really went out of her way to make us men—strong men. I don't think the emasculation of the male is very strong nowadays, I think the males now are hurting themselves. They just want to lay around—I call them twenty-five-year-old dependents. Still living at home and not contributing anything to the family.

In 1968 Len Davis felt personally frustrated, blocked in his desire to express his abilities, and bitter at the racial barriers that seemed to be keeping him down. The post office where he worked was "a Negro-type job" and a "headache." Now forty-five, he feels that he can do anything he really wants and no longer sees his fate determined by the color of his skin.

No one factor accounts for this transformation, but a pair of job changes certainly were key. In 1969 he left the post office when a social agency offered him a full-time position as a street worker. With years of volunteer experience, he worked well with young people. Before long he was promoted, placed in charge of a neighborhood center in northern California, and then appointed the organization's director in a major southern city—a very rapid climb in status, income, and authority.

That job was the greatest *experience* I ever had—outside of being brought up in the South. I learned a hell of a lot about myself. How I can switch on and off to different people . . . blend in with these dudes on the street and then go downtown . . . I didn't know that was important. A supervisor said, "Man, I really think you could talk to the president of the United States and feel comfortable." And he's right. I learned that I had a hell of a lot more tolerance than I thought. I had a secretary tell me once: "God, you really know how to say things." I didn't know that the way I was expressing myself was a good way to express yourself. I got plaques at home, and my wife keeps saying, "Why don't you put that stuff up?" I don't need that. I know what I got it for. There's a couple of lawyers here in Sacramento, one in San Francisco, a couple of guys that went into the air force, the navy, the coast guard, if I hadn't worked with them, they'd have wound up either dead or in the joint. That, man, makes me feel good.

But despite the recognition and other satisfactions, the job became frustrating. He missed being on the street, the direct contact with youth. And the agency's white middle-class emphasis bothered him. The constant pressures, the long hours, the traveling, and the moving around were beginning to hurt his family life.

I can name ten guys that are in management in the agency and *hate it*. But their terminology is, "Man, I can't afford to cut this loose, because I'm making big money." I've had a philosophy all my life that I'll never let anything control me. And I've never let money control me. So I gave up a lucrative twenty-six thousand dollars a year—that's what I was making in 1977—I gave that up for a sixteen-thousand-dollar job carrying mail. I've been back carrying mail for over three years now, and I'm happy as a lark.

You won't believe where I deliver, man. Just nothing but doctors, lawyers, you know, just very rich people. The tough thing is the damn houses are so far apart. It's a walking route. I like it because it's what we call a clean route. That means you don't have a lot of change of addresses. And the other part is no dogs. Everybody keeps them in.

Believe it or not, I had two of the same streets for five years before and I've got some of the same people still living there. The people that knew what I did—I had quite a few write-ups in the paper—they really come on different. They are aware of my color more. Every one of them come on with this "I hope he doesn't think I'm a racist" kind of mentality. (*Laughs.*) Every damn one of them. This doctor's wife, man, I was talking with her yesterday. She's intimidated by me. I really don't like that.

Some people are frightened of him because "I look like a big mean black guy. That really hurts deep down. Here I am a human being, sitting with another human being [at a human relations workshop] and he's afraid of me."

Still, people recognize his leadership, have tried to persuade him to run for city council. But he'd rather be on the corner working with kids than have to deal with "all of that minutiae at City Hall."

At work people have been pressing him to become a supervisor.

Post office management just stinks. They're managing by fear, there's no trust, and they're constantly threatening people. And the racism? God. It's the worst kind of racism, a very subtle kind. What I mean is smiling in your face and reach around behind you and sticking a knife in your back. Man, they are very good at that.

I think racism is at its highest level at the blue-collar level. The big rich guy, the money controls his thing, and there ain't a hell of a lot of blacks with that much money that can touch him anyway. And the real poor person, he's kind of being taken care of by some little government or somebody. But the guy that's fending for hisself out there every day, at the post office and all these other jobs—when I say "post office" I'm really talking about the whole blue-collar area—man, he has a fear that blacks are getting his job.

- *A lot of whites think blacks actually have a better chance today.*

Bullshit. They got some slots for you. And once they're filled, that's it. That's one of my criticisms of affirmative action. I hate to criticize something when I don't really have the answer to it. But that's not the way to do it, because that creates hostilities like what you're talking about. At the time I guess that was the only thing they could think of. But I think it's just as racist to kiss me because I'm black as it is for you to kick me because I'm black. Matter of fact, it might even be worse.

For a while we had a black supervisor. Man, you wouldn't believe how many guys bid out of that station. That's one of the reasons I got this route. None of the white guys high up on the list wanted to bid on it.

Affirmative action has brought [racism] a little more out in the open. Talking about welfare, they don't come out and say *black* or *Mexican*, but that's what they're talking about. And it's okay [now] for Bakke to say, "I want to get into medical school at Davis and take it all the way to the Supreme Court." That meant a lot to a whole lot [of people]. A lot of racists that said, "Hey, this guy's getting my job and he doesn't qualify for it."

I even got four welfare checks on this rich route. All of them white. I'm sick of this shit, it's *my* damned taxes. But it's crippling blacks more than anything else. The kid is brought up [to see] the mother sitting around on her dead rear end. Welfare and these damned social give-me programs made us very lazy.

Blacks have surfaced with a little more power politically. We're better educated, flooding the market with different skills. We had people with educational backgrounds, but where did they go in school? Some black school
down there. Now you got a cat walking around with an engineer's degree from
Georgia Tech, which is one of the top engineering schools in the country.
That's the difference. But that isn't saying it ain't racist.

*Davis thinks too many black kids are going to college these days, then thumb-
ing their noses at blue-collar jobs that might give them real security (like the
post office) or high wages (like plumbing and the trades). While more white kids
are going right to work after high school, for blacks "the corner has moved to the
campus" where they're still "bullshitting and jiving." The ones he's worked with
expect "a sophisticated job" to be handed to them, even though college hasn't
prepared them for the job market. He's tried to help them see this, but most
don't believe him.*

I think what tees me off as much as anything else is that we bought the
white man's system, you know, two cars in the garage and being in suburbia
and all of that bullshit. The young folk, they think black culture and soul is
walking around talking about I'm black and proud. And they're not really. It
really doesn't have any strength behind it at all now. I think it had a *little*
strength in the sixties.

I got an eight-year-old, okay? He doesn't know a damn thing about that.
But if he was born and raised in the South, in the forties and fifties, the things
that happened in the twenties were still being passed along in the fifties. But
the things that happened in the sixties, nobody knows any damn thing about it
in the seventies. That's why I'm saying it had no lasting effect. If anything it
affected whites more than it did blacks. It opened up a few doors that were
closed before. And it brought out some of the good in people. I think everybody has good in them, some human feelings for other people. I know some
white dudes that because of people like me and Harold [Sampson] and a lot of
other guys that they got to know during the sixties and seventies—I don't think
they'll ever go back to that nonchalant kind of attitude they had about blacks.
I don't think they'll ever do that.

Roots opened up a lot of folks' eyes. It even made some of them bitter. My
wife was born and raised in New York City, really no exposure to the black
culture to speak of. She got some of it in Harlem, but not a hell of a lot. And
it just burns her up to see how they were treating the slaves and all that stuff.
Black Power, that whole thing, probably hurt some folks in a way. If there's
any lasting effect, the greatest one might be they use racism as a cop-out.

■ *So they're bitter and feel this racist society owes them something?*

That's what I'm saying. When I did this (*points to transcript of first interview*) that was really affecting me, man. It was affecting me to the point that I wasn't getting things done because I'm saying, "If it hadn't been for this, I wouldn't be here." There were some things that happened to me from fifteen to early twenties, racial things that really kind of stifled me and a lot of the guys I grew up with. I just did not know how to deal with them. Had absolutely no help except from my mother. I had no male influence at all. Me and my father—we still don't get along.

When I went home to my mother's funeral, I started thinking about myself and where I was. And I made a pact with myself. I wasn't going to make no excuses about this and that and what the Man's doing to me. And I really haven't looked over my shoulder since. I still think about what I could have been . . . because it's a reality, it happened. But I will not let that happen to me now. Right now today, and I honestly believe this, I believe I can do any damn thing I want to do. I'm not saying I'm going to just carry mail the rest of my life. I'm forty-five, I'm not through yet. I believe I could accomplish pretty much anything I want to accomplish . . . over and above some white dude sitting on me. I just believe I can get around it. I think I'm smarter than he is. Because I know just about every move he's going to make. The sixties and the seventies really taught me to deal with some things.

January 1987. Now that I've reached fifty, things have got a little more personal. I've helped a lot of people, but I'm tired of chasing other folks' dreams. I don't get involved in things. I'm looking at myself, what's going to happen to me in five years. I might take an early retirement. Spend my time on some of my projects. Just dawdle a bit, go fishing.

Davis remains concerned about the family, "our greatest asset." Its disintegration is what's behind the drug crisis. Looking back on the sixties, he feels too much emphasis was placed on cultural differences between racial and ethnic groups, instead of on the commonalities we all share. And today we're stuck with that.

I resent somebody telling me Ben Hooks or Congressman Dellums is one of my leaders. Ron Dellums doesn't speak for me, he's not even my congressman. Damn, that's what racism is, man. You're going to slot me with all the other black folk?

I know damn well I'll never see it in my lifetime . . . I want one day somebody to call me Len Davis, American. Period. Now if you want to dig into it a little, you can say his ancestors came from Africa. Somebody else's ancestors came from Poland or whatever.

■ *What would a nonracist society look like?*

It would be the opposite of almost everything I see now. Institutional racism is so entrenched in this country that we pretty much accept it. Let's talk about kids, their imagination is stifled. . . . It has to get to the point where any person regardless of their race can sit here and just dream of being president or whatever position. That dream, to me, is as far off as the stars. Do you know how far away, how many light years away, the nearest star is? That's how I feel about your question. It's so damned far off, it's unimaginable. Personally I don't think it will ever happen.

Elena Albert

"I as an individual will continue to resist"

1978. Elena Albert, the amateur historian who described what it was like being black in Montana, has moved from an all-black neighborhood in San Francisco to a rural section of San Jose, to be closer to her grandchildren and the slow-paced life she knew growing up. At seventy now, she is enjoying this time of life "most intensely." Two years ago, after being out of school for fifty years, she enrolled in courses in French, English, and black literature. She's also teaching black history to senior citizens and is active in her historical society. The walls of her small house are covered with scenes from Africa, photos of black poets and leaders, and prints of the mother of Christ. She explains that these Black Madonnas are found all over the world. She's planning a book on them, and another on the legendary black queen Califia, for whom California was named.

Still, she misses the culture and political life of San Francisco, the community newspapers, and especially black people. She doesn't feel part of a community in San Jose, she hasn't joined a church, and in her neighborhood there's only one friend close enough to exchange kisses, and she's white. Living on the edge of town isn't what it was forty years ago, when everyone said good morning and offered you a ride if they saw you walking. And she misses the activism of the sixties.

When I was in San Francisco I was interested in everything and took part in everything. I used to go to bed at night and wonder when I woke up in the morning (*laughs*) what change to expect. Those of us who expected to make changes, social changes . . . we did see what *appeared* to be changes. But now in '78, and especially in San Jose, I don't see where there is a community expectation or experience of changes that are real.

I loved going out and picketing Bank of America. I used to love to say, "Picket Bank of America?" (*Laughs incredulously.*) But we did! And we did get hiring there. I remember we tried very hard to get justice for black people in the courts and we attempted to do something about the treatment of black prisoners.

There are some improvements. But so much that we had thought would make a great deal of difference, now I'm not sure of. For instance, in San Jose where my grandchildren go to school—they are including the history of black people in the United States. That pleases me very much, but I don't see a change for the black youth in job opportunities. I look at my grandchildren who are now nineteen, sixteen, and fifteen, I look at the kind of education they're getting in public schools, and I don't think there is much likelihood that my nineteen-year-old grandson will have really meaningful opportunities in jobs.

It seems to me that the gap between those black people who do not have jobs, who do not own property, and those who have their training is becoming wider. There are more in the upper middle class. I have many young friends who are in their late twenties and thirties and I feel it's excellent that many of the young black people who financially have profited from our attempt to open up better jobs are now living according to the American standard. They have the cars, the homes, they got their degrees without suffering. But when I look at *Ebony* magazine and read of the people who are written up, they are not people whom I admire a great deal. I think that many of them have become a part of the establishment. I have to admire their income, I have to look at their foreign cars and say "excellent," but I don't believe that many of them are dedicated to helping others of their own race or other people. I don't think they really think about us. When I walk into Bank of America and other banks now and see the wide ethnic variety there, I don't believe that the young people there in their twenties and early thirties realize that they are there because other people suffered so that they could be.

And when I marched and walked, I don't remember seeing Japanese and Chinese. And affirmative action was designed for black people, and other people have used it, haven't they? Now Mexican people with the legislation that we pushed through, they are rising. (*Chuckles.*)

I'm discouraged about some things. The laws which have integrated schools and the laws which have integrated hotels and restaurants have weakened black people. They weren't intended to, but they have. When I was young I used to dream of going to New York and staying at the Theresa Hotel. When I came [to Harlem], it was 1968, there was no more Theresa Hotel. There used to be a hotel out in the Western Addition. No more. The Negro college is in dire straits. Now one thing I am glad has happened. In every state now a white person can marry someone who isn't white.

My husband would talk about people who were working people, who were poor, who didn't own property, but their skin was white, and he would see that in individual cases they suffered lives that were full of pain and hard work. And he would say, "Well, they're white, and if they will treat them that way, how will they treat me?" And I think now my mind has expanded to grasp that. I must be concerned about people who are not my color, who are not my sex, who don't speak the language I speak. I must be concerned about Africans, I must be concerned about the struggle of people in South America. It is one world.

- *You've become more of an internationalist?*

Yes, definitely. I wasn't always concerned about what happened in Kenya. I didn't feel it touched my life and my life touched that. But now I do. And I am concerned wherever there are those who do not have power.

I'm very, very unhappy when I think of the increasing prison population. I believe that terrible things are being done to helpless people in prisons, in the state hospitals. And the people who have been released from institutions, they are not really being given treatment. I begin to wonder, am I a little mad? I am told, on the one hand, that life is sacred and, on the other hand, there are over four hundred people on death row. And here in our state, the attorney general is pressing for the death penalty. I have sent mail and I've tried to save lives and now I wonder—is my thinking at all of any value? Does it really have any force? (*Sighs.*)

I look at my friends who have been in the struggle for fifty years. They say to me, "Oh, yes, we have accomplished changes." Then I look at us and I think the same spirit against which we have struggled is alive and well—what some people call the system, the group that is in power. We think we have won a victory and we do win battles, but the *war* never ends. However, we do not stop our struggle. To the very *last* I *must* be interested in other people.

What I really feel disappointed about is that most ordinary people—not just those who do manual labor but those who have college degrees—are so willing to accept basic changes made by people where they have no part in decision making. Even though I may not influence decisions affecting my life, I will think independently. I as an individual will continue to resist.

- *Do you think the emphasis in the sixties on race and black consciousness might have been divisive?*

No, that was needed. We really needed to accept our differentness, to rejoice in it, to enjoy it. You have to realize how it is to be black in America. There was a time when you never *ever* would hear that a black woman was pretty or beautiful. And we did *everything* we could to try to be unlike what we were, and of course that's impossible, you know. When I was a young woman, I spent so much money and time to straighten my hair. My mother had hoped I would speak in a refined low voice—that if I would become as much like the ideal of white womanhood, perhaps I might be accepted. Well, that's not necessary. And when Marcus Garvey said that we were black and beautiful, and when he said, "Up ye mighty race, you could do what ye will" (*sung exultantly*), that made us look at ourself. And we are handsome, we are pretty, we are beautiful, we are lovely. Now that doesn't mean other people are ugly. I love to see the Spanish people. They are American and they are different. And we *are* different, you know (*with immense joy*), and that's all right, isn't it?

She laughs frequently, despite her pessimism. Her hair is natural, long, grow-ing up and outward. Almost white, it sets off her darkness. She is obviously no longer trying to reach "the ideal of white womanhood." She is a distinctive African-American woman, stately and very attractive.

American blacks are still in some way African. In the fact that we still think human values are valuable. I think we still enjoy music and we still really enjoy dancing. We still tend to choose the helping skills rather than business skills. And really, in America, what is sacred, what is right? Business . . .

I attended a conference in Los Angeles two weeks ago on the Afro-Ameri-can in our history. And we were told that we should turn from studying to be social workers, physicians, nurses, musicians, writers, poets, to go into the technical trades because that is what business wants. Now I tell my grand-children to resist this, because what is life if you are just an extension of a machine? This society needs also people who are dedicated to healing, to writing, to music.

We're criticized that more of us are not going into banking. I'm sure that's necessary in the world, but in my mind I resist it. And no matter whether it appears that the sign of a life that was worth living is the house that has all the latest gadgets, I don't choose it. I do feel that human values are the values that give life a reason. You don't work for the sake of the job, but you work for the values of life, of friendship and family and beauty and right and justice.

I don't admire scientists like Einstein as I did when I was a young woman. I often wonder if great intellectual advancement should be admired wholly for that reason without a consideration of how advances in technology destroy human life and human values. How can a person graduate from the univer-sity and then go to work for Nestle's, that corporation who makes the sub-stitute for mother's milk which they export to Africa and which is the cause of thousands of African babies dying?

I think an American, their ideals, their opinions, are the ideals and the opinions of their class. If you are a twenty-thousand-dollar-a-year man, this color or this color, you tend to live in the same neighborhood, you tend to think the same way, too. If you and I are high in the establishment, and we go to the conferences in Washington or New York or Hawaii that these high-level people go to, we both expect to stay at the Hilton and we *both* speak of "the natives," you know. (*Laughs.*) I guess it's natural, isn't it, and human?

I feel very close to people I have worked with in certain causes. And they're not my race. I feel I've been deprived because I have not grown up with people of my race, and in some situations I don't feel at home. My friends who come from the South have memories to share. They went to the same school, they went to the same church, they own property because southern black people own land. But there's no one here from the state of Washington who knew me when I was a child. When my class graduated from high school, I had no part in any of the social side of it. I didn't even go to get my diploma. So I missed something, you see.

Before she passed away in the early 1980s, Mrs. Albert continued her research on black pioneers in the West and prepared an exhibit on Black Madonnas, which was shown at the African-American Historical Society in San Francisco. James Herndon, an associate of hers, told me: "Just a remarkably spirited woman who took great delight in everything she did. She never had much money, she rose above money. We don't have that kind of individual now in the black community. We need to remember people who have contributed to other people."

Conclusion

Among the blacks we interviewed in 1968 there was a marked ambivalence toward integration. Ten years later this ambivalence had become a full-fledged disillusionment: neither integration nor Black Power had brought about the kind of fundamental changes in American society that people had expected. And despite some important reforms, it was clear that a racial revolution was not going to happen in the foreseeable future. In the late seventies, then, blacks were profoundly disappointed that racism remained pervasive in American society, that a nonracist society, in Len Davis's poetic imagery, remained "as far off as the stars . . . light years away."

In the sixties people viewed Black Power and integration as mutually exclusive strategies. In the nationalist mood of that era, the goal of becoming *integral* to American society was angrily denounced. By the late 1970s, however, it was becoming clear that Black Power and integration were not as antithetical as they had once seemed. Black Power and black nationalism had acted as a wedge, pressuring "the system" to open its doors to racial minorities, and Black Power had instilled a pride and confidence that enabled blacks to take hold of the new opportunities.

Since the early 1980s, black politics has been based on the recognition that a synthesis of the two strategies is needed. Integration alone cannot be expected to bring about racial equality because only a limited number, perhaps even a numerical minority of Afro-Americans, benefit from individual access and mobility. Today the people left behind have less hope of a better life than their counterparts did in the sixties: the urban ghettos are even more economically and socially depressed. And segregation—though no longer sanctioned by law—remains prevalent in schools and neighborhoods.

Even many of the successful have strong reservations about integration. They are not always judged and rewarded on "the content of their character," as King dreamed—or even on their work performance. Subtle and not-so-

315

subtle put-downs and, at times, active hostility make up much of interracial relations today. The progress of any minority brings the majority's deep-seated prejudices to the surface, though some of this tension reflects the painfulness of change and eases over time. (Harold Sampson was eventually accepted in the neighborhood where he at first felt he had been viewed as "a nigger with a Ph.D.," and Carleta Reeves came to terms with the university.)

While some people who were initially positive about integration have become disillusioned by its failures, others are disturbed by its successes. Many upwardly mobile blacks, especially the young, they complain, are too preoccupied with their own advancement to worry about race relations or the disadvantaged. The irony is that the racial consciousness expressed in the sixties' trinity of Black Power, black pride, and black culture has created opportunities for a generation that has largely rejected that consciousness. Even worse, too many middle-class blacks seem to have become "just like whites." The old fear that integration would lead to assimilation and the inevitable weakening of Afro-American ethnicity is apparently being realized.

The loss of community is seen as the most serious cost of integration. It underlies Howard Spence's question about whether the right to sleep in a motel or eat in a restaurant was worth the decline in land ownership, the closing of black businesses, and the difficulties faced by the traditionally Negro colleges and other institutions. Most of the other older activists share his doubts. They miss the solidarity of the communities they grew up in—or moved away from—and they recall with particular affection those dedicated teachers in all-black schools who cared about each child they taught.

But is integration the only culprit in the weakening of community bonds, or is some of this the inevitable workings of more general processes of social change in America? Strong evidence for the latter explanation comes from the general consensus among blacks and whites that the social fabric has deteriorated. Although blacks and whites in this study differed in their assessments of racial change, they generally shared a negative appraisal of overall social change: American society, they agreed, had become more violent and dangerous, more individualistic—even nihilistic—and less bound by traditional values such as hard work, personal responsibility, and respect for age and authority.[1] More specifically, whites made the same complaints as blacks about the decline of education and the worsening morale among schoolteachers.

Thus much of the loss of solidarity in black communities may result from changes in American society and not racial integration per se. For a long time segregation insulated black communities, particularly in the South, from the advantages and disadvantages of the postindustrial era. Now blacks are asking whether a cohesive community life might not have been too high a pay for social and economic mobility. But some whites are asking a question about suburban sprawl, the replacement of locally owned national chains and shopping malls, and the dominance of tract housing over villagelike neighborhoods. Many Americans, black and white, today feel cut off from their communities and their pasts, and they mourn the passing of traditional values and verities.

Although integration may have compounded this loss of cohesiveness, the advantages of participating in mainstream institutions are self-evident. How else can racial minorities have a good life for themselves and their families? Or as a group have some influence on the direction of the larger society and the local community? It is not equal opportunity but assimilation—the multiracial society as an end in itself—that has lost much of its luster. Still, integration and black nationalism remain effective tactics for achieving particular political objectives. In 1987 the Ku Klux Klan's disruption of a march honoring the birthday of Martin Luther King in Forsyth County, Georgia, was followed a week later by a much larger—and very integrated—march, one that recalled the mood of the early civil rights era. In the same month a demonstration condemning anti-black violence in Howard Beach, New York, had more of a late-sixties' nationalist cast, both in racial composition and in feeling.

That the Black Power slogan has rarely been heard since the mid-seventies does not mean that late-sixties black militancy has expired without a trace. The concept of Black Power has had a profound effect on the outlook of black people, on race relations, and on present-day racial politics (in the United States and throughout the entire African diaspora). Black Power, along with the civil rights emphasis that preceded it, brought about an irreversible change in the attitudes of Afro-Americans. Racism still exists, of course; substantive inequalities, especially in economic life, persist; and the problems of the underclass are overwhelming. But black Americans will never again accept the systematic denial of their basic rights, and their children are no longer socialized to "know their place." The belief in a right to dignity and fair treatment is now so widespread and deeply rooted, so self-evident that people of all colors would vigorously resist any effort to reinstate formalized discrimination. This consensus may be the most profound legacy of black militancy, one that has brought about a truly radical transformation in the relations between the races.

In the arena of electoral politics, the Black Power movement galvanized southern blacks who had been re-enfranchised by the Voting Rights Act, itself a product of the civil rights movement. Thus black militancy set the stage for impressive political gains within the system. Not only has the number of black officeholders increased, but the influence of southern black voters on national events also became apparent when the conservative southern senators whom these black voters had put into office felt constrained to oppose the nomination of Robert Bork to the Supreme Court. True, electoral strength and veto power do not constitute the community control that militants were demanding in the late sixties. With the notable exceptions of some southern counties and towns, black people as a whole have not been empowered. Indeed, in many communities blacks probably feel more powerless than they once did, as a result of the exodus of middle-class residents, who had been an important source of local leadership and who served as models for young people.

Despite the beneficial legacy of the militant era, people are more critical today of Black Power and black nationalism than they were in the late sixties, when their reservations about Stokely Carmichael, Huey Newton, and others were overshadowed by their admiration of the young radicals' fearless out-spokenness. (The exception to this change is Malcolm X, who is viewed with even greater respect today.) By the mid-seventies, black activists were disap-pointed that the militants' courageous talk included too much rhetoric and posturing and not enough practical, detailed planning. And the language of revolution raised unrealistic expectations of immediate fundamental transfor-mation—an attitude not conducive to the long-term commitment and orga-nizing required to effect enduring change. The dashed hopes and repressive retaliatory measures taken by federal and local authorities help explain why so many sixties' activists and sympathizers left the movement in the early seventies.

As a result, present-day black politics is pragmatic rather than ideological. Positions are taken issue by issue, judged by what has and has not worked. The orthodoxies of the militant era are shunned, and people are less con-cerned about whether a position squares with traditional racial liberalism. With rare exceptions, the new politics is nonconfrontational, aimed at devel-oping long-term coalitions as well as meeting specific needs in the black com-munity. Politically aware blacks have expanded their perspectives beyond race and a narrow domestic purview. Although the militants' emphasis on race and blackness was indispensable, many people now feel that it was pushed too far and too long, in the process antagonizing more moderate Afro-Americans and stiffening the opposition of working-class and ethnic whites to the black cause. Furthermore, they argue, the celebration of blackness in itself will not put food on the table or money in the bank, will not keep teenagers in school or get drug dealers off the street.

Another criticism of the militant perspective concerns its tacit sociological premises, its tendency to cite racism as a blanket explanation for all manifesta-ns of racial inequality. Such assumptions are not only overly simplistic, the 'cs charge, but they also suggest that the black community is powerless to we its social and economic conditions except through the conventional hts strategies of fighting discrimination and prejudice—strategies that sary but have proved limited. The mistaken assumption that racism anging monolith, rather than one powerful element of a fluid social ses twin dangers: it threatens to subtly erode the black commu- its own autonomy and capacity for self-determination and to minimize the value of individual responsibility. Too many young blacks during the sixties "used racism as a cop-out"—in Len Davis's words—to excuse their own personal failures.*

Today, black politics operates with a more sophisticated understanding of social causation and racial change. Race and racism are not the only structural realities that constrain the group position of Afro-Americans. The economy, the labor market, and the distribution of jobs and opportunities by region and urban location are also critical. Given these structural imbalances, the black community cannot by itself create enough jobs to ensure economic survival and stable family life. Government and industry must be persuaded to reallocate economic resources.

At the same time, blacks are turning their attention inward, to the task of strengthening the infrastructure of their community forms and preserving a dynamic cultural and institutional base while integration proceeds apace. Rebuilding inner-city neighborhoods and institutions is necessary both to counter the centrifugal effects of integration and to expand the scope of integration by addressing the problems—drugs, crime, teen pregnancy, and family dissolution—that demoralize and thwart young people. Community cohesion can also heal those divisions that weaken ethnic solidarity and consciousness: the gulf between the middle class and the poor, the tensions between men and women, and the gap between the generations.

The idea that blacks should take responsibility for the problems of their community, rather than relying on government programs and traditional civil rights strategies, may appear to signal a black conservatism, in keeping with the national mood of the 1970s and 1980s. But, in truth, the new position is really Black Power redefined, without the rhetoric and confrontation, and shaped by a clearer awareness of the complexity of social change. Indeed, blacks are the *least* conservative segment of American society, judging by their overwhelming rejection of Ronald Reagan in 1980 and 1984 and their virtually unanimous support for Jesse Jackson and his progressive politics in the 1988 primaries. And public opinion polls on social issues confirm that they remain by far the most liberal-progressive group in American society. When blacks invoke the traditional values of family, work, and responsibility, they are harkening back to Booker T. Washington, not jumping on the right-wing bandwagon. Integration and assimilation have not silenced the nationalist theme in Afro-American politics. As Florence Grier said in 1979: "Self-help—I think I was influenced by Elijah Muhammad."

Still, like other Americans, blacks are now more conservative in their views of government aid and intervention. In 1979 Howard Spence didn't

---

*A crucial distinction exists between the legitimate use of the concept of racism in the explanation of the lot of an entire ethnic group and the less legitimate use of the concept to explain an individual's fate.

sound that different from George Hendrickson on the topic of welfare dependency, although Spence's more humanistic outlook led him to regret the demoralization of young people's spirits rather than to dismiss welfare recipients as lazy. Blacks have also become more conservative on some law-and-order issues, most noticeably on the subject of the death penalty, which almost two-thirds approved of in one 1986 opinion poll.[2]

But these facts don't make blacks neoconservatives. They don't believe racism is a thing of the past. In fact, knowing that it's here to stay is what motivates the activists' decision to deal directly with their community's internal problems and not wait passively for the government to produce racial justice or for white folks to change their ways.

Racial Attitudes

The racial conflicts of the 1960s brought to the fore anti-white attitudes among many black Americans. Such feelings tended to be more prevalent among younger blacks, as the interviews in this book illustrate. Len Davis, Mark Holder, and Larry Dillard expressed a particularly intense racial bitterness in 1968. Yet ten years later each had made a striking turnaround in attitude. In part, these three young men changed with the times, as the extreme racial consciousness of the late sixties gave way to a more moderate, more individualistic, and less political epoch. But the changes in their racial feelings were also a matter of their growing older, part of a more general "mellowing" that people experience as they leave youth behind. Such effects of age are equally visible in Joe Rypins's newfound reluctance to get embroiled in fist-fights and in Bill Harcliff's more relaxed attitude toward authority. In the process of growing up, people also learn to take responsibility for their situation in life. For Holder and Davis, such personal accountability seems to have been an important part of the self-acceptance they gained during their thirties.

Davis, Dillard, and Holder each recounted pivotal experiences, turning points, that caused them to take stock of their lives, including their racial attitudes. Len Davis attributes his transformation to the death of his mother, after which he resolved to "make no excuses about . . . what the Man's doing to me." The recognition he gained at his new job, from whites as well as blacks, for his leadership and speaking skills was also important.

Larry Dillard felt himself fortunate to have come under the influence of an older black activist and theorist who convinced him of the futility of racial hatred. It was not easy for Dillard to follow his mentor's counsel during the racially polarized late sixties and early seventies. But it must have been a relief to Dillard, who expressed some ambivalence about the then-fashionable rejection of white people in 1967.

"Peoples of forty, they're no longer thinking about a race thing," said Mark Holder, of the three the most sensitive to the relationship between age and a person's outlook. In addition to growing older, he had found fellow workers with similar interests and attitudes, people who valued his abilities and took his opinions seriously, white people who did not discount or patronize him because he was black. The combined influence of personal insights and a less-charged racial atmosphere allowed him to drop his defenses and acknowledge a common ground with his white workmates.

Other young blacks, particularly Carleta Reeves and Jim Pettit, also became more relaxed in their racial attitudes during the seventies. The older people, none of whom were strongly anti-white in the sixties, maintained their open outlook—though Florence Grier's philosophy of universal love was sorely tested. Remarkably, no one, young or old, became more anti-white during the 1970s, not even Frank Casey, who would seem to have had the most cause.*

Not surprisingly, the sixties' emphasis on race affected whites less than blacks. With a few exceptions, the whites in this study did not participate as directly in the ferment of the sixties; the racial debates neither spoke to the core of their personal identities nor caused them to experience profound transformations. Still, the decade's openness to new ideas and life-styles affected everyone's consciousness. White blue-collar workers seemed particularly changed in their outlooks; for example, they have relaxed their traditional prejudices against women co-workers.

With political opinions no longer as polarized, whites today have a more balanced view of the sixties and its social movements. Many who had been fiercest in their opposition to sixties' activism at the time have come to concede that the protest movements did produce some positive results. There has also been a drift to the center in racial attitudes. Whites who were most hostile to blacks in the sixties have softened their feelings, in part because they are no longer confronted by a militant black movement that frightened and alienated them. On the other side, many liberals and radicals who had been strong advocates of racial minorities in the sixties have become less enthusiastic and in some cases even antagonistic to the black cause, partly from a greater fear of lower-class blacks. Perhaps the racial "rightists" have become less prejudiced because they have been pleasantly surprised by the competence of black people—which they underestimated—whereas the "leftists," who underesti-

---

*John Gwaltney, however, found considerable anti-white feeling among the predominantly East Coast blacks he interviewed in the early 1970s; see his *Drylongso: A Self-Portrait of Black America* (New York: Random House, 1980). Some of the difference between his findings and mine may reflect the contrast between the East Coast and California's relatively benign race relations. Also, Gwaltney is black and his respondents may have felt freer to discuss anti-white feelings with him than my respondents did with me.

mated the depth of black problems, have become less liberal as their disappointment hardened.[3] In this book, George Hendrickson and Bill Harcliff are the clearest examples of these two tendencies.

Even those whites whose understanding of racial matters deepened during the seventies retain significant blind spots. Joe Rypins is a case in point. No longer does he fear black people; he has learned on the job that blacks are people like everyone else—"There are good ones and there're bad ones and there's average ones." Like Mark Holder, Rypins exemplifies the venerable theory that prejudice breaks down when people of different races meet in situations in which their status is equal. But Rypins also illustrates the limitations of white racial perspectives. He has listened with interest as his fellow workers talk about the racism they experienced growing up in the South, yet he doesn't truly grasp its nature—otherwise he would understand why blacks did not fight back physically. When Rypins says he wouldn't accept a job offered to him just because he's white, he fails to realize how much his whiteness has already helped him—especially in getting so many second chances despite all his youthful missteps.

Rypins is certainly not alone here. Jim Corey has become more knowledgeable about race relations, but he is even more opposed to intermarriage than he was in the past. Maude Wiley would now accept a black son-in-law, but she continues to believe the old stereotype that blacks have more fun in life. George Hendrickson no longer talks about Zulus and Congos and sees environment as more important than biology in accounting for racial inequality, but he remains adamantly against intermarriage and equally intolerant of the minority poor. Whether or not Bill Harcliff is just being more honest than the others, he is the only one to declare that he has become *more* racist since the sixties.

Both Hendrickson and Harcliff describe positive relations with middle-class blacks, setting off the image of the "good" black from that of the "bad" by a class boundary—and, indeed, the white view of black people has become something like a split picture on a television screen. The mass media has brought up to date that old division between "good niggers" and "bad niggers," replacing the archetype of the docile, devoted house slave with the reassuringly "white" black professional (Bill Cosby's "Dr. Huxtable") and the aggressive, dangerous field slave with the hustler-criminal ("Superfly"). Rarely seen on television or in the movies is the broad range of working-class Afro-Americans, whose families, life-styles, aspirations, and values are as diverse as those of whites.

Such oversimplified images of blacks are not surprising given that the interracial experiences of most whites are quite limited. Of the ten whites in the second half of this book, only George Hendrickson unequivocally broadened his relationships with blacks in the twenty years of the study. Three people showed little change and six now have even less contact with blacks than they did twenty years ago. The commitment of Virginia Lawrence and her family to "an integrated life" remains highly exceptional.

Despite the pervasiveness of racism in American society and despite disquieting signs of a resurgence in overt bigotry, the struggles of the sixties and seventies profoundly changed the way Americans view racial oppression. Today there is a broad consensus in American public opinion that South Africa's apartheid is not only morally and politically reprehensible but also important enough for our nation and our corporations to actively oppose the Pretoria government. Such a united front of vocal opposition was unthinkable twenty years ago, when South African policy was of little interest to most whites and perhaps even to most blacks.

On the home front, pockets of white supremacist activity remain, but—as in Forsyth County, Georgia, in 1987—the local police and state troopers now protect the civil rights marchers and not the racist mobs. In 1987 the presumably defunct civil rights coalition emerged from a virtual hibernation to defeat the Bork nomination.

Progress, of course, is always uneven, and, as sociologist Herbert Blumer persuasively argues, the very gains of minority groups spur periodic increases in racial prejudice.[4] For example, in 1983 the mayoral campaign of Harold Washington provoked a kind of blatant racism in many Chicagoans that shocked even the most cynical observers. But after his victory life went on much as usual in Chicago, and Washington was reelected in 1987 in a campaign relatively free of racial animosity.

A Personal Closing

To me the most heartening lesson of this book is that ordinary people, working for social justice in their corners of the world, can make a real difference. I think of Dick Cunningham's efforts to integrate his printers' union, as well as Virginia Lawrence's example in her junior high school. And as Florence Grier, Howard Spence, and other activists showed me, it is possible to realize personal dreams without compromising one's commitment to the larger goal of a more just society. Despite the "me-decade," many people have maintained their faith in the value of helping others, doing so out of genuine concern rather than for the self-aggrandizing motives the "realistically cynical" Joe Rypins pointed to.

Not being a formally religious person, I did not understand at first how important religious belief and church membership can be for sustaining such commitment and concern—for whites like Lawrence and Cunningham as well as for blacks. The central role of religion in the lives of many of my black respondents was clear enough, but the larger point was lost on me until I read

Allan Bloom's discussion of how the Bible (or the worldviews of other great traditions) can provide those overriding values that both "furnish a mind" and build character.[5] This can be true both for churchgoers and for a man like Howard Spence, with his disdain for organized religion, who told me:

> I have to say something about the Bible every once in come-by, because I read a lot of it. I *have* to, 'cause I get lonesome sometimes, and I don't find in these books that you see stacked around here what I want. So I read the Bible. If Methuselah lived nine hundred years and died and that's all the Bible says about him . . . I never read where it said he done anything but live nine hundred years. I don't want to live seventy years and didn't do nothing but live seventy years.

One last thought. For almost twenty years now I've puzzled over the fact that more blacks than whites in this study had the kind of grace and grandeur of a Howard Spence: that on the whole—with important exceptions—the black life histories go deeper, are more firmly rooted in a philosophy of life, or are both more heartfelt and more persistent in an attempt to "see life steadily and to see it whole," as Matthew Arnold said. I have worried that this might be a result of some serious bias in the way we selected people. And I have wondered whether a better explanation might be that a life history focused on racial experience is not likely to elicit a depth of response or a measure of nobility from members of the dominant racial group.

But I have concluded instead that the differences have more to do with the dynamics of social mobility in a racist society. Studies suggest that for whites there is *some* truth to the popular idea that "talent rises to the top." But aside from a few notable exceptions, this has not been true for blacks. Because of racial oppression, many of the brightest and most talented blacks have remained in the bottom reaches of society. As Malcolm X said of his fellow hustlers trapped in the ghetto: "All of us, who might have probed space, or cured cancer, or built industries, were instead black victims of the white man's social system."[6] One of the truly significant things about the 1960s was that it opened opportunities, not just for the young and educated but also for many capable older people whose possibilities for achievement and self-realization had been limited by racial barriers.

If someone today were to do a study similar to mine, my hope would be that the whites would turn out to be as impressive as the blacks, no less and no more—and for the reason that the researcher would no longer find men with the vision and leadership potential of Howard Spence working as janitors, or women with the creativity and personal power of Florence Grier spending entire lifetimes cleaning, cooking, and caring for the children of white families. But considering the retrogressive trends in our policies toward racial minorities and the poor during the 1980s, I'm afraid this hope may be overly optimistic.

As I finish the work on this book, I'm aware of how I'm going to miss the people in it. They are an extraordinary group: resourceful and independent, thoughtful and articulate, deep and grounded in practical wisdom. Out of my penchant for identification, I've become involved with them vicariously, probably too involved. There's not one of their opinions—from the most noble to the most base, from the most humanistic through the most racist, and all that's in between—that I can't recognize as part of my mental makeup too. When my own life was stagnant, experiencing their changes kept me going. When my emotions were blocked, an incident from one of their lives would move me to tears. And still does, though I've read these stories at least fifty times or more. I've wondered why I spent twenty off-and-on years on *Black Lives, White Lives*, living with the same people, when I could have been out in the world, making new friends, gathering new experiences, advancing my career. I think it's because their lives are the stuff of literature and I was learning from them. I feel honored to have labored with the materials from these lives so that their experiences can illuminate others as well.

Appendix: Methodology

When we began interviewing in 1968, we used a "snowball" technique to find people. Beginning with respondents our interviewers knew well—Alex Papillon's fellow longshoremen, the political associates of Hardy Frye, and the friends and neighbors of Lincoln Bergman's hippy relatives—we asked each person we interviewed to suggest other names to contact. This method maximized rapport but not representativeness. In order to broaden our base we next organized group discussions at churches, union meetings, civic organizations, and youth clubs, and with gangs. Each group discussion led to one or two individual interviews and helped us achieve a better balance of class, age, life-style, and political outlook.

We conducted 264 interviews, both group and one-on-one. Of the nearly 400 individuals we talked to in the two formats, both blacks (58 percent) and males (69 percent) were overrepresented.* The age distribution was more balanced: a third of the interviewees were in their teens and twenties, a third were in their thirties and forties, and the remaining third were over fifty. We also achieved some range of economic status, though social and economic classifications are always arbitrary. Of the blacks, 11 percent were judged lower class, 40 percent working class, 38 percent middle class, and 11 percent were students. Of the whites, 33 percent were working class, 36 percent middle class, 15 percent college students, and 16 percent were unemployed or counterculture hippies whose class position was not clearcut.

The sheer volume of material was overwhelming. Transcribing the ten thousand pages and four million words from the 1968–69 interview tapes took four years, and I spent more than a year just reading them. The appearance of *Working* by Studs Terkel in 1974 fortunately suggested a solution to the dilemma of how to organize so much data. By selecting and abridging representative interviews, I could bring alive the racial politics of the late sixties through the voices of ordinary people. Instead of fragmenting their lives and thoughts, I would present them as whole human beings, letting them tell their stories in a way that would connect their politics and their consciousness to their life experiences.

For the second round of interviewing, I set out to locate fifty people who

*Because in its early stages the project had a special sociological interest in the experience of black men, we oversampled both blacks and men. David Wellman has discussed the shift in our theoretical orientations, as well as various issues of methodology, in his *Portraits of White Racism* (London: Cambridge University Press, 1977), an analysis of racial privilege and white racial thinking based on five case studies from the 1968 interviews.

met three criteria: (1) their life stories had been rich in detail and exemplified larger sociological themes (e.g., Howard Spence's return to his native South), or their ideas and reactions to events expressed more general patterns (e.g., Maude Wiley's fear of black domination); (2) they were particularly thoughtful and articulate—though for balance I chose several people who were not particularly good talkers and whose stories were fairly prosaic; and (3) they represented a spectrum with respect to age, class, life-style, and political attitudes.

I managed to locate and reinterview almost forty of the fifty. The missing cases include three blacks who died before the second interview, two who had returned to the South, and six or seven whites (mostly hippies) whom I could not find despite a five-year search.

Because people had already told us their most dramatic stories, the 1978–79 interviews for the most part lacked the intensity and passion of the earlier ones. For many people the interview in 1968 was clearly the single time in their lives when they had talked openly and fully about their personal histories, their hopes and dreams, and their political opinions. And by the second round of interviews the times had changed: people in the late seventies were more measured in their views of life and society. Ten years older, they were also more reflective; as one might expect, the outlooks of the younger people had substantially deepened.

In 1986, when I did the final round of interviewing, three more respondents had died, I could not locate two, and two others did not respond to my entreaties.

Shortly before the second round of interviewing, I began editing the first set of transcripts. At the time, little had been written about the methodology of editing.[1] I soon realized that the task was far from simple. The first issue was how to handle the speech of respondents whose language style deviated from so-called Standard English. Two schools of thought have emerged among those who produce oral histories and interview books. Robert Coles, for example, has written an eloquent defense of his practice of changing informants' speech into Standard English, while Nell Painter has persuasively explained why she preserves the phrases, syntax, sentence structure, and rhythms of her research subjects.[2]

For this book I adopted a preservationist philosophy. Not only do I value the richness of the varieties of American speech, the distinctiveness of Afro-American, white working-class, and late-sixties hippy language styles, but—beyond folkloric and aesthetic appeal—I felt that a book about identity and consciousness, about the way people see the world, had to respect and reproduce people's actual language. For our language symbolizes as well as expresses the distinctiveness of our personal identity and our most important group memberships and identifications: family, ethnicity, class, peer group, and life-style enclave.

The language style of black Americans in particular makes important sociological as well as personal statements. Most Afro-Americans are bilingual, capable of what linguists call rapid "code-shifting" from Standard

English to black speech patterns (southern black syntax in most cases, street talk in some, or a combination of the two). Their speech expresses both the tension of living in two worlds and what anthropologist John Gwaltney calls their "cultivated ease" in moving between them.[3] Had I translated Frank Casey's explanation for why he was fired from "They couldn't determinize distinctions from hostile to speaking their mind, because if you speak loud, you hostile" to "They couldn't distinguish between hostility and speaking one's mind, because to them talking loud means being hostile," the reader would have lost not only the immediacy of his anger and excitement but also that very style of expression that must have made him appear hopelessly unpolished to the bureaucrats who eventually fired him.

Therefore I did not alter either the words of people or their speech patterns (diction, syntax). But I gave myself considerable poetic license to *move* words around freely (as well as sentences and paragraphs) in order to bring out more sharply the "essence" of the person, sociological themes, or readability. And like any editor striving for economy and clarity, I have eliminated words and phrases, whole paragraphs and sections. When a speaker dropped a word that he or she clearly meant to say, I have supplied the word in brackets; clarifications of acronyms are also indicated by brackets.

Sometimes I found it impossible to coherently and economically edit a speaker's verbatim account of an important story, and I resorted to a third-person summary. A few interviews seemed to require a narrative voice to move things along, and I've also used the third-person voice to condense the longest interviews rather than cut their scope.

I eliminated most of the interviewers' questions and comments so as not to interrupt the flow of the speakers' thoughts. But I retained questions needed to establish the context (especially when the transition from one topic to another was abrupt) and those useful for enhancing immediacy or providing a change of pace in an otherwise lengthy monologue.*

Beyond these issues of form were difficult decisions about content. Every interview yielded much more material than I could use—typically fifty typewritten pages—and the raw material was a formless, often chaotic mélange of stories, incidents, and beliefs. In order to identify the main threads of a life story and get an intuitive feel for the whole person, I began by listening to the tapes in a loose way, almost as one listens to music. Then I read the transcript several times, immersing myself in the life space of the respondent.

Next I read the transcript in a more focused way, alert for details and sociological themes. I underlined passages that struck me as interesting and penciled out material that seemed tedious or extraneous or highly repetitive. I searched for passages with which to begin each selection, for transitions between topics, and for juxtapositions of personal and political material.

The first several drafts of each interview were trial-and-error experiments.

*For the sake of clarity and brevity, I have sometimes condensed the questions that were actually asked. Also, in a few spots I have borrowed Terkel's technique: instead of printing the interviewer's question ("What do you think about the riots?"), I have the speaker's answer begin with a rhetorical question ("The riots?").

The false starts indicated that I had not yet found the person's unique story, the special focus or issues that set this person off and added something new to the book's unfolding cast of characters. In most cases the critical task was to shape or create a story line, a frame for the central themes, an overarching emphasis. The false starts were also useful for condensing and clarifying the speaker's language and for pruning out repetitive phrases and eliminating superfluous material.

Some editors of oral histories use the same sequence of topics for each interview, but I decided to tailor the structure to the individual, letting my sense of each person determine the prominence or position of a particular topic. Life histories obviously invite chronological organization, but that can become tiresome and mechanical, and so at times I reversed time sequences.

Some interviews have an organic flow: the speaker introduces each new topic naturally and spontaneously, the interviewer's questions seem unobtrusive, and the transitions follow effortlessly. With only a few changes in sequence, the edited version of such an interview retains the immediacy and spontaneity of the actual encounter. But other interviews never develop an organic rhythm. They may be rich in content, but the sequence of topics reflects the conduct of the interviewer, not the mental rhythms or priorities of the speaker. In these cases reordering is necessary to create emphasis and movement, a sense of a beginning, a middle, and an end.

At bottom, the editing of interview transcripts comes down to two main points: thematic focus and substantive interest. The editor needs a clear focus, criteria that define what he or she really wants to know. In social research there's nothing more basic, but also problematic, than becoming clear about what one wants to know. But this issue of focus was especially difficult in this particular project because my own interests changed over the decades. In the sixties I was more interested in political and structural matters; in the late seventies and eighties, more in the personal and experiential. The decisions about how much political discourse to include in this book, about the balance of political and personal questions during the followup interviews, about discarding material that was no longer compelling to me were not easy ones. I can only hope that what speaks to me will speak to you and other readers.

Notes

Introduction

1. For the political difficulties of King and his nonviolent movement in the last two years of his life, see the definitive biography by David J. Garrow, *Bearing the Cross: Martin Luther King, Jr., and the Southern Christian Leadership Conference* (New York: William Morrow, 1986), especially chapters 9–11.

Integration or Black Power? The Great Debate

1. Thomas L. Blair, *Retreat to the Ghetto: The End of a Dream?* (New York: Hill & Wang, 1977), pp. 161–62.

2. See Todd Gitlin, *The Whole World Is Watching: Mass Media in the Making and Unmaking of the New Left* (Berkeley and Los Angeles: University of California Press, 1980).

3. Gallup poll, September 18, 1968.

4. Harris poll, August 9, 1967.

5. The following relies heavily on David T. Wellman's analysis in *Portraits of White Racism* (London: Cambridge University Press, 1977), pp. 218–22.

6. See William Ryan, *Blaming the Victim* (New York: Pantheon, 1971).

7. See Jonathan Rieder, *Canarsie: The Jews and Italians of Brooklyn Against Liberalism* (Cambridge: Harvard University Press, 1985).

8. Godfrey Hodgson writes that "in those feverish spring days" after the assassination, "black militancy . . . seemed to be building up to a climax, perhaps even to an ultimate test of armed strength"; *America in Our Times* (New York: Vintage, 1978), p. 263.

Chapter 1

1. Michele Wallace overlooks this association of manhood with rebellion and dignity when she interprets the aggressive masculine overtones of the black movement in the 1960s as a sexist endeavor to suppress black women on the one hand, and a device to legitimate relations with white women on the other hand; see her *Black Macho and the Myth of the Superwoman* (New York: Dial, 1979). In differing with Wallace, I do not mean to minimize the problem of black male sexism, or to underplay the importance and sensitivity of male-female relations across the color line.

2. In 1965 Daniel P. Moynihan, then an assistant secretary at the Department of Labor, wrote *The Negro Family in America*. Moynihan's report, a history of the debate on its findings, and a collection of critical responses are presented in Lee Rainwater and William L. Yancey, *The Moynihan Report and the Politics of Controversy* (Cambridge: MIT Press, 1967).

Chapter 3

1. *The Autobiography of Malcolm X* (New York: Grove, 1964), p. 36.

Chapter 4

1. Milton Viorst, *Fire in the Streets: America in the 1960s* (New York: Simon & Schuster, 1979), p. 378.
2. Max Hastings, *The Fire This Time: America's Year of Chaos* (New York: Taplinger, 1969), p. 115.

Chapter 6

1. For an excellent discussion of this "squeeze" on the white working class, see Godfrey Hodgson, *America in Our Times* (New York: Vintage, 1978), pp. 483–84.

Chapter 7

1. Andrew Tolson, *The Limits of Masculinity* (New York: Harper & Row, 1977).
2. Statistics from the following census publications issued by the U.S. Department of Commerce, Bureau of the Census (Washington, D.C.: Government Printing Office): *Sixteenth Census of the United States 1940*, vol. 3, *The Labor Force*, pt. 1, U.S. Summary, table 64, p. 97; *1960 Census of Population*, vol. 1, *Characteristics of the Population*, pt. 1, U.S. Summary, table 205, p. 546; and *1970 Census of Population*, vol. 1, pt. 1, sec. 1, table 81, p. 375.

The Ambiguities of Racial Change

1. A similar paradox was reported in a 1986 *Washington Post*–ABC News poll of 1,022 blacks: 48 percent thought income and living conditions were worsening for most blacks, and only 14 percent thought these conditions were improving. But 28 percent said that conditions were improving for them personally, while only 23 percent said they were getting worse; *San Francisco Chronicle*, January 20, 1986.
2. Reynolds Farley, *Blacks and Whites: Narrowing the Gap?* (Cambridge: Harvard University Press, 1984), p. 35.

3. See Steve Millner, "The New South: The New Racism," *Western Journal of Black Studies* 12, no. 1 (Spring 1987): 39–46.

4. Farley, *Blacks and Whites*, pp. 34 and 199. Farley's overall assessment of racial change, however, is less negative than these two citations suggest.

5. In 1969 there were 1,185 black elected officials; in 1979 there were 4,607; Joint Center for Political Studies, *National Roster of Black Elected Officials* (Washington, D.C., 1980).

6. Ibid.

7. Theodore Cross, *The Black Power Imperative: Racial Inequality and the Politics of Nonviolence* (New York: Faulkner, 1984), pp. 321–22. On the role of gerrymandering and other political strategies that work against black candidates, see Cross's discussion on pp. 142–48.

8. *San Francisco Chronicle*, August 10, 1987.

9. *New York Times*/CBS News Poll, reported in *New York Times*, November 8 and November 19, 1984. A California poll one week before the 1984 presidential elections found whites preferring Reagan to Mondale 62 percent to 33 percent; for blacks the ratio was 8 to 77 percent.

10. On February 7, 1983, the *New York Times* reported that strategic relocation has become a widespread practice, because, as one company official put it: "Black workers were less reliable, less skilled, and easier to unionize" and the firms "wanted to avoid affirmative action."

11. Personal communication from Dr. Lois Benjamin, Central State University, Wilberforce, Ohio, on her preliminary research findings.

12. As Bart Landry explains, analysts disagree about whether to define *middle class* as a function of income, occupation, or life-style; see his *The New Black Middle Class* (Berkeley and Los Angeles: University of California Press, 1987). Data on income from William L. Taylor, "Access to Economic Opportunity," in *Minority Report: What Has Happened to Blacks, Hispanics, American Indians, and Other Minorities in the Eighties*, edited by Leslie W. Dunbar (New York: Pantheon, 1984); data on middle-class jobs from Landry, *New Black Middle Class.*

13. In contrast, only 38 percent of black women were white-collar workers in 1972; see Diane Westcott, "Blacks in the 1970s," *Monthly Labor Review*, June 1982, p. 20. It is also true that black women are still overrepresented in such traditional occupations as private household workers, cooks, and housekeepers; see National Committee on Pay Equity, *Pay Equity: An Issue of Race, Ethnicity, and Sex* (Washington, D.C., 1987), p. 4.

14. Taylor, "Access to Economic Opportunity," p. 31.

15. *Time* Magazine, November 11, 1985, p. 84; *New York Times* (national edition), December 3, 1986.

16. Landry, *New Black Middle Class*, pp. 108–10, 196–98.

17. Farley, *Blacks and Whites*, chaps. 2 and 3.

18. For example, the proportion of college faculty who were black doubled (from 3 to 7 percent) between 1970 and 1977, but blacks suffered disproportionate losses (30 percent) when 17,000 teaching positions were eliminated between 1977 and 1979; Cross, *Black Power Imperative*, p. 440.

19. Landry, *New Black Middle Class*, p. 148. See also *New York Times* (national edition), July 19, 1986.

20. Data on black senior executives in the nation's one thousand largest companies from John Naisbit, "Not Much Progress for Black Executives," *San Francisco Chronicle*, December 31, 1986. Data on Fortune 500 from Cross, *Black Power Imperative*, pp. 274–75.

21. Data from Farley, *Blacks and Whites*, p. 200; Cross, *Black Power Imperative*, chap. 12; U.S. Department of Commerce, *U.S. Statistical Abstracts*, 108th ed. (Washington, D.C.: Government Printing Office, 1988), p. 435.

22. Charles Hardy, "Black America, New Opportunities and New Problems," *San Francisco Examiner*, July 21, 1986. By 1986 there was some improvement: from 1982 to 1986 median family income for blacks increased 14 percent, according to the *New York Times* (national edition), July 31, 1987.

23. Cross, *Black Power Imperative*, pp. 245–46. Almost half of these black teenagers live in the fifteen largest metropolitan areas, where jobs are few; only 23 percent of white teenagers live in these largest cities.

24. Troy Duster, "Social Implications of the 'New' Black Urban Underclass," in *Poverty with a Human Face* (San Francisco: Public Media Center, 1985).

25. Data from Uniform Crime Reports; Duster, "Social Implications of the Underclass"; *Christian Science Monitor*, November 13, 1986.

26. Census reports show that 66.7 percent of all black men of working age were in the labor force (either working or actively seeking work) in 1979. Since then, the percentage has continued to decline: "The proportion of black males over the age of 16 who were employed dropped from 74 percent in 1960 to 56 percent in 1982"; Taylor, "Access to Economic Opportunity," p. 41.

27. Hardy, "Black America."

28. *San Francisco Chronicle*, December 19, 1986.

29. Lillian Rubin, *Quiet Rage: Bernie Goetz in an Age of Madness* (New York: Farrar, Straus & Giroux, 1986).

30. William J. Wilson, *The Declining Significance of Race: Blacks and Changing American Institutions* (Chicago: University of Chicago Press, 1978). Michael Hout and other social demographers have supported Wilson's claims by documenting the increasing role of social class in the occupational placement of Afro-Americans. Until the 1960s, race was so all-determining that blacks born into middle-class professional families were just as likely to end up in low-status jobs as blacks who were born poor; Hout, "Occupational Mobility of Black Men," *American Sociological Review* 49 (June 1984): 308–22.

31. Alice Kahn, *San Francisco Chronicle*, November 23, 1986.

Chapter 8

1. In 1978 blacks held less than five million acres of farm land, down from twelve million acres at the turn of the century; Theodore Cross, *The Black*

Power Imperative: Racial Inequality and the Politics of Nonviolence (New York: Faulkner, 1984), p. 456.

Chapter 10

1. "Big Oakland Send-off for Slain Convict," *San Francisco Chronicle*, August 30, 1987.
2. *New York Times* (national edition), July 30, 1985, and August 25, 1986.

Chapter 13

1. Arthur Stein, *Seeds of the Seventies: Values, Work, and Commitment in Post-Vietnam America* (Hanover, N.H.: University Press of New England, 1985).

Conclusion

1. The yearning for community is shared by Americans regardless of color, as is stressed in Robert Bellah et al., *Habits of the Heart: Individualism and Commitment in American Life* (Berkeley and Los Angeles: University of California Press, 1985).
2. A Gallup poll in January 1985 found that 56 percent of blacks—compared to 75 percent of whites—favored the death penalty. A California poll in 1986 reported that blacks had changed their opinions on the death penalty dramatically since the early 1970s, from 64 percent of blacks opposed to it to 62 percent in favor (Field Institute, April 3, 1985).
3. For excellent material on the "defection" of Jewish liberals, see Jonathan Rieder, *Canarsie: The Jews and Italians of Brooklyn Against Liberalism* (Cambridge: Harvard University Press, 1985).
4. Herbert Blumer, "Race Prejudice as a Sense of Group Position," *Pacific Sociological Review* 1 (Spring 1958): 3–7.
5. Allan Bloom, *The Closing of the American Mind* (New York: Simon & Schuster, 1987), pp. 56–60.
6. *The Autobiography of Malcolm X* (New York: Grove, 1964), p. 91.

Appendix

1. Robert Coles had written of the "long and perplexing task of editing tapes, of arranging and rearranging sentences of talk, of adding sentences spoken on one or another occasion," but I had missed the reference in his "The Method," in *Explorations in Psychohistory*, edited by Robert J. Lifton (New York: Simon & Schuster, 1975), p. 178.

2. Coles, "The Method"; and Nell Irvin Painter, *The Narrative of Hosea Hudson* (Cambridge: Harvard University Press, 1979). For a fuller discussion of these issues, see my "Problems of Editing 'First-Person' Sociology," *Qualitative Sociology* 10, no. 1 (Spring 1987): 46–64.

3. John Langston Gwaltney, *Drylongso: A Self-Portrait of Black America* (New York: Random House, 1980), p. xxvi.

Bibliographic Essay

A comprehensive bibliography covering all the themes touched upon in this book would require a volume in itself. Here I have limited myself to the more salient topics and suggested a few readings for each. An excellent anthology, primarily theoretical, is Norman R. Yetman, *Majority and Minority: The Dynamics of Race and Ethnicity in American Life*, 4th ed. (Boston: Allyn & Bacon, 1985).

Integration or Black Power? The Great Debate

Two general treatments of the politics and culture of the 1960s are Godfrey Hodgson, *America in Our Times* (New York: Vintage, 1978), and Todd Gitlin, *The Sixties: Years of Hope, Days of Rage* (New York: Bantam, 1987). I also found useful Milton Viorst's *Fire in the Streets: America in the 1960s* (New York: Simon & Schuster, 1979); Harris Wofford's *Of Kennedys and Kings: Making Sense of the Sixties* (New York: Farrar, Straus & Giroux, 1980); and for the year 1968 Max Hastings's *The Fire This Time: America's Year of Chaos* (New York: Taplinger, 1969). Two books have recently appeared to mark the twentieth anniversary of that year: Hans Koning's personal report, *Nineteen Sixty-Eight: Its Mark on the Country, the Government, and You and Me* (New York: Norton, 1987); and David Caute's *The Year of the Barricades: A Journey Through 1968* (New York: Harper & Row, 1988), a comprehensive analysis that covers the Paris and Prague uprisings as well as the American crisis.

Stanley Karnow's *Vietnam: A History* (Harmondsworth, England: Penguin, 1984) is probably the best single source on the Vietnam war; Al Santoli, *Everything We Had* (New York: Random House, 1981) is an outstanding oral history of the war.

Harvard Sitkoff's *The Struggle for Black Equality, 1954–1980* (New York: Hill & Wang, 1981) has become a standard source on the civil rights movement. Valuable treatments of the southern-based movement include Aldon D.

Morris, *The Origins of the Civil Rights Movement: Black Communities Organizing for Change* (New York: Free Press, 1984); Howell Raines's oral history, *My Soul Is Rested: The Story of the Civil Rights Movement in the Deep South* (Harmondsworth, England: Penguin, 1983); and the definitive biography of Martin Luther King: David J. Garrow, *Bearing the Cross: Martin Luther King, Jr., and the Southern Christian Leadership Conference* (New York: William Morrow, 1986). Among the wealth of personal accounts, Anne Moody, *Coming of Age in Mississippi* (New York: Dial, 1968) is vivid on the outlooks of southern blacks in the years immediately before the movement. On the history of SNCC, including its changing racial composition and the emergence of Black Power, see Clayborne Carson, *In Struggle: SNCC and the Black Awakening of the 1960s* (Cambridge: Harvard University Press, 1981). The rationale for Black Power is set forth in Stokely Carmichael and Charles V. Hamilton, *Black Power: The Politics of Liberation in America* (New York: Vintage, 1967). Perhaps the best introduction of all is the six-hour video recording *Eyes on the Prize: America's Civil Rights Years, 1954–1965* (Alexandria, Va.: PBS Video, 1986), Henry Hampton's powerful and moving rendition of the civil rights years and the context of southern racism from which the movement emerged; the companion book, written by Juan Williams, was published by Viking in 1986.

Focusing more on the North, Charles E. Silberman's prophetic *Crisis in Black and White* (New York: Random House, 1964) remains a powerful account of racial polarization in the early 1960s. Thomas L. Blair, *Retreat to the Ghetto: The End of a Dream?* (New York: Hill & Wang, 1977) describes the pull between integration and nationalism during the late 1960s and 1970s. This issue informs Harold Cruse's seminal study of black nationalism, *The Crisis of the Negro Intellectual* (New York: William Morrow, 1967).

The best source on the Garvey movement is *The Marcus Garvey and Universal Negro Improvement Association Papers*, edited by Robert A. Hill (Berkeley and Los Angeles: University of California Press, 1983–). *The Autobiography of Malcolm X* (New York: Grove, 1964) remains indispensable. Two studies of the Nation of Islam are *The Black Muslims in America*, by C. Eric Lincoln (Boston: Beacon, 1961); and E. Essien-Udom, *Black Nationalism: A Search for an Identity in America* (Chicago: University of Chicago Press, 1962). Theodore Draper, *The Rediscovery of Black Nationalism* (New York: Viking, 1970) is a valuable critique of the major expressions of late-sixties' militancy. The most comprehensive study of the mid-sixties' riots remains *The Report of the National Advisory Commission on Civil Disorders* (New York: Bantam, 1968)—better known as the Kerner Report. John Hersey, *The Algiers Motel Incident* (New York: Bantam, 1968) covers the 1967 Detroit riots.

Works that concern the ferment in Afro-American culture in the late 1960s are Harold Cruse, *The Crisis of the Negro Intellectual* (cited above); *Afro-American Anthropology: Contemporary Perspectives*, edited by Norman E.

Whitten, Jr., and John F. Szwed (New York: Free Press, 1970); *Beyond Black or White: An Alternate America*, edited by Vernon J. Dixon and Badi Foster (Boston: Little, Brown, 1971); and my essay "Black Culture: Myth or Reality," in Robert Blauner, *Racial Oppression in America* (New York: Harper & Row, 1972). Lawrence W. Levine's *Black Culture and Black Consciousness: Afro-American Folk Thought from Slavery to Freedom* (New York: Oxford University Press, 1977) is an important study of folklore and music. For assimilation and ethnic pluralism, see Milton M. Gordon, *Assimilation in American Life: The Role of Race, Religion, and National Origin* (New York: Oxford University Press, 1964); Nathan Glazer and Daniel Patrick Moynihan, *Beyond the Melting Pot: The Negroes, Puerto Ricans, Jews, Italians, and Irish of New York City* (Cambridge: MIT Press, 1963); and Stephen Steinberg, *The Ethnic Myth: Race, Ethnicity, and Class in America* (New York: Atheneum, 1981). John C. Leggett's *Race, Class, and Labor: Working-Class Consciousness in Detroit* (New York: Oxford University Press, 1968) stresses the special class consciousness of Afro-Americans.

The relation between class and race is at the heart of the structural analysis of racism in Stanley B. Greenberg, *Race and State in Capitalist Development: Comparative Perspectives* (New Haven: Yale University Press, 1980), and George M. Fredrickson, *White Supremacy* (New York: Oxford University Press, 1981), two major theoretical and historical syntheses, both of which also compare the United States and South Africa.

An earlier classic, with a comparative focus on India's caste system, is Oliver Cromwell Cox, *Caste, Class, and Race: A Study in Social Dynamics* (Garden City, N.Y.: Doubleday, 1948). On the history of American racism as cultural ideology, see Winthrop Jordan, *White Over Black: American Attitudes Toward the Negro, 1550–1812* (Chapel Hill: University of North Carolina Press, 1968); George M. Fredrickson, *The Black Image in the White Mind: The Debate on Afro-American Character and Destiny, 1817–1914* (New York: Harper & Row, 1971); and Thomas Gossett, *Race: The History of an Idea in America* (Dallas: Southern Methodist University Press, 1963). The classic treatment of "liberal equalitarianism" is Gunnar Myrdal, *An American Dilemma: The Negro Problem and Modern Democracy* (New York: Harper & Brothers, 1944). See also David T. Wellman, *Portraits of White Racism* (London: Cambridge University Press, 1977), and Allen J. Matusow, *The Unraveling of America: A History of Liberalism in the 1960s* (New York: Harper & Row, 1984).

The psychological facets of racism are the theme of Joel Kovel, *White Racism: A Psychohistory* (New York: Pantheon, 1970). On institutional aspects, see Harold Baron, "The Web of Urban Racism," in *Institutional Racism in America*, edited by Louis L. Knowles and Kenneth Prewitt (Englewood Cliffs, N.J.: Prentice-Hall, 1969); and Stokely Carmichael and Charles V. Hamilton, *Black Power* (cited above). For working-class militancy in the late sixties and early seventies, see Stanley Aronowitz, *False Promises: The Shaping of*

American Working-Class Consciousness (New York: McGraw-Hill, 1973), especially chapters 1 and 2.

Chapter 1

The relation between racism and manhood is discussed in William H. Grier and Price M. Cobbs, *Black Rage* (New York: Basic Books, 1968). Robert Staples, *Black Masculinity: The Black Male's Role in American Society* (San Francisco: Black Scholar Press, 1982) is an excellent source on black men. Street models of masculinity are portrayed in Claude Brown, *Manchild in the Promised Land* (New York: Macmillan, 1965), and Charles Keil, *The Urban Blues* (Chicago: University of Chicago Press, 1966). Elliot Liebow, *Tally's Corner* (Boston: Little, Brown, 1967) is a classic study of street-corner men; Elijah Anderson, *A Place on the Corner* (Chicago: University of Chicago Press, 1978) is also useful.

Joel Williamson, *The Crucible of Race: Black/White Relations in the American South Since Emancipation* (New York: Oxford University Press, 1984) is an original psychological interpretation of black-white relations in the South from Emancipation through the 1970s, with an emphasis on the role of violence. He has abridged that longer work in his *A Rage for Order* (New York: Oxford University Press, 1986). For traditional race relations in the pre–civil rights South, see John Dollard, *Caste and Class in a Southern Town* (New Haven: Yale University Press, 1937); Allison Davis et al., *Deep South: A Social Anthropological Study of Caste and Class* (Chicago: University of Chicago Press, 1941); and Hortense Powdermaker, *After Freedom: A Cultural Study in the Deep South* (New York: Viking, 1939). Excellent social histories of northern urban black communities include Alan H. Spear, *Black Chicago: The Making of a Negro Ghetto, 1890–1920* (Chicago: University of Chicago Press, 1967); and Kenneth L. Kusmer, *A Ghetto Takes Shape: Black Cleveland, 1870–1930* (Urbana: University of Illinois Press, 1976). Class differences among Chicago blacks are emphasized in what may be the finest community study ever produced in the social sciences: St. Clair Drake and Horace Cayton, *Black Metropolis: A Study of Negro Life in a Northern City* (New York: Harcourt, Brace, 1945). Stanley Lieberson, *A Piece of the Pie: Blacks and White Immigrants Since 1880* (Berkeley and Los Angeles: University of California Press, 1980) is a detailed analysis of occupational and residential mobility among blacks and white immigrants in the urban North.

Chapter 2

The speeches and writings of Stokely Carmichael are collected in *Stokely Speaks: Black Power to Pan-Africanism*, edited by Edith Minor (New York:

Vintage, 1971). There are many personal memoirs about the Black Panther Party, but the scholarly literature is scant. An early journalistic account is Gene Marine, *The Black Panthers* (New York: New American Library, 1969). Gilbert Moore, *A Special Rage* (New York: Harper & Row, 1971) focuses on the 1968 trial of Huey Newton. On the "police riot" at the Chicago Democratic Convention, see Daniel Walker, *Rights in Conflict* (Washington, D.C.: National Commission on the Causes and Prevention of Violence, 1968) (known as the Walker Report). For the conflicts between the police and the black community, the Kerner Report (cited above) remains an excellent source.

On San Francisco's hippies, see Charles Perry, *The Haight-Ashbury: A History* (New York: Random House, 1984). Calvin C. Hernton, *Sex and Racism in America* (Garden City, N.Y.: Doubleday, 1965) is the classic work on interracial sexual relationships, though in recent years it has been criticized by black feminists. On positive interracial relations, including friendships, see Rhoda Goldstein Blumberg and Wendell J. Roye, *Interracial Bonds* (New York: General Hall, 1979).

The literature on race and racism in public education is enormous. Three influential personal accounts from the 1960s are Jonathan Kozol, *Death at an Early Age: The Destruction of the Hearts and Minds of Negro Children in the Boston Public Schools* (Boston: Houghton Mifflin, 1967); Herbert Kohl, *Thirty-Six Children* (New York: New American Library, 1967); and James Herndon, *The Way It Spozed To Be* (New York: Simon & Schuster, 1968). Three decades of school desegregation in the United States are thoughtfully appraised in Jennifer Hochschild, *The New American Dilemma: Liberal Democracy and School Desegregation* (New Haven: Yale University Press, 1984). J. Anthony Lukas's monumental *Common Ground: A Turbulent Decade in the Lives of Three American Families* (New York: Knopf, 1985) traces the impact of Boston's school integration crisis on the members of three families; it is also the most detailed study of race relations in a northern city in the 1970s.

Chapter 3

The treatment of domestic workers in black literature is the subject of Trudier Harris, *From Mammies to Militants* (Philadelphia: Temple University Press, 1982). *Willie Mae* by Elizabeth L. Kytle (New York: Knopf, 1958) is a wonderful, though hard to find, autobiographical memoir of working in the homes of white people. Two important studies of black women are Paula Giddings's political history *When and Where I Enter: The Impact of Black Women on Race and Sex in America* (New York: William Morrow, 1984); and Jacqueline Jones, *Labor of Love, Labor of Sorrow: Black Women, Work, and the Family from Slavery to the Present* (New York: Vintage, 1986), a history of black women as workers. Angela Y. Davis, *Women, Race, and Class* (New York: Random House, 1981) discusses historical and contemporary issues. Michele Wallace, *Black Macho and the Myth of the Superwoman* (New York: Dial, 1979) looks at gender conflict in the black movement. Important statements of black feminism include June Jordan, *Civil Wars* (Boston: Beacon, 1981); Bell Hooks, *Ain't I a Woman? Black Women and Feminism* (Boston: South End, 1981); Alice Walker, *In Search of Our Mothers' Gardens: Womanist Prose* (San Diego: Harcourt Brace Jovanovich, 1983); and Audre Lorde, *Sister Outsider: Essays and Speeches* (Trumansburg, N.Y.: Crossing Press, 1984); Lorde also offers a lesbian perspective. Male-female relations are also discussed in Robert Staples, *The World of Black Singles: Changing Patterns of Male/Female Relations* (Westport, Conn.: Greenwood, 1981), and Nathan and Julia Hare, *The Endangered Black Family* (San Francisco: Black Think Tank, 1984).

Chapter 4

On the white backlash and the Wallace vote, see Seymour Martin Lipset and Earl Raab, *The Politics of Unreason: Right-Wing Extremism in America, 1790–1970* (New York: Harper & Row, 1970); and on the white liberal retreat from civil rights, Oscar Handlin, *Firebell in the Night* (Boston: Little, Brown, 1964). For the seventies, the best source is Jonathan Rieder, *Canarsie: The Jews and Italians of Brooklyn Against Liberalism* (Cambridge: Harvard University Press, 1985).

The importance of numerical ratios in race relations is discussed in Hubert M. Blalock, Jr., *Toward a Theory of Intergroup Relations* (New York: Wiley, 1967), and in Marvin Harris, *Patterns of Race in America* (New York: Walker, 1964).

For the history of discrimination against nonblack minorities, see Robert F. Heizer and Alan Almquist, *The Other Californians: Prejudice and Discrimination Under Spain, Mexico, and the United States to 1920* (Berkeley and Los Angeles: University of California Press, 1971). Albert Camarillo, *Chicanos in a Changing Society* (Cambridge: Harvard University Press, 1979) is a social history of Mexicans living in Santa Barbara in the nineteenth and twentieth centuries; David Montejano, *Anglos and Mexicans in the Making of Texas* (Austin: University of Texas Press, 1987) covers the period from 1836 to 1986 in a brilliant mix of history and sociology. Victor G. and Brett de Barry Nee, *Longtime Californ': A Documentary History of an American Chinatown* (New York: Pantheon, 1972) is rich in historical and contemporary description of San Francisco's Chinese community; the Korean community in New York is the subject of Illsoo Kim, *New Urban Immigrants* (Princeton: Princeton University Press, 1981). Recent studies of Japanese Americans include Evelyn Nakano Glenn, *Issei, Nisei, Warbride* (Philadelphia: Temple University Press, 1986), a feminist analysis of family and work among domestics; and two oral histories: Eileen Sunada Sarahson, *Issei* (Palo Alto, Calif.: Pacific Books, 1983), and *And Justice For All*, edited by John Tateishi (New York: Random House, 1984), personal testimonies of detention in the wartime internment camps. Among the voluminous literature on the profoundly variegated Native American experience, Virgil J. Vogel, *This Country Was Ours* (New York: Harper & Row, 1972) is a useful documentary history on Indian-white relations in the eighteenth and nineteenth centuries; James S. Olson and Raymond Wilson, *Native Americans in the Twentieth Century* (Provo, Utah: Brigham Young University Press, 1984) continues the historical account. For the present-day struggles of Native Americans, see Alvin M. Josephy, Jr., *Now That the Buffalo's Gone* (New York: Knopf, 1982), a work also rich in historical background; and Peter Matthiessen, *Indian Country* (New York: Viking, 1984).

Chapter 5

On youth and personal identity, the pioneer theorist is Erik Erikson; see his *Identity, Youth, and Crisis* (New York: Norton, 1968). Daniel J. Levinson, *The Seasons of a Man's Life* (New York: Ballantine Books, 1978) focuses on the adult phases of the male life course, especially the midlife transition. John Irwin, *Prisons in Turmoil* (Boston: Little, Brown, 1980) discusses prison as a politicizing experience and race relations behind bars, issues treated also by Tom Wicker in his study of the siege at Attica prison in 1971, *A Time to Die* (New York: Quadrangle, 1975).

Chapter 6

I have not been able to find recent research on the racial climate of the workplace. However, Katherine Archibald, *Wartime Shipyard: A Study in Social Disunity* (Berkeley and Los Angeles: University of California Press, 1947) is a rich account of ethnic and racial interaction on the job. Political and cultural perspectives of white workers are described in *Blue-Collar World: Studies of the American Worker*, edited by Arthur B. Shostak and William Gomberg (Englewood Cliffs, N.J.: Prentice-Hall, 1964). Mirra Komarovsky, *Blue-Collar Marriage* (New York: Vintage, 1962), and Lillian Rubin, *Worlds of Pain: Life in the Working-Class Family* (New York: Basic Books, 1977) document the traditional values and kinship orientations of the white blue-collar class.

Chapter 7

William H. Harris, *The Harder We Run* (New York: Oxford University Press, 1982) is an important survey of the black working class from the Civil War through the 1970s. Joe W. Trotter, *Black Milwaukee* (Urbana: University of

Illinois Press, 1985) traces "the making of an industrial proletariat" between 1915 and 1945. On black militancy in the automobile industry during the late sixties and early seventies, see James A. Geschwender, *Class, Race, and Worker Insurgency: The League of Revolutionary Black Workers* (Cambridge: Cambridge University Press, 1977), and Dan Georgakas and Marvin Surkin, *Detroit: I Do Mind Dying—A Study in Urban Revolution* (New York: St. Martin's, 1975). Bruce B. Williams's *Black Workers in an Industrial Suburb: The Struggle Against Discrimination* (New Brunswick, N.J.: Rutgers University Press, 1987) is one of the few firsthand studies of the detailed workings of racism at the plant level; it also documents the new consciousness of the younger generation of black workers and their concern with manhood and dignity.

There is a rich literature on street hustlers, including Henry Williamson [pseud.], *Hustler!* (Garden City, N.Y.: Doubleday, 1965); Iceberg Slim, *Pimp* (Los Angeles: Holloway, 1969); Christina and Richard Milner, *Black Players: The Secret World of Black Pimps* (New York: Bantam, 1972); and the autobiographies of Malcolm X and Claude Brown already cited.

The Ambiguities of Racial Change

Two excellent social histories of the 1970s are Peter N. Carroll, *It Seemed Like Nothing Happened: The Tragedy and Promise of America in the 1970s* (New York: Holt, Rinehart, & Winston, 1982); and Arthur Stein, *Seeds of the Seventies: Values, Work, and Commitment in Post-Vietnam America* (Hanover, N.H.: University Press of New England, 1985).

General treatments of racial change since the 1960s include Reynolds Farley, *Blacks and Whites: Narrowing the Gap?* (Cambridge: Harvard University Press, 1984), especially strong on demographic data; *Minority Report: What Has Happened to Blacks, Hispanics, American Indians, and Other Minorities in the Eighties*, edited by Leslie W. Dunbar (New York: Pantheon, 1984); William J. Wilson, *The Declining Significance of Race: Blacks and Changing American Institutions* (Chicago: University of Chicago Press, 1978); Theodore Cross, *The Black Power Imperative: Racial Inequality and the Politics of Nonviolence* (New York: Faulkner, 1984); and Alphonso Pinkney, *The Myth of Black Progress* (Cambridge: Cambridge University Press, 1984).

Margaret Edds, *Free at Last: What Really Happened When Civil Rights Came to Southern Politics* (New York: Adler & Adler, 1987) examines black political gains since the 1960s in a comparative study of ten southern communities. See also Steven F. Lawson, *In Pursuit of Power: Southern Blacks and Electoral Politics* (New York: Columbia University Press, 1985). Studies of northern black politics and mayors include *The New Black Vote: Politics and*

Power in Four American Cities, edited by Rod Bush (San Francisco: Synthesis Publications, 1984); Michael B. Preston et al., *The New Black Politics: The Search for Political Power*, 2d ed. (New York: Longman, 1987); and Paul Kleppner, *Chicago Divided: The Making of a Black Mayor* (DeKalb: University of Northern Illinois Press, 1985), a thorough account of the election of the late Harold Washington.

The classic work on the black middle class is E. Franklin Frazier, *Black Bourgeoisie* (Glencoe, Ill.: Free Press, 1957). An early study of professionals is G. Franklin Edwards, *The Negro Professional Class* (Glencoe, Ill.: Free Press, 1959). Recent works include James E. Blackwell, *Mainstreaming Outsiders* (Bayside, N.Y.: General Hall, 1981), on producing black professionals; George Davis and Glegg Watson, *Black Life in Corporate America: Swimming in the Mainstream* (New York: Anchor, 1982), on black managers; and on the middle class as a whole, Bart Landry, *The New Black Middle Class* (Berkeley and Los Angeles: University of California Press, 1987).

The most recent work on the black underclass is William J. Wilson, *The Truly Disadvantaged: The Inner City, the Underclass, and Public Policy* (Chicago: University of Chicago Press, 1987). Other studies include Douglas G. Glasgow, *The Black Underclass: Poverty, Unemployment, and Entrapment of Ghetto Youth* (San Francisco: Jossey-Bass, 1980); Ken Auletta, *The Underclass* (New York: Random House, 1982); and Terry M. Williams and William Kornblum, *Growing Up Poor* (Lexington, Mass.: D. C. Heath, 1985). Wilson's book is a strong rejoinder to neoconservative Charles Murray's very influential *Losing Ground: American Social Policy, 1950–1980* (New York: Basic Books, 1984), which argues that increases in welfare dependency and female-headed families are the result of the liberal social programs of the 1960s. The underclass, welfare reform, drug use, and black families are also discussed in *The State of Black America, 1987* (New York: National Urban League, 1987).

Two recent studies of racial attitudes are Howard Schuman et al., *Racial Attitudes in America: Trends and Interpretations* (Cambridge: Harvard University Press, 1985), and Paul Sniderman, with Michael Hagen, *Race and Inequality: A Study in American Values* (Chatham, N.J.: Chatham, 1985). The relation between class and race is a leading theme in William J. Wilson, *The Declining Significance of Race* (cited above), as well as in Michael Omi and Howard Winant, *Racial Formation in the United States: From the 1960s to the 1980s* (New York: Routledge & Kegan Paul, 1986); Jack M. Bloom, *Race, Class, and the Civil Rights Movement* (Bloomington: University of Indiana Press, 1987); and the work of Edna Bonacich, for example "The Past, Present, and Future of Split-Labor Market Theory," in *Research in Racial and Ethnic Relations*, edited by C. B. Marrett and C. Leggon (Greenwich, Conn.: JAI Press, 1979).

Chapter 9

A balanced treatment of affirmative action is John C. Livingston, *Fair Game? Inequality and Affirmative Action* (San Francisco: W. H. Freeman, 1979). The argument that affirmative action has become essentially a reverse racism is advanced by Nathan Glazer, *Affirmative Discrimination: Ethnic Inequality and Public Policy* (New York: Basic Books, 1975).

Chapter 11

On the shrinking of the American working class, see Barry Bluestone and Bennett Harrison, *The Deindustrialization of America: Plant Closings, Community Abandonment, and the Dismantling of Basic Industry* (New York: Basic Books, 1982).

Chapter 12

Studies of the black family include Herbert G. Gutman, *The Black Family in Slavery and Freedom, 1750–1925* (New York: Pantheon, 1976); E. Franklin Frazier, *The Negro Family in America* (Chicago: University of Chicago Press, 1939); Andrew Billingsley, *Black Families in White America* (Englewood Cliffs, N.J.: Prentice-Hall, 1968); and Carol Stack, *All Our Kin: Strategies for Survival in a Black Community* (New York: Harper & Row, 1974). Daniel P. Moynihan's *The Negro Family in America* and much of the critical reaction to his report are presented in Lee Rainwater and William L. Yancey, *The Moynihan Report and the Politics of Controversy* (Cambridge: MIT Press, 1967). Reginald M. Clark, *Family Life and School Achievement* (Chicago: University of Chicago Press, 1983) looks at family patterns as the key to "why poor black children succeed or fail." An excellent anthology is *Black Families*, edited by Harriette P. McAdoo (Beverly Hills, Calif.: Sage, 1981).

Conclusion

John Langston Gwaltney's *Drylongso: A Self-Portrait of Black America* (New York: Random House, 1980) is a rich oral history particularly strong on black views of white people and of their own Afro-American culture.

Appendix: Methodology

The work of Studs Terkel has been important for me. His *Working* (New York: Pantheon, 1974) opened my eyes to the potential of oral history and the interview format for pointing up the connection between social structures and personal experience. Robert Coles has also been an inspiration, from his first book, *Children of Crisis: A Study of Courage and Fear* (Boston: Little, Brown, 1967). I particularly recommend his *Women of Crisis: Lives of Struggle and Hope*, written with Jane H. Coles (New York: Dell, 1978)—especially Lorna's story, "Eskimo Women Spirits," which shines in this gem of a book as the ultimate expression, for me, of the entire genre of first-person social science, or life studies, to use the term preferred by Thomas J. Cottle, another master of the form.

The Author's Story
(March 1990)

A few months after this book was published, I met a young African-American journalist who had been assigned to interview me. Her first question: "Why did you, a white man, write a book about race and black people? Did you witness a lynching at an impressionable age?" Today there are many young people like her, of all races, born long after the civil rights movement, who cannot quite understand why a white person would be concerned with racial justice.

No, I did not witness a lynching, but I did grow up in Chicago in the 1930s and 1940s under the cloud of Hitler's conquest of Europe, the Holocaust, and the Second World War. My parents were lower-middle-class liberal supporters of Franklin Roosevelt. They were also Jewish. But in their concern that my sister and I become "good Americans," they taught us almost nothing of our ethnic and religious traditions. Only when I found out in college that Marx, Freud, and other intellectual luminaries had been Jewish did I begin to see something positive in my heritage. But when friends in high school would discuss how hard it was to be Jewish, I would typically respond, "Things are much worse for the Negro people." Where this attitude came from remains a mystery. I do not recall that my parents explicitly taught me about race and difference, but they encouraged me to view all people as equals. Despite the considerable prejudice toward Irish Catholics among my ethnic compatriots in our north side neighborhood of Rogers Park, I played ball, traded baseball cards, and listened to Cubs games with Irish as well as Jewish friends.

Not only my Jewish affiliation but also my masculine credentials were problematic. Because my father was a somewhat shadowy figure in my life, from an early age I had looked for images of male strength to identify with. Sports figures loomed large in the imagination of a small Jewish boy somewhat disparagingly known as "the brain" in school. My first hero was Joe

Louis. He had come back from defeat to knock out Max Schmeling, the champion of Hitler's Reich. By the age of six I was listening to all of Louis's fights on the radio. He represented to me not only a model of masculine strength but also a persecuted race, not unlike my own.

But I did not have any first-hand contact with black people—or any people of color for that matter—until I entered the University of Chicago. Reading Gunnar Myrdal's *An American Dilemma* in my first semester was a turning point.* We were assigned only parts of the book, but I read all 1,483 pages voraciously. It provided a historical and sociological framework for an inchoate but developing personal interest in black–white relations. I also began to read African-American literature, and I urged my friends to read Richard Wright's *Black Boy* and works by other black writers and poets I was discovering. In 1950 I went to Washington as part of an NAACP mobilization for a national anti-lynching law. Passing through Virginia and Maryland, I saw southern-style segregation and noted the contrast between official Washington and the impoverished ghetto. For a twenty-year-old liberal who was already beginning to feel that need to be liked and accepted by blacks (a type well described by Bill Harcliff), it was heady stuff to stay in a black neighborhood and share a room with a radical African-American activist— and I congratulated myself on my presumed lack of racial prejudice.

During my college years I shifted my studies from literature, my first love, to sociology, which I decided to continue in graduate school. In Professor Everett Hughes's field methods course I chose an all-black census tract to study. A still somewhat innocent white boy, I walked around playing anthropologist, making "friends," attending church services, and being invited into homes to ask people their opinions about Paul Robeson, who was at the time under attack for his radical politics. In 1950, as Howard Spence recalled, you did not have to fear for your safety on the south side of Chicago.

Returning to Chicago in 1962 after a decade in northern California, I found that race relations had changed drastically, particularly on the border between my neighborhood, Hyde Park, and the black ghettoes that surrounded this white middle-class enclave. Largely because of the new civil rights consciousness, tensions between blacks and whites, even between passersby on the sidewalk, were now palpable. Our discomfort in this climate was an important factor in our decision to leave Chicago and return to California. I was teaching at Berkeley during the fall of 1964, when the Free Speech Movement erupted: this critical event sent me on the course eventually resulting in this book.

In Chicago I had taught a course on racial and ethnic minorities. But my research was on the sociology of death: in my personal life I was exploring

* Gunnar Myrdal, *An American Dilemma* (New York: Harper, 1944).

mortality and other existential questions. Inspired by this new student movement at Berkeley and by the civil rights movement then still largely in the
South, I decided that such personal preoccupations were too self-indulgent.
The voices from the urban ghettoes, which were beginning to express themselves in the riots of the mid-sixties, seemed to be saying that the problems
of the living, not of the dying, needed attention. So the death book became
an article, and in 1965 I began teaching and writing about race.

I had become interested in the question of why black Americans had not
risen as rapidly in the American class structure as had many other ethnic
groups. Obviously it had something to do with a unique history of enslavement and the continuing power and pervasiveness of racism—a slavery that
had damaged the African-American family and, along with racism, had im-
paired the capacity of black men to compete in the marketplace and provide
for their families. From the study of death and from my own personal quests,
I was also developing an interest in masculinity. I speculated about the concepts of manhood held by different ethnic groups. I wondered whether black
men, particularly in the lower and working classes, had developed a unique
sense of what it means to be a man, an ideal that while enriching black
ethnicity and fortifying individual identity might have a negative impact on
assimilation and upward mobility. At the suggestion of Nathan Glazer, I
sent a draft of an essay to his friend Daniel Patrick Moynihan, then an
assistant secretary of labor in Lyndon Johnson's administration. My ideas
overlapped in some ways with the soon-to-be-published Moynihan Report
on the Negro family. He sent me a note calling my article brilliant and
added, "You must be Jewish." Two years later I would send him a draft of
another paper in which I said that critics were wrong to call him and his
report "racist," since his position reflected instead an attitude I called "neo-
racist"! Moynihan, not surprisingly, responded with anger, saying that my
new term—and the whole article on black culture—would further polarize
race relations. It was the sixties, and things were changing fast, including
my ideas.

While much has been published about the failings of African-American
men, few writers have examined the prominent role many have played as
models of manhood to young people of all races. In my own personal and
political development Paul Robeson played such a role and in the process
fired my concern with racial justice. I attended many of his concerts and
speeches in the late 1940s. Through his songs and his words, he connected
the struggles of the Negro people against American racism with those of
Asians and Africans against colonialism and of workers throughout the world
against exploitation.* Hearing Paul Robeson sing and speak was as impor-

---

* See the recent biography by Martin Duberman, *Paul Robeson* (New York: Knopf, 1989).

tant in my radicalization as conversations with friends and the pamphlets from the Little Lenin Library they gave me. I remember him as an orator as powerful as Malcolm X and Martin Luther King, but some of the magic must have come from the psychological hunger of a young man for a larger-than-life hero to idolize.

Despite its paternalism, dogmatism, and other deficiencies, no other predominantly white organization at that time was as serious and successful as the American Communist Party in recruiting blacks, preparing them for leadership positions, and protesting racial injustice.* In weekly meetings we searched our souls and our practice for "white chauvinism," studied books like Carey McWilliams's *North from Mexico*,† and leafleted against "legal lynchings" in the South. Of course, the Old Left also tended to romanticize African-Americans as noble and virtuous. In Europe in 1951 I met a young communist from Brooklyn who told me how much he wished he had been born black. I was sophisticated enough to know that this was the worst kind of patronizing, but without a sure sense of my own ethnic roots and personal identity, I probably felt the same way on some deeper level. And we had to like Negroes just because they were black and oppressed. When I left the party in 1956, following Khrushchev's denunciation of the crimes of Stalin and the repression of popular revolt in Hungary and Poland, what a liberation it was to realize that the dislike I felt for a black person I worked with was perfectly legitimate!

During the 1950s the communist youth movement was encouraging middle-class students to leave the universities (where no serious political movement could be expected!) and join the working class in order to raise the consciousness of the only group with any real revolutionary potential. I cannot say that my five years as a proletarian made any detectable (or, for that matter, undetectable) impression on working-class consciousness; however, my own life and outlook were significantly altered. It was in the factory that I first observed the deep-seated racial bigotry that Myrdal had so well dissected, as well as the paradoxical on-the-job egalitarianism of white workers discussed in chapter 6. I have never forgotten a young white worker from Arkansas who exemplified this contradiction. As we rode to work together, he would spout off about how "the niggers should be sent back to Africa" because they were moving into the neighborhoods near the plant; an hour later he would be working in great friendliness and harmony with his young black partner on the assembly line. I myself tried to set a nonracist example by my questioning of blatantly prejudiced remarks and by my friendships

*Some of the best discussions of the American Communist Party and black Americans are found in Harold Cruse, *The Crisis of the Negro Intellectuals* (New York: Morrow, 1967), and idem, *Rebellion or Revolution?* (New York: Morrow, 1968).
†Carey McWilliams, *North from Mexico* (Philadelphia: Lippincott, 1949).

with Mexicans and blacks, the people with whom I actually felt most comfortable. These two ways of questioning not-to-be-questioned racial practices were enough to get me labeled as a "Jew-Communist college student"—which, of course, I was.

Returning to graduate school after five years as a worker-radical, I felt fortunate to have another chance to succeed within the system, and within a community of politically aware students and faculty at Berkeley who saw my political and working-class background as a positive experience. Reading the classics in political sociology—especially the works of Michels, Mannheim, and Bakunin, which were revelations to me—helped answer many of the questions I was asking about class, revolution, socialism, and bureaucracy. A strong need to settle down and develop a career also moderated my politics. In the early sixties I married again, revised my thesis into a book, and began teaching, first at San Francisco State, then at the University of Chicago, and finally at U.C. Berkeley.

But the social conflict of the 1960s put a halt to my settling down. Having moved toward liberalism, I once again became more radical. The late 1960s also intensified my personal and political ambivalence. I had to ask myself whether I should continue to pursue success and privilege at a time when the nation's most oppressed people were fighting for their basic rights. And whether power and position would better enable me to help bring about change from within the system. Or whether I should turn my back on success in order to work more effectively toward truly fundamental social transformation. It was a conflict by no means unique to me, but one that I never totally resolved.

In 1965 I was still enough of an insider to be named a consultant to the official commission investigating the causes of that summer's rioting in the Watts section of Los Angeles. My role was to find out how the citizens of Watts themselves felt about the uprising. But the law-and-order oriented commission kept throwing roadblocks in the path of the survey I was trying to carry out. When its conservative report was issued, I utilized my official position to publish a sharp critique of their "whitewash." * Tentatively suggesting an interpretation of the events as a kind of anticolonial revolt against the white institutions that controlled the ghetto, I was tilting to the left and toward the black militant perspective.

In 1966, during the same summer that Stokely Carmichael was raising the slogan of Black Power, my father died of a heart attack. In one of his last letters he had written me that the young blacks he observed in the parks of Chicago were hurting their group's just cause by acting so hostilely toward

---

* "Whitewash over Watts: The Failure of the McCone Commission," *Trans-Action* 3 (3) (March–April 1966): 3–9, 54. The essay also appears as chapter 6 in Robert Blauner, *Racial Oppression in America* (New York: Harper and Row, 1972).

white people. But in my writing and public action over the next few years, I increasingly championed the cause of these angry blacks, including the Black Power advocates, perhaps displacing some of my own anger at the loss of my father and at his unrealized life.

He had been fearful that I would be denied tenure because of my communist past. These anxieties were greatly relieved by a positive prognosis on my first promotion attempt. However, the tenure decision was postponed for a year because the university thought my new research was too vague. I was asked for a comprehensive methodological statement. I was a little annoyed, but, I reasoned, if they want methodology, give them methodology. Little did I know that I was beginning a project that would last more than twenty years.

I developed that statement into a grant proposal that the National Institute of Mental Health funded (about the same time as my tenure was approved). The proposal was entitled "Manhood Orientations and the American Race Problem," reflecting the Moynihan-like assumptions on which my work was still based. Before my research team began full-scale interviewing, we held weekly seminars to discuss the goals of the project and the sociological theory behind it. David Wellman, Hardy Frye, Alex Papillon, and others stressed that blacks and their ideas of manhood couldn't be studied in vacuo, that we had to look at minorities in the overall context of a racist society and therefore to focus on mainstream institutions and to interview whites as well as blacks. Reflecting the trends in the black movement and late-sixties racial politics, including the severe criticism leveled at the Moynihan Report—especially from blacks—we shifted ground and renamed the project "Racism, Manhood, and Culture." *

During the crisis-ridden year of 1968 I was still straddling the fence. But the radical outsider perspective was clearly winning. During the winter and spring I recruited minority students in my capacity as graduate admissions officer in sociology. I was interviewing prospective students at Tougaloo College in Mississippi when Martin Luther King was assassinated: it was not the most comfortable time to be a white man in a black institution. And I began my summer-long involvement with the trial of the Black Panther leader Huey Newton as an expert witness called to testify on white racism and its impact on the capacity of jury members to be impartial in a racially relevant case. That trial was probably the most important event that pushed me into unequivocal support of black militancy. Casting aside my characterological doubt, I joined the defense team after the attorney Charles Garry

---

* See David Wellman, *Portraits of White Racism* (Cambridge: Cambridge University Press, 1977), chapter 2, for an excellent discussion of this process.

asked me to help select the jury. I saw myself as a social scientist in the service of the black revolution and routinely referred to the police as "pigs."

The excitement of the late sixties invaded the classroom. Enrollments in my courses grew from sixty to three, four, and five hundred by 1970 and included sizable numbers of Native American, Chicano, and Asian students as well as blacks and whites. Students yelled and shouted at one another but almost never at me, as I managed somehow to mediate the clashing perspectives. (At times we discussed issues reasonably.) Outside the classroom, demonstrations and student strikes added excitement but also increased frustration as they shut down the campus and shortened the teaching term.

Attitudes toward the black militants divided Berkeley's sociology faculty. During my graduate student years and through the mid-sixties, there had been a strong sense of community in the department based in large part on a shared politics. There had been little distance between the most conservative and most radical professors because of the underlying liberal-left consensus among social scientists during the late Eisenhower and Kennedy years. This consensus began to crack with the Free Speech Movement. In the late sixties the department divided inexorably. Vietnam was the first issue, then student power, academic reform, and finally Black Power and black studies. Friendships of ten to twenty years' duration broke up. People stopped talking to one another, and bitter conflict, especially over personnel and curriculum, replaced what had been a benign internal politics. Several of the more moderate (and prestigious) faculty members resigned and found jobs elsewhere. Like many others in this book, I too had lost my little community.

For a period we radicals were buoyed by a larger community, that of "the movement." But when social protest was stilled by the combined effects of the conservative reaction expressed in Nixon's repressive politics and the mistakes of the movement itself, professors like myself, radicalized by the sixties, became demoralized. We had expected basic change, both in the universities and in the larger society. But without conceding more than minor reforms, social institutions had withstood the onslaught. So we felt isolated. And abandoned. White radical students were cutting their beards and getting "establishment" jobs. Black militants were trimming their Afros, downplaying the street talk, and getting accepted into law school now that affirmative action was in effect. But middle-aged professors had nowhere to go. We remained in the universities. Our late-sixties radicalism was no longer viable, but we were too committed to it to change easily.

As I became increasingly radical so did my theorizing and the articles I was publishing. The essays that I gathered in 1972 for a book entitled *Racial Oppression in America* dealt with internal colonialism, black culture, and institutional racism, including that of liberal universities like my own. They were not calculated to win friends within the academic mainstream. Yet a part of me also wanted to be rewarded by the system I was challenging. Within my own specialty I was at a further disadvantage. With the rise of black and third world consciousness, the spotlight shifted to minority scholars. They were getting the job offers and the invitations to conferences. At Berkeley I had served on a committee to plan a new research institute on race relations and to select its director. At a turning point in my career, I would have welcomed the directorship for myself. But I felt that I could not challenge the assumption that the post should go to a person of color—a position with which I also agreed. In short I was in the no-win situation of the "left colonizer" that Albert Memmi has so brilliantly described. *

Uncomfortable in conflict-ridden times, I was more than ready for the 1970s shift from political involvement to private life. I began spending more time with my children and for several years became the primary caretaker of my son. I became interested in inner experience, particularly my emotional life. Becoming health conscious, I gave up cigars, began running, and found the beauty of the natural world a source of inspiration and comfort. To make my teaching more personally meaningful, I devised a course on men and masculinity in which I minimized theory and formal lecturing. I taught instead from my life experience and encouraged students to talk openly about their lives. I still taught courses on race, but felt a little burned out, perhaps experiencing in my own way some of white America's retreat from racial issues.

After this mid-seventies and midlife transition, I was ready to get back to work. In the early seventies I had been writing a theoretical analysis of capitalism and colonialism and exploring the relation between class and race in American society. But I lost interest in that project. Theories now bored me, including the concept of internal colonialism with which I had become identified—too identified, I felt. That framework, like so many other "conceptual schemes," too easily turned into the kind of mechanical formula that often gets in the way of a fresh and creative approach. I was also troubled by the fact that the logic of internal colonialism—unlike classic colonial situations, in which the oppressors can be driven out—did not suggest any workable solutions to racial oppression in its unique American setting. I was still enough of a Marxist to believe that a correct theory must point the way to a workable political practice.

So I returned to the interviews that had been waiting in my files. It took more than a year to complete the first reading of the ten thousand pages, or four million words, of transcripts from 1968 alone. In 1977 I began editing them with the idea of a book on the late 1960s. I did not want to analyze

* Albert Memmi, *The Colonizer and the Colonized* (Boston: Beacon Press, 1967).

people and their racial perspectives; in fact, the feeling that such an analysis might be another form of exploitation was one reason that I had not written the book earlier. But I was fascinated by the life stories and by the way they made the racial politics—indeed the entire feel—of the late sixties come alive. Studs Terkel's *Working*, which I had been using in my classes, suggested an alternative.*

But the model of an interview book proved deceptive. I had naively assumed that producing a book based on first-person narratives would be easier than writing a conventional sociological analysis: every qualitative sociologist knows how difficult it is to make sense out of reams of interview material. Terkel, I thought, had played a practical joke on sociologists, creating a bestseller just by publishing the interviews. But the joke was on me.

It was not a simple task to make each person's story come alive. I wanted to suggest the uniqueness of their voices and bring out what the reviewer Kennell A. Jackson called their "very complex journeys to personal truths." † But at the same time I wanted to suggest some common experiences, highlight trends and patterns of change, suggest differences between blacks and whites, men and women, young people and old, as they negotiated twenty years of personal and social change.

The business of editing is inherently subjective. Given the same interview transcripts, each author would work up the material differently, on the basis of his or her professional interests, personal and political values, and life experiences, racial or otherwise. But for me the first step was still to get each person's account right. For some, like Vera Brooke, who told her 1968 story almost without taking a breath, I needed to do very little beyond the abridging, rearranging, and polishing involved in an author's normal three or four rewrites. But for others, like Joe Rypins, I had to revise the narrative at least a dozen times to achieve the proper flow and impact.

The decision to do a second (and later a third) round of interviews further complicated matters, not just because of the time and detective work needed to locate people but also because of the organizational problems this posed for the book. My original plan was to have each person's second interview follow the first so that a reader could easily see the changes and continuities in individual lives. But this "back-to-back" arrangement posed almost insuperable difficulties in organizing the book as a whole. There seemed no natural way to cluster people into thematic chapters because the groups they formed in the late 1960s did not necessarily correspond to those they fell into ten years later. And the back-to-back interview format highlighted personal changes rather than the larger social and political context. Dividing

---

* Studs Terkel, *Working* (New York: Pantheon, 1974).
† *San Francisco Chronicle Book Review*, July 16, 1989.

the book into two time periods solved these problems but made the individual lives harder to follow.

Because the organization of the book was unclear in the early 1980s, my publisher decided not to offer me a contract. I spent a year pursuing other publishers. An editor at one leading New York house liked my material but told me that the press already had a book about blacks on the following year's list and one was enough! Another publisher suggested that if I had a book on Hispanics, now that might be of interest. Most said that there was no longer enough interest in racial problems to risk publishing a book like mine. By the time I found a workable format, did a third round of interviewing, and completed the writing of my own interpretive chapters—the conclusion was the most difficult—the national climate was changing. In large part because of an upsurge of violence in the late 1980s, there was a renewed interest in racial justice and the mixed legacies of 1960s struggles.

Most rewarding in this long endeavor has been the opportunity to know the people, to share in their lives, and in a few cases to make those lives more meaningful. When I first began interviewing in 1978, the prospect of meeting them was a little scary as well as exciting. So at first I concentrated on people most like myself, the white liberals and the more educated, "assimilated" blacks. I was afraid that Will Singer and Joe Rypins, for example, might be hostile to a liberal-left Berkeley professor (they turned out to be warm and friendly) or that I might be the white man that Larry Dillard wanted to kill "just to put it on the books." And I put off interviewing Florence Grier for a long time, probably fearing that she would reject me as some kind of busybody white sociologist. I found instead that she was enthusiastic about sociology and its contributions to the understanding of racial conflict.

I was also awed at the prospect of meeting Howard Spence. If his 1979 interview is one of the best in the book, I don't deserve much credit. Exhausted by jet lag and traveler's insomnia, I was not relaxed enough to conduct a good interview. At a critical moment in his train of thought I introduced an irrelevant question and almost missed the story of his son's intermarriage. Today I play parts of that tape to my graduate students to illustrate interviewing mistakes they should avoid. Fortunately Mr. Spence is one of those people who is going to tell his story no matter who gets in his way. As one ages, it gets harder to find people of the next older generation who combine involvement in good works with wisdom and compassion. Visiting him was one of the high points of writing this book, and I have valued our letters and phone conversations since that weekend in 1979.

Over the years I was often struck by how the course of people's lives defied my expectations. Since lives are constantly unfolding, our fix on them is always tentative and time bound. That people keep changing may be confusing, since we seem to prefer the familiar and predictable, but I think ultimately it is cause for optimism.

As an undergraduate at the University of Chicago in the late 1940s, I read Carl Becker's classic article "Everyman His Own Historian." Becker called for the democratization of history, suggesting that all of us, ordinary people as well as professionals, have the potential to make valuable historical contributions. The growth of oral history has at least partly validated Becker's vision. One of my goals in writing this book has been to apply such a philosophy to my own field: to show, through the words of Florence Grier and others, how remarkably astute everyday people can be in their understanding of society—its inner mechanisms, contradictions, processes of change. Sociologists and policy experts should not only talk to ordinary people about their lives and opinions but also draw on their experience and wisdom in the search for answers to the difficult questions of social justice facing us in the 1990s. To paraphrase Becker for our times, we need to view "Everywoman (as) Her Own Sociologist."

Where Are the People Now?
(March 1990)

During some hard years of writing I was sustained by a daydream: after the book was published, I would host a reunion for all the people in it. There they would finally meet one another, the 1968 interviewers, and all my friends and students who had been reading and hearing about them for so many years. In October 1989 the fantasy became reality as eight of the "real authors" signed one another's copies and told a rapt International House audience in Berkeley what they were presently doing and how it felt to have their stories published in *Black Lives, White Lives*.

I began the formal proceedings with a brief history of the project, and then three of the interviewers, Hardy Frye, Alex Papillon, and Lincoln Bergman, talked about—even recreated—some of the atmosphere of heated debate and ideological ferment that marked our meetings in the late 1960s. Millie Harding reported on the book's reception in her own community, where "people who picked it up—whether in a bar, at church, on the street, or in the park—could not put it down" because they saw themselves in it. Lawrence Adams finally got his chance to ask me why he was in the book in the first place, what was so special about him. I hope I answered him satisfactorily. Maude Wiley, expressing her concern that some of her early (1968) remarks might be viewed as racist, told a hushed audience how over the years she had unlearned many of her old stereotypes about black people. Dick Cunningham made a moving statement about his daughter's intermarriage and his philosophy that color should make no difference. Frank Casey, injecting a little humor into the occasion, one-upped Virginia Lawrence: he bragged of fourteen grandchildren to her thirteen. But in a serious vein he expressed the hope that one day after he was gone they would "pick up the book . . . and know about their grandfather and what happened in this country three decades ago." (Two of these grandchildren came to the party with their mother, who until then had not known about the book or that whole part of his life.)

As Frank told the audience, he and I have been talking again, filling in some of those missing spaces from the ten to twelve years when "nobody knew where Frank Casey was." Although he had quite successfully held a number of human service jobs after he had left the school (working with mental patients in hospitals, with disturbed children in residential homes, and with the elderly), he had also backslid from the religion that had sustained him. But he found his way back from the streets and now spends six days a week at Bible school or his church, where recently he was ordained as a deacon. Getting closer to God has become even more important since Frank discovered early in 1988 that he is afflicted with a serious and totally unexpected illness.

In this kind of study one has to expect illness and death. George Hendrickson died in 1987 after a seven-year struggle with leukemia. His widow told me that one of his grandchildren was just like George; I sent her the transcripts of his life-history interviews so that his offspring could better know this memorable man. Harold Sampson was also stunned when early in 1989 his doctor told him he needed a triple-bypass operation. Fortunately Harold has had a "great recovery" and is working again as a dean of administration, learning now how to pace his activities. He particularly enjoys working with young black men, both at his college and in the community—this is the group he is trying to reach and motivate. A few months ago we had lunch with his friend Len Davis, who, because of some health problems of his own, is no longer delivering mail and is looking into other postal service or federal government employment.

At eighty-seven Howard Spence is "slowing down," but he is happy that he can still walk around unaided and stay on his land. He has had to give up trips and many of his activities. But people, all kinds of people—white, black, young, and old—are still drawn to him. He is living more in his mind these days: "It's a nice thing just to be able to live and remember" all that he has gone through. Mr. Spence reads a lot and meets every week with a group of like-minded people who study the Bible and the recent events in Eastern Europe and, above all, in South Africa.

Times have been good for Virginia Lawrence. In her mid-sixties, she has cut her work down to one day a week so she has time to relax and to travel with her new husband. He is white. When we appear together to talk about the book on local television and radio stations, she stresses education as the answer to today's problems of race and poverty more than ever. (Harold Sampson and Larry Dillard have also appeared.)

Henry Smith is still practicing medicine full time. He looked better than ever when I saw him at a book signing that Millie Harding had organized at her community center in Oak Park. Mrs. Harding is getting ready to leave her job at the center, having achieved most of the goals she set out to accomplish. She looks forward to returning to volunteer work, where she can once again advocate positions without reining in her natural outspokenness. Care of her husband, who suffered a stroke some years ago, absorbs much of her energy, but one of her future projects is to write her own autobiography.

Mrs. Harding told me that Richard Simmons has been in the state penitentiary for a number of years, so I haven't been able to speak with him. When I saw Larry Dillard just two weeks ago, he had been hassled by a series of arrests for penny-ante offenses, including talking back to a policeman. Because of the so-called war on drugs, he has curtailed some of his business activities. Dillard likes the way his children have grown up, and he is especially proud of the grandchild his son has recently fathered.

Joe Rypins is also very proud of his children, both of whom are military pilots. He continues to enjoy life, "fishing, hunting, and working a *little.*" Bill Harcliff too is happy with what he calls the "dull, good life" in his small town. Finally settling down "in his psyche" and with a vocation, he expects to be ordained a Zen monk soon. Bill also takes care of his three young children while his wife works.

Vera Brooke is back teaching in an inner-city school, and she loves it. She is by choice the single parent of two children now. Her youngest is three. Carleta Reeves has made a job change at the university, a step up that pleases her, at least for now. Jim Pettit also has a new job as a cook at a major university. He has been sculpturing as well, and he still lives in San Francisco with Martin. They have been together for almost twenty years.

And what has happened to the 1968 interviewers after more than twenty years? Hardy Frye is now a sociology professor at the University of California, Santa Cruz, where he teaches courses on politics, social movements, and race. He is writing a book about Berkeley politics, based on his years as a close associate of the former mayor Gus Newport. Lincoln Bergman now works as a science writer at the University of California, Berkeley; for a number of years he was director of the news department for KPFA radio. Married for the second time, Lincoln has two young children and is also writing a biography of a radical journalist. Alex Papillon is back working on the waterfront as a longshoreman. Over the past twenty years he has attended law school, worked as an administrative assistant to state senator Elihu Harris, and participated in a variety of community and political activities, including running for a seat on the school board. David Wellman is a professor of sociology and community studies on the Santa Cruz campus of the University of California, having taught for many years at the University of Oregon. He is completing a book on union democracy among San Francisco's longshoremen. I was pleased to meet Ed Price again at the 1989 sociology meetings in San Francisco. Since he left Berkeley, Ed has been teaching at Western Carolina University, where he does research on the peace movement. Sheila Gibson Stevens does management training and administration for a county social service agency. Her job gives her an opportunity to use concepts in social psychology and organizational dynamics and to deal with issues of ethnic diversity. She has two pre-teen children—and this spring will marry again. Maurice Haltom is now running a health and fitness center in Ithaca, New York, where he combines clinical psychology with martial arts and Eastern philosophy.

I thought finishing the book would bring me a life of leisure, but I have been busier than ever in the year following its publication. I have met some great people traveling and talking about *Black Lives, White Lives,* and I have been growing personally as I learn to speak effectively to broader audiences through radio and television. At that October 1989 celebration, Millie Harding wondered whether I would do a fourth round of interviews toward the end of the 1990s. I would not like to rule out anything, but I rather think it is time for me to move on to something else.